'Mark Smith has written a fluent meditation on Russian
history, a gallant attempt to reason with those who believe
that Russia is condemned to an endless cycle of failed
reform and resurgent authoritarianism . . . his propositions
are plausible, a welcome antidote to the overwrought
stuff about Russia so widespread in the West today'
Rodric Braithwaite, *History Today*

'Smith makes a very strong case that Russia's past needs to
be considered as much more complex than it generally is. For
that reason alone, this book deserves a large audience . . . *The
Russia Anxiety* is a very welcome book. It provides a provocative
and much needed analysis of Russian history which ably shows the
oversimplified nature of most Western understandings of Russia'
Paul Robinson, author of *Russian Conservatism*

'*The Russia Anxiety* is a valuable effort to assess the long history
of the West's Russia-related worries . . . Regrettably, more than
five years [since the annexation of Crimea], the United States
seems no closer to developing either a strategy or a policy to
manage its relationship with Russia. Mark Smith's provocative
book won't solve that problem alone, but it does offer
some valuable guidance in thinking about solutions'
Paul Saunders, *Russia Matters*

## ABOUT THE AUTHOR

Mark B. Smith teaches in the Faculty of History at the University of
Cambridge. He is the author of *Property of Communists: The Urban
Housing Program from Stalin to Khrushchev* and the blog *Beyond the
Kremlin*.

PENGUIN BOOKS

THE RUSSIA ANXIETY

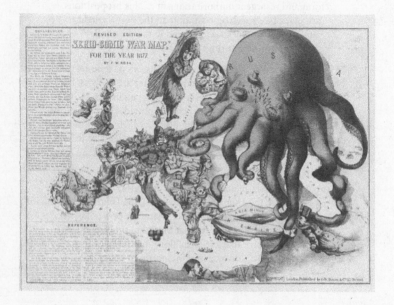

From the nineteenth century, the international press saw Russia as a furious bear, shaking its paws, baring its fangs, and waiting to be unleashed on its neighbours. Which is more frightening? The bear on the rampage, or the octopus spreading its tentacles, oozing through gaps and blending in with its surroundings? A well-known comic map of 1877 has Russia as an octopus. The other countries of Europe are drawn as human characters.

# MARK B. SMITH

# The Russia Anxiety

*And How History Can Resolve It*

PENGUIN BOOKS

## PENGUIN BOOKS

UK | USA | Canada | Ireland | Australia
India | New Zealand | South Africa

Penguin Books is part of the Penguin Random House group of companies
whose addresses can be found at global.penguinrandomhouse.com

First published by Allen Lane 2019
Published in Penguin Books 2020
001

Copyright © Mark B. Smith, 2019

The moral right of the author has been asserted

Typeset by Jouve (UK), Milton Keynes
Printed and bound in Great Britain by Clays Ltd, Elcograf S.p.A.

A CIP catalogue record for this book is available from the British Library

ISBN: 978-0-141-98650-0

*For Laura and Sonia*

# Contents

## PART III

# The Fireglow of History

# Maps

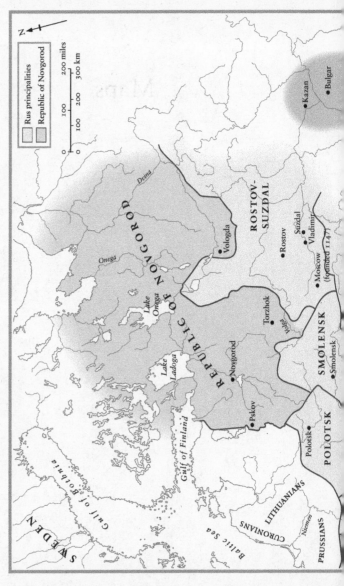

1. EXPANSION (1) The emergence of 'Russia': Moscow was founded in
been expanding and contracting for centuries, and other proto-states,
powers. Borders were never fixed, national identities were far from

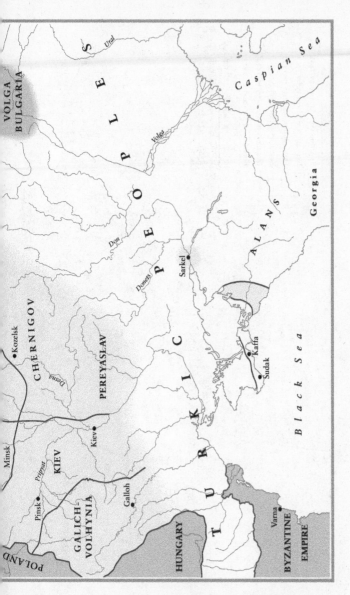

1147. At this time, other older principalities of Rus, notably Kiev, had such as the Republic of Novgorod and Volga Bulgaria, were regional primordial, and the medieval East Slavic world was multipolar.

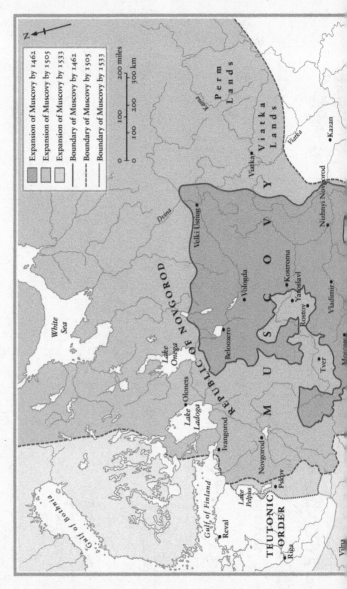

2. EXPANSION (2) The gathering of 'Russia': despite its late
Muscovy became the centre of East Slavic civilization in the fifteenth
success than previous or associated expansionary powers in the

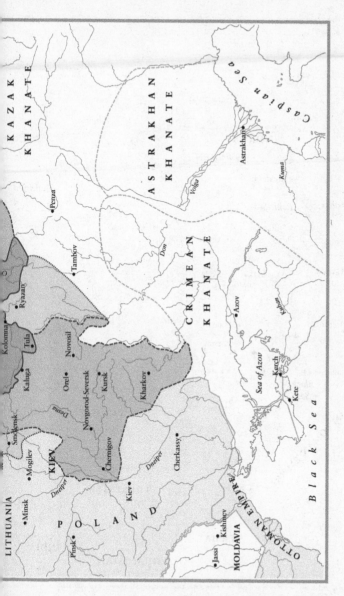

emergence and devastation at the hands of the Mongols in 1240,
and sixteenth centuries, expanding its borders with more durable
region, such as Kievan Rus, had managed to do.

3. EXPANSION (3) The vastness of Russia: the Russian Empire continued to
surface, by the time of the outbreak of the First World War. At this point it was
continued to grow after 1918.

expand, reaching its greatest extent, covering one-sixth of the world's land
approximately the same size as the British Empire, though the British Empire

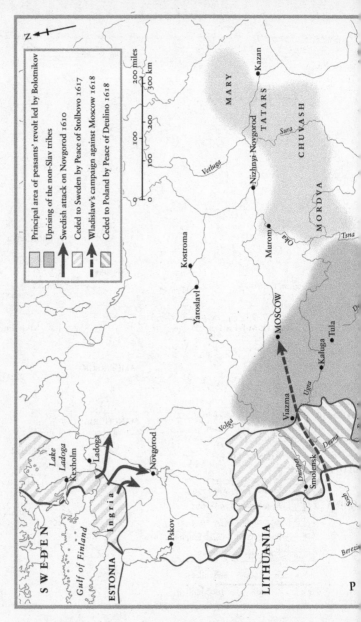

4. PRESSURE (1) From the north and west: in its various incarnations
total crisis included the invasion and occupation by the Mongols that began
the assault by Germany in 1941. One of the worst moments came during the
invaded, the Poles briefly occupied Moscow, and famine and dynastic crisis

The map legend reads:

- Principal area of peasants' revolt led by Bolotnikov
- Uprising of the non-Slav tribes
- Swedish attack on Novgorod 1610
- Ceded to Sweden by Peace of Stolbovo 1617
- Wladislaw's campaign against Moscow 1618
- Ceded to Poland by Peace of Deulino 1618

N

200 miles
300 km

MARY
Kazan
TATARS
CHUVASH
Sura
Vetluga
Nizhnyi Novgorod
MORDVA
Murom
Oka
Tsna
Kostroma
Yaroslavl
MOSCOW
Tula
Kaluga
Ugra
Viazma
Volga
Desna
Dnieper
Smolensk
SWEDEN
Lake Ladoga
Kexholm
Ladoga
Novgorod
Ingria
Gulf of Finland
ESTONIA
Pskov
LITHUANIA
Berezi
P

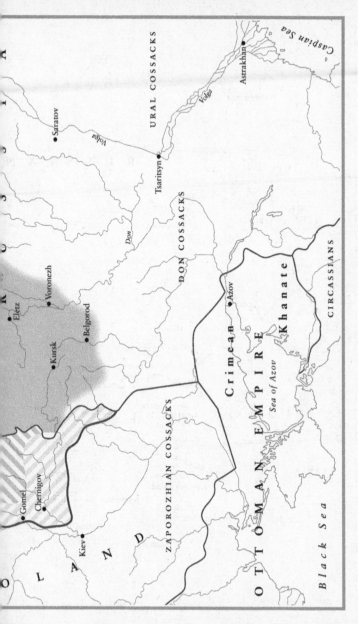

Russia has faced elimination at the hands of foreign invaders. Moments of
n 1240, the invasion by Sweden in 1708, the attack by France in 1812 and
Time of Troubles at the start of the seventeenth century, when the Swedes
converged.

5. PRESSURE (2) From the east and south: the sheer length of its borders
nineteenth century, Russia sensed threats from the Ottoman Empire in Asia
from the whole range of European, American and Asian empires.

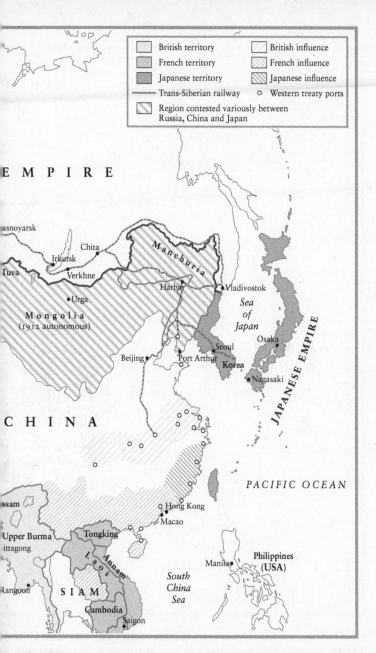

British territory · British influence
French territory · French influence
Japanese territory · Japanese influence
Trans-Siberian railway · ○ Western treaty ports
Region contested variously between
Russia, China and Japan

EMPIRE

asnoyarsk
Chita
Irkutsk
Tuva    Verkhne
•Urga    Manchuria
Harbin    •Vladivostok
Mongolia    Sea
(1912 autonomous)    of
Japan    Osaka
Beijing•    Seoul
Port Arthur    Korea
•Nagasaki

CHINA    JAPANESE EMPIRE

PACIFIC OCEAN

○ Hong Kong
•Macao

ssam
Upper Burma    Tongking
ittagong    Laos    Manila•    Philippines
(USA)
Rangoon•    Annam
SIAM    South
China
Cambodia    Sea
Saigon

gives Russia's policymakers unique strategic and defensive challenges. In the
from the British in India and Afghanistan, and from the Japanese – as well as

6. PRESSURE (3) Twenty-first century encirclement? The view from Moscow
anti-Moscow alliance – possessing a strategy of expansion, and the members of
are also located in Europe.

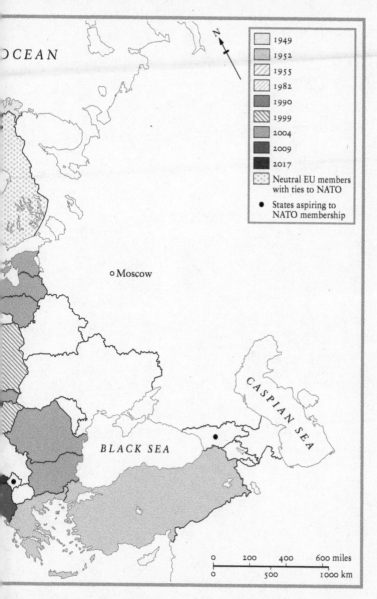

OCEAN

1949
1952
1955
1982
1990
1999
2004
2009
2017
Neutral EU members with ties to NATO
● States aspiring to NATO membership

o Moscow

CASPIAN SEA

BLACK SEA

| 0 | 200 | 400 | 600 miles |

| 0 | 500 | 1000 km |

s of Washington and Brussels getting ever closer, with NATO – historically an
he EU defining themselves as 'European' in distinction to non-EU states that

# *Preface*

I teach Russian history for a living, and I sometimes ask a class to tell me the first thing they think of when they hear the word 'Russia'. Students suspect a trick question and turn their gaze towards the middle distance. But what's the trick?

In the new age of Donald Trump and Vladimir Putin I asked a group of students a slightly different question from the one above: what they thought when they heard the name Putin. The image that one of them put forward was precisely what the media presented: a villain from a James Bond movie. His policies were violent and expansionist; his rule was arbitrary and coercive. He ran a kleptocracy and a mafia state based on a veneer of Russian nationalism. It was a house of cards, ready to fall. But then the student did what many excellent students do: mid-statement, uninterrupted, he pulled himself up short, breathed out and suddenly changed direction. He struggled to find coherence in terms such as 'mafia state'. Sensing the perils of received wisdom, he wondered if he was only saying what he was supposed to say, and he set about adjusting his position in full view of the rest of the class.

The question was not only about Russia, or about Putin: it was about the limits of how we understand the world around us. After all, observers had for years told different stories about Putin's Russia. For some, Putin had reshaped and modernized his country. Under his leadership, Russia emerged from the chaos and misery of the 1990s. He established a stable economy that was more flexible and open than before, and that raised living standards, at least in metropolitan centres, even after oil prices had long stopped rising. Presenting himself as dignified, articulate and decisive, he also stabilized the country's politics. Many Russians led normal lives, forming reasonable ambitions and plausible plans to realize them. It was easy enough to understand Putin's popularity. Was this another aspect of the truth?

I teach history, as I've said, and so the problems I discuss with my students concern the past, even if the conversation has turned towards the present day. When it comes to Russia, history shapes our imaginations – and defines our misperceptions. Was the present really the consequence of the past? Had Vladimir Putin made Russia modern, or had he allowed it to revert to type? In the age of Trump and Putin, did the West's Russia crisis come out of the past, or did it point towards a uniquely dangerous future?

Every day brought a new headline describing Russia as a hostile foreign power, with talk of annexation, fighting, mischief, hacking, hit jobs, sanctions, corruption and a short road to war. News programmes led with encroachments on airspace, interventions in elections and nerve poison in the medieval English town of Salisbury. In the years that followed Vladimir Putin's third election victory in 2012, Russia was cast as an extraordinary danger, and its president became Public Enemy Number 1.

Of course, people in 'the West' – itself not an undivided category or one that's clearly distinct from Russia – worry for good reasons about Moscow: its deteriorating relations with NATO, its scarcely transparent political system, its oligarchic capitalism, the allegations of political violence sometimes levelled against its government and its tensions with former Soviet republics, especially the conflict with Ukraine. In the present and the past alike, there have been moments of enmity, hostility and incomprehension that were real, not imagined or inflated. Think back to the closing in of the Cold War at the end of the 1940s and the start of the nuclear arms race. Imagine the need for answers in Salisbury in early 2018. But by then the anger on the TV screens was so loud that it was impossible to evaluate risks and reflect on motives. Incidents that were important but of a different order, culminating in the 'cyberwar' of the 2016 American election, were taken out of context, exaggerated, given strategic coherence and imagined as an ideological crusade. Among military and intelligence officers, politicians and journalists, and across the public squares of

America and Britain, it became acceptable to say what you wanted to say about Russia, and talking heads on Russian TV returned the compliment. One of the differences with the Cold War was that both sides, perhaps, seemed to forget that they were dealing with a massive nuclear power equal only to themselves.

Yet while the level of indignation was exhausting, it was not new. Perhaps because of its proximity to Western Europe (China is much further away), its size (the biggest country in the world) and its out-of-focus familiarity (no country is simultaneously so exotic and ever-present) Russia has sometimes seemed a unique menace in Western eyes. This feeling, usually based on error and even more often on prejudice, has come and gone for at least five centuries. We might call it the Russia Anxiety. At its worst, it creates a preposterous bogeyman and is itself a threat to world peace, most catastrophically so in July 1914.

This book analyses the history of the Russia Anxiety, but it does not only look backwards. It shows how history can be a platform from which to look at Russia more calmly, reasonably and accurately. But even when the discussion stretches to the time of writing, like it sometimes does in my classes, the judgements are historical, never contemporary. Their relationship to the present is suggestive, not decisive. This is a work of history with an unconventional structure and an open interest in current events. Telling stories from every age of the recorded past, it scrutinizes the patterns that connect Russia's history with its possible futures. But these patterns are obscure and unexpected. They defy predictability. And they make Russia seem more similar to other European countries and even the United States. Perhaps the Russia Anxiety cannot survive such a careful and critical way of thinking about history. In any case, this book invites you to make the journey back into the Russian past and to look at the present anew.

# PART I

# Fear, Contempt and
# Disregard

I had been afraid of Russia ever since I could remember.
*Colin Thubron, British travel writer, 1983*

The Russian peasant is indeed a barbarian at a very low stage
of civilization. In the Crimean hospitals every nationality was
to be found among the patients, and the Russian soldier was
considered far the lowest of all.
*Lady Verney, author and sister of Crimean
War nurse Florence Nightingale, 1888*

Look at the state of Russia now. They're in enormous decline.
By any definition, these guys are on a toboggan run. The
question is: when the run ends.
*Joe Biden, former US vice-president,
January 2018*

As I lay awake on my plank bed, the most unorthodox
thoughts came into my mind, about how tenuous was the line
between high principles and bigoted intolerance, and how
relative are all human ideologies, and how absolute the tor-
tures to which men submit their fellow men.
*Evgeniya Ginzburg, victim of
Stalinist repression, 1967*

[T]he next hundred years may become the golden age of civilization, of the human race ... [W]ith Britain and Russia as the pillars of this new Europe, it can be done.

*Alexander Werth, Anglo-Russian*
*journalist,* 1942[1]

More than a simple undifferentiated Russophobia, the Russia Anxiety, as I see it, is an historic syndrome that alternates between three sets of symptoms: fear of Russia, disregard of Russia and contempt for Russia. Western European countries and the United States have spells of the Anxiety, although it comes and goes, the symptoms switch about, and sometimes they disappear altogether. But the worst outbreaks of the Russia Anxiety exacerbate international disorder and risk war. In Part I, I explore the emergence and elaboration of the Russia Anxiety since the sixteenth century, when travellers started coming eastwards to Muscovy in large numbers. I discuss the 'black legend' of Russian history on which the Anxiety is based, the absolute categories that Western observers have often used to evaluate Russia, without much reflection on Russian conditions or even awareness of their own societies, and the particular view of how history 'works' that makes the Anxiety possible. And then I come to a narrative of Russian history: a story of what's happened in the last 6,000 years which corrects some of the Anxiety's assumptions. The chapters are designed to be read in order, but Chapter 3, which is a narrative of Russian history from the beginning to the present, is also a reference point for readers to return to. In other words, Part I recounts the history of the Russia Anxiety and hints that history itself – not only its attention to real facts, but also its cultivation of self-reflection, imagination and a sense of comparison and context – might be its remedy.

# I

# The Bear Phantasmagoria

*Did History Create the Russia Anxiety?*

Of all the love-hate relationships that have sprung up between Russians and outsiders, the one that was least troubled by love involved the French aristocrat and travel writer the Marquis de Custine. He visited Russia in 1839 and wrote a bestselling book about his experiences. Custine claimed in advance to love Russia, but these feelings did not survive his first encounter at the border. Even as he was going through customs, his contempt for the Russians had begun to show. On one journey, already frustrated by the poor quality of the road, he looked around him and spotted 'a large number of badly constructed wooden bridges, one of which seemed quite perilous'. On the basis of this, he concluded, as usual, 'Human life is worth little in Russia.'[1]

Nine years later, revolution spread across Western and Central Europe, shaking governments and sometimes briefly deposing them. But the revolutions of 1848 did not extend to the Russian Empire. *The Economist* was in no doubt why this was, claiming in its final issue of that year: 'her population is not yet civilized enough to feel those yearnings after freedom and self-government which have agitated Europe'. Over the next century and a half, *The Economist* would remain consistent in its use of adjectives. 'Russia's only aim in the 1990s was to become a normal, civilized state,' the newspaper insisted in September 2011, before describing how it failed. Reporting on the Sochi Olympics in February 2014, the same paper wrote that it was 'a dream' to consider Russia to be 'the sophisticated and civilized country' that was presented in the opening ceremony.[2]

A century earlier, on 28 June 1914, a Serbian-backed group of conspirators murdered the heir to the Austro-Hungarian throne, Franz

Ferdinand, during a visit to the imperial city of Sarajevo. As a result, the Austrians wanted to go to war with Serbia, to get revenge and kill off the irridentist menace to their empire in the Balkans. But the Austrians knew that the Russians stood behind the Serbs, their fellow-Slavs – and Russia was allied to France and Britain. Threatening Serbia was a high-risk strategy. Austria could only issue its aggressive ultimatum to Serbia because it was confident of the unconditional support of its German ally. Germany, famously, gave it the 'blank cheque' that partly made the First World War possible. Why would it do this? Because of the Russia Anxiety. The British and the French overestimated Russian economic power in the run-up to 1914, and this influenced their strategic judgements; but Germany made an even more dangerous miscalculation. Many influential Germans were convinced that Russia posed a far more deadly threat than was really plausible. Russia's economy developed very rapidly in the two decades before 1914, but it did so in a far more uneven way than many observers imagined it was doing, and it was scarcely the case that it was mere years away from becoming an unstoppable global powerhouse, as German policymakers feared. In fact, Russian GDP was still less than two-thirds that of Germany. Two weeks before the Sarajevo assassination, the German emperor, chancellor and foreign minister were all convinced of the grave threat posed to Germany by the Russian war machine: it was about to 'overwhelm' them if they did not take action.[3] The July Crisis opened up the opportunity for a pre-emptive war. It came just in time, as the Germans believed that a German-Russian war in, say, 1917 might already be unwinnable. Of all the various causes of the First World War, the Russia Anxiety is one of the most persuasive.

Custine, *The Economist*, Kaiser Wilhelm: they all felt the Russia Anxiety. They either expressed contempt for the barbarians in the East, denying them the attributes of civilization, and making their country a separate, 'other' place, or they worked up an exaggerated fear, based on the conviction that the biggest country in the world posed an imminent, even catastrophic threat. They used extravagant language – the end of the world is often nigh during outbreaks of the Russia Anxiety – and encouraged international recklessness. But the Russia Anxiety has another symptom: not just contempt or fear, but also disregard. After the end of the Cold War, Russia seemed to disappear from the calculations of Western policymakers. It was not considered to be an independent actor worthy of consideration. Following a pattern that recurred from time to time, after a Russian defeat or strategic overreach, 'the West' as good as said, 'We've won. That's it. Game over. We won't be hearing from them again.' According to one Washington analyst who worked in the Defense Department in the 1990s, America's post-Cold-War foreign policy (expansion of NATO, wars in the Balkans and the Middle East, forceful projection of US values and interests, including in Russia) completely disregarded the possibility that Russia had its own legitimate interests. 'We didn't do it because we wanted to hurt them,' she said. 'We did it because we didn't care if it hurt them.'[4] This more passive strain of the Anxiety can have the same effect as active contempt and fear: 'othering' the biggest European country and increasing strategic instability. But the Russia Anxiety is a cycle, and disregard can soon turn into contempt and then to fear. For centuries, outsiders have looked at Russia and felt superior or afraid. Years after the end of the Cold War, the sum of these feelings is as dangerous as ever, even though history shows that the Anxiety is almost always misplaced.

That might even be true in the great Russia crisis of the age of Trump and Putin. By taking a snapshot of this crisis, framing it between the US presidential election of November 2016 and the Russian election of March 2018, we can see what the Anxiety looks like, how it works, and the risks we take when we wilfully lose control of the way we talk about Russia.

## TRUMP-PUTIN: A TALE OF TWO PRESIDENTIAL ELECTIONS

All the elements of the Russia Anxiety converged during the election of Donald Trump to the American presidency. In the absence of a consensus to explain the rise of Trump, and lacking concrete evidence for widespread claims of Russian intervention in the election, Russia again became a proxy for evil in the eyes of Trump's opponents, most of the media and the wider American establishment, especially in the intelligence services and the Pentagon. Even to raise a doubt some-times seemed like treason. 'We are at war,' declared Morgan Freeman, the Hollywood actor, in September 2017, nearly a year after the election, using the language of the self-fulfilling prophecy.[5] He meant with Russia, though – it deserves emphasis – America and Russia have never been to war.

By the summer of 2016, Trump had secured the Republican nomination. It was around this time that allegations emerged about the involvement of Russians in his campaign. 'Vladimir Putin has a plan for destroying the West,' wrote the journalist Franklin Foer in July, 'and that plan looks a lot like Donald Trump.'[6] The evidence for all this was circumstantial, dating back to visits that Trump had made to the Soviet Union in the 1980s. But in July 2016, four months before the poll, Foer was clear. 'A foreign power that wishes ill upon the United States,' he wrote, 'has attached itself to a major presidential campaign.' It became an international scandal.

Was Trump the Kremlin's candidate? A series of reports by a former British intelligence officer, originally commissioned by the Democrats, was leaked at the start of 2017. 'The Russian authorities had been cultivating and supporting the US Republican presidential candidate Donald Trump for at least five years,' wrote Christopher Steele, the reports' author, in June 2016. He drew on the testimony of two senior Russian figures, a Foreign Ministry official and a former intelligence officer, who also told him that President Putin himself was involved in the conspiracy. And there were salacious details, apparently taken from cameras hidden in Trump's bedroom at the Ritz-Carlton hotel when he visited in 2013.[7]

On 6 January 2017, two weeks before Trump's inauguration, the director of national intelligence published a report on the Russians' cyber escalation of their 'longstanding desire to undermine the US-led liberal democratic order'. 'We assess,' the DNI wrote, 'Russian President Vladimir Putin ordered an influence campaign in 2016 aimed at the US presidential election.' Thanks to the efforts of the seventeen US intelligence agencies, his report expressed 'high confidence' that 'Russia's goals were to undermine public faith in the US democratic process,' while sabotaging Hillary Clinton's candidacy and showing 'a clear preference for President-elect Trump'.[8]

Secretary Clinton blamed Putin in significant measure for her defeat. 'In 2016 our democracy was assaulted by a foreign adversary determined to mislead our people, enflame our divisions, and throw an election to its preferred candidate,' Hillary explained in her memoir about the campaign. Her imagery turned medical. For Clinton, Russia had unbound a deadly contagion, and was itself suffering from the effects. 'Now that the Russians have infected us and seen how weak our defences are, they'll keep at it,' she wrote.[9] Americans have often seen Russia as an 'airborne pathogen', as the historian Sean Guillory put it. In the 1940s, the Cold War policy of containment was designed to protect against the infectious threat. He cites General Jack D. Ripper in *Dr Strangelove*, the black comedy of 1964. Ripper rails against the Soviet Union's attempts 'to sap and impurify all of our precious bodily fluids'.[10]

The late Senator John McCain and Senator Lindsey Graham spent the New Year of 2017 with Ukrainian soldiers and talked of Russia's 'act of war' against the United States. Congressman Pete King of New York professed 'no doubt' on live TV that 'Putin is evil'. *Vanity Fair* asked whether 'Putin's masterplan' is 'only beginning'. *Politico* wrote of 'the big war, being waged by Russia against all of us'. In Syria, where Russian forces supported the government of President Assad, the risks of an inadvertent collision with the United States seemed high.

But is Putin really as all-powerful as *Vanity Fair* suggested? Half a century of academic analysis shows that power has never been a unitary thing in either the Soviet Union or post-Soviet Russia, but that different government and economic institutions – not to mention interest groups, patronage networks and leading personalities – actively struggle to defend and extend their influence while monitoring and generally working with the grain of public opinion, at least in domestic policy. This is despite the appearance of total centralization, even in the hands of one man. Christopher Steele himself, in a report of 5 August 2016, pointed towards 'two well-placed and established Kremlin sources' who claimed that Sergei Ivanov, then head of the Presidential Administration, believed that Dmitry Peskov, Putin's press spokesman, had overextended himself into foreign affairs. According to the Steele report, Prime Minister Dmitry Medvedev took the same line as Ivanov. 'Talk now in the Kremlin of Trump withdrawing from presidential race altogether,' noted Steele, 'but this is still largely wishful thinking by more liberal elements in Moscow.'[11] In other words, it was never clear who initiated which policy, or which decision was made where and on the basis of what information.

During the first year of Trump's presidency, Robert Mueller began the independent judicial investigation into alleged collusion between the Trump election campaign and the 'hostile power' of Russia (the report was scheduled for publication after this book went to press). Speculation was periodically rife. 'When a country can come interfere in another country's elections, that is warfare. It really is,' said Nikki Haley, United Nations ambassador, on 19 October 2017. No Trump cabinet official had yet suggested a state of war. In January 2018, the defence secretary of the United Kingdom argued that Russia's aim for Britain was as follows: 'Damage its economy, rip its infrastructure apart, actually cause thousands and thousands and thousands of deaths.' Even the BBC was moved to suggest that this might be 'alarmist'.[12] It sounded like the Russia Anxiety in action. Foreign governments and writers were openly expressing contempt for Russia. Fear of Russian aggression motivated the construction of what looked like an anti-Russian alliance. In building that alliance, Western governments seemed again to be placing Russia outside their definition of civilization.

But then an attempt was made in Salisbury on the life of a Russian double-agent, Sergei Skripal, together with his adult daughter, days before the Russian presidential election of 18 March. The British government said that the weapon was a nerve poison – a chemical weapon – that could only have come from a Russian facility. In effect, they blamed Putin personally. Putin responded by asking what interest the Russian authorities could have in such an ostentatious attempted murder, just before a major election and weeks before the country was due to host the football World Cup, and demanded to see the evidence. The implication was that others – governments, renegade spies, expatriate oligarchs – had an interest in humiliating and sidelining the Russians even further, and that the fingerprints might belong to conspirators in other countries. Or was it a rogue element in Russian espionage, others speculated, implying that the Kremlin's control of its own secret services might be dissolving? It certainly seemed an elaborate and high-risk way of uniting Russian public opinion against the West days before polling. But the British foreign secretary kept going, comparing the forthcoming World Cup to the 1936 Olympics, held in Nazi Germany.

A few days later, President Putin was re-elected with 75 per cent of the vote on a 70 per cent turnout. 'The West turns on Russia,' announced the free *Metro* newspaper to British commuters on 27 March after twenty-nine NATO and EU countries worked in concert to expel more than 100 Russian diplomats and spies. The Russians reciprocated with their own expulsions. When the Americans closed the Russian consulate in Seattle, the Russians shut down the American consulate in St Petersburg. Perhaps only the fear of nuclear weapons could stop war from breaking out. Or perhaps the opaque bond between the two election victors might be a strange source of peace. Going against his advisers, President Trump congratulated Putin on his re-election.

The Trump-Putin crisis was real. In Washington it was a response to events in Ukraine, Syria and cyberspace, and in Moscow it was a push-back against the general treatment of Russia in world affairs since the end of the Cold War.

But it was also accidental. Whatever meddling had taken place in the US electoral process, and however precisely or skilfully it had been targeted, the outcome of the election came down to chance. Just a few thousand extra votes for Hillary Clinton in three swing states – out of 129 million that were cast in total, countrywide – and she would have matched her clear victory in the popular vote with a win in the Electoral College and been elected to the presidency. American politics would itself have defanged the crisis: with no need to paint Trump as a creature of Russian manipulation, or to argue that Russia had 'brainwashed' a fringe of voters, Democrats would not have called for the Mueller enquiry. With a president in office who respected them and gave them access, the American intelligence services would not have needed to express their view of Russia quite so openly and volubly. True enough, with Clinton as president, the underlying problem might have worsened – the sense in Moscow was that the American government would only view the world on its own terms, disregarded Russia's status, and that Russia was entitled to respond to perceived threats to its security – but there might well have been no full-scale flare-up of the Russia Anxiety in Washington. No historian, speaking as a historian, could evaluate the pictures painted by spies and cybernetics experts about the 2016 election, but the historic themes of the Russia Anxiety were nevertheless openly on display. The fearful assumption of unique malevolence and extraordinary capacity – the claim that the Russians could locate and change the opinions of selected groups of voters in carefully chosen electoral districts, often preoccupied as they were with local issues and personalities, as part of a masterplan to install their own candidate in the White House and sow doubts about the integrity of the voting system and the value of democracy – soon alternated with contempt for strategic overreach, tactical bungling and internal Russian weaknesses. The Russia Anxiety is cyclical, although the cycles can overlap and change their order, and the contingency of the Trump-Putin crisis only showed this up again. In the middle of 2018 it was even suspended, thanks to Russia's hosting of the World Cup, which charmed millions of visitors and hundreds of millions of TV viewers, with longer-term results that might be important.

Both real and accidental, the Anxiety's most important location was in the imagination, where the phantasmagoria took shape. In the age of Trump and Putin, it became ever more difficult to distinguish reality from rhetoric. 'Fake news' and 'post-truth' were supposed to be everywhere, their apparent ubiquity often blamed on Russian misinformation programmes, but the Russia Anxiety itself was, as ever, a conflation of fact and fiction. It seemed that many leading figures lacked the appetite for making the distinction. In fact, even the simplest distinctions became impossible. 'Russia' and 'Putin' were forever elided into each other, one easily standing for the other. Photos captured the president with sinister sunglasses, a withering look or an empty gaze. An *Economist* cover in October 2016 had a photograph of Putin's face coloured blue and shaded in black, with the background red; his eyes were missing, replaced by little red fighter planes. In the Western imagination, this confected image was the face of modern Russia.

For hundreds of years, such images have created and formed the Russia Anxiety. They have given energy to the cycles that push the

Anxiety from fear to contempt to disregard and back to fear. But these cycles do not always follow the same pattern, and the Anxiety has never been a permanent or fixed condition.

# FIVE HUNDRED YEARS OF THE RUSSIA ANXIETY

The Russia critics of the early twenty-first century sometimes had a good tune, but they were often singing from an ancient songbook. Those who have written books about Russophobia have tended to emphasize that it is age-old, even if they are themselves prompted to write by a present-day crisis.[13] Some date Russophobia to partings of the ways between East and West in Europe, beginning with Constantine's decision to move the capital of the Roman Empire eastwards from Rome to Byzantium (Istanbul) in 330 AD.[14] Soon enough, the division between an Eastern and a Western Europe was politically defined, though in early medieval times, it was the Byzantine East that possessed the richer culture and the greater power. When Grand Prince Vladimir of Kievan Rus, the forerunner of the modern East Slavic states (the largest of which is Russia), was christened in 988, it was Orthodoxy, taken from Byzantium, rather than Catholicism from Rome which was adopted across the realm. Was this the moment when 'Russia' chose East, not West? In 1054, the Schism between Orthodoxy and Catholicism seemed to place Kiev and, soon, Moscow (which was founded in 1147) on the proverbial wrong side of history. And then the invasion of the Mongols in 1240 effectively increased the distance between Moscow (and Kiev) and 'the West', a distance which facilitated the assumption of barbarism.

Despite its shortcomings, this argument is attractive for one big reason: it emphasizes moments of decision and external ill fortune, not genes or geography, in erecting barriers between the Russian lands and what would become the West. Russophobia – and the Russia Anxiety as a broader phenomenon – was not inevitable. But in the very length of its chronology, it implies a way of thinking which by now can't or won't change. This is a fallacy. The backdrop of the Russia Anxiety is old, but it's not that old. In its recognizably modern form – as a specifically anti-Muscovite syndrome of disregard, contempt and fear – the Russia Anxiety dates to the sixteenth century, when merchants, government officials and churchmen travelled eastwards to Muscovy in much larger numbers and for lengthier stays than before, partly thanks to improved communication links via the White Sea. The accounts of visitors from Western and Central Europe became well known. Some of these were marked by calm observations and careful scholarship, others by sensational hearsay and plagiarism. No wonder that contemporary audiences found much to be anxious about, or that posterity had access to a useful mine of prejudices. The relative remoteness of the Russian lands made them an easy screen on which readers could project their wildest fantasies.

Sigismund von Herberstein represented the Holy Roman Empire in its Muscovite embassy between 1517 and 1526. This was during the reign of Vasily III, just before Ivan the Terrible came to the throne, at a time when Muscovy was becoming a significant European power. Muscovy was expanding its borders. Its economy was more deeply integrating into regional, continental and even transcontinental trade routes. Herberstein was a sharp-eyed resident of this changing society. Twenty years after his departure, his account of Muscovy was published. It soberly described Muscovy's history, political rituals and religious practices. And it resorted to fantastical anecdotes and generalizations. Herberstein tells a story that has entered the folklore of Russia-watchers, about a blacksmith of German extraction who was married to a Russian woman. Their marriage seems satisfactory, until the woman claims that her husband does not love her. Why do you say such a preposterous thing, he asks. Because, she replies, 'you have never beaten me'. When the blacksmith went on to do this 'most cruelly', he told Herberstein that 'his wife showed much greater affection towards him. So he repeated the exercise frequently; and finally, while I was still at Moscow, cut off her head and legs.'

Such stories furnished the emerging legend of a special Russian predisposition to violence and cruelty. Herberstein used them too to conjure aphorisms about a national character of passivity, reducing the complex Muscovite economy of unfree labour to the idea that 'this people enjoy slavery more than freedom',[15] a notion that some journalists and academics borrowed to describe Russians in the Stalin era, and even the early twenty-first century. A German theologian, Sebastian Franck, drew together various first-hand accounts and then elaborated on them in a work of 1534. 'In sum,' he wrote, 'the people of the Muscovite state are rude, and furthermore they are subject to great servitude and tyranny, such that, as is the case among the Turks, anything anyone has is considered to be the king's own, and the king holds everything as his property.'[16] Franck's assumptions about the relationship between the manners of the people, their location beyond the realm of civilization and the implicit threat of tyranny have shaped 500 years of perceptions, on and off. Take Giles Fletcher, the English merchant who wrote of 'the Russe commonwealth' in 1591. In his opening epistle, he addressed the queen, Elizabeth I, telling her that Muscovy was 'a Tyrannical state (most unlike your own) without true knowledge of God, without written Laws, without common justice'. Its people were 'poor' and 'oppressed'.[17] Yet much of the latest research into Muscovy places its economy on a European continuum and its justice system within European norms.[18]

In the seventeenth century, the range of contacts between Muscovy and the West increased, shifting perceptions. Peter the Great (1682–1725) dramatically increased the significance of the process, setting Russia on course to be a modern state, a world empire and a European power. Being part of Europe and closer to 'the West' meant two different things. It was the chance to borrow administrative practices, legal principles, architecture and fashion. But it was also the necessity of engaging in the violent struggle for mastery that periodically characterized relations between the powers. Peter's armies were at war with Sweden, Catherine II's armies would fight the Turks, while Elizabeth and Alexander I found themselves preoccupied with pan-European conflicts. This new era of war and diplomacy was one in which Russophobia would have to be reconfigured, or at least superficially so.

The British, for example, might still have looked down on the Russians, but they were no longer on opposite wartime alliances as they had been in the Petrine era, and by the middle of the eighteenth century they saw the Russians as useful and effective partners, with a strong army, a massive territory and an invulnerable geography, potentially the key to their continental policy. According to a British writer, describing the contemporary history of Europe in 1748, 'Experience has taught us what

Effects a Shew of Liberty only could produce in a Country accustomed to Slavery, and groaning under the Yoke of Tyranny and Oppression: for in less than half a Century the Empire of Russia, from a poor contemptible people scarce spoken of in History, became a Nation formidable in War, and great in policy.'[19] A large and established expatriate British community lived in St Petersburg in the eighteenth century, including men of business, doctors, gardeners, soldiers, technical experts and their families. They assembled in the city's English church, several of whose chaplains travelled widely in Russia and wrote extensively about its history and culture for an audience back home. One of them, the Reverend Daniel Dumaresq, was especially proficient at developing links between the scholarly worlds of Britain and Russia. After 1800, chaplaincies in Moscow, Archangel, Riga and Odessa made cooperation and mutual understanding better. Among eighteenth-century tourists, a number of upper-class British men of letters wrote conscientious and well-informed accounts of Russian life, while the penal reformer John Howard investigated Russian prisons and chose to live in comfort in Crimea before his death. Casual Russophobia, the oxygen of the Russia Anxiety, was not abundant in this milieu.

It was not that the Russia Anxiety disappeared. After all, it is always a stubborn and dangerous survivor of world history. But it is a contingent one, activated by politics or personal dislike. It comes and goes, often rising and falling in the cycle that goes from fear to contempt to disregard. Edward Clarke, a Fellow of Jesus College, Cambridge, proved in his own narrow way that it was probably always just below the surface even when it was not in view. 'They are all,' he wrote when he visited Russia, 'high and low, rich and poor, alike servile to superiors; haughty and cruel to their dependents; ignorant, superstitious, cunning, brutal, dirty, mean.'[20]

Likewise, the Anxiety was a force of variable strength in France. Russia and France enjoyed a 'golden age' of relations between the Seven Years' War (1756–63) and the French Revolution.[21] The Russian nobility was increasingly Frenchified. They spoke French, embraced French culture, set up salons that let them inhabit a version of Paris. The common language and shared cultural sensibility allowed them to fit in with the European aristocracy, although not always as equal partners. Voltaire and Diderot symbolized the links between the French and Russian Enlightenments. But Catherine the Great reacted to the Revolution with deep mistrust, and the execution of Louis XVI brought the golden age to a close. Within a few years, the countries were at war. Unsurprisingly, France's defeat by Russia in the Napoleonic Wars unleashed the Anxiety for years to come.

The most elaborate display of the Russia Anxiety in the nineteenth century was the so-called Testament of Peter the Great, published in France in 1836. It enumerated Russia's fourteen-point plan for world domination. Even long after it was proved to be a forgery, it continued to be published and discussed as if it were genuine. War scares, Polish rebellion, flare-ups of the Eastern Question, in fact any moment when Russia caught the public's attention – during all of these episodes, the fake Testament was prime evidence for the prosecution. It had an afterlife in Cold War debates in the 1970s.[22] It remains a reference point in the imaginations of some policymakers – whether or not they have ever heard of it. Lighter but no less pernicious was Gustave Doré's *History of Holy Russia,* a grotesquely illustrated historical caricature published in the 1850s, in which the pornography of violence substitutes for Russian history, in a mean-spirited parody of apparent Russian barbarism over centuries. It was not a great success. But it was republished in Germany in 1917, 1937 and 1970, in France in 1967, and in the USA in 1971, in part as propaganda, in part as scholarly evidence for the back story of a particular definition of Soviet politics (one in which Ivan the Terrible and Leonid Brezhnev were actually the same man).[23]

But that came later. In their own time, such works as the 'Testament' of Peter the Great and Gustave Doré's *History* were the context in which France went to war against Russia in Crimea. By the 1850s, fear of Russia had given way to disregard and contempt, manifested in the conviction that French political culture was superior; in fact, anti-Russian feeling helped to define France's sense of its own politics. After all, backward old Nicholas I was on the throne in Russia, suppressing the Poles, when the French were establishing their newly liberal 'July monarchy'.[24] Similarly, by the 1830s and 1840s, some British elites began to define their own qualities – in their land of liberty and civilization – in distinction to Russia. The consequences of all this were grave geopolitical risks. One of many propaganda tracts on the subject from that period was *On the Designs of Russia* by the Member of Parliament and army general, George de Lacy Evans. It contained an eight-point plan explaining how to defeat Britain's greatest enemy. Top of the list: attack it pre-emptively.[25]

Britain's Russia Anxiety survived the Crimean War and made Britain reckless in its imperial dealings with Russia. The Anxiety has often distorted how policymakers interpret the risk that Russia poses to them, collapses the timeframe in which a Russian threat can be resolved and exaggerates their country's capacity to defeat it (it was the same for Germany in 1914). In the second half of the nineteenth century, there was little prospect that the British could fight a successful war against the Russians in either Asia or Europe, because of the configuration of alliances and the distribution of military and naval resources. Knowing this, but partly blinded by the Russia Anxiety, the British rolled the dice, but drew back, in two dangerous war scares of 1878 and 1885.[26]

The Anglo-Russian encounter between the 1840s and early 1900s, marked by rivalry over India, espionage clashes and alliance-building in Europe, is one of the most potent historical sources of the Russia Anxiety. Yet the Anxiety was not hard-wired: even at this time of imperial competition and European tension, the Anxiety came and went, had consequences of varying seriousness, and was contingent on events. Even in the run-up to the Crimean War, both governments were capable of cordial and careful relations, as they worked out exactly how to pursue their interests in south-east Europe. Nicholas I made a successful visit to England in 1844. The war was not the consequence of an inevitable contest between incompatible societies. During the fighting, British subjects in Russia were largely allowed to go about their lives peacefully and normally.[27] While hatred there might have been, and extravagant language there certainly was, actual examples of physical violence between the two countries after the Crimean War ended were zero apart from during the exceptional circumstances of the Russian Civil War, when British troops fought for one group of Russians in opposition to another.

Historians have come to argue that the 'Great Game' – the probes and counter-strikes, the espionage and the strategic competition between Britain and Russia over north-west India, Afghanistan and

Turkestan – has therefore been overblown, and even the term 'Great Game' was largely a later invention.[28] The two countries might have come close to war in the region in 1878–9, thanks not least to the tension-raising and misunderstanding-inducing Russia Anxiety, but local leaders, such as Abd al-Rahman Khan, had a much better grip on strategy and policy than the sometimes hapless great powers, who looked more like blunderers than master planners.[29] One of the reasons why the Anxiety can be so virulent but also fleeting is that it represents an accumulation of Russophobic rhetoric rather than real conflict. This was not a 'clash of civilizations' in any strategic or substantive sense,[30] though the language of British politics often placed Russia outside the boundaries of civilization. Yet Russia was not at war more often than the other great powers, not least Britain itself.

France, Britain and Russia ultimately became allies, fighting the First World War together. By then, though, Germany's fears of Russian conquest help to explain the reckless calls for a pre-emptive war in 1914. The German court had been divided in its attitude to Russia during the nineteenth century, with one side strikingly pro-Petersburg. Bismarck, the pragmatist, joined Germany to Russia in two major international agreements which helped to determine the course of European affairs, the Three Emperors' League in 1873 and then the Reinsurance Treaty in 1887. But general cultural attitudes in Germany were not so positive. In history and geography textbooks used in German schools between 1890 and 1914, Russia was usually shown to be 'backward', 'barbaric' and 'Asiatic'. 'We do not love the Russians, certainly not,' stated the *Frankfurter Zeitung*. 'They are dangerous to us and doubtless in their thinking and morality true Asians.'[31] Yet when war broke out, it was the Austrians who surpassed themselves in the atrocities they committed against local populations on the Eastern front (the Russians were also far from innocent).[32]

In the United States, meanwhile, sympathy and understanding towards Russia were not uncommon in the nineteenth century, partly promoted by the Russian connections of two presidents, Thomas Jefferson and John Quincy Adams. The Russia Anxiety was a force, once again, that was dependent for its existence on specific events. For many, such as the poet Walt Whitman, a sense existed that Russia and America were similar places, possessing a continental destiny, a messianic approach, even an instinct for liberation (serfdom and slavery were famously abolished at almost exactly the same time). By the later nineteenth century, though, this very similarity generated a more insidious understanding of Russia: that it was a bit like America but could be much more so if only it tried harder. It was not yet really civilized but it had the promise to become so. Plainly, there was a measure of contempt in this, and it was a variant of the Russia Anxiety. The great Russia expert of the time, George Kennan, whose namesake and relation became the country's leading Russia hand of the twentieth century, turned Russia into America's 'double', demanding that it mimic the United States.[33] In turn, this was one of the dimensions of America's twentieth-century Russia Anxiety. Looking through American lenses and deliberately not seeing the country on its own terms, Anxiety-prone observers were bound to see Russia as alien and malign or a disappointment and a poor learner.

After the First World War and the Russian Revolution, the Anxiety turned into the Red Menace, which was the background to the rise of fascism in Italy and of Nazism in Germany. This was the Russia Anxiety for a new generation, partly reprogrammed in the ideological language of urgent anti-communism. The Bolsheviks were the latest incarnation of the Russian barbarian. Hatred of the Left and hatred of Russia reinforced each other in what became, for the far Right, a virtuous circle. Italy's 'two red years' between 1918 and 1920 prompted an aggressive reaction that caused Mussolini to come to power by 1924. Although there were a number of reasons for the growing success of the Nazi Party in the 1920s, one of them was widespread fear of the extreme Left and the Russian Revolution. British and French bad feeling towards communism and Russia itself – which by the 1930s was a blend of reasonable moral judgement and age-old prejudice – contributed to the failure to form the pragmatic anti-Nazi alliance in 1939 that might have prevented a regional conflict becoming a world war. But for all its deepseated prejudices and the high-risk approach to foreign affairs that it engendered, the Anxiety could quickly dissolve when circumstances demanded. Few people and places were more popular in Britain and the USA during the Second World War than Uncle Joe, 'the Russians' and the Soviet Union.

*

At its heart, the Russia Anxiety is a Western phenomenon. The view onto Russia from other parts of the world has often looked quite different. Despite the long Russian border, China has not suffered from the Russia Anxiety. Relations date from the seventeenth century, when Muscovite expansion reached the Amur River.[34] For about 200 years, through to the middle of the nineteenth century, relations were calm and productive, facilitating trade. Neither side assumed it was superior to the other. This changed during the nineteenth century, as China was opened up and exploited by the great powers. Such notorious episodes as the Opium Wars of 1839–42 and 1856–60, prosecuted by the British, left deep anti-Western wounds. As a European power, Russia was implicated in an anti-Chinese superiority complex. It took part, for example, alongside Britain, France, Germany, the United States and several others in the suppression of the Boxer Rebellion, a prolonged cry of anguish against Western imperialism. But Russia was not only of the West, it was also Eurasian, with much of its territory lying in Asia; its imperialism was not quite so based on scientific racism.

Chinese elites became increasingly interested in Russia from the late nineteenth century. They learned about Russian culture, as more works of Russian literature were translated, and they pursued diplomacy, with the opening of more consular missions. What they saw were similar problems. Russia offered the Chinese an example of the perils and possibilities of modernization on a transcontinental landmass. And within a few years, it gave Chinese communists a model of revolution. China and the new Soviet Union formalized diplomatic relations in 1924, though Chinese forces had intervened against the Reds during the Russian Civil War. By 1929, massive instability across Eurasia, not least tensions over Mongolia, would interrupt diplomacy again. The People's Republic sought the friendship of the USSR after 1949, and many of its leading cadres had personal links to Moscow, even maintaining a love affair with the Russian Revolution,[35] but relations worsened after Khrushchev's condemnation of Stalin in 1956, even descending to a brief border conflict in 1969. It was only really with the Soviet collapse of 1991 that a new Chinese-Russian *modus vivendi* could emerge, leading to a Treaty of Friendship in 2001. In the Xi-Putin era, the level of military cooperation and arms trading, and the quality of cautiously amicable relations on the border, increased, at the same time that they were declining with the West.[36] Whatever each side might say about the other in private, this was a more polite and less risky relationship than Russia has with the Western powers, perhaps because no Asian military alliance defined itself against Russia in the way that NATO did.

And what about Africa? Russia did not have an empire in Africa, so it didn't exploit Africans, as the British did across the continent; it didn't massacre them, as the French did in Algeria; nor did it exterminate them, as the Belgians did in the Congo or the Germans tried to do in their south-western colony. In the twenty-first century, Russia was not buying up land and resources in the quasi-imperial manner of contemporary China. So there were no historic or present-day circumstances in which the Russia Anxiety could take hold. Nor did the Cold War create them, though the continent was a theatre in which soft power was exercised and proxy wars were waged, not least in Angola, Liberia and Ethiopia. The Soviet Union's development programme, in projects such as the Aswan Dam in Egypt, created positive associations. In the 1985–6 academic year, 18,118 black Africans came to the Soviet Union as students, with stipends and fees paid by Moscow (in a policy not calculated to reduce racism, the stipends were three times the level granted to Soviet students).[37] The end of the Cold War dramatically reduced these connections. Russia's image in Africa probably depends upon present-day initiatives rather than on history.[38] But the Russia Anxiety is unlikely to get in the way.

And why be scared of Russia in South America? Congenial relations, fleshed out with a record of cultural exchanges and personal links, extend back to the nineteenth century, sometimes boosted, as in the case of Brazil, by modest migration from Russia.[39] The Russian Academy of Sciences has a Latin America Institute with close ties to similar scholarly bodies in South America. Spanish and Portuguese were significant languages in Soviet higher education. In 1985–6, 17,277 Latin Americans came to study in the USSR; just over one-third of them were Cubans.[40] But things can change fast, for worse as well as for better. Mexico has no heritage of the Russia Anxiety, and yet a cut-out of one was quickly assembled for it. 'The Russians are coming to get our oil. Russia already controls Venezuela's oil,' claimed an audio message, sent to hundreds of thousands of mobile phone users via the WhatsApp messaging service during Mexico's presidential election year of 2018. The then American secretary of state Rex Tillerson warned the government about likely Russian interference in the poll.[41] It was unclear whether anyone would take any notice, or whom the Russians were supporting, though the American stance towards the Mexican poll was obvious in April 2017, when John Kelly, then secretary of homeland security in the US government, had let Mexicans know that a left-wing president 'would not be good for America or Mexico'.[42]

But they have taken notice in other far-flung places in the past. Russophobia became a global industry thanks to the British Empire. Yet what, really, could be more preposterous than Russophobia in New Zealand? British culture in the colony transmitted a tendency to feel the Russia Anxiety, one that was exacerbated by pre-1914 imperial rivalry and then by anti-communism. It came and went: during the First World War, in which soldiers from New Zealand fought in disproportionate numbers, public feeling was anti-German, not anti-Russian. And it had specific qualities, such as worries about undercutting by Soviet trade, especially after Soviet dumping of butter on the UK market in 1931. Hounding of pro-Soviet academics – McCarthyism before McCarthyism – gave way to inter-governmental cooperation, when the finance minister, Walter Nash, travelled to Moscow in April 1937. When war broke out in 1939, Russophobia was less evident in the life of New Zealand than at any time in the previous forty years.[43] Again, the virulence of the Anxiety quickly dissipated when the time was right.

Let's draw some preliminary conclusions. The Russia Anxiety is a historically deep-seated feature of international relations. Western commentary since the end of the Cold War has often been 'hysterical and one-sided', according to one of the most respected of writers on the subject – and he was describing the 1990s, not the Trump-Putin years.[44] 'Healing its imperial and Russophobic complexes is going to take time,' wrote one expert on the American 'anti-Russia Lobby' – in 2009.[45]

This is not an imaginary construct in the heads of Russians. Among

Westerners, feeling the Anxiety can seem instinctive and natural, even a careful response to events, but it is usually irrational, a displacement, a political choice rather than a necessity; and when there are good reasons to be worried, the Anxiety distorts and exacerbates them. Fear of Russia among its immediate neighbours on the western border is, by contrast, involuntary, while fear elsewhere, even among former adversaries in Turkey or Afghanistan, is minimal. Meanwhile, no one can predict the international effects of the Russia Anxiety; they can amount to nothing, or they can contribute to the outbreak of war. Either way, submitting to the Russia Anxiety is a decision, and a high-risk one.

But it's easy to succumb. When people do, and whether they realize it or not, they often draw on a set of categories devised by a nineteenth-century French aristocrat who freelanced as a Russia expert. Writing about his Russian adventures during the reign of Nicholas I, Astolphe de Custine compiled the most enduring taxonomy of the Russia Anxiety.

Custine, whose vituperation began this chapter, was perhaps the most important link between the bald Russophobia of the sixteenth century and the more differentiated Russia Anxiety of the twenty-first. The account of his journey to Russia of 1839 was based on a simple narrative arc of revelation and disillusion. A fan of Nicholas I from afar, and smitten once he met him in person, Custine claimed a pro-Russian agenda for his trip. He shared with other French aristocrats the sense that Nicholas embodied a stable compact between sovereign and nobility. Custine was anxious about the consequences of tyranny, which, he fretted, derived from too much democracy. Perhaps Russia offered answers that France had failed to find. But from his arrival in Russia he was convinced it did not. The aggressive anti-Russian qualities of his book were hardly captured in its original title: *Russia in 1839*. It became a success in its own time. Edited and republished more than a century later during the Cold War, when it was stripped of historical context and read in a literal manner,[46] its messages carried to new generations. It is still lauded on 'must-read' lists about Russia and cited in travel guides.

Custine's book elaborated a Russian phantasmogoria but it was not entirely the result of misplaced fears and unfair judgements. Although

Custine described a personal and intellectual journey, it was not an idiosyncratic one. It made sense to his fellow countrymen. He had come of age during the Napoleonic Wars. As a result of their invasion of Russia, the French had suffered half a million casualties. They had experienced the humiliation of Russian soldiers parading through Paris and the presence of a triumphant tsar. On French soil, Alexander celebrated Russian nationhood and mocked the French. Even twenty-five years later, it was not surprising that Custine's position turned anti-Russia, or that there was such a big audience for his observations. Custine's description of Russia was a caricature, but anti-Russian feeling in France was not only the result of an irrational Anxiety.

He was born in 1790. Three years later, his father – himself sympathetic to the Revolution, but nevertheless an aristocrat – was executed during the Terror. His mother had tried to save her husband's life and then after his death to revive her family's prospects. She forged contacts across high society, starting a long-running affair with Chateaubriand, not least for the purpose of saving her remaining family. But despite his advantages – being an aristocrat in the era of France's monarchical restoration, not to mention having a modest fortune and a brilliant mother – Custine did not live up to the promise of his circumstances. He spent a few years in the diplomatic service, but back in France he drifted from salon to salon in search of a wife. He and his mother didn't have the resources to keep up their estate, and a good marriage was the best prospect of boosting their income. His mother eventually found the perfect match for him, a very young woman called Léontine, whose family lived not far from them in Normandy. Her fortune was adequate, and they married in 1821. They immediately had a child. She died a year after that, pregnant again, at the age of twenty.

Custine had felt affection for his wife. She had not only been a source of financial salvation but an alibi, because Custine was gay. His mother lived a worldly life, so she was aware of the reason for her son's frequent trips to Paris. Shortly after the marriage, a young Englishman, Edward Sainte-Barbe, moved into the household in Normandy. When Léontine died, the two men stayed together until Custine's death thirty-four years later. Their home was as openly a homosexual one as was consistent with propriety. Both men had affairs with others, but they stayed true to each other. In 1835, they admitted a young Pole, Ignatius Gurowski, to their household. Ignatius's family had been sent into exile from the Russian Empire following its participation in the Polish uprising of 1831. Custine was interested more generally in the exiled Polish community and knew Chopin.

Keen to learn more about the Russian Empire of which his friends had been a part, seeing literary opportunities after completing a successful travelogue on Spain, and ready to make a case, if he could, to end the enforced exile of the Gurowski family, Custine set off from Paris for the German Baltic coast in June 1839, where he caught a steamship from Lübeck to St Petersburg. After spending time in the capital and then in Moscow, he more briefly visited the nearby provincial towns of Yaroslavl, Nizhnyi Novgorod and Vladimir. He was usually surrounded by French-speaking high society. Just over three months later, on 26 September, he left the Russian Empire and arrived in Tilsit.[47]

*Russia in 1839* was published in 1843. Priced at 30 francs for four volumes, it quickly sold out its run of 3,000 copies. A second edition sold out, too. Translations soon appeared in English, Swedish and German. A Belgian publisher printed a pirated edition. Over the next decade, further editions – legal and not – enjoyed success, until Custine put together an abridged version for propaganda purposes during the Crimean War.[48]

The record of Custine's experiences, styled as letters home, merged Russophobic comments in a compelling travelogue. On display are all the strands of the Russia Anxiety. For a start, there was fear. Custine was always uneasy during his Russian travels. He projected his worries onto a wider argument about international affairs that carried great weight throughout the Cold War and again in the 2010s. 'I can see the colossus from nearby,' he wrote. '[. . .] It seems to me that it is principally destined to punish the evils of European civilization by another invasion.' His fear easily elided into contempt. Russia was a 'colossus', and the European civilization of which it was not a part had its own failures and 'evils', but Russia was separate, different. 'Between France and Russia there is a Great Wall of China,' he surmised: 'the language and character of the Slavs.' His contempt for the people behind the wall was boundless. He consistently denied that they were civilized. 'Imagine a half-savage people who have been regimented, without being civilized,' he wrote: 'then you will understand the moral and social state of the Russians.' In turn, contempt shifted towards disregard. 'The Russians have nothing to teach us,' he sniffed. Civilized Europeans could turn their backs on the Russians and get on with their own plans for carving up the continent. But not quite, because the cycle of the Anxiety turned disregard soon enough into fear. Custine himself immediately finished the thought: they might not have anything to teach us, 'but there is much that they can make us forget.'[49]

Custine's was a pathology born of lack of national self-awareness. His own father had been consumed by the French Revolution at a time when the 'heart' of Europe – Paris – was experiencing a total collapse into brutality and lawlessness. Yet he had no doubt that his own people were entirely civilized, and that this gave him the ability to see that civilization was never more than a veneer in Russia. Whatever the rights and wrongs of their case, and knowingly or not, Cold Warriors in the 1950s followed Custine's script, as did the received wisdom of the 2010s. The script itself drew on centuries of similar descriptions, and ultimately on an appeal to history itself.

Custine's journey was across time as well as space. His case against Russia rested not simply on what he saw in 1839, but on an argument about the structure of history over the *longue durée*. Another dimension of the Custine taxonomy was chronological, about the essence of history and the historical process.

He pointed to Russians' problem with history, 'with no Middle Ages, with no ancient memories, with no Catholicism and with no chivalry behind them'.[50] It was as if nineteenth-century Russia lived against a backdrop of oblivion. Russia had plenty of history compared with, say, the United States, but the design of its past – the periods and labels that one might use to describe it – were quite different from that of France. Greeks and Romans had made it to Custine's homeland (admittedly the former rather tangentially), leaving an imprint, not least in the historical imagination. The Greeks had established colonies in the southern Russian lands, but the Romans had not, and so the 'ancients' were indeed a less obvious historical presence than they were in French self-understanding. Before the Riurikid dynasty and the foundation of Kieven Rus in 862 AD, the territory was governed by tribes which left no written record. In this sense, Custine was not wrong about Russia's lack of 'ancient memories', even if the connection between the ancient Mediterranean and the prospects for modern civilization, either in 1839 or the twenty-first century, is only a debating point.

Custine's claim that Russia had no Middle Ages, though, is a different matter. By any reasonable measure, medieval Russia lasted for centuries and has a rich historiography to describe and explain it. But this period was invisible to Custine when he looked back on Muscovy, because, for him, the Middle Ages were created by Catholicism. The East Slavic lands were formally Christianized during the reign of Vladimir the Great in 988, but theirs was the Orthodox Christianity of the Byzantine Empire. It came ultimately from Constantinople, the 'second Rome' that was the seat of the Roman Empire from the fourth century until 1453. No matter that for hundreds of these years Byzantium was a flourishing and complex civilization at a time when Western Europe was experiencing the 'Dark Ages', and Rome was permanently under threat from 'Barbarians'; for Custine, it was St Peter's Holy See in the Italian peninsula that was the guardian and creator of Christian culture.

Few would deny that the Orthodox and Catholic traditions contributed to social and cultural differences inside Europe. But to exaggerate the distinction is to follow Custine down a rhetorical approach to history whose effect is to exclude Russia and perhaps also Greece and Bulgaria from Western civilization. It seems reasonable enough, too, to say that different parts of Europe experienced the Middle Ages in different ways. For instance, the East Slavic lands did not have a direct analogue of self-governing city-states or of guilds, which offered groups of craftsmen some organized autonomy from the state in northern Europe.[51] But how much difference this has made to historical change over the long term is really just a matter of speculation.

For the Marquis de Custine, Russian history was inadequate. It got low marks. He passed this viewpoint on to later Western Europeans and Americans. The Russia Anxiety is exacerbated by a confusion about history: not just a matter of mistaking the historical facts one could invoke to explain current events, but of imagining a whole historical process that was apparently guiding events in an undesirable direction. We might call it the fallacy of 'instant history'. Used right, history might resolve the Russia Anxiety. Used wrong, it makes the Anxiety much worse.

At the heart of the Trump-Putin crisis as it played out between the two elections of November 2016 and March 2018 was the seductive peril of assuming that events were not complex or contingent at all. Instead, they were unprecedented in their course or ancient in their causes. They might even be simultaneously both. After all, Vladimir Putin and Donald Trump have one thing in common: a rise to power that was both unimagined and inevitable.

What could this mean? Both men enjoyed political success against all the odds. Their rise was completely unanticipated. Appointed prime minister in August 1999, a position from which he was catapulted to acting president within months, Putin confounded the global industry of Kremlin-watchers. And Trump: well, the possibility of his election was an international joke until election night itself. But once they had assumed the presidency of their respective countries, their triumphs became somehow inevitable, explicable by the deep social and cultural forces of the time. More than this: they both fitted into the deep patterns of the past. They were History Men. Putin was the product of centuries of Russian violence, expansionism and greed. Trump was the manifestation of America's original sin, the unresolved issue of race, and of its great contemporary struggle, the challenge to its supremacy in a globalized economy, historic forces which together secured the loyalty of his electoral base.

We might call it instant history, instant in the speed of its analysis, and instant too in how it imagines the passage of time. Instant history assumes one of two things, depending on what needs to be explained. Sometimes, it instantly and unreflectively assumes inevitability, drawing straight lines between what happened in the past and what is happening now. Or, at other times, it draws an instant cut-off, following which things today are completely new. Both halves of instant history generate the Russia Anxiety. Take 'hybrid warfare', the idea that Russian foreign policy brings together episodes of armed force with campaigns of fake news, aggressive digital interventions with the cultivation of political extremists. Hybrid warfare is warfare without conventional war. Arguing that such a strategy is brand-new and uniquely pernicious is what instant history is all about. Instant history allowed people to say that Russia was at war with America when on calmer reflection this was simply not the truth. America–Russia relations might not look like a war – battles between soldiers, bombs out of the sky – but that is because, the instant historians say, it is a new type of war. But no one who lived through a war would recognize this as a war, and most military historians do not see the strategy as a new one. While the technologies and the term might be novel, the principles of hybrid warfare are as old as the hills, used in the ancient world as well as during the Cold War (not least by the United States).[52]

Perhaps more common, though, is the assumption of inevitability caused by the intransigence of history's deep structures. This is instant history, too, though in another way, because it often represents an instant historical judgement on current affairs, a reflex in our historical imaginations: it must be like this now because it has been before; perhaps it's always really been like this. And yet much of what happens in the present looks like the result of our own actions now: our good intentions, malice and luck. A family of Soviet celebrities illustrates the point.

They were a grand Soviet family. Sergei Mikhalkov was a famous children's writer of the Stalin era. His younger son, Nikita, was a ubiquitous actor in the post-Stalin years. He became a film director and then a part-time politician after 1991. His credits include *Burnt by the Sun,* an award-winning film about Stalin's Terror. Nikita's elder brother, Andrei, took their mother's surname, Konchalovsky. He was another major figure in the film industry, working with Andrei Tarkovsky and directing adaptations of Chekhov and Turgenev that won international prizes, before going to work in the United States. With their creative talents, resourcefulness and ideological adaptability, the Mikhalkovs showcased some of the themes of Soviet life.

Although famous for his children's poetry, Sergei's most influential work was the lyrics of the Soviet national anthem, composed in 1944.

This stirring tune became part of the soundscape of the Cold War, the soundtrack to Communist Party congresses and Red Square parades, Olympic medal ceremonies and documentaries about the space race. When Khrushchev denounced the crimes of Stalin in 1956 the lyrics were no longer appropriate. The music remained, but without words to accompany it. Two decades passed before a new version was approved in 1977. After the collapse of Soviet power in 1991, when many of the symbols of the old regime were removed, some music by the nineteenth-century composer Mikhail Glinka became the new national anthem. But it didn't tug at the heart strings in quite the same way. In late 2000, in the months following Putin's first election to the presidency, the Soviet anthem was reintroduced.

Of course, it needed new words – it made little sense to praise the Communist Party of Lenin – and Sergei was brought out of retirement to compose new lyrics. He was eighty-seven. One of its original signature lines, 'raised up by Stalin, we're true to the people' (you can hear the words if you know the tune as it scans the same in Russian) had become 'raised up by Lenin to follow a just cause' in its late Soviet variant. Of course, all this went from the text of 2000. For instance, one famous line – 'the party of Lenin, the strength of the people' – was replaced by another: 'the wisdom of ancestors, borne by the people'.[53] Those words – *the wisdom of ancestors, borne by the people* – lie at the heart of this book. Let's call them the Mikhalkov Line.

Do historical events and personalities really walk along the Mikhalkov Line? After all, the notion of 'the wisdom of centuries, borne by the people' is influential rhetoric in some Russian circles. For others, of course, history walks along a path parallel to the Mikhalkov Line, and contemporary Russia enjoys not the consolation of historic wisdom but the burden of centuries of backwardness, or anti-democracy, or coercion. At the heart of the Russia Anxiety is usually an assumption that contemporary Russia is not the distillation of hundreds of years of wisdom, but rather an awful accumulation of error, passivity and violence. This is the reasoning of instant history: if something is not brand new, it's probably deeply ancient. But it is implausible that the historical process resembles a one-way road. Russians have spent their history straying from the Mikhalkov Line and its parallel pathway, just as the populations of all societies have strayed from their equivalents. The German 'special path', or *Sonderweg*, is a poor kind of explanation for German history, and Russian history also deserves a more sophisticated reading.

This is partly because historical change is so often the result of chance. In a country whose history is marked by big events – invasion, war, revolution – *contingency* has played an outsize role in shaping its development. The direction of the Mongol invasion in the thirteenth century was partly determined by the weather, so that, as it turned out, Moscow would overtake Kiev for good as the metropolis of East Slavic civilization. Personality-driven, cloak-and-dagger conspiracy was the only reason for the elevation to the throne of the most influential Romanovs, Peter in 1682 and Catherine in 1762. Later, the Bolshevik seizure of power in 1917 depended on the most improbable combination of circumstances.

And it is also because of all the obstacles that clutter the Mikhalkov Line, making easy transit along it impossible. It can be tempting for historians, under pressure to justify the purpose of their work or keen to push a political agenda, to simplify the link between the past and the present. In 1811, Nikolai Karamzin, the writer who has a claim to be Russia's first great historian, found himself in conflict with Tsar Alexander I's leading adviser, Mikhail Speransky. Karamzin believed that Speransky was proposing reforms that compromised the principles of autocracy. Seeking to defend autocracy, Karamzin wrote, 'the present is a consequence of the past. To judge the former one must recollect the latter.'[54] But reading the connections between past and present is fraught with risk. For a start, historical sources are products of their time – not our time. And the present cannot only be the consequence of the past. Too many unique contingencies are at any moment in conflict with each other. Countless pasts, near and distant, long ago and recent, and often contradictory to each other, simultaneously contribute to the fleeting present. The relationship between past and present has aspects that seem solid and logical, possible to describe. But it has other dimensions that are simply inscrutable, to historians and to anyone else. And, complicating everything still more, Russia, like many other countries, has had moments when its rulers self-consciously embarked on a new start, wilfully discarding their relationship to the past, or partly claiming to do so – most of all, Peter the Great in the late seventeenth century, and the Bolsheviks in 1917. The Mikhalkov Line – a transit point for the Russia Anxiety – is quickly blocked off by this more careful analysis of history.

Back in the 1840s, Custine's French audience gleefully consumed his conclusions about the country that had roundly defeated it two decades before. He also had a rather more select audience back in St Petersburg. Nicholas I rose above the reaction to the book of his former guest – a man he had invited to his daughter's wedding and entertained in high style – and did not dignify it with a response. But he apparently read the book and threw it to the ground in fury.[55] Custine's work and that of others, and their recycling in wider conversations, have always redounded on the country they describe. Faced with the Russia Anxiety, Russians have reacted in a number of ways, some of which have made the Anxiety sharper. Worst of all, some of them have swallowed the Anxiety whole. If the Russia Anxiety has had a 500-year history, it's no wonder that the Russians themselves have been affected by it.

## UNCLE BORIS

'It is embarrassing to be Russian these days,' says Uncle Boris, shortly before his grisly demise in the BBC's 2018 international gangster drama, *McMafia*. He's talking to his Anglicized nephew, a smooth-talking banker indistinguishable from his public-school contemporaries. Uncle Boris wants to remind the younger man of the feelings inspired by his post-Soviet family heritage, which created such a sense of awkwardness when his *nouveaux riches* relatives dropped him off at his boarding school at the start of term. But in early 2018, any lingering embarrassment was only the start of the problem for expat Russians (99.99 per cent of whom were peaceable souls and not oligarchs, spies, gangsters or prostitutes). At the time the TV series aired, Russians were objects of suspicion, and contact with some of them raised doubts about one's patriotism. In the United States, where the series did not show, news media and politicians were still speculating about whether any official who had recently had a conversation with the Russian ambassador might be a potential traitor. Within weeks, the concerted international response to the attempted murder in the United Kingdom of the double-agent Sergei Skripal had led to dozens of diplomatic expulsions and threatened a major international crisis.

Faced with hostile rhetoric and worse, Russians at home and abroad had a choice of answers. One response was to fight fire with fire. Vladimir Medinsky, who would soon become minister of culture, completed a three-volume bestseller called *Myths about Russia* in 2011. By then, post-Soviet Russia's disillusion with the intentions of the West was already solidly established. Medinsky combined sober analysis with rhetorical broadsides, plausibility with tendentiousness. He argued that 'the creation of black political myths' about Russia in the West extended as far as 'total hatred' and 'Russophobic paranoia' whose aim was to weaken Russia's international standing and domestic cohesion, allowing 'the seeds of self-disparagement and complexes' to germinate. Such an approach takes reasonable points – that the historical relationship between today's Russia and Latvia is not simply a matter of the former crushing the latter, or that the Russian defeat of Napoleon was due to human effort and not just a result of the weather – and extracts from them an angry challenge to the West.[56] Another popular author, the TV host Igor Prokopenko, took a similar idea and expressed it more concisely. 'This is not the first century,' he wrote, 'in which Western intellectuals have pedantically taught us to be ashamed of the fact that we are Russians.' Prokopenko's myth-busting agenda was still more explicitly driven forward by the notion of national revival than Medinsky's. His aim, he wrote, was to confirm in the reader's mind the 'necessity to love the motherland'.[57]

This populist tone and language recall some of Donald Trump's speeches during the election campaign of 2016. Vladimir Putin has drawn from a more subtle repertoire of similar sentiments. Commentators interpreted his election victory of 2018 as a success for the 'patriotic majority'. But most of this majority are quiet folk, keen to avoid international politics, or, if they must face them, to pull up the drawbridge, at least psychologically. Given centuries-long anxieties about foreign invasion, and decades-long fears about the good faith of the West, a fortress mentality is a natural Russian response at moments of international crisis. But perhaps the most common response is fear

of war. In Russia's past and present, war scares don't generate jingo-
ism, but they compound the existing fear of war. The idea that
nationhood is more powerfully felt and expressed in Russia than in
other countries, that the Russians are forever on the lookout for a
chance to sacrifice all for Mother Russia – that all it takes is for the
right leader to tell them what to do, or the right combination of insults
and incentives to drive them forward, pitchforks raised – is one of the
most misguiding clichés in European history.

Still, the character of Uncle Boris reminds us that some Russians are
embarrassed about their national origins. Others are ashamed or angry
about the actions of their fellow citizens. There are people everywhere
who condemn their own country for its sins, look down upon their com-
patriots, even renounce their citizenship. In the case of Russia, these
self-critical arguments have often been conducted in exile. A common
message is love for country but hatred of its government. This was the
mission statement of Alexander Solzhenitsyn, writing in his Vermont
compound in the two decades after 1974. But it also informed the émigré
characters who populate the novels of Vladimir Nabokov or Ivan Bunin,
or the Russian intelligentsia-in-exile that was so significant in American
university and government departments during the Cold War.

Some Russians have taken renunciation to its bitter conclusion. The
philosopher Pyotr Chaadayev was the most famous example of all.
'Alone in the world, we have given nothing to the world, learnt nothing
from the world, and bestowed not a single idea upon the fund of human
ideas,' he wrote in 1836. 'We have not contributed in any way to the
progress of the human spirit, and whatever has come to us from that
progress we have disfigured.'[58] This caused a major scandal in St Petersburg. It is a fearsome charge sheet. Russophobia is perhaps most
pungent when it takes the form of a dialogue of agreement between
insiders and outsiders. Chaadayev's argument that Russia was uncivi-
lized was an historical one: he claimed that Russia lacked a history; it
did not possess organic or useful traditions. 'Russian civilization is still
so close to its source,' wrote Custine, whose trip to Russia was three
years after the Chaadayev *cause célèbre* – 'that it resembles barbarism.'[59] When he set off for Russia, Custine carried in his pocket a letter
of introduction to Chaadayev.[60] Custine had read widely in Russian

sources, and before setting out he must have come across the writer and social critic Alexander Radishchev's work of 1790 about his journey from St Petersburg to Moscow.[61] 'A barge-hauler who goes to the tavern with downcast head and returns blood-spattered from blows to the face may help to explain much that has seemed puzzling in Russian history,' posits Radishchev.[62] This is merely silly, but it is right up Custine's street.

The comic novels of the Soviet period put this self-critical strain of the Russia Anxiety under the literary microscope. 'I wish I'd been born in a small French town,' says Nikolai, the lazy and incompetent main character of Yuri Olesha's *Envy* (1927), 'grown up on dreams, set myself some lofty goal, and one fine day left my little town, and walked to the capital, and there, working fanatically, achieved my goal. But I wasn't born in the West.'[63] In Mikhail Bulgakov's *Black Snow*, a satire on Soviet theatrical life, written but not published in the 1930s, one's origins are always something to be denied, modified or completely rewritten. The characters in Vladimir Sorokin's *The Queue*, first published in Paris in 1985, are waiting in line for they know not which deficit item, but the more foreign it is the better. Perhaps they are coats with Astrakhan collars. 'Sure they're not Bulgarian?' asks one character. 'Of course not. Real Turkish. That's why there's such a queue,' says the next person in line.[64]

Less ironic self-criticism came from out-and-out opponents of communist rule: not those like Solzhenitsyn, who made a distinction between people and system, and retained affection for one while condemning the other, but those who came to see the West as a much preferable alternative to their homeland. Such people included 'White' émigrés, fleeing the Revolution to Prague, Berlin, Paris or Shanghai, and then scattering around the world, together with their sons and daughters born in exile. And there was a much smaller group, of political dissidents, Jewish 'refuseniks' who had been allowed to emigrate in the 1970s, and even defectors. Some of these people were critical of the West; others idealized it, and defined the Soviet Russia they had left behind in contradistinction to it. Oleg Gordievsky, a KGB spy who defected to Britain in the 1970s, later wrote of the Soviet population that it 'was composed entirely of Homo Sovieticuses: a new type had been created, of inadequate people, lacking initiative or the will to work, formed by Communist society.'[65]

The recycling of outsiders' Russophobia by insiders is a toxic process. Perhaps no one worked harder to avoid such an outcome, or inadvertently contributed to its realization, than the American diplomat and writer George Frost Kennan. He's our first lesson in how history can dissolve the Russia Anxiety.

## THE PARADOX OF GEORGE F. KENNAN

The most significant encounter between Russia and 'the West' in the twentieth century took place in the imagination of George F. Kennan, America's leading expert on the Soviet Union and Russia during the Cold War. Kennan was a true Russia expert, a man of deep thought and good faith, and as such was immune to the Russia Anxiety. His worries about the intentions of the Soviet leadership were rational, the result of knowledge, experience and reflection. In some ways he loved Russia. 'Outside the little oasis of the diplomatic colony,' he wrote of the pre-war Moscow embassies, 'there stretched still, fascinating and inviting, the great land and life of Russia, more interesting to me than any other in the world.'[66] But even as he presented a sympathetic view of Russians, the result could be alienating. 'The air of Russia is psychically impregnated,' he wrote, 'as ours is not.'[67] Gifted as he was, he saw the oppressive patterns in Russian history of common cliché, and though he added fine grains and paradoxes to the picture, he sometimes presented a grandiose and emotional view of the country, which only added fuel to America's Russia Anxiety during the early Cold War. He gave a generation of Americans the intellectual tools to exploit the Russia Anxiety in ways that he himself came to deplore.

Yet his achievement in the interface between Russian scholarship and high diplomacy in America's Cold War was formidable. Unlike narrower minds, he framed a critique of Soviet policy and then doubted it, remaining true to his scholarly instincts yet retaining his political influence. In so doing, he came to suggest a cure for America's Russia Anxiety through greater national self-awareness. This was an intellectual trajectory which his harder-line admirers came to see as the result of a blind spot.[68] In the career of George F. Kennan we might bring together the strands that run through this chapter.

His life and work remind us that the Russia Anxiety is an historic condition that's existed for centuries but which we shape ourselves by our own interpretation of history; they permit us to observe the logical conclusion of the Anxiety, the risk of mass destruction; and they show us a way to reduce the Anxiety safely.

Kennan was born into a prosperous Wisconsin family in 1904. His father was a lawyer, and his mother died when he was very young. The family looked outwards. They travelled to Europe, learned languages and found out about an ageing relation, also called George, who explored Siberia, wrote major books about it, and became one of the most influential Russianists of his day. The younger George studied at Princeton and spent a summer footling around Western and Southern Europe. After he graduated, he passed the exams for the Foreign Service. He remained a diplomat for a quarter of a century. In the 1950s, he began a second, long career as a scholar and public intellectual at Princeton's Institute for Advanced Study, though he twice emerged from academic life to take up ambassadorial appointments, including briefly to the Soviet Union in 1952. He lived to be 101, the ultimate Russia hand.

Even if the elder George's Russian exploits were only peripheral to his childhood, Kennan's whole life was a meditation on, and an intervention in, Russia and the USSR. When he had the chance, after postings to Geneva and Hamburg, he began to study Russian. The Service gave him three years to do so, funding his time as a student of Russian language, literature and history in Berlin. Then they sent him to Riga to try out his expertise. It was the nearest he could get to Russia, and the place where he started a family with his Norwegian wife. Two years later, in 1933, Kennan was part of a small team setting up an embassy in Moscow, after Washington finally established diplomatic relations with the Soviet Union. He stayed for five years, after which he was posted to Prague. Kennan's war was a mixed one: he endured internment in Germany for several months, served in the diplomatic mission in Lisbon, worked back in Washington, DC, and then returned to Moscow. After a last spell back at Washington, followed by his resignation and translation to Princeton in 1950, he returned briefly to diplomatic life in 1952 as ambassador to Moscow.

Kennan had wide experience of Stalinism in its three acts: the 1930s, the Great Fatherland War and after 1945. He was not encumbered by a revolutionary past, and his viewpoint did not emerge from detailed knowledge of Marxism. 'Distaste for the Stalin regime,' Kennan later wrote, 'did not come by way of disillusionment of an earlier enthusiasm.'[69] He knew the Soviet Union from within and without, from above and below, or at least as much as a Stalin-era diplomat could; he had an independent understanding of the country's domestic life and its international politics, and a scholarly appreciation of its literature and history. Stalin himself praised Kennan's language skills. They said he sounded like an intellectual from the age of Pushkin.

Despite being declared *persona non grata* after some undiplomatic utterances while visiting Berlin, following little more than a summer as ambassador between May and October 1952, Kennan's reputation was secure. It rested on the so-called Long Telegram. On 22 February 1946, labouring under the effects of a bad cold, and with Ambassador Averell Harriman away, Kennan wrote a 5,000-word analysis of the Soviet threat to the US and the West and sent it to his colleagues in Washington by telegram, partly to be sure of attracting their attention. It was the longest telegram in the history of the State Department. In it, Kennan argued that the time had come to draw a line in the sand. It was impossible to negotiate with the Soviet Union, whose government was trapped by a combination of Russian history and Marxist ideology. But he also argued, in a quieter and somewhat contradictory key, that compromises might be possible, that the Soviets had no interest in advancing any further, and that their government was rational in its intentions, if conspiratorial in its organization.

The Long Telegram was keenly read back in the State Department, where officials focused on the essential differences it portrayed between the USSR and the West, and the futility of accommodation. It articulated a sense that already existed, and prefigured Churchill's speech about the Iron Curtain that he delivered in Fulton, Missouri, the following month. The Telegram was transmitted to a wide and enthusiastic audience through an anonymous article Kennan wrote for *Foreign Affairs* the following July, where he talked more explicitly about 'containing' the USSR.

When his authorship was revealed, Kennan became a diplomatic celebrity, and remained one for the rest of his life. He influenced President Truman, for whom the Telegram was the analytical basis of the containment policy. Most of Kennan's admirers today perceive him as the *de facto* author of the policy that saved the Western world. Before the Long Telegram, the narrative goes, the Americans were wobbling, trying to see the best in Uncle Joe. After the Telegram, the scales fell from their eyes, and the outlook was clear. There was no truck in dealing with the Soviets. But war was too dangerous. So the adversary had to be *contained*. Kennan wanted the Americans to stand up politically to Stalin's government, and to establish a common defence, based on a shared political agenda, with their European allies. 'Never,' he wrote later, '[. . .] did I consider the Soviet Union a fit ally or associate, actual or potential, for this country.'[70]

Kennan neither wanted war nor wished to court it. The paradox was that he provided the intellectual rationale for a US policy that transcended his intentions. He fretted about a 'Truman Doctrine' of ostentatious containment, with its 'universal and pretentious note, appealing to the patriotic self-idealization which so often sets the tone of discussion about foreign policy in our public life, but which is actually unrealistic and pernicious in its effect on the soundness of public understanding of our international situation'. Kennan wrote derisively about John Foster Dulles, Eisenhower's secretary of state, who 'spoke of that "liberation" and that "massive retaliation" which, in reality, he had no intention of inflicting on anybody'.[71] He was very cautious about the military and did not want any talk of war, which was one of the reasons why he helped to design the Marshall Plan as a scheme to which the USSR and Eastern bloc were invited, even though he knew that the Soviets would decline the invitation and force their satellites to do the same. But Kennan's ideas were taken further and pushed out of context. Determined that the Soviets should advance no further, the 'Truman Doctrine' underwrote the CIA's anti-communist intervention in Western European elections, and the attempt to shore up the anti-communist opposition in the Greek civil war. In time, it would be the basis of interventions in Latin America, the stand-off with Khrushchev in Cuba and the war in Vietnam. But long before then, the Russia Anxiety had turned to panic in Senator McCarthy's anti-communist hearings. Russian émigrés in the United States might have feared McCarthy, but many of them felt the Russia Anxiety. Kennan contributed to the intellectual licence that enabled this.

George Kennan, with his training and wide-ranging experience, looked at Russia in layers. The result was his profound alarm about the Russia Anxiety. First was the layer of deep historical structures. Here Kennan implied a paradox. On the one hand, the Soviet leadership's behaviour was predictable, deriving from ingrained cultural patterns, as well as the imperatives of Marxist ideology; it was very likely to perceive certain kind of threats, to express itself volubly as a result, to ready itself for war. On the other hand, it was open to negotiation and compromise. This was precisely because it had no intention of launching a war. Instead, it was a formidable political and ideological adversary that had to be opposed by political and ideological means. Second were the social layers, of people and government, which Kennan believed did not overlap and possessed different characters and aims. The people were peaceful, independent-minded and terrified of war, while their government uttered bellicose rhetoric when it had the chance.

In short, it was the Soviet government that was the opponent of its American counterpart, but not the Russian people (or, presumably, the Soviet peoples).[72] A third layer was the international status of the Soviet Union. Here, Kennan made a distinction between political adversary and military enemy. He always argued that the Soviet Union was the former, by virtue of the formal logic of its ruling Marxist ideology, which posited the failure of capitalism, but should never be the latter. A fourth layer, related to this, was the nature of its political system, totalitarianism. Kennan was clear: despite the claims of the totalitarian theorists of the early post-war years, Stalin was not Hitler, the Soviet Union was not Nazi Germany, and post-war 'Russia' was different from pre-war Germany because it did not pose a plausible military danger to the United States or its European allies. When he was ambassador in 1952, Kennan deplored the use of his embassy for the posturing of military visitors and spies. Why did US intelligence officers have to stand on the roof of the embassy and take photographs of Soviet spies taking photographs of them? Why did the State Department, the Pentagon and the White House have to gather American forces near to the Soviet border? He hated the Stalinist political order. But he thought that Washington was courting war.[73]

So what was the answer? Political pressure: yes. Military planning: no. '[M]ilitary plans had a way of giving reality to the very contingencies against which they purported to prepare,' he warned. Korea laid out the terrible risks. The US aerial bombing of the eastern Korean city of Rashin was 'frivolous and dangerous', it was 'so close to the great Russian port of Vladivostok'. He interpreted the majority support in Congress for expanding the Korean War as a *de facto* call for war with the Soviet Union and China, and imagined that Stalin would see it the same way.[74]

In 1948, the Americans were deciding on the precise form of the peace treaty that they would impose on Japan. Kennan tried to see the problem from the point of view of Moscow. What about making a treaty to which the Soviets would also assent, rather than simply deny that they had interests in the region too? True enough, the Americans had borne the sacrifices of the war against Japan together with their Western allies, but the Soviets had the rights of proximity: the Sea of Japan was as close to the USSR as the Caribbean was to the USA. In 1945, Soviet forces had occupied islands in Japan's Kuril chain, off their own Far Eastern coast, and they had taken back South Sakhalin, which stretched from the Soviet mainland almost to Japan, and had been lost in the war of 1904–5. Most important, revolution in Korea brought the peninsula into a Soviet-Chinese sphere of influence that threatened conflict with the United States. Was the Japanese peace treaty an opportunity to solve these problems in one go, by trading off the demilitarization of Japan for that of Korea, and the withdrawal of American and Soviet troops alike from the region? Why should the Soviets exit Korea unilaterally while the Americans were making it increasingly clear that they were in Japan for the long haul? He argued that the Soviet government was not duplicitous in negotiations, or at any rate not about specific issues of arms and territories (vague big-picture commitments were another matter). Nor did it want to go out and occupy other countries: there was simply no evidence that it sought to expand, at least beyond the position of its armed forces in Europe in May 1945. Kennan's argument did not get very far. The USSR and China soon formed an alliance, and the Korean War broke out in 1950.[75]

*

As the Cold War went on, and Kennan spent more time at Princeton, at his second home in rural Pennsylvania, and in many trips to other parts of the United States he came to know America better than before. He was a patriot, but he found deficiencies in American democracy and society that led him further to question the bipolar morality of the Cold War. In 1967, in his memoirs, he wrote of how 'American statesmanship' always seemed doomed to suffer the effects of 'neurotic self-consciousness and introversion', with foreign policy focused not on the world outside, but on domestic opinion and the machinations of Congress.[76] And it would be better not to make extravagant moral claims on behalf of oneself and one's policies.

By the time of *perestroika*, Kennan had come half-circle. In the spring of 1987, he wrote that the threat of forty years before had been ideological, not military, but now 'the situation is almost exactly the reverse'. And yet it was not Moscow as such that threatened the United States. '[W]hat most needs to be contained,' he claimed, 'is not so much the Soviet Union as the arms race itself.' Nuclear weapons and the expansion of military technologies on both sides were threatening the world. At a time of global fluidity, when no one could be sure of Gorbachev's intentions, let alone predict the end of the Soviet Union, Kennan was prepared to dissolve the Russia Anxiety by a process of self-examination. On the one hand, he wrote, 'we are going to have to learn to take as the basis for our calculations a much more penetrating and sophisticated view of that particular country than the one that has become embedded in much of our public rhetoric'. And on the other: 'we are going to have to recognize that a large proportion of the sources of our troubles and dangers lies outside the Soviet challenge, such as it is, and some of it even within ourselves'.[77]

Kennan amplified these arguments once the Cold War was over. The United States should reject an interventionist foreign policy. Its leaders should not get carried away with a messianic vision.[78] If the attachment to Western values was eternal, NATO need not be. The long-term endurance of alliances such as NATO had unpredictable effects. 'Their very existence creates new situations, which their creators could never have envisaged,' he wrote in 1993.[79] And America should look to itself. '[T]he greatest service this country could render to the rest of the world,' he went on, 'would be to put its own house in order and to make American civilization an example of decency, humanity, and societal success from which others could derive whatever they might find useful to their own purposes.'[80]

But Kennan's prescription was not followed. Perhaps it never could have been. And so the Russia Anxiety was revivified, even during the 1990s. As others pointed out, America pushed a democratizing agenda on Moscow, but with little concern for the particularities of the Russian case, so that it came across as patronizing and triumphalist. There was little material support or institutional encouragement; no great global settlement emerged.[81] Instead, Russia was just a 'bad learner' who didn't become like us because of its historic burdens, even its genetic deficiencies (it was common to speculate on just how much had been lost from the gene pool during Stalin's Terror and then the Second World War). By extension, Russia's presence at the high table of diplomacy, when it was invited, was merely a matter of begrudged courtesy.[82]

With the end of the century in sight, when Kennan was approaching his own centenary, he found it 'distressing' that 'anxiety and suspicion of the new Russia' were widespread in the Western press. For him, there was no plausible threat that Russia would want to extend itself beyond its borders. Even Crimea, which he saw as a special case, was not an open target of Russia's leaders. 'There is,' he argued, 'no country anywhere in the world whose inhabitants, including what the Communists used to call its "ruling circles", have less to gain and more to fear from new military involvements than do those of the Russian Republic.' Kennan's critics were quick to point out the implausible optimist, or the Russophile of good faith betrayed by the ill intentions of what came next, or the 1940s visionary who could not apply his brilliance to an entirely new and even worse world.

Twenty years on, it remains easy for Kennan's critics to dismiss him. But since he wrote these comments in the 1990s, Russia's fundamental interests remained the same, though it began to defend them aggressively. What changed the most were the circumstances outside its borders, including the rise of interventionist dogma in American foreign policy and the expansionary logic of European institutions. Kennan argued that Europe was a patchwork of exceptions and geographical absurdities that could be happily maintained if policymakers retained a sense of rationality and contingency. Serious discussion of extending NATO towards Russia's borders was 'unreal, unnecessary, and in highest degree deplorable'. It was not that Russia would ever be an American-style democracy; but it was not a threat. The problem was the Russia Anxiety. '[L]et us ... not confuse ourselves, and let us not unnecessarily complicate our problem, by creating a Russia of our own imagination,' he pleaded.[83] Would he have thought the same today, after Ukraine, Crimea, the 2016 election and the 2018 mass expulsions of diplomats? When he wrote the Long Telegram, he saw a clear and present ideological danger, an adversary that needed to be told clearly of American resilience. He was not the type to take a soft line. Yet he would certainly have deplored the language with which Russia was demonized in American politics and media in the age of Trump and Putin. He would have looked for greater clarity and less politicking in the investigation of events. And he might have thought that the Russian crisis was in part one of America's making.

If the shade of Kennan could not meet Trump or Putin, to everyone's detriment, what would we learn from an encounter between him and the ghost of Custine?

In 1963, Kennan gave a lecture at the University of Belgrade. Six years later, visiting All Souls College in Oxford, he gave that year's Chichele Lectures. In 1970, he left his base at Princeton to give a talk at Harvard. In each case, he was refining the same subject: the Marquis de Custine. Could Kennan resolve Custine's Russia Anxiety, or would Custine play on Kennan's Anxious moments?

Kennan exposed the contradictions and inaccuracies in Custine's book, its derivative nature and its reliance on rumour, and the extent of what Custine missed. For Kennan, Custine was not wrong in his descriptions of corruption, or the 'pretentiousness of high society', or the gap between Russia and the West, as they existed in 1839. But he missed the complexity of Russian society. He did not see that many Russians themselves understood their problems all too well. Kennan approvingly quoted one of Custine's Russian critics. 'We do not propose to place ourselves, on our own initiative, at the head of civilization: we do not claim to be the tutors or regents of other nations,' this critic wrote. 'But we too have our place in the sun, and it is not Monsieur de Custine who is going to deprive us of it.'[84] This is a familiar source of Russian *Angst*: of being talked down to, excluded from the room, ignored or misinterpreted. Putin understands it well; his speeches are often designed to hit the exposed nerves of his fellow citizens.

So Kennan concluded that Custine's was not a good book about Russia in 1839. But it was 'an excellent book, perhaps the best of books, about the Russia of Joseph Stalin, and not a bad book about the Russia of Brezhnev'. What the imaginary Russia of 1839 and the real Soviet Union of 1939 had in common, for Kennan, was a lack of social dynamism, suggesting that change could only come through revolutionary violence. Custine missed the emergence of liberalism and other-thinking in Russian society, which would in time generate the great reforms of the 1860s and the emergence of 'society' in the late imperial period; but these were precisely what was absent under Stalinism. And Custine's Russia of 1839 came to pass a century later not because of inevitable patterns of Russian history but because of chance: the unlikely combination of circumstances that caused the Russian Revolution. In other words, Russian realities were not caused by instant history, the assumption that events are either unprecedented or provenanced by antiquity. Custine created a phantasmagoria, but he was right about the failures of Russian monarchy. He glimpsed a possible future, but only by chance, as the Russian Revolution did not need to happen. And even in Soviet society, Kennan concluded, there existed, as isolated elements, the same positive, regenerative forces that existed in nineteenth-century Russia.[85]

In this way, Kennan entered into Custine's Russia Anxiety, faced its worse prospects for the 1930s and the 1970s, but then dismantled the Anxiety from within. He was unlike his successors. Determined to see Russia and the Soviet Union on their own terms, willing to be critical of America, uncomfortable with absolutes, and prepared to change his mind when he was wrong, he showed how past and present could combine to diminish the Russia Anxiety.[86]

Kennan was gone, and there was nobody to replace him. In the second decade of the twenty-first century – the age of Trump and Putin, of Crimea and cyberspace, of recklessness and hatred – the Russia

Anxiety has reached an almost unprecedented size. And yet the Russia Anxiety is not a permanent condition. It's a syndrome whose symptoms come and go. Some people and countries are not susceptible to it; others can control the symptoms when they start. The Russia Anxiety is partly formed by history, but, as Kennan showed, history also offered possible ways to resolve it.

Instant history and wilfully misunderstood history have been environments in which the Russia Anxiety has thrived. They have made possible the widespread myth of a special path of Russian history, a specially bad path, of barbarism, poverty and un-freedom. This black legend of Russia's damaged destiny has been a risk to world peace in the past and it might be again, as we'll see in the next chapter.

# 2

## The Destiny Problem

### Does History's 'Black Legend' Set Russia Up to Fail?

Grand Prince Vladimir (r. 980–1015) faced an exceptional choice in the 980s, according to the *Primary Chronicle*, the most fundamental source for the history of Kievan Rus. Representatives of four great monotheistic religions – Islam, Judaism, Roman Christianity and the Christianity of Byzantium – came singly to his court to ask for a hearing. In this 'Investigation of the Faiths', Vladimir listened and pondered the virtues of each. He was drawn to the idea of a single God who would be worshipped by all his subjects, rather than the plethora of gods and spirits which currently provided the religious life of the Rus lands, because this might bring all his people together and legitimize his own single-person rule. Embracing God, not the gods, was a turn towards the future.

Christianity seemed to have advantages rather than drawbacks. Islam's prohibition on alcohol was unappealing. The fact that the God of the Jews had not given his people their own land was unpromising. By contrast, Vladimir's grandmother had been a Christian, and a Christian church had been at work in Kiev for half a century. And geopolitics held out a trump card. By the end of the first millennium AD, Kievan Rus looked south, towards Byzantium, for cultural resources, commercial advantages and political friendship. Newly baptized, and Christianizing his people *en masse*, Vladimir sent an army of 6,000 men to relieve Basil II, emperor of Byzantium, who was under strain following an uprising in the Balkans by the Bulgars. In return for Vladimir's support, Basil offered his sister's hand in marriage. Strengthened by his Christianizing programme and his powerful ties to Byzantium, Vladimir consolidated the rule of the Riurikid dynasty over Rus, assuring the status of Kiev.[1]

In November 2016, 1,001 years after Vladimir's death, President Putin and Patriarch Kirill unveiled a statue to the grand prince a short distance from the Moscow Kremlin. Putin praised Vladimir as a great unifying figure. He drew attention in particular to his introduction of the Christian faith. 'This choice,' Putin declared, 'was the common spiritual source for the peoples of Russia, Belarus and Ukraine, laying valuable foundations which define our life, right to the present.'[2] The unveiling took place on 4 November, itself a symbolic date, which marks the anniversary of the expulsion of Polish forces from Moscow in 1612. This had become a public holiday, the Day of National Unity, in 2005. (Here 'national' comes from the word *narod*, which could also be translated as 'people's', so the idea is more cultural than geopolitical.) The public holiday is more happenstance than the consequence of a nationalist agenda. It emerged as a convenient way of resolving a banal dilemma: how to cancel the celebrations that anachronistically marked the anniversary of the Bolshevik Revolution without dispensing with a popular day off in early November.

The statue was controversial. Ukraine's government claimed that Russia was expropriating a great Ukrainian hero; a similar and much more venerable statue stands in Kiev. Even the formulation of the name could sound like cultural appropriation; in Ukrainian, 'Vladimir' is 'Volodymyr', though the grand prince in question ruled a sovereign territory that was neither Ukraine nor Russia, and the name in the *Primary Chronicle* is 'Volodimer'. Western commentators wondered what to make of this latest gesture of braggadocious nationalism, as many of them saw it. Muscovites were unsure of the monument's aesthetics. Local residents had successfully petitioned for the statue not to be erected in the city's Sparrow Hills.

However one might disentangle the symbols and the politics, it seemed clear that the Russian government was making its own use of a millennium of history, explicitly drawing a 1,000-year line between Kievan Rus and the Russian Federation.[3] Talking about the long-range connections between Russia's past and present is an understandable political strategy at a time of national and international uncertainty. Governments in other countries do the same (think of today's politicians' grand statements about Magna Carta, the French Revolution, the Founding Fathers). But it's also a strategy that outsiders have used many times to make Russia seem a uniquely dangerous and repressive place.

The myth of Russia's special, undeviating path to misery is at the heart of the Russia Anxiety. Misread from historiography and repeated endlessly by journalists and foreign statesmen, and agonized over by Russians themselves, it has shaped understanding of the Russian past more than anything else. 'Strains of xenophobic paranoia and a gravitation to autocracy are embedded into the [Russian] cultural DNA in a way that long predates the twentieth century,' tweets a journalist in New York City with 127,000 Twitter followers, as the Russia Anxiety grew during the Trump election campaign. 'It's incredible,' tweets back a writer in Ontario followed by less than 1 per cent of that, 'what the media can say about Russians that would be quickly denounced if you used a different group.'[4]

This is Russia's black legend, the idea that centuries of oppression have created a servile population forever fated to be hoodwinked by a tyrant. It's the historical mood music of the Russia Anxiety.[5] The purpose of this chapter is to describe the legend and to offer other ways of understanding Russian history, closer to the facts and more promising for the future.

## RUSSIA'S BLACK LEGEND

'Russia lives in history – and history lives in Russia,'[6] wrote *Time* magazine when it announced Putin as its Person of the Year in 2007. 'Of all the burdens Russia has had to bear,' wrote Tibor Szamuely, casting the same idea in a more pessimistic light, 'heaviest and most relentless of all has been the weight of her past.'[7] History is always alive in contemporary Russia, just as it is in much of the Middle East as well as other parts of Eastern Europe. In luckier places, history has been tamed and housebroken, confined to ruined castles, books of photographs and days of remembrance. But in those societies where the whole future – the borders of the country, the national way of life, the entire way of doing politics – is permanently up for grabs, history is a living actor.

Sit round a family's kitchen table in Russia, and at the moment when the conversation turns to politics, history will pull up a chair. And history will contribute not just decorative precedents, loosely parallel personalities or killer factoids. It will invoke whole structures of historical time, in which a millennium of Russia's past makes possible a democratic future or foreshadows inevitable dictatorship. Using and abusing the deep past in everyday political discussion is embedded in Russian culture.

A few distinguished scholars have written convincing millennium-long histories of Russia that make a structure of the Russian past.[8] Such historians point to long-range continuities, and some of them are pessimists, but it is only by caricaturing their work that it can be turned into the black legend. Instead, they often emphasize a particular variable as the key to Russia's development. It might be the 'strong leader', or religion, or the relationship between nation and empire, or property relations, or patron–client ties, or the exploitation of the periphery by the centre. In an earlier age of historiography, especially as practised by Soviet historians, it could even be class. This way of doing Russian history has made centuries of history look comprehensible, but it comes at a cost. History is made up of layers and is prone to interruption and sudden change, so the structural, big-picture approach must show the variable at stake following false starts and hitting dead ends as well as travelling down a broad highway of historical development. Only by doing that can the historian who links present to past convincingly show an obvious truth: that the Russian present is a complicated place that can give rise to different futures.

Russia's black legend, by contrast, does not do this. It's certainly clever. Many of its details are accurate. But ultimately it's based on a blunt understanding of historical change. It pulls off a brilliant rhetorical trick, but its overall argument is misleading.

Here it goes. Geography is the black legend's starting point. The harsh climate of the central Eurasian landmass, with its long, freezing winters, means that the Russian lands have always had a short growing season, sometimes half the length of Western Europe's. Fields can be rotated less frequently, diminishing their fertility. But Russia is unlucky too in its rainfall: it rains the most where the soil is worst. The good-quality black earth soil can't yield its potential. Harvests, as a consequence, are low. Unable to scratch much more than a subsistence living, peasants were averse to risk. They spent the long winters cooped up with their animals, breathing in too much carbon monoxide from the stoves in their wooden houses. As a result, they became passive, failing to develop and innovate. They were almost congenitally backward. Peasants relied on each other, through bonds of mutual responsibility, and while their collective identity was strong, they had little sense of individual personhood, or so the legend claims.

Nevertheless, some of them had enough initiative to seek out the open route to a better life in the south and east. In order to maintain production levels, extract taxes and recruit enough soldiers, the sovereign found such mobility intolerable. Peasants had to be prevented from moving on. They had to be tied to the land. This was the basis of serfdom.

With or without serfdom, the very small agricultural surpluses inhibited urban growth. Production of finished goods was low, and the country relied excessively on raw materials and natural resources, in the first instance fur. The problem of weak urban development was worsened by geographical isolation, insufficient waterways and poor roads, all of which suffered when the snow and ice melted in the spring. Poor communication links reduced access to trade.

Towns lacked an independent spirit. By international standards, there wasn't much of a bourgeoisie: a class which owned capital, drove forward trade, turned professional, gained qualifications and administered public offices effectively. The nobility was also weak, because property law was tilted dramatically in favour of the sovereign. In fact, law was a misnomer, as the sovereign's authority was unlimited. He owned everything inside his realm, and his subjects were *de facto* (and sometimes *de jure*) slaves. Officials who administered central government and the provinces quickly resorted to corruption. The term to describe this system is patrimonialism. Over several centuries, the black legend goes on, the system of Russian oppression was extended in all directions, as Muscovy and then the Russian Empire grew at extraordinary speed. Eventually, the empire reached the Pacific Ocean. In this system of power, ethnic Russians were colonized – exploited – as much as other ethnicities. Meanwhile, the long borders that resulted were difficult to defend, generating all kinds of geopolitical challenges. The eastern, southern and western borderlands were all zones of suspicion and threat. Foreigners routinely insisted that Russia was a menace to its neighbours.

As a result, a willingness to sacrifice the people for the good of the sovereign has been the common thread that's run through Russian political life. This contention is perhaps the core of the black legend. Ivan the Terrible exemplified Muscovy, Peter the Great defined imperial Russia, Stalin was the ultimate truth of the Soviet Union, and Putin was the only reality of post-Soviet Russia. They were all variations on the same principles and practices of total sovereign power.

In these circumstances, opposition has been difficult. The archetypal opposition movement emerged in the nineteenth century. This was the intelligentsia. Frustrated by its stunted professional chances, and angered by its exclusion from the political nation, it turned against the autocracy. Obsessed with German philosophy, it explained the world in abstracts that were a poor match for Russian conditions and had no organic connection to the reality of the people who lived there. Violent, black-and-white radicalism resulted. It led naturally to the Bolshevik Revolution. Meanwhile, the characteristics of the Russian political tradition – patrimonialism, corruption, the cult of a leader, repression, censorship, the absence of rights and civil society – transmitted themselves across the revolutionary divides of 1917 and 1991.

This is the black legend of Russian history. It is not a straw man, but a clever and coherent explanation. Not all of it is wrong. The relationship between ecology and society, for instance, contains important truths. Some of the legend's insights have animated the best of historical writing. Taken whole and uncritically, however, it generates a dark reading of Russian society that has little explanatory power.

There's a better way of understanding Russian history. For a start, we might reflect on the layers that construct it, which give it variety and energy. The Russian past should be thought of as a cake, not a legend.

## THE LAYERED CAKE

Imagine an old-fashioned English cake, a sponge with a vanilla centre, topped with pink icing. However much you look at the cake from above, deconstructing the swirls of icing, and sampling occasional bits of pink, there is no way that the bird's eye view will give you a sense of what the whole cake is all about. To get that, you have to cut a slice, look at the layers, reflect on how they ooze into each other, and then take a bite from the bottom to the top.

Russian history, like this cake, is a layered confection. You will not get very far towards understanding its complexity by only gazing down on it from above. Although the black legend has plenty to say about different groups in Russian society, ultimately it's a story of top-down power, concerned with the sovereign's repression of his people, his 'paranoia' and his international ambition. The legend squashes the cake out of all recognition.

One way to understand what is right and wrong about Russia's black legend, then, is to look at the layers beneath. We might illustrate the point with three of them: serfdom, the Orthodox Church and the intelligentsia, all of which have given grist to the mill of the legend in one way or another. Yet these three examples – one could offer many more – show that Russian power has been much more interactive and dispersed than the legend suggests, creating space for individuality and unpredictability.

Early in 1847, the future novelist Ivan Turgenev published one of his first literary works, the short story 'Khor and Kalinich'. Turgenev had already travelled abroad to complete his education, and was starting to know Western Europe well. But he was also deeply and instinctively in tune with the countryside and the people of Oryol Province, where he had grown up on his mother's estate. For him, the world of serfdom was instantly clear. It was reprehensible, for sure, but it was also varied, complex and not simply an expression of the tsar's power.

In this story, Khor's house had burned down fifteen years earlier. It was usual in those circumstances for the serfs in a village community to bind together to help the victim. Their economy of mutual responsibility demanded this: the village as a whole shared certain financial obligations, which meant that it was in the interest of everyone to help a neighbour who had fallen on hard times. But Khor made an offer to the noble who owned him, Polutykin. I will pay you whatever rent you choose if you let me build a house out in the marshland. Why not? Polutykin agreed. A clever individualist, Khor became rich, paying more in rent as the years went on. Polutykin was a reasonable man. He told Khor to buy his freedom: he would be able to afford it many times over. But Khor protested that he lacked the means. He was being wily: it was obviously in his interest to remain where he was. Serfdom seemed to facilitate his autonomy and even to reduce his obligations. In Khor's world, the Russian autocracy was built on far more compromises than anyone could readily describe. Out in the backwoods and the marshland, the arm of repression could be feeble. Serfdom was plainly a flexible instrument with diverse effects. It created multiple realities. 'A Russian is so sure of his strength and robustness that he is not averse to overtaxing himself,' wrote Turgenev's narrator. 'He is little concerned with his past and looks boldly towards the future.'[9]

Yet by the time that Turgenev was writing, many people in Russia's educated and even noble society had become opposed to serfdom as an offence against human dignity. The history of serfdom makes it clear why this should be the case. Serfdom was imposed from above, mostly in the sixteenth and seventeenth centuries, and it endured until 1861. It did not just exist from time immemorial. Instead, it was a result of political and legal decisions, not of a culture of passivity by the peasants or unlimited ownership by the tsar.

Muscovy's rulers needed a stable workforce, not one that was mobile, ready to up sticks and seek out a new chance, if the productivity and tax potential of the peasantry were to be maximized. One answer was to turn peasants into slaves. Not serfs, but *slaves*. This cruel institution had existed for centuries. By its nature, it was exploitative; it was unfree labour, the selling of one person to become the property of another. But Russian slavery was unusual. It did not follow military conquest, and it was not usually the subordination of one ethnic group to another. On the contrary: many Russians willingly sold themselves into slavery. At times of emergency – famine and war, or as a result solely of personal misfortune – it was a way of guaranteeing one's basic survival. The initial transaction, at least, was contractual, though scarcely a deal between equals. The usual type of Russian slavery was for a fixed term of one year. A desperate peasant would take out a loan from a landowner, offering labour instead of paying interest. Should he default on the principal, which was sometimes as little as one ruble, the term was extended to life, and could be hereditary. By 1550, between 5 and 15 per cent of the population were slaves, and a government office existed to deal with this aspect of Muscovite society. For government, it had a plus side: it kept peasants working in a given locality. But slavery was inefficient. Slaves could not be taxed. A law of 1597 allowed them to be freed when their owner (formally speaking, the creditor) died. But freed slaves often struggled to adapt. They quickly reverted to slavery, and were once again peasants from whom the state could not extract revenue.[10] To repeat: this was the institution of slavery, not serfdom.

The existence of slavery in Russia seems to go with the flow of the black legend of Russian history. Slaves willingly gave up whatever rights they might have had before. Many must have suffered beneath the Muscovite 'power vertical'. But this system lacked the dehumanizing and disorienting forced movement of the transatlantic slave trade, the expatriate fortunes that resulted from it, and the violent racism which was its hallmark. Russian slavery, moreover, was phased out and then abolished in the seventeenth and eighteenth centuries; it had slowly been turning into an anachronism since the fifteenth century. The tsars preferred serfdom, though it took until 1724 for Peter the Great to change the status of all remaining household slaves into serfs.

In the middle of the fifteenth century, an idiosyncratic rule was introduced: that peasants who worked monastery lands were only allowed to move on and find residence elsewhere once a year, on St George's Day. In the law code (the Muscovite-era term is *Sudebnik*) of 1497, the mobility of all peasants was constrained in exactly the same way. The point was to keep them in one place, working as part of functional and effective village communes, which collectively contributed to the state budget. But within a century, this safety valve had been turned off. In the 1580s and 1590s, peasants were denied the right even to move on St George's Day. Boris Godunov, as regent then tsar (1598–1605), was set on recovering the capacity of the state after the chaos that Ivan the Terrible had brought to the rural economy. But he also reduced the penalties for fleeing from one's owner.

If a fugitive serf was not recaptured within five years, he was legally free. Why? The Muscovite territories to east and south were expanding and were too empty of Russian peasants to be economically productive. The statute of limitations allowed a minimum of labour mobility to cultivate this land.[11] These different laws were consolidated in 1649, with the approval of a major new law code (the *Ulozhenie*). But for all its awfulness, serfdom was varied and complex in ways that the black legend doesn't explain.

The legal scope for serfs to exercise any control over their own lives, or to extend protection to their family, was minimal.[12] Still, not all peasants were serfs. In the eighteenth and nineteenth centuries, state peasants had a different status, though their lives were often similar. They still faced limits on residence and mobility, and worked with their fellow villagers in a system of collective responsibility. And there were some peasants who had more rights, notably special categories of settlers: the military settlers, and those from outside, including Germans and Mennonites.[13] The life of Turgenev's Khor suggests that serfdom was built on compromises and concessions as well as on repression. Despite the legalities, there were serfs, like Khor, whose lives resembled those of prosperous smallholders. Others were educated and trained, in estate management, say, or in music or acting, and seemed indistinguishable from free men or women.[14] However improbable it seems, there were also serfs who became major business magnates, leading wealthy lives and controlling millions of rubles. But they were still the property of their owner, their formal rights over their own commercial enterprise were very insecure, and their success depended on the progressive attitude of the noble family in charge of them. The Sheremetyev family, spectacularly rich and managing in turn a network of many thousands of their own serfs, were such a family.[15] Meanwhile, traditional peasant culture disregarded aspects of the law, making an entirely different set of assumptions about ownership of land and resources. Many peasants led their lives wilfully, according to their own customs and mentalities, their communities seeking to avoid the arm of the state.

Perhaps the variety of serfs' lives only exposed the indignity and growing inefficiency of an awful institution. By the nineteenth century, serfdom was failing to match the needs of an industrializing economy or a modern conscription system, and it was partly blamed for the defeat in the Crimean War in 1856, soon after which it was abolished. But emancipation came in 1861 for two reasons. First, Alexander II was convinced of the moral case for change. Second, he could implement it in practice because of the progressive administrative work that had already been undertaken by some leading bureaucrats during the reign of Nicholas I, a time which is often seen as merely dark and reactionary.

All of this – the way that serfdom was introduced, the varied forms it took, the process of emancipation – reveal the layered quality of Russian history. This is the antithesis of the black legend. Carefully studied, even serfdom offers correctives and precedents that should reduce the Russia Anxiety. We can say the same about Russian Orthodoxy.

The legend goes like this: the state triumphed over the Orthodox Church, and for centuries thereafter religion has lacked spiritual coherence and practical effectiveness, with little ability to hold power in check. After introducing the great law code (*Ulozhenie*) of 1649, Tsar Alexis turned his attention to the febrile spiritual atmosphere abroad in his realm, with the help of a six-and-a-half-foot Volga-region monk called Nikon. Having gained Alexis's ear, Nikon promised to achieve religious harmony and uniformity across Muscovy, and soon became patriarch. He edited a new psalter in October 1652 and new books for services three years later, revised the words of the Lord's prayer, and changed the way that worshippers made the sign of the cross, with three fingers rather than two. The reforms caused great unease and generated resistance. For example, when they crossed themselves with the traditional two fingers, believers were calling out to God and Jesus; three fingers, by contrast, were symbolic of the Trinity, and that seemed more Roman than Muscovite, an affront to Orthodoxy and a needless concession to Catholicism. A priest called Avvakum, who came from the remote north, became the centre of opposition. His traditional and even fundamentalist followers were persecuted. Some of them were rounded up and burned to death. Others were excluded en masse from the Orthodox Church. Fleeing to the interior, they became known as Old Believers, and practised

Orthodoxy in the way they were convinced was right. Their leaders, though, were exiled to the Arctic coast and jailed. Avvakum was comparatively lucky; the authorities cut out the tongues of two of his co-conspirators.

Nikon's triumph was an empty one. Tsar Alexis took the chance to tighten control over Nikon's Church, to end old talk of patriarch and tsar enjoying equal authority over Muscovy. Having overplayed his hand, Nikon was exiled. Alexis turned increasingly towards Western influences and celebrations of secular power. The process was taken to its logical conclusion by Peter the Great in 1721, when the office of patriarch, and the supreme Church council, or *sobor*, were eliminated. Any semblance of religious autonomy was apparently ended. The Orthodox Church was now administered by a government office, the Holy Synod.[16]

But the Old Belief fought back. It became a layer of Russian life – an alternative authority, a centre of civil society. Under the leadership of Nikolai Dobrynin, Old Believers took part in a major uprising in Moscow in 1682. Later, they became more respectable. In the nineteenth century, the Old Belief possessed a major presence in public and commercial life. Clustering in the Zamoskvorechye district – the area 'beyond the Moscow river', across from the Kremlin – were entrepreneurial families of the Old Belief, such as the fabulously wealthy Morozovs, who had made their money in the textile business in Moscow Region.

Meanwhile, the Orthodox Church itself was not a mere government department. It continued to direct the spiritual affairs of the nation, and played a significant part in the last decades of tsarist power. True, in April 1905, when he was under great pressure from revolutionaries, Nicholas II declared his Manifesto on Freedom of Conscience, which for the first time gave an easy green light for apostates to leave the Church. In these fluid times, some priests saw a chance, asserting themselves by campaigning for the calling of a council. There had been no such gathering since before Peter's reforms.[17] It eventually took place in the revolutionary year of 1917, when it elected the first patriarch for two centuries, Tikhon, who would face the Bolsheviks' brutal campaign for atheism.[18]

Orthodoxy therefore took part in the political contests of the early twentieth century, though it had to fight for attention. In the heartlands, it remained at the centre of people's lives. From the great social realist painters of the nineteenth century, with their eye for a useless, drunken priest, to the historians of the Soviet Union, with their Marxist agenda, the coherence and significance of Orthodoxy has been understated by observers. The religion of the peasants has often been described as a 'dual belief', part-pagan, part-Christian. Already hinting that official Russian Orthodoxy was a fake version of Christianity, in a way that they would not think of, say, the Church of England, some Western commentators claimed that these everyday religious practices were hardly Christian at all, with the Scriptures and the saints a veneer over longer-standing rituals and simple fatalism. But Orthodoxy, far more than any other source of knowledge, left its mark on the peasant mentality, whose traditional beliefs were reconciled to the demands of Christian faith.[19]

Orthodoxy, meanwhile, is not the only religion in the Russian lands. Other versions of Christianity played an important part in imperial Russia and the Soviet Union. Some were inflected by Roman Catholicism, such as the Uniate Church, especially important in Ukraine, and others by Protestant beliefs and practices.[20] Islam has been a crucial feature of Russian civilization since the Mongol invasions. Buddhism is historically one of Russia's major faiths. Many other forms of spirituality have proliferated among the 'small peoples of the north' and in Siberia. In the most difficult circumstances, religion has given many Russians the ability to endure. It has also provided them with ways of understanding secular power, accommodating themselves to it and even standing up to it. The sheer variety of Orthodox experience is another layer of the Russian past that the black legend cannot process or describe. And then there's the intelligentsia.

Yuri Trifonov spent eight or nine days of March 1955 in Nebit-Dag, the largest city in the west of Turkmenistan. Trifonov was still enjoying the success of his first novel, *The Students*, which had been published in 1950 and for which he had won a Stalin Prize. He had come to Nebit-Dag to visit the literary critic Tsetsilya (Cecily) Kin. She had spent eight years in the Gulag, the wife of an enemy of the people, and had ended up, by a roundabout route, living in Nebit-Dag. They stayed in her cramped accommodation. He told her all the big political and literary news from the capital. She talked to him about the poet Pasternak, and Trifonov recited his poems from memory. Later, their conversation ranged more widely. 'We did not hide our heads under our wings,' she said. There was no point in being coy. This was two years after Stalin's death, and they had a common history of unhappiness. She had been in the Gulag. Trifonov's father had been shot and his mother had been arrested when he was a child.

These scenes – reciting Pasternak spontaneously, the talk of life and death, the mood hovering between anguish and joy, the life of exile, in a room far away – look like the Russian intelligentsia at sharpest focus. As such, the picture seems a bit too familiar. Cynics will point out that the Russian intelligentsia has always been capable of vanity and snobbishness not less than long, unselfish exchanges of the highest intellectual standards. But these moments in Nebit-Dag, in the uncertain time between the death of Stalin in 1953 and Khrushchev's condemnation of him in the Secret Speech of 1956, were fretful ones, and the conversation was no doubt an honest attempt to come to terms with events. The exchange also reflected the ethics of the intelligentsia. 'Our pains, misfortunes and grievances were not simply and not only our own,' Cecily said. 'Our personal fates were like grains of sand. Our personal tragedies were the pain and tragedy of the motherland.' What is the motherland? It 'isn't the landscape, not the silver birches, not the cornflowers in the rye'. Instead, 'it is the victory over fascism. It is the immortal tragedies of the Russian novel, of great Russian poetry.'[21]

Cecily Kin's words capture part of the mission of the Russian intelligentsia: to show how the lives of individuals can represent the experiences of society as a whole, to make the case that the collective achievements of the people belong to the people and not to the state, and, therefore, to hold power to account. The Russian intelligentsia historically exists apart from the state. It is in another layer. The black legend might respect the achievements of Tolstoy and Tchaikovsky, and it might admire the manners of intelligentsia types and the quality of their conversation, but it sees them as prone to extremes, quick to exaggerate emotions, possessed of a fake morality, attracted by violence, naturals for Bolshevism.

In other words, the legend turns the intelligentsia into another act in the long history of repression by the Russian state. Yet the political record of the Russian intelligentsia veered to moderation as much as extremism; it generated liberalism as well as Bolshevism. And the fact that Bolshevism won was a matter of chance.

The origins of the Russian intelligentsia have been traced to the Enlightenment in the late eighteenth century,[22] but it recognizably emerged during the reign of Nicholas I, when poets, writers and critics such as Pushkin and Herzen were writing for the new literary journals and exchanging ideas in salons and 'circles' of the like-minded (*kruzhki*). There were not many of them; but they made an historic splash. Some of these men were nobles, and the literary salons that they attended in St Petersburg or provincial outposts were often run by high-born women. But many among the intelligentsia had little class or estate affiliation, and little loyalty to the state; they were 'people of various ranks', who sometimes had a university education, were always engaged in the world of ideas, but lived in a society that seemed neither to respect nor need their accomplishments. Nicolaevan Russia had plenty of bureaucrats, but it lacked a clergy with university degrees, or ostentatiously learned lawyers for hire, or a coffee-house culture and a fairly free press. It didn't have the obvious ways of absorbing and calming down a middle-ranking awkward squad who might think differently. Instead, lacking opportunities, those people often turned against the monarchy.

The intelligentsia spread wide and deep, oozing across social and political layers of Russian life. It was an 'everyday' part of society, determined by manners and culture as much as by political opposition, located in provincial towns and country estates, as well as in the capitals of the empire and their grand salons. And it also included great artists such as Chekhov and Tolstoy who worked out how to publish works of conscience that the censors did not touch.

But for much of government – not all, as the state itself contained multitudes – there was no concept of a 'loyal opposition' in Russia; opposition could not improve government, but was inherently disloyal. Pushkin and Herzen both spent time in exile. Turgenev had a brief spell in prison. Dostoevsky was incarcerated for longer in Siberia. They took risks to talk freely and to publish even mildly subversive works. Tasked with maintaining public decorum and loyalty, the Third Section, as Russia's first secret police force was called, worked with the censorship authorities to reduce the public space in which the intelligentsia could operate. Perhaps this uneasy world of conflicting pressures and anxieties was a promising one in which ideas could proliferate in attractive ways.[23]

By definition, these ideas existed not to prop the government up, but to make it accountable. This is the real distinguishing mark of the Russian intelligentsia: sociologically and intellectually it existed as a layer outside of the state. During Nicholas's reign, the 'enlightened bureaucrats' were an essential part of government, the men whose patient work designing possible reforms to the rule of law and serfdom would come to fruition twenty years later under Alexander II. Some of them had university degrees and deep interests in culture, not to mention a progressive worldview. But they worked for the state. In the later nineteenth century, some members of the intelligentsia would find careers on the edges of local government, bringing enlightenment to their provinces through the expansion of education, healthcare and welfare, the systematic study of regional life, and the protection of the environment. But in the absence of an independent judiciary, parliament or political parties (the first of these would be established in 1864, the other two in 1906) it was only books, paintings and music that could challenge central power. Working within the interstices of the censorship rules, the intelligentsia found inventive ways to do this. The black legend promotes the idea of a defunct or dangerously radical intelligentsia, but cannot explain the varied layers that this complicated group of people occupied in Russian society.

In Eastern European cultures, 'intelligentsia' is a wide-ranging concept, incorporating all kinds of people who have made a commitment to the life of the mind. The adjective *intelligentnyi* in Russian does not refer to intellectual capacity, but to a set of moral qualities. In the Soviet Union, the intelligentsia took different forms; the likes of engineers, for example, were sometimes referred to as a 'technical intelligentsia'. A person who worked directly for the authorities, in a ministry or party organ, even though he might be entirely *intelligentnyi* at home in the evening, was not a member of the intelligentsia.

But the state was so capacious that almost everyone worked for it in some way or benefited directly from it. Meanwhile, the organs of repression were much more violent and the networks of censorship much more highly oppressive and sophisticated than they had been under the tsars. The Soviet intelligentsia could never have been a direct continuation of its predecessor in the age of Turgenev. Understandably enough, many among the intelligentsia enjoyed the perks that came from membership of, say, the Union of Writers, and settled for a quiet life.

Yet some of the intelligentsia still sought to hold power to account. After Stalin's death, in the Khrushchev-era 'Thaw' and later, their chances to do this increased. Risk-taking editors like Alexander Tvardovsky at *Novyi Mir* (*New World*), a progressive journal, found such authors as Alexander Solzhenitsyn and published them. *One Day in the Life of Ivan Denisovich* appeared in 1962, apparently after being personally approved by Khrushchev. The novel went with the grain of official de-Stalinization. But it also gave readers a way of thinking about government policy towards the Gulag and the Stalinist past, and of articulating ways of agreeing and disagreeing with that policy. After Khrushchev fell, Solzhenitsyn ended up on the wrong side of the KGB, writing in elaborate secrecy. He was thrown out of the Soviet Union in 1974.

Even so, Brezhnev and his colleagues could easily accept an intelligentsia that was capable of showing, as Cecily Kin pointed out, how the sufferings of a person were the same as those of the motherland – rather than, she might have added, of the state. It prescribed severe limits in which the intelligentsia operated. But the relationship between intelligentsia and power was complicated and mutually dependent. It was even the case that semi-independent organizations that originated in the state but had some similarity to the pressure groups of civil society were founded in these years. Using such institutions as VOOPIiK, which campaigned for the preservation of historical monuments, the intelligentsia was simultaneously coopted by power and held power to account.

It was in this environment that Yuri Trifonov wrote his greatest works, a sequence of novels about the everyday dilemmas of Muscovites of the 1960s and 1970s. All of these were published. Trifonov's works were very widely read. He was one of the big literary names of the late Soviet period. Whether showing how people responded to the housing shortage, or the pressures on the healthcare system, or the encroachment of the city on the countryside, or the need to make use of the shadow economy, he put forward an accessible vision of how one might reconcile idealism and pragmatism, mind and body in the paradoxical world of late socialism. Many (far from all) of his characters were from one or other layer of the intelligentsia. He described how their families, neighbours, friends and acquaintances related to collectives of colleagues, to the state and to the Revolution that was now decades old and which still structured everybody's lives. This was not dissident literature. By contrast, the dissidents were a very minor branch of the intelligentsia, albeit one which had an important impact at the end of the 1980s. Their bitter opposition to dictatorship, focus on abstract ideas, fearlessness and self-evident different-thinking were much easier first for the black legend to incorporate – and then to rewrite as a fairy tale of freedom's inevitable triumph.

But the very fact that Trifonov was not a dissident was the point. It was as the archetypal late Soviet *intelligent* that Trifonov made his extraordinary contribution to Soviet literature and life. He was part of a group which knew how to make its way successfully in this society, not to reject it. He discovered a way of writing stories that power could accept, but which gave readers a way to critique power. Scholars have called the works of Trifonov and similar writers 'permitted dissent'.[24] This placed him in the long tradition of an intelligentsia that went back to Pushkin, was located in the overlapping layers of Russian history and society, but lay beyond the black legend's line of sight.

Let us imagine a different cake. The *medovík* – a honey cake – is made of countless thin, fine, biscuity layers, a bit spongy and a bit crunchy, joined together with a honey mixture, the whole coated with honey-flavoured crumbs. Like this honey cake, Russian history is made up of very many layers; serfdom, Orthodoxy and the intelligentsia are only three. We could, for instance, have talked about the many layers of the state itself, whose competing interests defy the legend's assumption that one-person rule explains everything. Or we could have analysed the different historic communities in which Russianness has been incubated: village, nation and empire. These too represent indistinct layers, melting into each other, that the black legend of Russian history cannot make sense of. But these are things we will come back to later in the book.

The historical stories that give the Russia Anxiety life come from the black legend. These stories provide historical fuel for the cycle of fear, contempt and disregard that alternate within the syndrome of the Russia Anxiety. The black legend of Russian history assumes a barely deviating, even inevitable route to misfortune for the Russian people, connecting past to present and future in an unbreakable structure. We have already seen some of the problems with the notion of inevitability in chapter 1. But to challenge the legend further, we need to establish whether contingency might have played a bigger role than destiny in the Russian past.

## THE CHERNOMYRDIN DICTUM

In a moment of what seemed like accidental honesty, Viktor Chernomyrdin, Yeltsin's prime minister for much of the 1990s, voiced an immortal Russian sentiment: 'We wanted better, but things turned out like always.' It was one of the most laughed-at but revealing of Yeltsin-era soundbites. The fall of the Soviet Union might have offered a fresh page on which to write a new Russian future. But instead of initiating a fair reset for the Russian people, Yeltsin and his circle sidestepped the Russian sense of social justice. Their reforms seemed to reward the most those who behaved the worst. Even so, Chernomyrdin's phrase long retained its cachet, not least because he himself never seemed completely insincere. The first part of what we might think of as his dictum – *like always* – sounds as if the Russian people were on their special path. But Chernomyrdin pointed out that the collapse of the Soviet Union offered the chance of a different outcome: *we wanted better* than the post-Soviet transformation that did occur. This is a quite different way of imagining Russia's historical development, one that conceives of new beginnings and various futures, even if the 1990s were a false start.

Russian history has plenty of what-ifs, the short moments or indeed quite extended periods when the direction of the whole political culture was under negotiation. There are even instants when the weather takes on the burden of determining the shape of future geopolitics. It might be the case that the onset of a quick thaw in March 1238 deterred the Mongols from striking at Novgorod; concerned that their horses would be bogged down in the melting ice, they paused, then turned south and west, and, in 1240, attacked Kiev instead.[25] In turn, the demise of Kiev made possible the rise of Moscow. This was only the most outlandish and speculative of the extraordinary combination of circumstances that contributed to Muscovy becoming the political heartland of the late medieval and early modern Russian lands.

Contingency – the importance of events, decisions, and blind chance – complements structural change in historical explanations. The more you think about contingency, the more the grip of the black legend loosens, and the less sustainable the Russia Anxiety as a whole becomes.

Medieval Novgorod, for example, was built on a relatively participatory and responsive political culture which facilitated its status as a major trading centre. It would be eclipsed when Muscovy became the Mongols' main point of contact, and there was nothing predetermined about that. After all, Moscow's geographical location was more problematic than Novgorod's: it offered only mixed economic potential and was vulnerable to invasion. And even as the Mongols diminished Kiev and Novgorod, they also placed heavy burdens on Moscow, exacerbating its weaknesses with demands of tribute. Even if Moscow was an unlikely capital for East Slavic civilization, it was strengthened and partly formed by the useful legacies that Novgorod transmitted to it. Meanwhile, the fact that Moscow was a hungry state, eager to extract ever greater payments from its population and from surrounding territories, scarcely made it unique in medieval Europe.

Social scientists call what might have happened next 'path dependence', suggesting that once a society finds itself on a particular road, it can be difficult to get off it. The basic assumption is that once Muscovy was in the driving seat, the future Russia was doomed. Sure, there might have been forks in the road earlier on, when there was a real chance of taking a different route – when there was a signpost in Russia's historical development towards Novgorod, say – but as time went on, the number of forks decreased, and sheer momentum would anyway make it tricky to negotiate the turn.[26]

True enough, what happened in the past sets limits on what's likely to happen in the future. But history is chaotic. Multiple futures exist at every present moment. Even British history, often perceived as taking a straight line, is marked by ruptures rather than continuities in political culture and defined by moments of decision, not least since 1914. Or take the Bolshevik Revolution, one of the most unlikely events in world history. How could a small group of extreme Left radicals seize power in a country which only a few months before had been ruled by a 300-year-old dynasty? How could a Marxist clique, with an ideological agenda designed to overturn a capitalist economy, set about a socialist revolution in a largely rural society? The ultimate answer lies in the political skills of the Bolshevik leaders, rather than in the age-old inadequacy of Russian political culture, or the inevitable demise of capitalism.

In the months between February 1917, when the tsarist order fell under the weight of the massive crisis of the First World War, and October, when the Bolshevik Revolution took place, the Bolsheviks accrued a large following in major urban centres and in parts of the Imperial Army. This was no national majority, but it was a credible base of support at a time when the Provisional Government which had replaced the monarchy was no longer capable of retaining any kind of authority.

The Bolsheviks benefited from widespread sympathy for socialism in general. Their extremism flourished while politics were polarized, when law, civil society and government were being fatally undermined. But it was they who rose to power and not another socialist groupuscule – the Mensheviks, say, or the Socialist Revolutionaries – because it was their leaders who rose to the occasion. There was Lenin, with the clarity of his vision: support revolution now, and get bread, peace and land straight away. And there was Trotsky, with his rhetorical brilliance and capacity for organization. They were able to learn from mistakes, such as the false start of their failed uprising in July. And they were willing to act decisively when the next opportunity presented itself. We know from the records of the Party's Central Committee that other decisions were possible in October 1917, but that Lenin and Trotsky led the charge to take control at the moment of maximum possibility.

Even then, on the eve of the Bolshevik coup, when the Provisional Government had already been humiliated, and the problems of waging war and recovering the economy seemed intractable, a liberal alternative future was not impossible. True, the political system was broken; anger, hatred and extremism were rife throughout the country. True, too, it was only the circumstances of a total European war that stopped the other allied powers from intervening and crushing a dangerous socialist revolution before it took hold. Germany even fomented revolution in Russia as a way to finish off the conflict on the Eastern front, not least by transporting Lenin back to Petrograd from his Swiss exile. But after they took power, the Bolsheviks looked exposed and vulnerable.

By contrast, constitutional moderates – liberals and gentler socialists – were educated in the ways of administration, familiar with running the professions, equipped to deal with their peers in other countries and capable of devising the laws that might guide the country forward. The monarchy had gone, and no one was campaigning for its return: Russian conservatism was as weak as ever (a counter-intuitive theme to which we will return). A socialist majority might well have existed in the country, but it was fragmented between competing parties. The liberals became irrelevant, but that was the consequence of the accumulation of historical tragedies and accidents between 1917 and 1920. For a time, they were an alternative.

And imagine, before that alternative was eviscerated: without Bolsheviks in power in Russia, there would have been no red menace in the East for Hitler to fulminate against, the German far Left would have lacked momentum, and the Nazis would have matched them for insignificance in a more moderate political landscape. European politics would have been less violent, and international threats much less potent: Russia could have belonged to the moderates indefinitely. To extend the counterfactual speculation, Russia in the 1920s could have become dependent on a different path and looked like a 'normal' European country, part of the West, supported and encouraged by Western European semi-democracies, at least as quickly as Poland, say, managed it in the 1990s. Just imagine how Russian political culture might have developed in the 1920s without the Bolshevik proclivity to extremism, suspicion and violence. Imagine if the revolution had come in 1914, preventing the Great War from breaking out, and the extremists had been destroyed by foreign intervention. The imaginary political culture that could have followed might well have been pluralistic and dedicated to the protection of secure rights for all citizens. Those 'long centuries since the Mongols' need not have doomed this counterfactual future to failure.

But the Bolsheviks were better at politics than the liberals. Lenin and Trotsky made the liberals irrelevant. The Bolshevik leaders possessed the nerve to override the will of the people, who voted for a broad-based, multi-party socialist future in the elections of January 1918. Instead of accepting the verdict, the Bolsheviks quickly closed down the Constituent Assembly. And they embraced the opportunism that could craft an exit from the First World War under the bemusing slogan 'neither war nor peace'. Even then, there was no inevitability that they would win the Civil War and push forward the extremism of their vision into the rest of the twentieth century. But they plainly had the ruthlessness to do it.

Viktor Chernomyrdin was an archetype of post-Soviet life. As the country's senior gasman, he embodied the entitled corruption which allowed a Soviet bureaucrat to cash in his connections and become a wealthy businessman and politician. Such transactions destroyed the chance for a post-Soviet settlement founded on social justice. The reasonable expectations of most of the population, who wanted to preserve the social settlement of Soviet life while discarding its limits on personal freedom and economic improvement, were dashed. But Chernomyrdin had a lack of guile that was somehow bearable. For all the misery of the early 1990s, it was still possible to possess, like Chernomyrdin, a shadow of optimism, based on the recognition that the past does not own the future, and that the next chance that comes along might be the one that turns into a lucky break. Drawing on the black legend for support, the Russia Anxiety misunderstands the flexibility of history. The Chernomyrdin Dictum, with its emphasis on the contingent and conditional, is one device for deflating the legend's fallacies; the Speransky Conundrum, which shows the flexibility of Russia's governing institutions, is another.

## THE SPERANSKY CONUNDRUM

Russia's black legend gets the structures and shapes of Russian history wrong. It can't account for the complex layers of Russia's past. It doesn't take account of how contingency vies with structure in the Chernomyrdin Dictum. And where it rightly sees autocracy and dictatorship in Russian history, it fails to grasp that they make little sense if they are only viewed as top-down forces. But Mikhail Speransky, the great statesman of early nineteenth-century imperial Russia, demonstrated otherwise. We might call the problem with which he grappled the Speransky Conundrum.

If the black legend has struggled with the layers and contingencies of history, it has also misinterpreted the flexibility of autocracy and dictatorship in Russian history. Russia's subjects and citizens have possessed rights at particular times, usually in vulnerable forms. Limited rights have facilitated aspects of a responsive political culture. This was probably even the case in Muscovy between the fifteenth and seventeenth centuries, where subjects seem to have had a sense of belonging and participation, and were capable of making claims on the state. One distinguished historian even calls this 'rights without freedom', experimenting with the idea of pre-modern 'Muscovite citizenship'.[27] Assuming Russian power to be rigid, the legend has not seen its suppleness. Russian rulership has struggled with an historic puzzle, of how to incorporate forms of popular rights, however limited, into an autocratic system. No one came closer to solving the puzzle than Mikhail Speransky, Alexander I's indispensable adviser.

Tsarist Russia had its equivalents of the fabled journey from log cabin to White House, though it didn't embed them in an attractive master-narrative of politics. The story goes that Alexander Menshikov sold pies on the streets of Moscow as a child; he would become one of Peter the Great's leading advisers, elevated to the status of prince. Or take the striking story of Mikhail Speransky. He was born on 1 January 1772 in a village in the province of Vladimir, east of Moscow. His father was a priest. The priesthood had some of the qualities of a closed caste, and so Mikhail set out on his father's path. In the villages of imperial Russia, priests were poor, like the peasants to whom they ministered. At the seminary school in the town of Vladimir, Mikhail endured harsh poverty. None of that stopped him from displaying his dazzling gifts. He was sent on to complete his schooling at the Alexander Nevsky seminary in St Petersburg. Here, in Catherine the Great's capital, he received an Enlightenment education, learning languages and reading foreign texts as well as receiving religious instruction. Unsurprisingly, his talents were spotted and he acquired a patron: Prince Alexei Kurakin. Speransky became his private secretary, which opened the door to a career in government.

At the age of twenty-six, just a few years distant from village life, Speransky was appointed a collegiate councillor. On Peter the Great's Table of Ranks, this made him the civil equivalent of a colonel. He married a young Englishwoman, the love of his life, who died after giving birth to a daughter. It was the workaholism that accompanied his lengthy grief that turned his already spectacular career into an historic one. Alexander I (1801–25) soon appointed him as his chief adviser. There were progressive influences on Alexander: his childhood tutor, his young noble friends, and his aunt. But the biggest influence on Alexander was his grandmother, Catherine the Great.[28]

Catherine's reign (1762–96) offered Alexander the example of Enlightenment rulership. She aimed for rationality and order, distrusting superstition. Catherine sponsored the development of modern medicine, city planning, the arts, the care of orphans and well-organized schooling. Her reforms did not seek universal rights or the demolition of hierarchies. But they showed that Russia was becoming a modern state. For sure, actual democracy and republicanism scared Catherine rigid. The French and American Revolutions made the last years of her life uncomfortable. But the sum total of rights increased during her reign. Her Instruction (Nakaz) of 1767 was her major political declaration. It offered a prototype for increasing the size of the political nation and bending the autocracy in the direction of participation and rights. She also introduced the Charter of the Nobility in 1785. As a concession from the autocrat rather than a durable two-party contract, it was no Magna Carta, and it was vulnerable to a future sovereign's whims (as the nobles would find out during the brief reign of Paul, between 1796 and 1801, before they murdered him). But no longer could nobles simply be placed at will in particular civil or military roles by the tsar. Instead, elements of civil society sprang up around them, with the formation of noble assemblies and boards of public welfare.[29]

Following his accession to the throne in 1801, Alexander called on the administrative and legal skills of Speransky to investigate and implement a redesign of Russian government. Speransky had big aspirations, but his achievements were piecemeal. This was his conundrum: how to rationalize government without infringing the status of the Tsar, and how to enhance the status of subjects without diminishing the autocracy. The reforms were unmistakably modern. Speransky established new ministries in the place of Peter the Great's enduring administrative 'colleges', notably the Ministry of the Interior and the Ministry of Justice. They were led by substantial and able men. Gavril Derzhavin was the country's first minister of justice. His worldview was expansive, and he was a major poet. There was now a Committee of Ministers. In 1810, Speransky's State Council came into being. It was designed to be a forum for debating the quality of laws, and was divided into three sections, for economic, judicial and military affairs. The aim was to offer a bird's eye view from which legislation could better be drawn up. Meanwhile, Speransky helped to devise measures for enhancing the education of government officials. He established clearer lines of contact between ministries and provincial government: when it worked at its best, this decentralization had the potential to make central government more capable and 'enlightened'. Speransky also explored the possibility of a parliament whose basis would not contravene the norms of autocratic government, though this was a reform too far for Alexander.[30] There were faults and contradictions in all this, but the measures created a clearer and more rational administrative order than had existed during the reigns of Peter and Catherine, and provided the shape of the central administration through to the 1905 Revolution.[31]

In so doing, he solved his own conundrum. Speransky understood reform and revolution in Western Europe and the United States. He appreciated that Alexander's sense of constitutionalism had vanishingly little in common with the constitutional monarchy of Britain, where institutions and conventions placed limits on the power of the sovereign, and it had nothing in common with America, where people's entitlements were all written down, or France, where the king had recently been guillotined. By contrast, Speransky worked with the grain of Alexandrine constitutionalism. Alexander argued for constitutional reforms, but he had no intention that the constitution should place limits on his own power. What he meant was that the administration should be transparent and rational in new ways. He meant that this system should create predictable and rights-backed transactions between people and power. But he did not mean that these rights should come at the expense of the power of the sovereign. It was a dilemma in Germany, too, where the law-based rule of Frederick the Great's Prussia a few decades earlier, and the universal suffrage of Bismarck's unified empire a few decades later, represented the coexistence of some rights with autocratic power in a 'well-ordered police state'.[32]

In rationalizing the state administration, Speransky promised to change the form of the autocracy, to prime it for the challenges of the future.[33] But the idea of autocracy was not under debate, and Speransky himself did not imagine a world without it – precisely because autocracy was a political order which helped everyone. It was not the same as unlimited central power; when power had been exercised despotically in Russian history, such as during the reign of Ivan the Terrible, the principles of autocracy had not been observed. So Speransky's new Committee of Ministers and State Council were not prototypes of cabinet government, composed of independent men of power. Each minister was responsible to Alexander; they were not collectively responsible for anything. Their power was diminished too by their overlapping areas of authority and by the stubborn strength of provincial governors. But a glimpse of the rule of law was emerging out of the fog of Russia's opaque institutions. It could co-exist with autocracy because the Tsar, so the claim went, would by his nature not make decisions that went against the interests of his people; the system dealt with bad apples like Paul I, Alexander's father, who was murdered by a group of nobles after five years on the throne. There was nothing disingenuous about this description of autocracy. Speransky believed in the coexistence of autocracy, rational administration and law as much as Alexander did, arguing that nothing better served the Russian people. For him, it really was possible that the autocracy could be ruled by law.[34]

The conundrum was not resolved to everyone's satisfaction, though. Nikolai Karamzin was the father of Russian historiography and a leading conservative voice. He was associated with the tsar's younger sister, Catherine, who opened her salon to conservatives in her home in Tver (her husband was the province's governor). Karamzin wrote in 1813 that 'Russia is not England ... In Russia the sovereign is the living law.'[35] The tsar was the organic meeting place of past and future, of people and power, and the substance he was made of was the Russian tradition itself. Karamzin argued that Speransky's reforms were made of something anti-traditional, artificial and even foreign. They were a bit like Napoleon's law code, which had transmitted administrative regularity to his conquered territories. Napoleon was of course the anti-Christ, recently ejected from Russia. For Karamzin, the reforms placed a bomb under the nobility's prospects; the seamless relationship between nobles and tsar was the guarantee of the people's wellbeing. Turning one's back on the Russian tradition would destroy Russia's greatness and lead her to international irrelevance. Karamzin's message was tactless – he was arguing that Alexander was making a mistake – and the great work in which he made the case, his *Memoir on Ancient and Modern Russia*, was not published until much later.

So what about Speransky? Beset by conservative enemies, he fell out of the tsar's favour. Alexander sidelined him, removing him from office in 1812. Speransky spent years working in provincial government, partly in Siberia, before coming back to Petersburg to take up a less powerful role in central government. When Nicholas I came to the throne in 1825, a group of noble officers known as the Decembrists rose up against him, seeking the more thorough constitutional arrangements with which Alexander had briefly flirted a quarter-century before. The coup failed, and the perpetrators were executed or exiled. From these scary beginnings to its end amid the disasters of the Crimean War, Nicholas's reign (1825–55) is remembered as a time of conservative reaction against rational competence and enlightened hope. And yet it was also the age of Pushkin, of showy beauty and clever talk, of Russian Romanticism and the birth of the Russian intelligentsia – and it was still the age of enlightened and rational old Mikhail Speransky.

Nicholas I was responsible for one of the great legislative feats of Russian history. He owed it to Speransky, whom he brought out of premature retirement. Under Speransky's direction, the new Second Section of the Imperial Chancellery codified Russia's laws for the first time since Tsar Alexis had done so in 1649.[36] Speransky also saw to it that a new generation of officials was properly trained and curious. Such men as Nikolai Milyutin were the 'enlightened bureaucrats' who designed the reforms that would be introduced, for the most part, only after their reluctant but not completely obstructive tsar had died.[37] It was under his son, Alexander II, that the Great Reforms of the 1860s were brought into being. At their heart was the emancipation of the serfs of 1861. In that way did the Russian Enlightenment, and Mikhail Speransky, devise their ultimate legacy: the great 1860s, a brief coincidence of political stability and expanding rights. No wonder that the black legend of Russian history struggles to explain him.

The new statue in Moscow of Vladimir the Great, grand prince of Kievan Rus and bringer of Christianity to the East Slavic lands, symbolized the meeting place of past and present in third-term Putin's Russia. But this symbol did not mean that contemporary Russia was locked into the fulfilment of a dark historic destiny laid down by a thousand years of history. Not only did the Russian past offer many possible futures, thanks to its complex, layered form, but the Chernomyrdin Dictum showed the unpredictable force of events and what-ifs, while the Speransky Conundrum revealed the complexity of authoritarian politics, where power flowed in various directions. Russia's black legend is weak on analysis – and therefore strong on promoting the Russia Anxiety.

Not long before the new statue of Vladimir was built, President Putin inaugurated another monument near the Kremlin. In November 2014, he unveiled a statue of Alexander I, and invoked Speransky's measures in his speech.[38] His interest was the patriotic dimension,

200 years after Alexander's army occupied Napoleon's Paris. Configuring historical memory only slightly differently, Russians and foreigners can look at the statue and recall the domestic politics of Speransky, not just the wartime leadership of his tsar.

Speransky showed that Russian history is not about inevitability, or destiny, or legends. Those things offer Russians a licence to give up, and allow outsiders a free rein to fear Russia or treat Russians with contempt. Speransky's career and the Speransky Conundrum show something else: that the past can set Russia up to succeed in ways that are entirely unpredictable. The next chapter presents a narrative of Russia's history, from the beginning to the present, that corrects the excesses of the black legend, cutting out the fake history on which the Russia Anxiety depends.

# 3

# The Narrative Correction

*What's Really Happened in the Last 6,000 Years?*

The black legend needs a narrative correction: a chronology for Russia's story that's true to the agreed-upon facts.[1] This chapter divides that narrative of Russian history from the beginning to the present into ten sections. It focuses on Russia itself, not the Empire, and offers, for purposes of clarity, a story that is mostly about politics and 'big events', though it does not mention every tsar or battle. Each of the ten sections is headlined by a principle that sums up that period in a nutshell. But those ten principles also throw light on Russian history as a whole – and cast some darkness on the Russia Anxiety.

## I (PREHISTORY):
## EVERYTHING IS POSSIBLE

Imagine a vast space in the heart of the Eurasian landmass. The sun rises over a towering sky. Summer is blistering. Winter is lethal. Rich forests, wide rivers, endless grasslands stretch to the horizon. But there are hardly any people. In this empty place of beauty, wealth and danger, the possibilities are limitless. Any kind of civilization might emerge here.

Homo Sapiens were in the Siberian regions of what would later become Russia 40,000 years ago. Others were in western Russia shortly after. It might even be the case that early humans lived in the north Caucasus more than a million years ago. They must have been tough, resourceful, adaptable and on the move – like many human beings everywhere, and not least their Russian descendants. Six thousand years ago, farming communities were settling in southern Siberia, the Far East as well as the southern steppes and the river valleys of western Russia, Ukraine and Belarus. In the easier-living south, men and women advanced into the Bronze Age, using metal tools and devising metal decorations. In the Iron Age, from around 1000 BC, an ancient people known as the Cimmerians came to rule these lands to the north of the Black Sea, until they were defeated by the Scythians sometime around 700.

If the Cimmerians would become known for their Greek connections, with Greek colonies emerging in the southern Russian lands, the Scythians – nomadic warriors who did not even fear the superpower Persians – were nothing if not Asian. From around 300 BC, the Sarmatians, who had similar origins, displaced them. But for all the stereotypes conjured up by the Anxiety, it was not a backward anti-culture that was emerging in what would become Russia. The Black Sea offered crucial links to Greek culture and Roman power, while the route to Persian civilization was wide open. These two influences diffused into each other, creating complex forms of cultural and economic life.

The future Russia had both European and Asian roots. But so did many other countries – not least Hungary and Finland, even Portugal and Spain – and these were all located further to the West. The Russian lands were never part of the Roman Empire. They shared the shock, though, of the barbarian migrations that broke the Empire, smashed the European economy and caused, if not the dark ages, then certainly a long era of misfortune. From the start of the third century AD, the Goths swept down from the Baltic. Their eastern branch, the Ostrogoths, dominated the great swathe of today's Eastern Europe. By the end of the fourth century, the Huns, coming from the East, had pushed them out, though when Attila died in 453, they too started to lose their power. The Avars, another Eastern, even Asian, group were next to dominate the region. They had fought their way to the south-western territory of today's Russia by the mid-sixth century, and they ruled as far west as the Danube. Meanwhile, the most important group of all – the Slavs – were entering Eastern and South-eastern Europe from further west. They fought the Avars. The Slavs even reached the north-west forests, which contained the toughest of Uralic-speaking settlers, related to the Finns, who hunted and gathered in these inhospitable conditions, hitherto without disturbance, until the agriculturally more 'advanced' Slavs displaced them further to the north.

Two powerful groups faced the Slavs in the strategically contested south: the Bulgars and the Khazars. Eurasian in origin, Khazars came to rule the lower Volga and Black Sea region in the seventh century. They were strong enough to withstand inroads from other invaders, notably Islamic forces, and they promoted urbanization, eastward trade and legal protections for cultural diversity. The Bulgars were entrenched further south, nearer Byzantium, helping to run major east–west and north–south trade routes. Again, the zone north of the Black Sea, up the Volga, around the Don – a crucial part of Russia (and Ukraine and Belarus) before the Russians (and Ukrainians and Belarusians) – linked the entrepôts of Arabia and Byzantium. Slavs were entering the area in larger numbers, intermarrying, diversifying and enduring. This was the origin of a fluid, diverse, flexible and necessarily cosmopolitan attitude to life.

## 2 (862–1240): POLITICAL CULTURES ARE PLURAL

But diversity also implied a lack of order. Medieval chronicles claimed that the leading tribes – the Ves, the Krivichians, the Chuds and, most importantly for history, the Slavs – asked Vikings to rule over these lands for the sake of proper government. The Vikings who went east and south from Scandinavia were known as Varangians; those who went on to Byzantium, having raided and colonized the future Russian lands, and settled among the Slavs, were called Rus (or Rhos) by the locals. They came in significant numbers, just as they went westwards too, to shape the Anglo-Saxon kingdoms and elsewhere. But the idea of a compact with local tribes is probably a legend, elevating the Rus to historic peacemakers and overselling the coherence of the 'state' that resulted. They took control of settlements in the region, including Kiev, and, before that, Novgorod. Still, Riurik, who is sometimes described as the father of today's East Slavic civilization, was a Viking, and while 862 was only a symbolic date for the foundation of Rus, it suggested a plural and contingent basis of politics, and not one that was culturally or ethnically exclusive.

For years it was assumed by scholars that Riurik was a Slav, but the names of the rulers tell their own stories. Riurik, ruler of Novgorod, had a Norse name, showing he was a Varangian. His two successors – Oleg, who might have ruled from 879 to 912, starting in Novgorod and ending in Kiev, and Igor, who reigned in Kiev from perhaps 912 to 945 – had Slavic versions of Norse names, Helgi and Ingvar respectively. The generations after that were completely Slavic in their choice of names: Sviatoslav (945–72), Yaropolk (972–80), Vladimir (980–1015). The future Russia would be a Slavic country, just like Poland, Serbia, Bulgaria and others. Today's Russians, Ukrainians and Belorusians are East Slavs.

The *Primary Chronicle* attests that Riurik and his Varangians ruled Novgorod from 862 and Kiev from 882. Moscow would not be founded for another three centuries. These northern towns had complex economies; trade and culture were lively. But they were frontier outposts. They were not a country, nor were they the repository of a cohesive culture. Riurik's Varangians were called the Rus, and his dynasty would control these lands in one combination or another through to 1598.

Kievan Rus was Russia's first incarnation. This is a statement about powerful symbols and myths rather than straightforward political history, as there was no direct continuation between the earlier Kievan Rus (882) and the later Muscovy (1147), or indeed other East Slavic polities, including modern Ukraine (1991). (I refer to 'Kiev', not 'Kyiv', for reasons of historiographical convention, name recognition, and consistency, not because of a political bias; 'Kievan', in any case, is a later terminological addition to a territory known at the time as 'Rus'.) Over the next hundred years, Kievan Rus became the driver of a unifying East Slavic politics. It did this by fighting wars, paying and receiving tribute, keeping its leading princes on the move, and by each prince bequeathing the throne to a plausible successor. But it did not create a durable sovereignty or an unquestioned legitimacy. Neither did it found a recognizable overall culture, though it created individual triumphs in architecture, icons and chronicles, and achieved quite widespread popular literacy. It was a capital city, and it was led by a grand prince of great symbolic power, but other major towns, and their princes, exerted authority in their own right. Kiev did not have a bureaucracy or anything recognizable as a government. This made it difficult to bestow real as opposed to symbolic legacies to its modern successors. Still, Kievan Rus is claimed as the first Russian state and the first Ukrainian state, although both these things are total anachronisms. But although the Mongols completely destroyed Kiev in the thirteenth century, by which time it had long become a political backwater, Kievan Rus is a common origin, a civilizational fount, of Ukraine, Belarus and Russia. Of the first rulers, Prince Sviatoslav (945–72) pushed its borders the furthest, down towards Byzantium, today's Istanbul, where the capital of the newly Christianized Roman Empire had been relocated in the fourth century. Sviatoslav was repulsed, but a complicated pattern was set. Kievan Rus, like its successor states, would be expansionary in ambition, though no more so than comparable imperial powers.

Rus looked outwards. It was sophisticated. The Russian lands were Christian. In 988, during the reign of Sviatoslav's third son, Vladimir, Kievan Rus entered Christendom: or rather it joined its eastern sector, Byzantium, not Catholic Rome. In 1054, the Eastern and Western Churches split in the Great Schism. Religion therefore placed the future Russia, Ukraine and Belarus in Europe, but in a different kind of Europe than that which was focused on Rome. Yet Rome was not bound to be the heart of Europe. It was not inevitable that centuries later the Islamic Ottomans would conquer Byzantium but not Rome too. And why should there be anything automatically less European about the Orthodox civilization of Greece-Serbia-Bulgaria-Russia-Ukraine-Belarus than the Catholic civilization to the West? Meanwhile, members of the dynasty were related by marriage to the ruling houses of what would become Sweden and Norway, as well as Poland, France and Hungary, not to mention Byzantium. It was also during the reign of Yaroslav the Wise (1019–54) that Kievan Rus adopted the law code *Russkaya Pravda* (which can be translated as either Rus Justice or Rus Truth). This was a foundation stone in East Slavic civilization and its legal history.

Grand Prince Vladimir Monomakh (1113–25) saw off the Polovtsy, a leading steppe people with whom there were sporadic skirmishes, and fought across the Baltic region, as well as in the south. He might have established the great city of Vladimir (the sources are too difficult to be sure), and he became known for progressive welfare measures. Legend traced the Cap of Monomakh, used in Russian coronations from the fourteenth century, to Vladimir, who was thus one of the many founders of the Russian state in both practical and symbolic senses. Within a couple of decades of Vladimir Monomakh's adventures, Kievan Rus was irrevocably split by civil wars. Little more than a century on, in 1240, it was no more, effectively eliminated by the Mongols.

## 3 (1240–1462): HISTORICAL LEGACIES HAVE THEIR LIMITS

Across China, Central Asia and the Caucasus, Chinggis Khan and his descendants launched invasions that were ferocious, superbly organized and vast in scale. They first broke Rus resistance at the disastrous Battle of the Kalka river in 1223, in the south, near the Sea of Azov, but did not press the point further. Seventeen years later, under Chinggis's grandson Batu, an army as big as four Kievs took control of the East Slav lands. The locals called the Mongol invaders Tatars and referred to their empire as the Golden Horde. Its headquarters was established in Sarai on the Volga, in the south.

The Mongols were initially destroyers, but they were builders, too, placing the Russian lands in a web of Eurasian networks, facilitating trade and providing administrative models that would help Muscovy to construct its state. But Russians did not become Mongols. Rule was indirect. The Mongols, at one time or another, controlled many of today's great states without Mongolizing them either – China, Turkey, Iran, and into Central Europe. Here they smashed Cracow and Moravia, defeated today's Hungary and fought in what we now call Austria. The decades following 1240 are often known as the Appanage period. 'Appanage' describes a form of inheritance in which all the sons of a prince or other landowner received a share. The opposite of primogeniture, of the first son getting everything, it was a response to political events. The consequence was division of territories and landholdings, a centrifugal process inimical to centralization and shared identities. If Kievan Rus had been a fragmented realm, then its successor was even more so.

Novgorod was one of these new centres of power and culture. It had been independent-minded long before 1240, but now it displaced Kiev as the incubator of Russian civilization. Thanks not least to the diplomatic skills of its great prince, Alexander Nevsky, Novgorod held out against the Mongol threat and was never attacked, though it was forced to pay tribute. Nevsky became one of the heroes of Russian history, also fighting off repeated threats from the West, especially from Swedes, Teutonic Knights and Lithuanians.

Kiev had no Alexander Nevsky to defend it. The Grand Duchy of Lithuania took control of Kiev, Minsk and a significant part of old Rus. In the late fourteenth century, the union of Lithuania and Poland under the Jagiellonian dynasty brought much of this territory, including Kiev, under sustained Polish imperial control for more than two centuries.

Novgorod had something of the self-governing city-state about it. It was famous for its *veche*, a city assembly which oversaw the energetic urban life of 30,000 Novgorodians. Similar assemblies, of varying powers, existed elsewhere in the region, too. Novgorod was a major centre of trade, expansive in its commercial aims and general outlook. These characteristics blended with others in an emerging Russian tradition.

But if Novgorod held out successfully against the Golden Horde – as the khanate established by Batu in the region was sometimes called – it succumbed to Moscow. The city that would become known as the Third Rome, and the capital of half the world during the Cold War, had been founded in 1147 by Yuri Dolgoruky, a prince from Suzdal. Less than a century later, it was smashed to pieces by the Mongols. Moscow gradually recovered, restoring robust but supplicatory relations with the Golden Horde and growing in size. Grand Prince Ivan Kalita (1325-40) was a brilliant exponent of tribute-driven diplomacy, taking money from the lands just outside his seat, and giving some of it to the Mongol overlords in Sarai. ('Kalita' can be translated as 'Moneybags'; he was entitled to the title Grand Prince thanks to his overlordship of Vladimir too, from 1332.) He encouraged the metropolitan, the head of the Church in what was no longer Kievan Rus, to live in Moscow. Ivan's successors continued to bolster Moscow's position as the emerging political and religious centre of the Russian lands.

One of them, Grand Prince Dmitry (1350–89), secured Moscow's great victory against the Mongols, at Kulikovo in 1380. The battlefield was above the Don river, and the grand prince is known to history as Dmitry Donskoi. It took another century of ebbs and flows in Mongol authority before the Golden Horde finally lost control completely, but Mongol rule was never secure after Kulikovo. The intervening time was not lost. Economic capacity, political identity and cultural virtuosity all grew. Andrei Rublev, painting in the late fourteenth and early fifteenth centuries, was one of the greatest exponents of the Russian icon tradition. As Muscovy emerged, then, it blended antecedents from Kiev, Novgorod, the other Rus cities, Byzantium, the Germanic hinterland of North-east Europe and the Mongol Horde. Not one of these legacies was decisive in Moscow's development.

With the Mongols gone, Moscow grabbed the Russian future.

# 4 (1462–1598):
## THE DANGEROUS TIMES ARE THE EXCEPTIONS BECAUSE MOST TIMES ARE 'NORMAL'

Ivan III – Ivan the Great – reigned from 1462 to 1505. He finally saw off the Mongols, so Moscow was fully free of foreign tutelage. And he went on with the 'gathering of the Russian lands', extending Moscow's power ever further, notably over rival power centres such as Novgorod and Tver. The fractured authority of the Appanage period had come to a close. Ivan was a convincing holder of the new title Sovereign (*Gosudar*) of All Russia. His realm was Muscovy, and it was becoming a major power.

Posterity, not least in the new historiography of the nineteenth century, looks down on the Muscovite period, inventing one of world history's major villains: its long-lived ruler Ivan IV (the Terrible, 1533–84). In 1885, the painter Ilya Repin constructed the modern period's lasting image of mad-eyed Ivan, shortly after he had murdered his own son.

Evidence indeed suggests that Ivan's ghastly childhood was followed by a life of cruelty and redemption, a miserable cycle that might have been patterned by psychotic episodes. He became monarch at the age of two, following the death of his father, Vasily III. His paternal uncle, a potential rival, was imprisoned and died of hunger; his mother died next, possibly poisoned, when he was eight. Her relatives could no longer protect him; and his younger brother, deaf and dumb, was in no position to offer much fraternal help. Ivan responded by hurling small animals off the towers of the Kremlin. As a sixteen-year-old, preparing to get married, he arranged for the impaling and beheading of selected relatives of the men who had made his infancy unhappy. All this had profound consequences for Russia, not because Ivan's possible mental illness was in some mysterious way emblematic of the country's condition, but because Ivan's political and strategic achievements proved durable. They included imperial expansion, consolidation of government and foreign ties. But progress was matched by terrible violence.

Translating more specifically from the Russian, his name is better rendered as Ivan the Awe-inspiring. The first to be crowned tsar, or Caesar, Ivan secured the authority of the monarchy against the sometimes recalcitrant nobles, or boyars. He established a state-within-a-state, the *oprichnina*. This was a separate realm lorded over by a personal police force, the *oprichniki*, which terrorized his real, potential and imagined opponents. Meanwhile, he extended the boundaries of Muscovy. In 1552, he conquered Kazan, which ensured that Russia would always have a substantial Muslim minority. He also fought the Livonian Order and reached the Baltic, and waged a running war against the Crimean Tatars, coming close to annexing the Crimean peninsula. The route to Siberia was opened up by merchants and musketeers, led for a time by the famous figure of Yermak.

Muscovy was now a major power, inspiring feelings of fear and thoughts of mystery among outsiders. Direct sea links with England were discovered, promoting extensive trade with Western Europe, whose merchants emphasized its submissive people and tyrannical ruler, having no knowledge of his normal, spiritual or incompetent predecessors. Relations with foreign governments were secured. But it was an 'other', not quite respectable, inconsistently powerful, and more than slightly barbarous. The Ottomans were still the real territorial successor to Byzantium. And the Poles were waiting for their chance to invade. Kiev and other cities that would be integral to the empire were not yet under Moscow's control. Politics was unstable, resting on an uncertain succession. Twenty years after Ivan the Terrible's death, Muscovy faced elimination. Ivan IV left a range of legacies, some of which weakened Muscovy disastrously, while others looked towards a stronger future. Ivan was an exception. After the worst of his effects had subsided, most of Russian history looked completely different. But Muscovy went through purgatory before something like normality could return.

# 5 (1598–1676):
## RUSSIA IS A EUROPEAN COUNTRY

The Time of Troubles (1598–1613) became one of the recurring nightmares of Russian history. Dynastic crisis, invasion and famine combined.

In 1598, Ivan's son Tsar Fedor died. He left no obvious successor. Boris Godunov seized the moment, emerging from behind the throne to reign in his own right for the next seven years. But he was not joined to the bloodline of the House of Riurik. Instead, this capable man had been elected by his peers in the proto-parliament called the *Zemsky sobor*, so his rule was always bitterly disputed. He faced challenges from pretenders such as the 'False Dmitry', who claimed to be Ivan's son. Meanwhile, the peasants who made up almost the entire population were under extraordinary pressures: state officials enforced new forms of serfdom and tax, while landowners extracted other payments. Large numbers of desperate peasants gave up and hit the road. Many died from hunger, especially between 1601 and 1603. Lacking food supplies, Moscow succumbed to catastrophe.

With tens of thousands dying of starvation and disease, Godunov's rule was under threat. The False Dmitry gathered forces in Poland.

He fought his way into Moscow, briefly winning the throne. The ruling establishment struck back. Their representative, Boris Vasily Shuisky, became tsar. If Godunov had had the formal backing of the *Zemsky sobor*, and Dmitry had claimed to be the lost son of Ivan the Terrible, Shuisky's authority seemed much less clear. Sweden and Poland-Lithuania prepared to strike. Polish forces under Sigismund III tried to take enduring control of Moscow.

They failed. Muscovite civilization was still in free-fall.

In 1613, popular resilience and dynastic decisiveness saved it. The *Zemsky sobor* put its faith in young Mikhail Romanov. This was a vital moment not just because of the dynastic decision, but because an embryonic Russian nation became visible. It was headed up by the townsfolk of Moscow, and was distinct from the monarchy. With the Poles gone and other enemies exhausted, the Time of Troubles slipped away. It left its mark: the institutions of the Muscovite state had evolved and survived; the Russian tradition of protest had been invented; and the Western border, vulnerable to Poland's and Sweden's interference, would thereafter always define the Russians' own anxiety. But Mikhail brought recovery and stability.

Tsar Aleksei (1645–76) succeeded him. He consolidated Muscovite laws in the code (*Ulozhenie*) of 1649, a legislative feat which was the first of its type for a century and which survived intact for nearly 200 years. Serfdom was clarified at this time but it was only ever ambiguously laid down in law. Meanwhile, religious conflict caused great distress but not war. Muscovy was riven by schism (*raskol*). Patriarch Nikon introduced reforms in the early 1650s which would lead to the exit of the Old Believers, more orthodox than the Orthodox, from the Church. Aleksei, meanwhile, took his chance to centralize his power over religious institutions which had overstepped their authority. He came to terms with the Poles in the Ukrainian lands, and saw off rebellions from Cossacks in the west, and from the great peasant violence led by Stenka Razin in the south. Fascinated by what he knew of Western Europe, Aleksei was keen to import some of its cultural products. Russia did not experience the Reformation – that was true of large other parts of Europe, too; and while it did not go through the Renaissance, it enjoyed some of its benefits. Aleksei's reforms were substantial, modern and even cosmopolitan, and the recovery of classical learning would be an important part of eighteenth-century Russian culture. More foreigners than ever before were in Moscow, negotiating business deals and cultural exchanges. Peter the Great's future transformation of Russia, making a modernizing state that was open to the West, was the central fact of the next 200 years of Russian history, but it grew logically out of the past.

## 6 (1676–1762): RUSSIA IS A MODERN GREAT POWER

After two great reigns, it was time for a dynastic crisis. Aleksei had three sons. His eldest was Fedor, who ruled weakly for six years (1676–82) as a teenager. Aleksei's second and third sons then ascended the throne together. Ivan V was sixteen: like Fedor, he was not really capable of exercising power. Peter I was ten, too young to rule in practice if not in theory. Ivan and Peter were proxies in a power struggle between two clans, centred on the aristocratic families of the Miloslavsky and Naryshkin lines, from which Aleksei's two wives had come, the first giving birth to Fedor, Sophia and Ivan, the latter to Peter. Sophia served as regent between 1682 and 1689, representing the Miloslavsky clan and taking advantage of Ivan V's infirmity. Working together with Prince Vasily Golitsyn, her rule was in many ways enlightened, even if it was bookended by brutal power-grabs.

Bloody political infighting led to her fall and the establishment of Peter as tsar in his own right. In 1696, the co-tsar Ivan died too. There was nothing to stop Peter setting his own agenda: the modernization of Russia, his revolution from above. The medieval-seeming world of old Muscovy faded quickly.

Like any project for a new world, it was defined by violence. Soon Peter ordered a massacre of the *streltsy*, the stormtroopers who had terrorized his childhood years as tsar. The scene was forever captured by the great history painter Vasily Surikov in 1881. His image of state violence was the fate of a child. In the foreground of his painting of the massacre, a little girl in a red headdress is lost and alone, terrified and confused, her brightness surrounded by muddy ground and the plain blouses and furs of defeated men. Like the little red-coated girl in the black-and-white film *Schindler's List*, she is a haunting sight of innocent suffering. On the right, Peter sits imperious on horseback, with the Kremlin towers at his side and St Basil's Cathedral behind him, indifferent to her, overseeing the act of revenge on Red Square.

This was a reign of unlimited authority by a supremely effective practitioner of power. He was massive in physical size, geopolitical ambition and ideological vigour. In 1697 and 1698 he travelled around Western Europe, seeking to learn about new technologies and modes of power. It was a further turn towards modernity and 'the West'. On his return, Russia became a land of foreign experts, beardless nobles, a new navy, a streamlined government and a weakened Church. In 1703, Peter started building the new capital city of St Petersburg, his 'window on the West'. His armies fought major wars against Sweden and the Ottoman Empire. He redesigned the channels of power: nobles were obliged to perform civil or military service to the state in accordance with their place on the new Table of Ranks, while peasants had to pay a new poll tax. But as with all Russia's rulers, Peter's reach into the provinces was not as sure as it looked from outside.

Peter's successors continued his task of making the court at St Petersburg one of the great centres of European power and culture, a place where the nobles of the eighteenth century, in their new uniforms, looked somewhat French or Prussian. Many spoke foreign languages. Catherine I (his wife), Peter II (his grandson), Anna (his niece) and Elizabeth (his daughter) pursued the Petrine inheritance between 1725 and 1762. During Elizabeth's reign (1741–61), the country's first university was founded in Moscow in 1755, under the guidance of the brilliant polymath and self-made man Mikhail Lomonosov, who possessed a glittering vision of Russian learning. Ideas about native 'Russianness' came into vogue, but Russianness also looked ever more westwards while Elizabeth was on the throne. Entering the Seven Years War (1756–63) alongside Britain and France, the Russian army scored brilliant victories against Prussia, and occupied Berlin in 1760. But the tableau of court, metropolitan and diplomatic life made almost no sense in the Russian countryside. Peasants often called their nationality 'Orthodox', referencing their religion, and tended to say 'round here' when asked by outsiders where they were from. Russian nationhood had little common meaning, but the Russian Empire was already a great power, an indispensable part of European culture and politics.

# 7 (1762–1825):
## RUSSIA IS A POSITIVE FORCE
## FOR EUROPEAN SECURITY

Catherine the Great (1762–96) was born a German princess, which did not make it easier to say what 'Russian' meant. Married to Peter's grandson in 1745, who became Peter III in 1762, she ascended to the throne herself when he was murdered a few months later. For all her German heritage, she became a Russian speaker of the Orthodox faith, surrounded for much of her life by Russians, the mother and grandmother of future tsars. In all her glitter and brilliance, she really was a Russian tsaritsa. She expanded the empire in all directions, waging wars with the Turks, transforming cities such as Odessa and establishing whole new Russian regions, such as New Russia, or Novorossiya, on the Black Sea coast. She was the fourth major tsaritsa of the century. Russia accepted female rulers in a way that eighteenth-century France, for example, found impossible. This new modern Russian Empire was one in which laws were properly codified, medicine was improved, welfare was expanded, universities were created, and an Academy of Arts was established to match the Academy of Sciences started by Peter a half-century before. Catherine was Russia's leading Enlightenment ruler. But the execution of Louis XVI haunted Catherine at the end of her life. Her son, Paul, who reigned between 1796 and 1801, was the manifestation of Catherine's doubts and failures. A martinet who lacked the feel for power, he wanted to tighten his authority at the expense of the nobility, and he alienated his natural supporters. Paul regulated serfdom and introduced a law of royal succession, but he was a tyrant. He was murdered in a palace coup.

Within a few years, under the rule of Alexander I (1801–25), Paul's son, Russia was in a fight for its life with Napoleon. War had come and gone between the former allies since 1807, but the Fatherland War, Russia's national struggle, only began when the French invaded in 1812. Falling back and gathering strength, Russian forces faced the

*Grande Armée* near Smolensk, when the two armies pulverized each other at the Battle of Borodino. The Russians licked their wounds, and the route to Moscow was open. But the French were exposed, under-supplied and vulnerable, while the Russians were recovering, consolidating and growing stronger. With the old capital in flames, and a terrible winter coming on, the Napoleonic Army's occupation of the city was only brief. By 1814, the Russian Imperial Army had chased the French all the way back to Paris. Waterloo was just the *coup de grâce*. Russia was the indispensable nation. Alexander I had a seat close to the middle of the top table at the post-war Congress of Vienna in 1815. The message was clear: Europe is at its safest when Russia is at its heart.

Russia defeated Napoleon because of Napoleon's hubris and errors, but above all because of the quality of Russia's generals, the determi-nation of its soldiers, the suppleness of its transport and logistics, the scope of its war economy, the endurance of its soldiers and the sacri-fice of people of all classes, not least in Moscow, when it was burned to the ground. Victory seemed to mark the height of Russian national feeling. Tolstoy argued that Marshal Kutuzov embodied the Russian virtues, and so did the peasant-soldiers, with their patience, stoicism and faith, and their mysterious bonds with God, sovereign and fellow subjects.

These bonds were the essence of the Russian autocracy. The tsars styled themselves 'autocrat of all the Russias'. Their power was unlimited, derived from God. But they could not do as they pleased: that would have made them tyrants. Everything the tsar ordered must be in the interests of his people as mediated by God; arbitrary rule and autocracy were, in theory, antithetical. Some even believed that autocracy guaranteed freedom. Practical life in the biggest country in the world, meanwhile, limited the tsar's reach. 'God is in his heaven and the tsar is far away,' ran a peasant saying.

In the early years of his reign, Alexander's brilliant adviser, Mikhail Speransky, experimented with constitutional reforms. But, as Speran-sky knew, a constitution would have formally limited the tsar's power. You could not reform the autocracy into a constitutional monarchy: it was like turning an apple into a pear. Or was it? This remained a life-and-death question for the next hundred years.

The ambitions and experiments of Alexander's first years on the throne faded. Alexander came to rely on Aleksei Arakcheyev, whose understanding of the world was military and rigid, where Speransky's was civil-minded and compromising. Alexander abandoned Speransky, and with that he exchanged imagination and talent for fearfulness and superstition. Unsurprisingly, Alexander's rulership deteriorated. He ended his days in mysterious circumstances in the south of Russia. The war against Napoleon had shown that Europe was secured by a strong and confident Russia, but Alexander did not learn from its success.

## 8 (1825–1917): REVOLUTION IS UNLIKELY – BUT IT HAPPENS

His brother Nicholas I (1825–55) took the throne, defeating in the process an anguished conspiracy of liberal guards officers known as the Decembrists. Military in bearing and severely conservative by temperament, Nicholas oversaw the creation of the secret police (the 'Third Section'), tightened censorship and approved the mantra 'Orthodoxy, Autocracy, Nationality'. But this was also the age of Pushkin (1799–1837), Russia's greatest poet, inventor of its literary language, a mercurial talent capable of holding power to account with verse, dead in a duel at the height of his powers. He was much the greatest of a new group that emerged under Nicholas and would later come to determine Russia's fate: the intelligentsia. In the 1830s and 1840s, writers on left and right, Western sympathizers and 'Slavophiles', provincials and metropolitans became the first generation of politically engaged intellectuals. Nicholas had little time for them, but he was not a wicked reactionary who put in train the long-term origins of the Russian Revolution. Instead, he charmed many who met him, had a sense of Western Europe and ruled over a government that was itself multi-layered and complex, some of whose officials were enlightened, reform-minded and interested in the operation of the law inside the autocracy. Nicholas's greatest failure was the Crimean War, an exceptional and unnecessary conflict with Britain, France and Ottoman Turkey, ending in awful defeat.

Of all Russia's lost worlds, the 1860s have always offered the richest starting point for those who dream of a 'better' Russian past and a missed alternative to 1917. In 1861, Alexander II, who reigned from 1855 to 1881, signed the decree that emancipated the serfs. Emancipation was the fundamental fact of nineteenth-century Russian history. It hinted that constitutionalism and autocracy might be reconciled, because it implied the existence of rights and even citizenship. By formally untying the peasants from the land, it was the precondition of modern urban growth and large-scale industrialization. When taken together with Alexander's other reforms, which introduced partly representative local government (the *zemstvos*), trial by jury, self-regulating administration for universities, more humane terms of army conscription, an end to corporal punishment and a reduced regime of censorship, it promised a harmonious and evolving form of autocracy, suitable for a modern age.

In March 1881, members of the radical and unmoored branch of the Russian intelligentsia assassinated Alexander II, blowing him up in the centre of St Petersburg. Nothing more significant could have happened. The revolutionaries were radical socialists, tracing a genealogy back to the reign of Nicholas I and a web of influence out into Western Europe. This seemed, in retrospect, a decisive step towards the Russian Revolution. But it was a chance disaster. It ended an alternative future of effective monarchy and humane reform. Alexander III (1881–94) learned the lesson he wanted to learn: that the past was better than the future, that Muscovy was more moral than Petersburg, and that opposition was always disloyal. Bearded and big as a Russian bear, he was the model of monarchical intransigence. He died quite young, in 1894.

His son came unprepared to the throne as Nicholas II (1894–1917), a slighter man in every sense. He continued the tenor of his father's policies: stamping on reform, stepping up repression, 'Russifying' the borderlands. The confident flexibility of the autocracy that Catherine the Great, Mikhail Speransky and Alexander II had exercised was no more. Instead, the autocracy of the last two tsars was blunt. More and more people were alienated from the autocracy – and from each other's social classes and ethnic identities. It was an insensitive time of lost potential, when the monarchy was inadvertently put at risk.

At the heart of this period of reckless reaction, between 1881 and

1904, was a problem. The tsars were determined to guarantee Russia's geopolitical future. They wanted secure borders, a more powerful empire, world-class armed forces and a dynamic economy. But they could not do this without rolling the dice. Only by loosening the ties between peasant and land so that new factory workers could staff an industrial revolution could they build the economy that would make modern Russia great. And that meant pushing Russia forward to modernity: to cities that could not be controlled, where time was speeding up and normality was fracturing.

Russia's expansion in Asia led to war with Japan in 1904. Defeat at Asian hands was inconceivable for the European empire that had triumphed against Napoleon. It exposed Russian weakness. The humiliation nearly destroyed the monarchy. In 1905, workers struck and peasants rampaged. They were offended not only by poverty but by lack of justice. Revolutionary chaos began on 9 January, Bloody Sunday, when a peaceful demonstration was massacred near the Winter Palace in St Petersburg. If the elements of truth and fairness – *pravda* – were in doubt, then autocracy had malfunctioned, and the bond between people and sovereign had frayed. Radicals seized the day and liberals tried to catch up. The army couldn't stop the revolution: it was fighting and being defeated in Japan. Elected councils (soviets) of workers were founded in St Petersburg and Moscow. By the end of the year they would be crushed, but not before Nicholas II had signed the October Manifesto, promising a parliament, or Duma. In early 1906, the Fundamental Laws defined the exercise of power in Russia. The laws should have been the basis of a constitutional monarchy. Trade unions and a diversity of political parties were now legal and openly competing with each other. The first Duma was elected in the spring. There were millions of voters.

Confusingly, the Fundamental Laws promised the coexistence of autocrat and parliament. Monarch and Duma danced uneasily around each other. In 1907, Pyotr Stolypin, Nicholas's powerful prime minister, took matters in hand. A conservative of great imagination and ability, dedicated to saving the tsar, Stolypin limited the Duma's troublesome potential, sponsored repression and boosted defence spending. Industrial development accelerated. He also supported welfare reform for factory workers and land reform for peasants. Above all, he made it much easier for peasants to leave the village commune and set up as smallholding farmers in their own right. By giving them a stake in tsarist Russia, he tried to invent the conservative-minded majority that would prop up the tsar in a refurbished autocracy. Pessimistic historians would later suggest that he had the weight of the past against him, but Stolypin had intelligence and vigour on his side.

Meanwhile, the future was destroying the past. On the one hand, the economy was expanding, prompting allies and enemies to see Russia as the superpower of the future. On the other, more and more peasants were on the move, crowding into the great cities of the empire. The predictable round of elegant city living was disintegrating. Life was more difficult to understand than ever. At its most extreme, avant-garde culture was incomprehensible. Within a few years, the brilliantly talented Kazimir Malevich had reduced painting to a black square.

An epidemic of suicide spread across the Empire. Terrorist attacks by radical socialists were costing the lives of many thousands of government officials. Society was divided against itself. On 14 September 1911, Stolypin was assassinated at the theatre. Vladimir Kokovtsov was a worthy successor. When he was removed from office, those who were left, such as the new prime minister, Goremykin, who lacked robustness and vision, were a weak team to field in the terrible challenge of 1914. But Russia had faced emergencies before.

The First World War changed everything. It made the world modern. Between 1914 and 1918, all the great powers were transformed by citizen warfare on an industrial scale, as peasants and workers in military uniforms were slaughtered from Ypres to Tannenberg. Nationhood assumed new contours, accommodating women workers and angry soldiers. States expanded their reach, collecting more data than ever about their populations. Economies changed their shape. Monarchs were humiliated. Empires collapsed. Russia was never more European than when the contemporary world was coming into being.

Nicholas II took on the mantle of Russia's war leader, but it made him look foolish. It was a genetic accident, an historical contingency, that he had neither the intellect nor the bearing for such a role. The Imperial Army retreated miserably in the face of the Germans, though it held its own against Austria-Hungary. Famished and furious, soldiers and workers, many of them women, rose up in the country's capital, which had been renamed Petrograd (less German-sounding than Petersburg) for the duration. In February 1917, the tsar abdicated. Nobody missed him. A Provisional Government, made up of leading members of the Duma, came to power. On the other side of central Petrograd, the Soviet of Workers and Soldiers' Deputies was formed. The Provisional Government promised to govern in an open and reforming spirit, paving the way for eventual elections to a Constituent Assembly. Prime ministers changed, from Lvov to Kerensky, and the liberal-conservative-socialist composition of its ruling coalition modified itself several times between February and October. But it was always committed to the one policy that made its survival impossible: keeping Russia in the war. The Soviet (or Council) represented the working class and the solidarity of the lower orders, shouting out opposition, pushing the Provisional Government and making it answerable; it had power but not responsibility. Its democracy was defined by the loudest voices in the room, which called for an end to the war, an eight-hour day, and equality between officers and soldiers. Their members were socialists of different stripes, whose technical differences mattered less to ordinary people than their common home on the Left.

Lenin came back to Petrograd in April 1917. He was barely known, his Bolsheviks a tiny splinter group. But he and the other leading Bolshevik, Trotsky, had things in common: the gift of words, the ability to captivate a crowd and organize a movement, the demagogue's willingness to give facile answers to the most complicated problems that Russia had ever faced. They took their message of urgent socialist revolution across the city. Offering the desperate population bread, peace and land, while more moderate socialists tied themselves in Marxist contortions, and liberals and moderate conservatives tried to make complex policies hit moving targets, they whipped up support. The Provisional Government missed a chance to crush them after a failed rising in July. But the Bolsheviks lacked their scruple and self-doubt. When they grabbed power in October, they already had substantial support in Petrograd, Moscow and some other cities. It was not quite a *coup d'état*. The Provisional Government had given up, and Kerensky fled the Winter Palace disguised as a woman.

Very soon, the Bolsheviks introduced decrees fulfilling their wild promises, and also setting up their secret police. They organized elections to a Constituent Assembly and then crushed it when they came second to the Socialist Revolutionaries. With their enemies at the gates of Petrograd, Lenin and the Bolsheviks fell back to the Kremlin. Moscow was again the capital. The impossible had come to pass.

## 9 (1917–1991): PERIODIZATION IS THE FRAME THROUGH WHICH YOU LOOK AT RUSSIAN HISTORY

The Empire struck back. Civil War started. Between 1918 and 1920, the Russian Revolution was up for grabs, but the victorious Red Army sealed the Bolsheviks in power. Their geographical advantage, access to industry and ideological clarity resulted in victory, but it was only after defeating many millions of Russians (and those from other nationalities) who hated and feared them. Although many cultural norms transmitted themselves across 1917, the Bolsheviks set about building a completely different world. They were guided by 'democratic centralism' – the principle that free debate ended at the moment when a resolution was accepted – and so pointed towards a future where you could say what you liked as long as you agreed with everyone else. Not quite an empire, the Soviet Union was constituted in 1922 as a federation of republics like Russia, Ukraine and Transcaucasia, rather than the more centralized Russia-focused state that Stalin really wanted.

Lenin died in 1924, and though Petrograd was renamed Leningrad for Soviet perpetuity, the future was undecided. Economic recovery and stable rule came in the era of the New Economic Policy (1921–8), when private trade and steady socialist development coexisted. A future that emphasized the plural rather than the singular briefly seemed possible. Stalin crushed that possible future. He outmanoeuvred all political rivals during the 1920s, eventually taking up a position on the extreme Left. Staying there, always revolutionary, he dictated the Soviet Union's future from 1928 until 1953. Stalinism was a likely outcome of the Bolshevik Revolution, but it was not the only one. The New Economic Policy had been another. And de-Stalinization after 1953 was a third.

Between the 1920s and the 1980s, there were several Soviet Unions. Soviet life looks quite different depending on the start and end dates of your story. Periodization is the key to Soviet history.

And Stalinism was not a single period. It took place in three acts. Act One was the Stalinist 1930s, a forcing house of modernity that squeezed a century's transformations into a decade. In an epic cycle of creation and destruction, new cities rose up out of nothing, factories were built, agriculture was collectivized, peasant traditions were liquidated, millions of people migrated, famine struck, propaganda was ubiquitous, literacy escalated, the Gulag expanded, the bitter but addictive taste of a new world was everywhere. Stalinism had one aim – building this new world inspired by Marxism-Leninism – and it had one ethic: that anything could be done to make it happen. Between 1936 and 1938, Stalinism reached its logical high point, when 700,000 people were shot on trumped-up charges whose overall pattern seemed entirely plausible to many Bolsheviks. Never before or after had the ends justified the means quite so transparently. Stalin had fulfilled his destiny and defended the revolution. It was by far the greatest catastrophe and worst exception in Russian history.

Stalinism's second act began on 22 June 1941, when Nazi Germany invaded the Soviet Union, bringing to an end the brief Nazi–Soviet pact which Stalin had concluded, *faute de mieux*, as the best chance of delaying an almost inevitable war with Hitler, and picking up some low-risk spoils – the Baltic states, eastern Poland – along the way. The Germans battered their way far into Soviet lands, rolling through Kiev and Minsk, besieging Leningrad, reaching the gates of Moscow. They killed Jews and communists wherever they went, razed villages, torched cities, massacred civilians and starved prisoners of war. Stopped by winter, they then turned south, until defeat at the Battle of Stalingrad in January 1943 made their ultimate victory impossible. Yet it took another twenty-six months for the Red Army to push the Nazis back all the way to Berlin. The war to kill off Slavs and grab their territory – the fight to the death between Nazism and communism – was the bloodiest in history. The Soviet side responded with atrocities of its own. But Red Army veterans and their descendants are entitled to remember their victory as the culmination of a moral struggle with the darkest forces of the twentieth century.

Nothing could be the same after victory in the Great Fatherland War. (Calling it the 'Great Patriotic War' over-translates the keyword – *otechestvennaya* – which relates to 'Fatherland', not 'patriotism', and conveys the idea that the war was fought defensively on the territory of the Fatherland and for its survival. It is the same term used for the war against Napoleon and precisely does not mean that the war was a patriotic crusade.) This was the third act of Stalinism, its 'late' period, between 1945 and 1953. Twenty-seven million Soviet soldiers and civilians were prematurely dead. The survivors lived in a wasteland: 70,000 villages burned down; 1,700 towns destroyed; infrastructure wrecked; food supplies and public health in jeopardy. To keep its grip on power and make the economy work, Stalinist government had to build new housing, train new doctors, fund new pensions. The ends continued to justify the means – Stalin had no interest in improving people's lives for their own sake – but the new policies set a precedent. They created capacity for future reforms. And so the coherence of Stalinism slipped after 1945. Post-war society paid greater attention to living conditions – at the same time that the Gulag reached its peak size. Countless voices insisted that wartime sacrifice demanded a return to the liberating spirit of 1917 – but the dictatorship exercised power arbitrarily, especially towards administrative elites and Jews. Meanwhile, the political system now promised permanence: the old commissariats were restyled as ministries. Controlling Europe as far as Berlin and Prague, and acquiring the atomic bomb, Soviet power consolidated itself behind the Iron Curtain. The wartime alliance ended and the Soviet Union found itself in a costly Cold War with American-led NATO.

Stalin's sudden death from a stroke on 5 March 1953 was a total system shock for the Soviet Union. Unrestrained grief was widespread though scarcely universal. With the tears still wet, no one knew quite what to do. Georgyi Malenkov (chair of the government) and Nikita Khrushchev (head of the party) killed the favourite for the succession, Lavrenty Beria (security chief), as the post-Stalin Thaw began. They supported similar reforms, such as increasing peasants' economic rights, loosening censorship and stepping up Gulag releases, but Khrushchev won out politically. He presided over a decisively different Soviet Union.

On 25 February 1956 in a closed-off Kremlin, Khrushchev stood up at the Twentieth Congress of the Communist Party of the Soviet

Union. Speaking for four hours, he delivered the Secret Speech, which cautiously and selectively condemned Stalin for the crimes of his era. Yet ten months later, soldiers from the Soviet-led Warsaw Pact were sent to crush the Hungarian uprising. Thousands were killed. Neutrality or independence were impossible for the 'satellites', which all remained police states, but de-Stalinization was pursued in most of them. Reform followed in much of the Eastern bloc, though its pace and variety were inconsistent. Throughout the post-war world, planning was crucial to reconstruction and recovery. Growth was high in the industrializing communist bloc for two decades. In economic terms, it was not immediately clear that the Soviet approach was 'wrong', practically or intellectually.

After the Secret Speech, the Soviet Union turned its back on Stalinism without changing so fast that the whole country unravelled. Much of the Gulag was dismantled. A more open public culture gave people some of the tools to come to terms with the traumas of the past. Cracks were opened in the Iron Curtain, and Russia's complex relationship with the West was debated again by a new generation. Big social reforms were enacted, headlined by a massive housing programme. The economy was partly reoriented towards people's individual needs. Meanwhile, Yuri Gagarin conquered the cosmos.

Khrushchev was a mercurial character, witty and clever but with little schooling, committed to improving popular living standards and renewing the Soviet settlement, while engaging in reckless diplomacy and driving his colleagues to distraction. During his term of office, economic growth slowed. People noticed not only this, but also his incapacity to listen, his vulgarity and the lack of force that underwrote his power. He was shunted into retirement in 1964 and replaced by Leonid Brezhnev.

After many years of wild hopes and endless tragedy, the country settled into its long illusion of permanence. Life became as close to normal as it ever did in the Soviet Union. Shortages and queues partly defined the daily round. Bosses lived distinctly well. But life was marked by high levels of equality and followed a sustainable rhythm. The KGB no longer seemed a threat to most people most of the time. Like in all modern societies, people were preoccupied with private life and getting on. Still, many citizens possessed a particularly Soviet vision. Above all, they assumed the existence of certain social rights.

They took for granted that everyday life was stable, that the rhetoric of peace and internationalism could coexist with the consolations of national culture, and that the great achievements of Soviet history – 1917 and 1945 – somehow offered the means for holding power to account.

Nothing lasts for ever. Brezhnev died in 1982 and was briefly replaced by first Andropov and then Chernenko. The past had run out of options, and the Soviet Union again bet on the future. Mikhail Gorbachev came to power in 1985. Compared to his predecessors, he was young and dynamic. He had arrived in the Politburo a few years earlier from Stavropol in the south of Russia. Like Khrushchev, who had governed the Ukrainian republic, he was a reformer who was partly shaped by the view from the periphery. Ambitious and worried, he wanted to reform the economy and flirted with a new type of politics. The American president, Ronald Reagan, had reignited the Cold War arms race. Gorbachev knew that the Soviet Union could not keep up. He also feared for world peace. The international détente of the 1970s had already given way to new Cold War crises, prompted not least by the needless Soviet invasion of Afghanistan in 1979.

Growth had slowed still further in the USSR. It was behind Western countries in the development of electronics and computers (though it was training the world's best programmers) and living standards across the breadth of the USSR were very uneven. Gorbachev would later claim that the country he came to rule was enduring a time of 'stagnation'. But that is not quite how it seemed at the time: the long 1970s in the Soviet Union, the 'late socialism' that stretched from 1964 to the mid-1980s, also possessed social complexity and cultural dynamism, educational and scientific achievement, social guarantees and a measure of ideological legitimacy. Left to its own devices, and underwritten by nuclear weapons and natural resources, it would probably have lasted for decades to come, but at the cost of impoverishment and growing dislocation in the absence of carefully conceived market reforms.

Thanks to Gorbachev, though, the Soviet Union committed suicide by accident. His reforms were designed as a restructuring (*perestroika*) of the Soviet system, not its demolition. Where Khrushchev succeeded in pointing the Soviet Union in a new direction, and reforming it to survive in a new form, Gorbachev's reforms blew the top off the system. On the one hand were democratization and *glasnost*, giving the people a voice; on the other were market reforms. It was too much. At the same time, the Eastern bloc opened up to the West. Arms control treaties ended the Cold War. The Iron Curtain rose and the Berlin Wall fell. Gorbachev proved he was a man of peace and the Soviet peoples showed that they feared war at all costs. Soviet elites began to jump ship, seeing a hazy horizon of post-communist business. The Soviet republic of Ukraine turned towards independence. Boris Yeltsin, who had been elected president of the Russian republic in 1990, cultivated a rival centre of power in Moscow to Gorbachev's, claiming to represent Russians rather than Soviet citizens as a whole; he now exploited the situation mercilessly in the name of Russian independence from the Soviet Union. Gorbachev resigned on Christmas Day 1991. The red flag was pulled down from the Kremlin. After seventy-four years, the Russian Revolution was over, and the Soviet Union had ceased to exist. If ever anything was an accident in the history of Russia, it was the collapse of the USSR: the consequence of a badly designed reform programme and political vanity, not of fearless diplomacy, careful strategy or structural inevitability.

## 10 (SINCE 1991): THE FUTURE IS NOT DEFINED BY THE PAST

It was another Time of Troubles. During *perestroika*, Boris Yeltsin had been elected president of the USSR's Russian republic. He was now president of the Russian Federation, the main successor state of the Soviet Union. Russia had a parliament (attacked by Yeltsin's tanks in 1993) and elected local government. But democracy was put in the service of new economic reforms which led to hyperinflation and unpaid wages. Pensioners lined the streets to sell their possessions. Crime and violence infested public life. Unfair privatizations created 'new Russians', a *nouveau riche* class, and impoverished the masses. Mafias and corrupt officials were ubiquitous. The new Russia was founded on an historic injustice. Freedoms to travel and read what you wanted, and shops full of goods which you couldn't afford, were not enough to recover democracy's reputation. Bankrolled by oligarchs, who were terrified of the real chance that the communists would win, Boris Yeltsin was re-elected in 1996. Perhaps it was no wonder that people remembered Brezhnev with nostalgia.

Sick, alcoholic and incapable, Yeltsin looked for a successor. He eventually fixed on Vladimir Putin, a former KGB colonel who had advanced through the jungle of post-Soviet officialdom to the chairmanship of the country's security services. In line with the workings of the Russian constitution, Yeltsin appointed him prime minister in the late summer of 1999, and so he became acting president when Yeltsin resigned that New Year's Eve. Putin was elected in his own right three months later, and re-elected in 2004. His energy and clarity inspired many Russians. The economy recovered and stability returned. Wages were paid on time, pensions grew, and people went on holiday. He formed close ties with foreign leaders, including George W. Bush. But compared with the era before *perestroika,* economic life was ever more unequal and persistently corrupt, dependent on the oil and gas that came out of the Siberian heartlands. Meanwhile, the political pluralism that had characterized the chaotic Yeltsin years began to disappear. Putin stepped to one side in 2008 to respect the constitutional limit of two presidential terms. As prime minister again, he ruled alongside President Medvedev. In 2012, he was back as president. The Duma did little to restrain the executive. Conflict in east Ukraine and the annexation of Crimea aggravated tensions with Western powers. Western economic sanctions exacerbated the aftershocks of the 2008 global financial crisis to create a major economic slowdown, but also, in time, new opportunities for small businesspeople. A major international confrontation between Russia and 'the West' set in between the election of Donald Trump in November 2016 and the re-election of Vladimir Putin in March 2018. Yet for all the air of crisis, many Russians lived better than ever before, in a much more open society than the Soviet Union, driven by consumerism, and, most of the time, unhindered by government, sometimes helped by it, but alert to the need not to cross the wrong road.

From the Western perspective, Putin was a new tsar, or a new Stalin, and sometimes, amazingly, both. The evidence for this was inconsistent and unclear: the inner core of the Kremlin was closed, and judgements about it could not be verified. Kremlinology could prove anything. High-level corruption, unstable personal networks and the overlapping of business and politics made it impossible to read how power was dispensed, precisely which decisions Putin made himself, and why he did so. Russian power was not simply high politics in action, but was, as ever, also a force of society and culture, whose layers together pushed historical change. The process was unpredictable. No one had the least idea what could happen next.

# PART II

# Normality, Friendship and Liberty?

We are Europeans.

*Mikhail Gorbachev, 1987*

You will find that I have no other view than the greatest welfare and glory of the fatherland, and I wish for nothing but the happiness of my subjects, of whatever order they may be. All my thoughts are directed towards the preservation of external and internal peace, satisfaction and tranquillity.

*Catherine the Great, 1764*

Neither [the USSR nor the West] can accept friendly criticism, and each makes wild pronouncements about the other because of ignorance. In fact, our worst enemy is not the other side, but our own intolerance. If we want peace, which now means the survival of the world, no less, we must recognize truth – about ourselves and others.

*Sally Belfrage, British writer and journalist, 1958*[1]

No one is going to write a history of Russia, its power, people and place in the world, that claims to be an unvarnished story of normal life, international friendship and popular freedom. Russian history is far from the sum of these qualities – and yet they are much more common than the Russia Anxiety can account for. Russia is an exceptional country, the biggest in the world, and almost everything about its past and present can seem outsize and extraordinary, often not in a good way. In many ways, moreover, the Soviet period was an historic outlier, creating a unique world. But on almost all levels, Russia's experience has often been 'normal'. Its economic performance, the everyday operations of its legal system and its cultural norms historically fit within a European framework. Russia's political system, though not democratic, has usually been flexible, capable of evolution, and based on a measure of legitimacy. The country's internal life has usually not been ostentatiously coercive. Its empire expanded like other empires did, and often less violently. Russia has not been at war more frequently or posed a greater international danger than the leading Western powers, and has often been the ally of half or more of them. In other words, Russia's experiences mostly fit within reasonable international comparisons. Over a millennium, Russians have lived out lives not dramatically different from those of other Europeans. The age of 'tears without end', between 1904, when war with Japan broke out, and 1953, when Stalin died, is a unique dark age, but even those terrible years fitted into a wider European and global story. Understanding Russia's history and its present-day predicaments is enriched by changing perspective, giving a little ground, and looking again at one's own national culture, too. The Russia Anxiety, of course, is based on the opposite approach. In Part II, we explore five of the Anxiety's *bêtes noires* – issues of democracy, violence, 'the West', expansionism and war – to show that normality, friendship and liberty are solvents in which the Anxiety might dissolve.

# 4

## The Dictatorship Deception

*Does Russia's Past Offer Democratic Prospects?*

Soon after New Year in 1881, in deep midwinter, a man called Kobozev was running a phantom cheese shop at 56 Malaya Sadovaya Street in St Petersburg with a woman who was pretending to be his wife. Suspicious neighbours and angry competitors brought the shop to the attention of the authorities. A health commission from the St Petersburg city government called in unannounced. It must have been a heart-stopping moment for Kobozev, because his real name was Yuri Bogdanovich, and he was a senior agent of Narodnaya Volya, the People's Will, the most murderous of Russian revolutionary societies.

The cheese shop was in fact a front for a plot to assassinate the tsar, but then the inspectors were not from the municipal government. They were members of the Imperial Corps of Engineers, charged with protecting the tsar. With their backs to the wall – there had been half a dozen assassination attempts since late 1879, including a massive bomb in the cellar of the Winter Palace, two floors below the tsar's dining room – the security outfit was acting on connections between tip-offs. The would-be health inspectors, who included an incognito general, didn't notice some debris in the corner of the shop and left Bogdanovich in peace, for now. It was one of the most catastrophic mistakes in Russian history.

What they missed was the entrance to the tunnel that the terrorists were digging. The tunnel was nearing completion. It was intended as the site of a subterranean explosion when the tsar's carriage was driving past. Conspirators at street level would then throw the home-made grenades that were designed to finish him off. But despite this missed chance, the police still seemed to be closing in. On 27 February, one of the leaders of the People's Will, Andrei Zhelyabov, was arrested. His fellow conspirators, still at liberty, decided to activate the assassination plot with the utmost despatch. The following night, fuses were set in the tunnel leading from the shop. In a secret rendezvous at a nearby café, the men who were to throw bombs at the tsar's carriage were given parcels containing their armaments.

On the next day, on Sunday 1 March, at a quarter past two in the afternoon, Alexander II and his entourage travelled along their customary route, so well known to the People's Will. They went by the Catherine Canal and past Malaya Sadovaya Street. The assassins were waiting. They set off the bombs in the tunnel. The first bomb that they threw missed, killing a young boy at the side of the road. The tsar went out to try to help. Stranded, he was killed by a second bomb.[1]

Ivan Turgenev was in Paris when he heard the news. The great Russian novelist, one of the giants of nineteenth-century European culture, was a liberal by sensibility and political conviction. It was a devastating shock. Alexander II was, to him, Russia's great hope: the tsar who had emancipated the serfs, sponsored a durable experiment in local democracy and seemed set on new reforms. The assassins were villains who had betrayed Russia's future. 'Yes, it's an unhappy country, our motherland,' he wrote to his friend Pavel Annenkov, five days after the bombing. He added more to the letter the following day: 'Will Russia fall into the abyss and break its neck on account of this? That's nothing to our assassins!'[2] For Turgenev, the revolutionary terrorists were using violence to destroy the gradual, constitutional reform that had a mild democratic flavour. They only had contempt for the Speransky Conundrum, making autocracy more likely to clamp down aggressively than to mould itself naturally to the demands of a new age. A couple of weeks later, Turgenev wrote an article for *La Revue politique et littéraire* about the new tsar. He had some upstanding personal qualities, and there were specific policies initiated by his father that he might be hoped to pursue. But the assassins had blown Russia off the general path that Alexander II had set it on. 'Those who are expecting a parliamentary constitution from the new Tsar will soon be deprived of their illusions,' he wrote. 'We are at least convinced of that.'[3]

For Turgenev, revolutionary terrorism was the opposite of democracy. Seven years earlier, he had written *Virgin Soil*. Many of the novel's characters were young radicals who aspired to take part in the 'going to the people' movement. This heavy-handed scheme encouraged radicals to spend time in the countryside and teach the peasants about politics. Throughout the novel, the main character, Nezhdanov, struggles with the empty moral quality of this encounter. The young urbanites might be literate, educated, and know about the outside world, but they are also narrow-minded, convinced of their own rightness. By contrast, the peasants' worldview knows more of human life. Their attitude to these strange outsiders is sceptical, worldly wise. So where does democracy fit in? 'I see though you are a revolutionist you are no democrat,' someone says to Nezhdanov early in the novel.

Nezhdanov sees for himself that the radical intelligentsia of which he is a part doesn't care what people want. As the novel progresses, the weight of this insight becomes an intolerable burden. Faced with the humiliating coquetry of his patron's wife, and the fact that the ruling-class milieu that she represents holds him in contempt, Nezhdanov's underlying democratic instincts overcome his revolutionary mission. 'That bitter feeling which he always had, always carried about in the depths of his soul,' Turgenev wrote, 'again stirred within him; the reproachful suspiciousness of the democrat awoke.'[4] For Turgenev, the struggle between organic, reasonable, progressive inclusiveness and radical, intolerant exclusivity, between the listener and the knower-best, played out inside Nezhdanov. It was too much: he kills himself at the end of the book.

When the proponents of the Russia Anxiety turn to Russian democracy, Nezhdanov might be their exhibit A. He embodies the violent, disabling struggles that Russia, like all the great powers, faced during modern Europe's first age of democratization in the decades before the First World War. In Russia, more than elsewhere, the process led to self-destruction. It was a struggle that seemed to show Russia lacked the historical basis for organic democratic development. Nezhdanov brought together within himself a national past of democratic trauma and a future of totalitarianism. For the Anxious, Nezhdanov is a prototype of Russian anti-democracy. He confirms a common understanding about the history of Russian politics, which we might call the dictatorship consensus.

It is an irreducible truth that nearly all of Russia's history, over hundreds of years, has unfolded in autocratic or dictatorial political orders. But democracy has for long periods been important within these non-democratic political systems. The dictatorship consensus that is so common in Western popular commentary and foreign-policy decision-making might better be considered a dictatorship deception.

Turgenev offered his readers access to such complexity. Even characters that seemed sinister or dangerous possessed different sides and the capacity to change. Nezhdanov died, but not before imagining a calmer and more flexible version of human relations than the revolutionaries wanted. The very fact that he understood the struggle that was going on inside himself offered readers hope. In this chapter, we'll confront the paradox that democracy is an important way of understanding Russia, even though the political system has scarcely ever been democratic. This is one of the ways that history can reduce the virulence of the Russia Anxiety.

The terrible events of 1 March 1881 marked the collision of two visions of democracy: a representative vision associated with Alexander II's reforms and a total vision vouchsafed by his assassins. I'll start by exploring the history of these two understandings of democracy in Russia. Then I'll discuss two of the biggest obstacles to Russian democratization, the weaknesses of liberal and conservative party politics. And finally I'll place Russia's democratic dimensions in an international framework, one that illustrates what democracy does and doesn't do in Western societies, and clarifies what democracy can mean in Russia. But let's start with the representative vision of Russian democracy, which we can see, strangely enough, if we peer between Turgenev's thighs.

## TURGENEV'S THIGHS

'Look at him now, pacing up and down,' wrote Leo Tolstoy to the poet Nikolai Nekrasov, 'deliberately waggling his democratic thighs in my face.'[5] The thighs belonged to Ivan Turgenev, and he was waggling them in 1855. Tolstoy had finally come to meet the older and more famous writer. But where Tolstoy wore his Russian heart on his sleeve, Turgenev possessed a different character. Tolstoy was mercurial, changeable, prone to extremes – the hedonist who turned ascetic. Turgenev was also a man of appetites. But his temperament tended to moderation and consistency. Less prone to shoot off an impulsive put-down, he was more inclined to a 'democratic' outlook.

Born in 1828 in Oryol to a peaceable provincial noble who died young and his angry, self-centred wife, Ivan Turgenev was skilled at bringing people together and finding a middle way. After all, he negotiated himself into a *ménage à trois* with his great romantic love, the French opera singer Pauline Viardot, somehow befriending her husband in the process. As a twenty-year-old, studying in Berlin at the end of the 1830s, Turgenev was part of a circle of young Russians who passionately debated how German philosophy could justify their two contrasting outlooks: conservative support for the Russian autocracy and revolutionary opposition to it. Turgenev shunned the two extremes. Back in Russia, he found friendship with moderate opponents of Nicholas I's 'reactionary' version of autocracy, such as the famous writer Belinsky.

Later, Turgenev was in Brussels when revolution came to Western Europe in January 1848. Louis-Philippe abdicated from the French throne. Turgenev came back to Paris, where he had many friends. The Second Republic was declared. He settled easily into the revolutionary rhythms of everyday Paris life, but he disliked the self-regarding balkanization of French revolutionary politics. Worse than the infighting of the Left, however, was the brutality of the Right. In June, revolutionary arguments came to their head: working-class forces rose up. General Cavaignac's army came in to fight them. Not only did deadly fighting paralyse the city, but so did an awful rash of arbitrary arrests and executions without trial.

Turgenev now knew for sure that he hated revolution. But he hated it in a different way to Nicholas I, who had signed an edict demanding that 'all loyal subjects combat the French Revolution'. Turgenev believed that the Russian autocracy should be flexible enough to accommodate reform. Democratic aspirations, if reasoned not forced, might even shape its future. Fanaticism of any stripe was the enemy of human dignity and progress.

Even during the reign of 'reactionary' Nicholas I, the tsarist social and political order was supple. It allowed some people to make their way successfully, despite the labels it ascribed to them. Most of the time people simply got on with their lives and set about achieving their aims exactly as they did in republics or constitutional monarchies in other parts of Europe, at least until they tried to cross a social boundary.[6] Turgenev's subtle mind could recognize this. He acknowledged the greater dangers of rapid change. But there was a bottom line. Serfdom lacked dignity. It could not go on. With the accession of Alexander II in 1855, Turgenev believed that reform would soon come. As a landowner, he anticipated emancipation, setting about the division of the land that his own serfs tilled in 1859. He was in Paris when the emancipation edict was finally announced in 1861, and he went off to give thanks at the Orthodox church nearby. His vision of reform was coming to pass.

Alexander followed his emancipation edict with the introduction of *zemstvos* in 1864. These were elected councils in the (large) provinces and (much smaller) districts of much of the Russian Empire. *Zemstvos* were chaired by marshals of the nobility. Their deputies were chosen through *de facto* electoral colleges. This made for an in-built bias towards the nobles, enough to offset some of their ill feeling about emancipation. (The ill feeling was also reduced by the redemption payments that the now 'free' peasants were required to make to their former owners.) Still, the first time that elections were held to the district *zemstvos*, 38 per cent of the elected members were peasants (42 per cent were nobles), an astonishing number in European comparison.[7] In Nizhnyi Novgorod, a typical example, the assembly worked with the grain of democratizing reasonableness, changing the character of local politics and social policy.[8]

Even late imperial politics, therefore, sometimes dissolved the dictatorship deception. Over the next fifty years, *zemstvos* enacted a vast array of social legislation, especially in healthcare, that made a fundamental difference to local life. The *zemstvos* were responsive to local needs. While their elected composition did not mirror local society, they were in an important sense participatory and representative assemblies. Some of Russia's regions incubated significant democratic habits in the decades before the Revolution.

\*

The *zemstvos* moved the Speransky Conundrum onto a new plane of action. They showed that the Russian autocracy of the later nineteenth century contained within it an element of democracy. It existed only in the realm of local government, it did not formally act to restrain the tsar's power, but it had an enduring practical and educational influence. The *zemstvos* helped to take Tsarist society in a new direction, which, convoluted and beset by violence as it proved to be, led towards the convocation of a national parliament, or Duma, in 1906. But the *zemstvos* did not emerge from nothing; they drew on previous experiences. For instance, in 1785, Catherine the Great granted a charter to cities, giving rights to urban dwellers, who could vote for municipal assemblies and mayors. Those who lived in towns, at least those above a certain level of respectability, were divided into six groups, and they elected the town duma, with one representative from each group. There were limits both to the capacity of what a local municipal assembly could do in the face of a provincial governor, who was appointed by the monarch, and there was an issue of legal philosophy, too: town dwellers might have been invested with some rights, but so too were the towns themselves.[9] When it came to the promises of her 'Great Instruction' of 1767, it was clear that Catherine's manifesto was not anticipating democracy, for all her interest in rational government and the rule of law. 'There ought to be some to govern, and others to obey,' the Instruction declared.[10]

Catherine was a deliberately European monarch. She started life as a German princess and in later life became friends with the likes of Voltaire and Diderot. But her experiments with popular representation drew on the precedents of Rus and Muscovy as much as on the atmosphere of the Enlightenment. The medieval East Slavic lands were well known for the irregular town meetings at which significant issues concerning the common weal were debated by residents. One such gathering of burghers, known as the *veche*, took place in Kiev on 15 September 1068 on the market square. They resolved to expel Prince Izyaslav and to welcome a successor (though Izyaslav was soon back).[11] More famously, a *veche* met at Pskov and Novgorod periodically from the ninth century on. Novgorod was well known too for the practice by which the city's boyars elected their prince. In a reform of 1354, the process was formalized, with the election too of representatives among the boyars. Of course, their interests were not the same as those of many of the town dwellers, even the most privileged ones, but the *veche* itself was a forum for the wider community.[12] This was a prototype of modern urban government, as important in later myth as historic reality, and an obvious point of comparison with Western Europe. But the reality did not survive invasion by the Mongols and the growing rivalry with Moscow. Another body was the Boyars' Duma, variants of which met between the ninth and eighteenth centuries. A collection of the realm's top magnates, it received officials, visiting dignitaries, and supplicants, and might even have passed laws, but despite what seems like its importance, its work is difficult to make out from the sources.[13]

During the reign of Ivan the Terrible, another public assembly emerged. In a different way and on a different scale, it represented powerful classes and protected their interests in cooperation with the monarchy. The origins of the *Zemsky sobor*, or Assembly of the Land, are not clear, and the term itself is a coinage by historians writing in the nineteenth century. Our knowledge about it is full of gaps. Still, such an assembly was called in 1566 and met between 28 June and 2 July. It included the Boyar Duma, as well as representatives from the Church, the more minor gentry and urban merchants. Their debate covered a limited but vital agenda. Ivan asked the assembly how and whether he should make peace with the Lithuanians, who shared a powerful and expanding Commonwealth with Poland and Livonia (or Latvia). A range of views was brought to the table. Representatives from the Church, for example, insisted that Ivan should press on and go for Riga. On the basis of this consultation, Ivan then returned to his discussions with the embassy from Lithuania.

The *Zemsky sobor* of 1566 showed that some diffusion of power was possible in the Russian lands. Elections took place – but opposition to the Tsar was not their purpose. Representatives had the authority to act on behalf of their social estate – but never in a way that would conflict with the interests of the government. The process increased the involvement of 'society' in government – but did not make society independent of government. Assemblies of the Land were summoned thirty-seven times between 1549 and 1684, choosing tsars, advising about wars and approving the historic law code of 1649. The most important convened in 1613, tasked with the crucial work of deciding whether to hand power to the Romanovs. In general, the *Zemsky sobor* shared with the French Estates General and the English parliament the basic function of generating a monarch-led consensus, making it easier for a king to rule (though it shared the limits of the Estates General rather than the deeper roots that the English parliament was growing).[14] Or think of central Europe. In the Polish-Lithuanian Commonwealth, the parliament-equivalent (the Sejm) met 235 times in the 300 years from 1493. It was one of the most dramatic arenas of proto-democracy in pre-modern Europe. On 6 April 1573, for instance, seven years after Ivan the Terrible called his most significant *Zemsky sobor*, 40,000 electors gathered in Warsaw to choose the next king.[15] But the resolutions of the Sejm required unanimity for much of the seventeenth and eighteenth centuries: the so-called *liberum veto*. Convening the Sejm was at the discretion of the king, who determined the agenda and chaired the upper of the two houses, the senate.[16]

However imperfectly, the Muscovite assemblies fitted inside this tradition. The *Zemsky sobor* drew on Mongol examples, too. 'Quriltai' had earlier emerged on the steppe, and the lessons of these assemblies transmitted themselves to Muscovy.[17] This would-be democratic heritage, whose potential can be wildly exaggerated, corrects the assumption that unlimited power resided in the person of the tsar.

Within forty years of the great 1566 Assembly of the Land, Muscovy had become impossible to rule. The Riurikid dynasty had petered out. Political crisis followed. The absence of effective government coincided with invasion and economic dislocation. This was the Time of Troubles of the start of the seventeenth century. But the most influential historian of the period saw in this catastrophe a democratic hope. Vasily Klyuchevsky was a near-contemporary of Turgenev's, born twenty years after the great novelist; he was elected to the Chair of History at Moscow State University while Turgenev was still an active writer. He saw autocratic rule as a flexible and collaborative instrument that was socially and geographically inclusive.

During the Time of Troubles, power changed hands several times. No doubt, this was dangerous. Power can be exercised in especially cruel ways during times of instability. The risk of misrule greatly exacerbated social and economic crisis. It made life miserable for many people. But it was precisely the rapid changes of ruler that allowed people to imagine a different kind of politics. For Vasily Klyuchevsky, the Time of Troubles created a new way of seeing political sovereignty. It was now possible to think that the people, not the tsar, might be sovereign – because rulers were so temporary and dispensable, while the people were eternal. The 'will of the people' might even dislodge a dynasty. A new blueprint emerged in 1610, when Muscovy came to terms with its Polish invaders. For Klyuchevsky, it was 'a complete draft of a constitutional monarchy', recognizing individual rights, and limiting the power of the tsar. This idea did not survive the accession of the Romanov dynasty in 1613. But Klyuchevsky drew attention to a ruling class that seemed to be made up of independent-minded magnates who understood sovereignty in their own way, and who were part of a newly bolstered *Zemsky sobor*. All this, wrote Klyuchevsky, 'seemed to promise well for the development of the state and the community'. What's more, he argued, it 'provided the new dynasty with abundant spiritual and political resources that the old dynasty had never possessed'.[18] At the same time, it gave scope to the people, too, to rise up against power when it was being abused, as they did repeatedly for much of the seventeenth century, until Peter the Great came to the throne.

Klyuchevsky's vision gives historical force to the democratic possibilities that Turgenev hoped for. Seventeenth-century Muscovy was at the cusp of many possible modern futures. Back then, Klyuchevsky showed, Russia had as much or as little democratic promise as many other countries. But Klyuchevsky also taught an important practical lesson to his immediate audience in the late nineteenth century. He demonstrated how a reasoned belief in Russia's 'democratic' precedents might shape the country's contemporary and future political development at a time of uncertainty and reaction following Alexander II's assassination. If you're thinking about embarking on a risky political experiment, it helps to imagine that the past offers you something to hold on to.

In the turbulent period following Alexander's assassination, it took the Revolution of 1905 to prompt the tsar to make democratic

concessions. The Fundamental Laws of April 1906 signalled the creation of a parliament composed of two chambers: the Duma was the
lower house, elected on a mass franchise, and most recognizably a
national assembly; the State Council was a nominated upper house.
Elections were via an electoral college, which favoured rural interests.[19] Suffrage was not universal or equal, but it was widespread, and
extended into all groups in society, though not to women. Overall,
this picture compared favourably with many other parts of Europe,
including Britain. Political parties were now legal and enjoyed some
protections. Elections were free and not noticeably corrupt. Debate in
the Duma and direct reporting of it was not hindered by fear or censorship. Nicholas remained an 'unlimited' autocrat, but this was a
theoretical posture. If pushed, Nicolaevan autocracy might break the
new semi-constitutional order; if flexed gently, it could resolve the
Speransky Conundrum for a new generation. So while ministers
remained responsible to the tsar alone (and individually so, not collectively), the Duma and State Council were allowed to challenge and
question them. And while the tsar had a legislative veto, Duma deputies effectively did too; they could go back to a vetoed law and discuss
it again.[20] Members formed legislative committees that could call on
expert witnesses.[21] At their best, the Fundamental Laws of 1906,
headlined by the Duma, had elements of a constitution about them.
While they might not have held the tsar to account, they did check
the government at times. They offered a compelling framework for
constitutional development, in which the extremes of conservatism
and radicalism, the wilfulness of tsar and parliament, provided
mutual restraint.[22] But the framework needed time to become secure.
It was too immature to withstand the social storms of the decade
before 1917, and it could not bend with the transforming forces of
popular politics and political violence. Instead, it was blown over.

The Constitutional Democrats (Kadets) dominated the first Duma,
with 179 of 478 deputies. They were joined by other liberals, as well
as by moderate and extreme socialists – the Social Democrats had ten
seats. The Socialist Revolutionaries, the popular peasant-facing radicals, boycotted the elections, so the Duma was probably more
moderate than the electorate. The country was veering leftwards as it
would in 1917.

Unsurprisingly, government and parliament shared no common ground. In July 1906, the Duma was dissolved. The Kadets fled to Vyborg, near the Finnish border, where they issued a democratic manifesto. The organs of the state struck back. With half their deputies arrested, the Kadets lost their plurality in the elections of summer 1906, and conservatives gained some ground. But the second Duma remained a progressive forum, committed to prolonging the achievements of the 1905 Revolution. This was of symbolic importance, but the Duma could not hold government to account. State coercion, which only irritated the wounds of the country, went on, regardless of the Duma's composition.

In 1906, Pyotr Stolypin became chairman of the Council of Ministers, or head of government. He had been governor of Saratov Province. Saratov was one of the furnaces of the 1905 Revolution, troubled by many peasant attacks on nobles' property. Stolypin headed the Ministry of the Interior from April 1906, and three months later became prime minister. He had a rounded view of Russian life and politics, but was convinced that Russia could not progress while parliament and government were in vicious conflict. His electoral law of 3 June 1907 has often been described as a 'coup'. It fiddled with the electoral college enough to make a permanent conservative majority, but the conservatives were a mixed bunch, ranging from quiet centre-right critics of the monarchy to furious anti-Semites. They were not the material out of which to build a democratic pro-monarchy consensus. Stolypin wanted to manipulate the 'constitution' to give people a stake in the ruling order, something he backed up with his 'wager on the strong', a reform to rural land law whose aim was to turn the more ambitious peasants into property-owning farmers.

In the end, though, it was self-defeating. The revised Duma made it less likely that a sustainable political order would develop, one which could resolve the Speransky Conundrum by making democracy safe for autocracy. Duma and government were conspicuously on different sides and lacked the most basic of common goals. Political elites were so divided that they had no common loyalty.[23] Meanwhile, many people found themselves alienated from all political institutions, while sharing little common ground with those from other classes. True enough, the right to vote and the opportunity to participate to protect one's interests were strengthened in the last years before 1917. For instance, a major social reform of 1912 concerning workers' social insurance established welfare boards that were partly made up of elected worker representatives. But here the expansion of civil society actually promoted political instability, because these boards became incubators for revolutionary politics. In a sense, the government could not win. But the potential of non-revolutionary Russian democracy was not exhausted. A wise leader during the emergency of the First World War might have harnessed it. But Nicholas II did not trust his people, and as the war ground on, the prospects of revolution – in which democratic progress would be in peril – gathered pace.

From Rus to the Revolution, amid the long development of autocracy, the Russian lands underwent various experiments in limited constitutionalism and democratic participation. The temporary success and ultimate failure of these experiments largely depended on circumstances. The worst bad luck of all was the assassination of Alexander II. Russia has at times possessed institutions that reflected Turgenev's vision, based on a measure of individual rights, promoting the interests of different groups, facilitating open discussion. Other countries have built modern democracies on slighter historic precedents. But the more important point is that these traditions, memories and cultural resources still today modulate the operation of institutions, create accommodations and compromises in the interactions between people and power, and make for a legacy that can be useable whenever the political system might evolve more substantially. In the 2010s, the Duma is controlled by the government, but is still a forum for balancing the interests of competing claims by interest groups, at least elite ones in different branches of government and business. The 'dictatorship deception' ignores this major element of Russian history, which makes it easier for proponents of the Russia Anxiety to treat the country with disdain or disregard. But the history of Russian would-be democracy gives warnings, too. There is also democracy's dark side: the spectre of total democracy.

# STORMY APPLAUSE

Alexander Solzhenitsyn was the most famous of Soviet convicts, spending a decade in prisons and labour camps following his arrest in February 1945. He fought in the Second World War as a junior officer (he'd been a schoolteacher before 1941), but the secret police confected a case against him based on a cynical over-reading of his censored letters to friends and family. Solzhenitsyn went on to write *One Day in the Life of Ivan Denisovich*, a novel of Gulag life, which was published in the USSR in 1962 and was a milestone in the country's coming to terms with its Stalinist past (more on this in chapter 9). He then wrote the non-fiction *Gulag Archipelago* about the country's whole network of political violence and incarceration, which was published in the West and won its author the Nobel Prize. It also cost him his Soviet citizenship. He was exiled in 1974.

In the first volume of the book, he describes a characteristic arrest during the Great Terror of 1936–8. Imagine the scene (this story is a great favourite of teachers of Russian history). It's a large meeting of Party members and officials in a provincial district close to the city of Moscow. Everyone there is a person of some substance in the locality: the people who run the provincial government as well as its factories and collective farms, those responsible for schools, hospitals and university departments, ambitious industrial workers, even one or two peasants who had somehow done well out of collectivization. In the chair sits a newly appointed district party secretary. His predecessor is already in the hands of the secret police. As the meeting comes to an end, with the business complete, a paean to Stalin is read out. In these circumstances, the minutes and newspaper reports always record the same response: 'stormy applause'.

The applause went on. And on. People looked around, ecstatic expressions in place. They carried on applauding because they were afraid to stop. There were NKVD officers in the room, also clapping, looking around. Inside the hall were reasonable people with a sense of proportion and responsibility. There were others who were malicious, quick to denounce those around them. Others panicked easily. They were all applauding.

After eleven minutes, one of the reasonable people in the hall stopped applauding and sat down. It was the signal that everyone had been waiting for, and they followed his example. The man who stopped first was the director of a paper factory, who was sitting on the platform with the local political elite. He was a robust person who knew his own mind. You will already have realized what happened to him next. In such a way, Solzhenitsyn wrote, 'they discovered who the independent people were. And that was how they went about eliminating them.'[24]

The scene in that hall, out in an obscure corner of Moscow's greater region, is emblematic of the dark side of democracy in the Soviet Union. If elections to *zemstvos* were a hint of representative democracy, the endless applause of 1937 was the extreme point of total democracy: where everyone has a say but everyone agrees, and the only reason to disagree is because you are the enemy of everyone else.

Turgenev was afraid of stormy applause. His most famous novel, *Fathers and Sons*, analyses its echoes in the Russia of Alexander II. The novel's central character is a medical student called Bazarov. He has charmed one of his contemporaries, Arkady Kirsanov, and the two friends go to visit the modest Kirsanov estate in May 1859. Arkady's widowed father, Nikolai Petrovich, owns 200 serfs in this idyllic backwater. On the estate, the gentle Nikolai has taken up with a young peasant woman, whom he loves and treats as properly as convention allows; they have a small child. Nikolai's brother, Pavel Petrovich, who has travelled widely but never found his place, is also in residence.

Bazarov disrupts this harmonious existence. Where the 'fathers' of the novel see the world as an organic place, governed by compromises, improved by goodwill, characterized by the different and the unique and subject to gradual reform, the 'sons' see it as a laboratory in which radical theories can be tested and extreme change brought about. Pavel Petrovich is so mortally offended that he and Bazarov end up fighting a duel. 'It's a waste of effort studying separate individuals,' says Bazarov. 'All human beings are like one another, in their souls as much as in their bodies. People are like trees in a forest. No botanist is going to study each individual birch tree.'[25]

But Turgenev showed that uniformity, breakneck change and forced consensus fell outside the boundaries of normal human responses. Bazarov never formally abandons his beliefs, but their collision with reality only reveals their incoherence, something he begins to understand. He falls in love with the owner of a nearby estate, Anna Sergeyevna Odintsova. In theory, love should not exist in Bazarov's material world: it should be an illusion. Bazarov goes out to work among the local peasants, bringing them some rudimentary medical care, in a risky way that contravenes his apparent views about human nature and implies a wider sense of love. At the end of the novel, Bazarov dies because of an infected cut; the local doctor does not have the right equipment and bungles the treatment. On his deathbed, nothing seems more real than Bazarov's need for Anna or his parents' devastation at the pointless loss. In a letter at this time, Turgenev called Bazarov 'a democrat to his fingertips',[26] and not in a bad way: in the end, Bazarov honestly grappled with the implications of his own worldview, finding complexity and peace where before he had imagined uniformity and violence. Turgenev fell out with lots of people because of *Fathers and Sons*. Not only did he anticipate Russia's violent struggle between organic pluralism and stormy applause, but he suggested that you might never be sure who would be on which side.

Variants of these two types of democracy – that which claims to respect all individuals, and that which wilfully tramples on some of them – exist in many places. Turgenev's own life, much of which was poised between Russia and France, showed that. Not only did he witness the democratic violence of the 1848 Revolution, but he also spent a lot of time in Napoleon III's strange plebiscitary dictatorship. Coming to power following a *coup d'état* in December 1851, during which his forces took control of the National Assembly and seized leading deputies in their homes, Louis Napoleon called a referendum to approve his new political system. All men were allowed to vote, to 'make the entire people judges' of political life; a new parliament was convened, elected too by universal male suffrage; and a follow-up plebiscite in November 1852 confirmed the return to an Empire, with Louis now crowned as Napoleon III. The 'democracy' of the Second Empire looked two ways. It manipulated popular sovereignty, but it allowed rights to develop, especially in the late 1860s, when there was a limited liberalization of the Second Empire. But the core feature of this version of democracy was that Napoleon's massive majorities underpinned his personal authority, which rested on a high level of state coercion and the suppression of opposition.[27]

The total and representative dimensions of politics in the Second Empire help to normalize Russia's democratic limits and potential. But French history of this period also directly influenced early Soviet 'democracy'. The Second Empire ended in defeat at the hands of Bismarck in the Franco-Prussian War of 1870–71. In the capital, the Empire gave way to the Paris Commune, an exercise in a particular type of democracy that Lenin greatly admired and referred to many times during 1917.[28] For a few weeks in the spring of 1871, the capital was run as a participatory community – officials were elected, citizens did guard duty, and institutions were run in accessible and experimental ways. There were shootings and intolerance, too, and the eventual pacification of the city by government soldiers was extremely violent, an example of civil war.[29] The Paris Commune was a democracy with a bright side and a dark side. It was about power in the hands of the people, government being run from below, and the central state disappearing. It was also about the emergence of a determined revolutionary government with its own rigorous agenda. But for one of its most prominent historians (no radical socialist), 'this distinction is clearer in retrospect than it was at the time'; for him, the carnivalesque and the optimistic were the dominant keys of the Commune's music.[30]

This had a Soviet legacy. In *State and Revolution*, which Lenin wrote in 1917 as a sideline while he was organizing the most improbable revolution in world history, the Bolshevik leader drew on the lessons of the Paris Commune to argue in favour of a form of direct, revolutionary democracy that required mass participation. In the immediate aftermath of the Revolution, the mystique of the Commune sometimes inspired experiments in communal living, whose inhabitants adopted the neologism *kommuna* to describe their environments, avoiding obvious Russian equivalents such as *obshchina* or *mir* (the words used for the traditional peasant commune).[31] But the biggest lesson for the Russian Revolution was not what the Paris Commune did, but what it didn't do. It was the relative moderation of the

Commune's leadership, keen to avoid terror and violence where possible, that provided the most powerful lessons for Marx and Engels, as well as Lenin, Trotsky and Stalin (and their French socialist descendants). Given the chance to build socialism, the Commune had fudged it, according to the Bolsheviks. Too focused on immediate morality to execute all their opponents, the Communards had taken their eyes off the ball. They had missed the chance to be ruthless and therefore to defeat their enemies. Utopia justified violence; socialism justified a dictatorship; the ends justified the means.[32]

The October Revolution was accompanied by stormy applause. Of all the competing voices in revolutionary Russia, the Bolsheviks' was the loudest. It prevailed over the others. Some of these voices attracted more people, notably that of the Socialist Revolutionaries, but carried less far, thanks to a lack of clarity and boldness. It was understandable, then, that very early after assuming power the Bolsheviks should compensate for this, introducing the most populist of measures, giving land to the peasants, and the most coercive of decrees, forming their secret police (the Cheka). Peasants hoped to be left alone, to have the chance to follow their own will (*volya*) and do what they wanted with their lives, but the Bolsheviks and their organs of state coercion soon got in the way. The Cheka was Bolshevik democracy in action: it was the violent tool whose purpose was to make the people agree with the will of the people.

In the year from February 1917 to January 1918, Russia was the setting of an increasingly desperate conflict between the two types of democracy. At the end of it, stormy applause won out decisively: there were elections to a Constituent Assembly in which the Bolsheviks came second, but they shut the institution down and carried on ruling regardless. The Bolshevik Party organized the Red Army and won the Civil War, bolting enforced popular sovereignty onto the dictatorship of the proletariat. In time, stormy applause would find its ultimate manifestation in the vicious public meetings of 1937, where denunciation followed by self-criticism of a victim were met by the unanimous approval of the audience.[33] Turgenev's nightmare had come to pass.

Stormy applause understandably echoes loudly in the ears of those who feel the Russia Anxiety. It's an important sound in Russian history, most especially in Soviet history, and is an essential accompaniment to totalitarianism. This is a complex term that historians do not use lightly, but it certainly carries weight when one imagines that room in Moscow Region during the Great Terror. Yet the mentality that causes stormy applause probably comes and goes within most people in modern societies across the globe. It is present in the top-down consensus formed in committee meetings; and its natural consequence, when a group rounds on the person who disagrees, is a feature of high-octane residents' meetings about parking. What makes stormy applause lethal is its political context, which in the case of the Soviet Union derived from the chance combination of events that caused the October Revolution. Stormy applause can't be the soundtrack of a national character. It was an indispensable feature of Soviet politics until the 1980s, but even then it was never the only feature.

Probably no country held more elections than the Soviet Union. People were always voting in one institution or another, not least for the national parliament that was created by the Constitution of 1936. The Soviet Union called itself a democracy. Famously, Sidney and Beatrice Webb, British socialists, came to visit and believed it; they called Stalin's rule 'the most democratic in the world'. This was, of course, absurd. But why did the Stalinist government bother with so many public polls? Was holding elections in the Soviet dictatorship really for the purpose of hoodwinking the Webbs?

One of the fallacies of Soviet history is that it was all about politics. According to the theorists who set up the totalitarian paradigm for interpreting the Soviet system, the government exercised total power, and Soviet life was relentlessly political. Politics flowed in the same direction as power did: top to bottom. Ideology was designed at the top and the population was indoctrinated with its messages. Yet the Soviet Union changed over time, becoming a looser and less politicized dictatorship; and even in the Stalin period, the 'total politics' view of Soviet life is exaggerated. During the height of Stalinist rule in the 1930s, politics and ideology on the grand scale were often the last thing on people's minds. They were frantically busy just getting what they needed to survive.

Nevertheless, Stalinist society contained laboratories of political experience, participation, discussion and conflict. Take trade unions, of which the Soviet Union had 157 in 1937. In that year, there were central committee elections featuring secret ballots and a choice of candidates in 146 of them. The person at the top was often replaced. There were elections to other committees too, at all levels of the unions. Six per cent of the total union membership – 1.23 million out of 22 million – were elected to some position or other in their union hierarchy.[34] This was a deliberate reinvigoration of an apparent oxymoron, Stalinist democracy. Meanwhile, elections were held for political posts, from those in 'primary party organizations' in workplaces right up to the national assembly, the Supreme Soviet, the 'parliament' established by the 1936 Constitution.

So Soviet democracy was about participation. Only exceptionally, though, was it about choice. If the main function of an election is to choose the government, with a realistic possibility of changing it, this was not possible in the Soviet Union, where almost all elections lacked more than one candidate. On 5 October 1945, Mikhail Kalinin, chairman of the Presidium of the Supreme Soviet of the USSR, signed the decree that called Supreme Soviet elections for 10 February on the following year.[35] 'The forthcoming elections won't give us anything,' said a citizen from Penza Province in January 1946, 'but if they were conducted like they are in other countries, that would be a different matter. We only had free elections in Russia under Kerensky.'[36] Russia's 'freest year' of 1917 contained examples of total and representative democracy alike, but the idea of choice and pluralism was still a powerful folk memory after the Second World War. The absence of choice was evident by 1946, and the formal existence of non-Party candidates on the list was a patent illusion – though, for some, the leading role of the Party might not be a bad thing. 'Why do we have to have a bloc of Communists and non-Party members at the elections,' asked someone in Voronezh, 'when the Bolshevik Party is the only governing party in the USSR, it leads all organizations and the people trust it with their fate?'[37]

Probably more important than what happened at the ballot station was the campaign that preceded it. Campaigns provided a powerful mechanism for two-way communication between the authorities and the population. The most significant campaigns were for elections to the Supreme Soviet. Elections were first held to the Supreme Soviet in 1937. Then came the war, and the next election took place in February 1946. After that, they were held approximately every four years. The election campaign that preceded voting day lasted around a month. It was a widespread feature in newspapers, radio, and, later, TV news programmes. Candidates had to be nominated at the level of constituencies, and sometimes by institutions like trade unions or the Academy of Sciences. The process of nomination could be competitive. Candidates made their case at public meetings. Between their formal nomination and polling day itself, they continued to make speeches. Some famous candidates, including Stalin, who stood for election in a Moscow district, did not campaign as such. But many Party officials campaigned on their behalf. Ideologists crafted the message. Banners announced the Party's favoured slogans. Journalists shaped the message's delivery. The campaign penetrated all institutions of work and study, not least schools, which sometimes acted as polling stations. Election day itself was a ritual of mass involvement. According to a worker at one of Moscow's engineering plants in 1946, Comrade Lebedev, 'the elections are a real festival for us.'[38] Especially during the Stalin and Khrushchev eras, but to some extent too in the more sceptical period that followed, electioneering was a total performance.

The election campaign was, therefore, an important way for ordinary people to read signals from the authorities about how they should express themselves. But the communication operated both ways. In formal terms, candidates were asking something of the electorate: their votes. As a result, they had to listen to them. They did so in election campaigns, which featured countless public meetings, many on the factory floor or inside the collective farm. The questions people asked or the opinions people shouted out – on how policy affected their lives not on who should be in charge – gave officials the chance to gauge public opinion. Especially in the years of Khrushchev and Brezhnev, when the dictatorship was more responsive to people's needs, this was a crucial feedback mechanism.[39]

In the end, though, on extremely high turnouts and with no choice on offer, elections gave people the chance to agree with power. They were a parade of unanimity. The Supreme Soviet and other elected institutions were not simply representatives of the people, therefore:

they were the people. They articulated the unanimous and undisputed views of the people, their collective class interest.[40] As Bazarov said: the trees in the forest could not be distinguished from each other, the individuals became a mass. For all the apparent pointlessness of a single-candidate election that can't change the government, elections without choice helped to make Soviet politics work under Stalin as well as in the much less repressive years of Khrushchev and Brezhnev. An extra point was that elections without choice had a useable, valuable legacy. Experienced in political participation and voting, however mechanically, people very quickly adapted during *perestroika* to the politics of pluralism and to elections that did offer a choice. For all the unreasonable contempt with which the Soviet person came to be regarded – not least by those Russians themselves who coined the term *sovok* to describe the 'typical' Soviet souls they disdained the most – it was obvious that stormy applause was never a hardwired state of mind.

Sunday 9 April 1989 was election day in the USSR. It was a new type of election for a new institution, the Congress of People's Deputies. The elections were complex, with contests for different types of seats held on different days. As one candidate for election, Anatoly Sobchak, pointed out, 'it was a cumbersome and not very democratic system [that] Gorbachev had concocted'. But it was unlike elections for the Supreme Soviet: it was an election that offered a choice.

Sobchak was an academic lawyer at Leningrad State University, which was located in the city's Vasilevsky Island district. The district had always returned a worker from the Baltysky shipyard to the Supreme Soviet. It seemed likely that the shipyard would continue to dominate the working-class politics of the district in the newly competitive era of the Congress of People's Deputies. At a nomination meeting of his trade union in early 1989, Sobchak decided to buck convention and stand himself. He took part in the packed hustings that would nominate the candidates for the whole-constituency election, standing against representatives from the shipyard. 'Words about the need for a law-governed state, the priority of common human values over class interests, the necessity of a new approach for ensuring human rights, rolled off my tongue,' he recalled later. 'I spoke enthusiastically about reforming the economy, of new ideas for industrial accountability, and of independence for the republics.' Following voting at the nomination hustings, he became one of four candidates for the district.

Across the constituency, he canvassed for votes, making speeches through a loudhailer near metro stations, debating with the other candidates on local TV, and sharing platforms in public meetings. Honing his arguments in his encounters with the electorate, he engaged keenly with the 'civil society' campaign groups that were springing up across the city. He lacked much organization. To some voters, Professor Sobchak was no man of the people, but a journalist called him 'the voters' advocate'. He won with 76 per cent of the votes.[41]

In 1989, Leningrad fulfilled again its independent political spirit. 'The people have spurned their trust in the city's party and soviet leaders,' declared one leading group at the end of the election campaign. 'We have voted against, because we don't believe the promises of the *nomenklatura* to end arbitrary administration, economic irresponsibility, and social injustice.'[42] It wasn't just Leningrad, the cradle of the Revolution: the politics of pluralism were now on display throughout the country. Clubs, pressure groups, and political groupuscules that might be the building blocks of a democratic order proliferated.[43] But they were weak. Few lasted. They often seemed to promise anarchy rather than reasonable government. 'It's just accidents, rallies and strikes,' wrote a man called Osipov who lived in Astrakhan. 'No, we can't be given democracy; we don't know how to handle it.'[44]

By the late 1980s, the deepest question of all was about the meaning of Soviet democracy. It had to remain rooted in the decentralization of economic power, or it would mean nothing at all. 'It is only through democratization that the workers can be included in the process of *perestroika* because only democracy can give all power to the people,' wrote Abel Aganbegyan, one of the economic designers of Gorbachev's reforms. What could this democracy be? Mystifyingly, it was not about elections to a parliament. 'We must involve the masses in management, ensure that they participate in discussions about possible

developments, about the deployment of funds, or about which measures should be carried out first and which second.' This was an ideal
of grassroots democracy that drew on the half of Leninism that had
promised personal liberation. Aganbegyan emphasized that late Soviet
democratization was quite different from 'liberalization' on a Western
model. 'Liberalization means allowing things; it means power being
granted from above,' he wrote. 'The people do not participate in liberalization, though some parts of the population might benefit from the
process.' Democratization was about giving power to the people, not
about granting concessions from on high or imposing more and more
laws on the people. Supporters of *perestroika* 'wish to widen and
deepen the process. We stand for genuine democratization.'[45]

In such a way, the designers of *perestroika* looked back to the legacies of the Revolution and its aftermath to help them steer a route
between the hazards of stormy applause and the chaos of Turgenev's
thighs. But *perestroika* happened much too fast. Its badly conceived
policies transformed property relations in perverse ways, giving incentives to political and industrial bosses to bet on a pseudo-Western-style
democracy that forsook Soviet and Russian legacies, encouraging them
to enrich themselves dramatically. Unsurprisingly, they acted against
the real spirit of democracy and the rule of law. As the big-business
'democrats' prevailed, small-scale democratic participation, rooted in
economic life, had no chance of prospering. And the complete incomprehension of Western outsiders only made the situation worse.

In Western parliamentary and presidential democracies, 'economic
democracy' remained a niche idea during the 1990s. Only seldom did
it influence corporate life, such as in the Mondragon Cooperative Corporation, one of Spain's biggest conglomerates, never touching the
mainstream brokers of Western power politics, and only becoming a
populist Leftist dream after the financial crisis of 2008.[46] After 1991,
the Western powers – the 'Washington Consensus', made the most
short-sighted of errors when they assumed that democracy only meant
a very limited range of institutions and practices, a vaguely and lazily
understood version of their own. By using a cookie cut-out of
democracy-building, failing to support it with full-hearted help, both
material and moral, and ignoring the democratic resources that the
complicated Russian past made available, the would-be democratic

transition was never likely to be a transition to actual democracy. The 1990s were a time of freedom of speech and democratic participation, but they were marked by President Yeltsin's military assault on his own parliament in 1993, a new constitution which focused power in his hands and an economic system in which politics and big business could overlap. This gave stormy applause a new chance. It ushered in a new phenomenon: sovereign democracy. As the Putin era went on, state and power, sovereignty and democracy became the same thing.

Viktor Chernomyrdin, prime minister to Yeltsin's president, oversaw the turbulent relations between government and Duma in post-Soviet Russia. In those days, the Duma was a competitive arena, the home of bitter debate, where communists, nationalists and liberals vied to hold the government to account. But what was the natural party of the governing-minded, people like Chernomyrdin himself? In the 1990s, there was, in turn, 'Russia's Choice', led by the architect of the free-market reforms, Yegor Gaidar; the 'Our Home is Russia' Party, of which Chernomyrdin himself was chair; the 'Fatherland' party, headed up by Yuri Luzhkov, Moscow mayor, and Yevgeny Primakov, prime minister; and then the 'Unity' Party, whose leading figure was Sergei Shoigu, who later ran the Ministry of Emergency Situations before becoming defence minister. All these men were tough executive politicians, not natural parliamentarians equipped to serve in opposition, though Primakov arguably had it in him to be the exception.

By the new decade, the 'United Russia' Party had assumed the mantle. It swept all before it in Duma election after Duma election. In the September 2016 poll, it was returned with 343 out of 450 seats. 'Whatever party we create,' mused Chernomyrdin, years before that, 'we always end up with the Communist Party of the Soviet Union.'

United Russia was a vehicle of power, designed to govern, to support careers, and to distribute perquisites; the idea of serving as the opposition or holding the government to account was oxymoronic. But unlike the CPSU, it lacked an ideology and a heritage of grassroots participation. Neither liberal nor conservative, United Russia was the institutionalized consensus of the Russian political and business elite. Should the government change, it would be difficult to see what purpose the party would have.

The only really organic mass party in contemporary Russian life is the successor of the CPSU – the Communist Party of the Russian Federation. Although its connections with 'power' are no longer transparent, it has been a coherent opposition voice and the consistent runner-up to Putin and United Russia. The other large group is the Liberal Democratic Party, a populist-nationalist vehicle for the perennial comic turn of post-Soviet politics, Vladimir Zhirinovsky.

As time went on, parties of the centre and centre-right were marginalized. Some gave up. The reasons for this were both contemporary and historical. In fact, the long-term weakness of such parties in Russia, of liberals and conservatives alike, has placed an historic limit on Russia's democratic prospects. But does it suggest, as the Russia Anxiety would have it, that Russians lack the instincts of decent liberalism or reasonable conservatism, and are prone instead, as anti-democrats, to extremes and submissiveness? Has their history missed the crucial steps embodied by a liberal like Gladstone or a conservative like Bismarck?

## THE GLADSTONE GAP AND THE BISMARCK LACUNA

It became a ritual of post-Soviet politics. Every few years, Grigory Yavlinsky would limber up and run for president. Summoning up a lugubrious authority, displaying an ostentatious grasp of economics, and ruffling his full head of hair – he had something of British Prime Minister Gordon Brown about him – he would deliver his nomination papers. But if Brown was a tough machine politician with a vicious temper, Yavlinsky was the opposite. His Yabloko Party, Russia's leading liberal group, was grounded in grass-roots politics, but it was vulnerable to the massive and unpredictable head-winds of post-Soviet life. There were no party machines in the new Russian politics. Power-broking took place in government offices, not party meetings or smoke-filled rooms of election operatives. Politics offered nothing resembling a career structure. Running for parliament gave little advantage to independent-minded careerists, whose prospects were better served in officialdom and big business (though sometimes they stood for parliament later, a Duma seat conferring legal immunity and proximity to power). And throughout, for better or worse, Yav-linsky conducted himself in a professorial and cool-minded manner, even when tested in the most extreme way: his son was kidnapped in 1994. Yavlinsky became a fixture in post-Soviet politics: the high-minded, apparently incorruptible, quixotic, courageous critic of power who never had a chance.

In June 1996, Yavlinksy scored 7.3 per cent in the first round of the presidential election. Yeltsin and Gennady Zyuganov, the Communist boss, both attracted around one-third of the electorate, and went on to face each other in the second round, which Yeltsin won in contro-versial circumstances. In March 2000 – the election was slightly ahead of time, because of Yeltsin's resignation on the previous New Year's Eve – Yavlinsky came in at 5.8 per cent. Putin beat Zyuganov substan-tially, scoring over 50 per cent of the vote and winning outright, without the need for a second round. In 2004, Yavlinsky stayed out of the fray. He claimed that there were so many electoral abuses that it was not worth running. Putin won with 72 per cent. With Yabloko boycotting the poll, the closest to a liberal candidate was Irina Khakamada, a less disciplined politician than Yavlinsky, and a lead-ing figure in the small centre-right bloc, Union of Right Forces.

Next, in 2008, Yavlinsky stood aside in favour of the dissident Vladimir Bukovsky, who was disqualified on a technicality. Dmitry Medvedev attained 71 per cent of the vote, easily sidestepping Gen-nady Zyuganov, the long-running Communist leader, while Putin, having already been in office for the maximum of two consecutive terms, assumed the role of prime minister. In 2012, however, Yavlin-sky tried again. His candidacy failed. The authorities insisted that almost a quarter of the necessary 2 million signatures on his nomina-tion papers were forged. (He had to jump such a high bar because Yabloko was no longer in the Duma, having fallen below the 5 per cent threshold.) Putin beat Zyuganov on a slightly reduced but still overwhelming majority, and then the Duma extended the presidential term to six years. Yavlinsky came back to run again in March 2018. His hair had silvered a bit and he'd grown a smart beard, and now he walked around without a tie. He polled at 1.05 per cent. Although the opposition vote was split between seven candidates, who shared the quarter of ballots that were not cast for Putin, the liberal constituency seemed to have shrunk. Ksenia Sobchak, daughter of the Leningrad professor, stood too, and divided the natural Yabloko vote further, gaining 1.68 per cent. Despite Yavlinsky's gifts and grit, his political CV was an exhausting record of mixed accomplishments.

Grigory Yavlinsky was Russia's most famous post-Soviet liberal. Born six months before Vladimir Putin, he shared with him some of the experiences of their generation: coming of age and higher education in the Brezhnev era, career progression during *perestroika*. If Putin was a man of state service, Yavlinsky seemed more a man of the Soviet intelligentsia. He trained as an economist and worked for research institutes that were focused on national economic problems. He critiqued policy. But he did not stand completely outside power, and so he was not quite the classic Russian *intelligent*, the type who, however feebly, could claim to ask questions of government because they were not within it. By the end of the 1980s, Yavlinsky was one of Gorbachev's most senior advisers, and he became a prominent politician in his own right in the 1990s.

A cautious man, seeking to build coalitions rather than to grab headlines, he was a founder member of the Yabloko Party, post-Soviet Russia's most distinctive liberal group.[47] But Yabloko had a problem. It was the home of 'social liberals', those who were critical of the devastating social consequences of Yeltsin's breakneck economic reforms. As in other countries, though, liberals, who shared a commitment to civil liberties, were divided between supporters of economic deregulation and advocates of social welfare. 'On the one hand, we in Yabloko want Russians to be able to get rich, we want them to be able to earn high pay, we want to foster competition, and we want to exploit our country's natural resources and untapped potential for wealth creation. In that sense, we are a "bourgeois" party,' Yavlinsky wrote in 1997. 'On the other hand, when we see the government spending vast sums on official silverware and candelabras and see legions of public officials driving around in Audis and Mercedes-Benzes, we may sound a bit more "socialistic". So be it.'[48] In the face of this challenge, Yavlinsky consistently failed to press his point home. True enough, by 2018, he had managed to summarize his message in a single word. 'The most important word' – he told a Moscow audience, gathered in the snow on a Saturday three weeks before voting – 'is respect, respect of power for the people.' On a cold Moscow day, he wasn't even wearing gloves, taking energy instead from his supporters.[49] For a moment, he had the charisma of clarity, but it was too late. Yabloko only got a reasonable shout-out during national elections, though even then the main TV channels were open in their support for Putin. Vladimir Pozner, the veteran TV presenter and an authoritative neutral voice, interviewed Yavlinsky a few months before polling day, and wondered whether the younger generation had ever heard of him.

The after-life of communism has played an outsize role in shaping political values in post-Soviet Russia, which did not make for a promising environment for liberalism. This was partly because a Soviet education encouraged people to think in the structures of Marxism, in ways that seem antithetical to liberalism: in the polarized categories of socialism versus capitalism, or West versus East, or enemy versus loyalist. Most important of all were the enduring habits of mind that defined a citizen's relationship to the state. Post-Soviet Russians have shown a combination of attitudes to the state: anxiety about its coercive potential, anger about its corrupt tendencies, but also the enduring expectation that it will fulfil its beneficent promise, and remain as a court of final appeal about living standards and social provision. It can be difficult to disentangle the state and the nation in the imaginations of the older post-Soviet generations. Among the opposition parties, the Communists have therefore been best placed to make a straightforward and comprehensible case that can attract substantial support. Paradoxically, the same applies to the successive parties of statist power, which lack a recognizable ideology on the left-right spectrum, such as Our Home is Russia, under Yeltsin and Chernomyrdin, and now Putin's United Russia Party. The centre and centre-right have little chance by contrast. Alexei Navalny, the most distinctive opposition voice of the 2010s, whose presidential candidacy in 2018 was foxed by put-up criminal charges, was no liberal, but a populist-nationalist anti-corruption campaigner.

And yet the basic message of liberalism, about the special status of the individual, was a neat fit with *perestroika* and the transition to the post-Soviet period. Discussed in a Soviet tone, with messages paid to the centrality of social and economic rights, Gorbachev's own ideas were not inconsistent with aspects of a liberalizing agenda. From property rights to human rights, the spectrum of liberal sympathies enjoyed much support. But the devastating economic whirlwind of the 1990s seemed to put paid to Russia's liberal prospects. The Chernomyrdin Dictum reminds us about the interplay of structure and contingency in Russian history. And so it was events, the chances of politics during *perestroika* and transition, that kept Yavlinsky and others like him miles from power. Yavlinsky was not the victim of an inbuilt Russian problem with liberalism, as the Russia Anxiety might assume, but of policy failures and political calculations with which he could not contend.

If the glimmers of democracy – reflected when nobles once elected a monarch, or the burghers of a town gathered to make decisions about urban life – date back into the distant past of Rus and Muscovy, then so does the idea that the individual is a person of status in his own right. Vasily Klyuchevsky, one of the nineteenth-century titans of Russian historiography, argued that 'the very idea of personal rights, scarcely noticeable in Russian political thought before, is for the first time more or less definitely expressed' in the agreement with the Poles of 4 February 1610 that ended the threat of their takeover of Moscow.[50] Under Tsaritsa Anna (1730–40), reforms to property law protected the status of ownership. Peter III (1762) introduced measures defining the legal status of nobles. The instincts and necessities that underlay liberalism existed in the Russian lands just as they did in the West, even if they were not properly elaborated or securely defended.

A more systematic approach to liberal reform began during the eighteenth-century Enlightenment. Catherine the Great developed policies that looked towards civil rights, such as the Charters to the Nobility and to the Towns. She also imposed a rational approach towards elementary schooling and social protection, especially for orphans and the sick. Meanwhile, the loosening of censorship allowed a more systematic dialogue with liberal ideas from abroad, notably those of Montesquieu. It also made possible the publication of journals that put forward social criticism, and even attempted subtly to criticize the authorities, such as Novikov's *The Drone*. Catherine's Russia was an autocracy, but the scope of freedom had expanded there. Her reign anticipated a reformed autocracy that might one day be based on the rule of law, with a promise of liberal constitutionalism. Then, during the first years of Alexander I's reign, Mikhail Speransky established the terms of his 'Conundrum', aiming for an autocracy governed by laws as well as by a man. As he wrote in the law code of 1809 that was never formalized, 'What is the point of civil laws if their "tablets of stone" can break at any time on the rocks of the autocracy?'[51]

By the start of the nineteenth century, the opportunities for Russian liberalism seemed real. But the structure of Russian politics created problems and shaped mentalities in unhelpful ways. For all the rich potential of the Speransky Conundrum, the autocracy was hostile to Russian liberalism. Three out of the four tsars who reigned between 1825 and 1917 made it difficult for liberal ideas to develop naturally. As a result, with its options narrowed, part of the intelligentsia became dramatically more radical, committed to violent revolution. This liberalism was squeezed between an uncompromising state and an extremist opposition. One tendency that flowed from the noble officials of Peter the Great directly to the assassins of Alexander II was the uncritical assumption of Western ideas, the tendency to believe in utopias and the willingness to make use of whatever means might be necessary to achieve the desired ends.[52] This anti-liberal tendency was only one part of eighteenth- and nineteenth-century Russian political culture – the liberal tendency itself was another – but it was a powerful one, and it diminished liberalism's prospects.

It was not as if liberalism did not have a rocky path in other European countries. At best, 'liberalism' and 'democracy' everywhere suffered from grotesque lapses; more likely, they were never truly capable of protecting rights for all. Nineteenth-century Spanish history was partly an unsatisfactory dialogue between liberals and the monarchy, starting with the abortive proclamation of a liberal constitution in 1812. More generally, liberalism adopted uncertain forms across the southern European periphery, in the lands of today's Portugal, Italy and Greece, a zone of slower development and dramatic politics whose modern history can usefully be compared with Russia's, and which are no less European than France or Denmark.[53] Or take the prototypical example of liberal politics: Britain. For all the coherence of John Locke in the seventeenth century or John Stuart

Mill in the nineteenth, and for all the increasing influence of liberal ideas on politicians as the Victorian age went on, modern British liberalism was founded on an original sin: the coexistence of civil and political rights at home for those of the right gender and class with their deprivation from the non-white inhabitants of the colonies. Encoded deeply in liberalism's practice was the assumption that there existed a few people who possessed rights and many others who didn't. Russia's liberalism fitted on the European spectrum.

Alexander II's great reforms increased the space for Russian liberals to breathe and even flourish. The emancipation of the serfs had been the liberal nobles' preoccupation, and now they could put its possibilities into practice on their estates. Liberals made use of the *zemstvos* to promote their own values. Reforms to universities and the judiciary made it possible for liberal-minded professionals to honour their political convictions in the institutions in which they worked. The spirit of the 1860s was a brief thing, curtailed by Alexander's own doubts and then by his assassination, but its influence survived in the more hostile conditions of the later nineteenth century. It cultivated convictions about the status of the individual in law, and expressed a desire for the peaceful, gradual and limited reform of the autocracy, an approach that Turgenev and his 'fathers' would recognize.

By 1905, however, the old liberalism had been outstripped by events. Its agenda belonged to a slower-moving world. If liberals were to enjoy relevance in a time of revolution, they had to change gear. Most of them had been long-lasting constitutionalists, but now they had to accept that the Revolution had moved the goalposts, requiring them to back a range of social and economic rights. But in the end, why should a radical vote for the liberal Kadets in the Duma elections when he could opt for something more authentic? Like in any political situation that was becoming more revolutionary, the centre could not hold. This was not really a failure of the liberals, or of liberalism. It was the result of circumstances beyond their control: the exceptional, unanticipated, febrile politics of the decade before the First World War.

And they were undone by the genetic accident of monarchy. Nicholas II was incompetent enough to alienate support when it was offered to him. Shortly after the outbreak of the war, the Duma's moderates coalesced in the Progressive Bloc. Its aim was to combat extremism, reflect public opinion, enhance the status of the Duma and provide patriotic wartime support to the tsar. Keen to help the government direct the war effort, it was rebuffed: Nicholas signed a decree to adjourn the Duma until September 1915. 'The extended hand was rejected,' wrote Pavel Milyukov, the leader of the Kadets.[54] The monarch's intransigence not only reduced the goodwill of the moderates and the capacity of Russia's war machine, it also strengthened the opportunities of the far-left socialists at the expense of the liberals.

Milyukov had argued before 1905 that Russia had missed its real chance a century earlier, when Alexander I rejected Speransky's original programme for a reformed autocracy and embraced conservative and mystical visions in the second half of his reign.[55] In November 1916, Milyukov made his famous 'stupidity or treason' speech in the Duma, in which he outlined the monarchy's incapacity to fight the war effectively. In both cases, Milyukov pointed out that the failure was the monarch's. Alexander I and Nicholas II alike were unable to forge the obvious alliance with the liberals, constitutionalists and moderates that would have contributed to the monarchy's survival. It was not that Russian political culture was naturally hostile to liberalism, but that a succession of tsars made bad decisions. Put it another way: bouts of dangerous political weather, rather than a permanently unmanageable political climate, shipwrecked Russia's liberals. Milyukov was right that liberals historically fell victim to political circumstances, though in 1916 his own speech was one of those circumstances. In the midst of such a storm, Milyukov's contemptuous words were reckless. The monarchy fell a few weeks later, but the liberals never had control of events during 1917, and the Bolsheviks destroyed them. Milyukov fled Russia in 1918 and spent the rest of his life in exile.

The Russia Anxiety points to the absence of political pluralism in Russia, sometimes justifiably so, but where it tends to underestimate Russian liberalism, it exaggerates the significance of Russian conservatism. Liberalism might be necessary for a lasting democratic culture, but democracy-building is based on a different truth: it needs conservatives. In mid-Victorian politics, the great political rivalry was between Gladstone and Disraeli, alternately prime ministers for the Liberals and Tories. Benjamin Disraeli was the prototypical modern

Conservative; it was no accident that it was he, and not his rival, who was responsible for the Second Reform Act of 1867, the period's most influential democratizing stride. The Act enfranchised the upper echelons of the male working class, and entrenched an influential relationship between Conservatives and certain types of manual workers that would in some ways shape modern Britain.

Disraeli was a mercurial politician of great talents. But the most brilliant democratizing conservative of the nineteenth century was Otto von Bismarck. He built a country: as minister-president of Prussia, he won the wars, conducted the diplomacy and designed the institutions that unified the German states. Under the sovereign power of the Kaiser, this 'Second Reich' came into being in 1871. Bismarck possessed a mastery of tactics: without it, he would not have been able to find his way through the thicket of international and domestic politics that stood between himself and his aim of unification. But he also exercised a strategic vision. This extended not only to the creation of Germany, but to the type of politics that would govern it. More radical than the Second Reform Act, the constitution of the new Germany allowed for a Reichstag that was elected on the basis of universal male suffrage. There were political parties of various stripes, and trade unions. Meanwhile, the status of conservative Prussia in the new 'democratic' Germany was assured, and the Kaiser remained powerful in practice; Wilhelm II dismissed Bismarck in 1890. This was practical authoritarian politics vigorously pursued, by a statesman whose authority went beyond the patronage of the emperor (until Wilhelm II came to the throne). Russia's struggles to make autocracy workable seem like arcane theology by comparison.

Late imperial Russia lacked a statesman of Bismarck's calibre, who could make democracy and autocracy coexist. It was not that Bismarck solved Germany's Speransky Conundrum. Instead, he showed it was irrelevant, making democracy safe for conservatism – and conservatism safe for democracy. Marxists argued that he tamed democracy and hoodwinked the workers. He gave them the vote, allowed them to organize and supported them with generous social security and welfare measures, but extracted a cost, obtaining their quiescence. For better or worse, this compromise grew into the dynamic and intermittently durable mass democracy of Germany's modern age. It began as an illiberal democracy under Bismarck, but it had liberal potential, eventually realized.

Bismarck was greatly admired in Russia. Policy enthusiasts wrote tomes about his welfare programme.[56] In 1912, a major social insurance law was introduced in Russia; one of its leading proponents in the Duma tried to win traditionalist deputies round by comparing it with the German welfare laws.[57] No one thought more of Bismarck than Sergei Witte, prime minister in 1905, when Russia was going through a failed revolution. Witte encouraged Nicholas II to make the political concessions that culminated in the creation of the Duma, first elected the following year; but his premiership was otherwise a failure, because his grip on the politics of the street was so weak, and the monarchy might have collapsed had he remained in office beyond the autumn. His biographer claimed that he even felt 'adulation' towards Bismarck. It was partly a matter of the German's unique mastery of international and dynastic politics: his unrivalled capacity for state building. More deeply felt, though, was Witte's admiration for the particular type of democracy that Bismarck designed. He had found a way of preserving the magic and authority of the Kaiser while bringing all adult men inside the political nation. Witte called it a 'social monarchy'. The Russian statesman would have loved to build an analogue of the German social monarchy in St Petersburg. Witte thought that the German model facilitated 'the defence of the rights of the weak' in such a way as to make the state stronger.[58] This was a conservatism of extraordinary possibilities.

Bismarck's conservatism channelled the forces of modernization in the direction of monarchism. This was a model too for Pyotr Stolypin, prime minister from 1906 until 1911. But Stolypin's tactics were different from Bismarck's, reflecting a fear of democracy rather than the confidence to use it. In 1907, Stolypin was responsible for changing the electoral rules so that the Duma would be dominated by supporters of the monarchy, a move which reduced rather than extended the political nation. But he did so in a way that assumed that prosperous peasants, and not regular industrial workers, must be the bedrock of the monarchy. This seemed the wrong bet at a time when it was the cities of the Empire which were deciding the future of politics. Stolypin's 'wager on the strong' extended individual property rights by diminishing the power of the village commune. His law allowed ambitious peasants to set up shop as small-holding farmers. This petty-bourgeois class, Stolypin believed, could help to save imperial Russia: it was bound to be conservative, just as it was in Western Europe and the United States, and would thus support the monarchy. The vulnerability of Stolypin's experiment with dynamic conservatism was revealed by his assassination at the theatre in Kiev in 1911.

But at least Stolypin tried. In Russia, much more often, conservatism was all about vacuously turning one's back on the forces that were creating the modern world. By the early twentieth century, the potential of conservatism was unrealized. In the place of a dynamic and strategic vision from the centre-right, Russian conservatism was static, and where it was radical, it was violent and intolerant, believing Russian politics was a conspiracy of Jews and Freemasons. In the polarized conditions of the First World War and the Civil War, this was the ugly face that Russian conservatism presented to the world.

The historic root of Russian conservatism, though, was the autocracy, and the function of conservatism was to provide extra ideological justification for the monarchy. This gave conservatism a static quality, as if it was merely the sycophantic servant of the monarch. Count Sergei Uvarov served Nicholas I as a minister for education. In 1832, he came up with the famous summary of the monarchy's purpose, 'Orthodoxy, Autocracy, Nationality', which became a slogan for conservatism. It did not offer a way of making the government accountable, or representing specific interests, or promoting the status of the bourgeoisie or defending organic, age-old rights; instead, it suggested that conservative politics were simply a way of explaining and supporting autocracy. Konstantin Pobedonostsev, who was the most influential conservative voice in late imperial Russia, had this stationary worldview. He tutored the last two tsars in their youth and was also procurator of the Holy Synod – the government official in charge of the Orthodox Church – between 1880 and 1905. Lacking the privileges of most high officials, he was brought up in the ranks of the intelligentsia; his father was a professor at Moscow University, though the atmosphere at home was devout rather than sceptical, perhaps reflecting his grandfather's modest service as a village priest.

Pobedenostsev believed that democracy was always wrong, whether it was calmly representative or the forum for stormy applause. 'For-ever extending its base, the new Democracy now aspires to universal suffrage – a fatal error, and one of the most remarkable in the history of mankind,' he wrote. In a democracy, it was the demagogues and shady operatives who had the power. Politics became debased and vulgar. The wise reforms of a statesmanlike elite were no longer pos-sible. Parties bribed and manipulated the voters. Parliaments served not the public good, but 'the triumph of egoism'. Showing he had totally misunderstood the way the wind was blowing, Pobedenostsev even called out Bismarck. 'In Germany,' he wrote, 'the establishment of universal suffrage served merely to strengthen the high authority of a famous statesman who had acquired popularity by the success of his policy.' For Pobedonostsev, democracy was so malign that it was unspeakable even when it was serving a conservative agenda. Obliv-ious to the path on which Nicholas II had set the monarchy – 1905 was just round the corner – Pobedonostsev ended his tirade against Bis-marck: 'What its ultimate consequences will be, Heaven only knows!'[59]

But conservatism did not have to be static and stupid. At its best, but in scattered and unrealized form, nineteenth-century Russian conservatism might have saved the monarchy. It could offer prescrip-tions that were by their nature particularly Russian, rather than generic and international, as Enlightenment-inspired liberalism inevi-tably was. As a result, Russian conservatism could sometimes sound inventive, flexible, and responsive to local conditions.[60] Take the struggle between Mikhail Speransky and Nikolai Karamzin during the reign of Alexander I. Karamzin deplored Speransky's instinctive but scholarly desire to reform and thereby renew the autocracy. For him, it missed the point. He thought that Speransky marked a fash-ionable shift towards abstract ideas and universal theories at the expense of organic, tried-and-tested practicalities. Karamzin argued that the tsar's power must be undivided: it should not be compromised by elected institutions or curtailed by written-down constitutions. But he also argued that it was not, by definition, unlimited: it was not arbitrary, ungenerous or personalistic.[61]

Such a conservative view was not a cheap catch-all defence of a tsar. It offered scope for political evolution and practical criticism. Karamzin was a deeper thinker than the usual blind adherents of power.

He offered the possibility of a conservatism that did not emerge from within the autocracy itself. Instead, it was a conservatism that might advise the autocracy as a candid friend, point towards a fresh direction or even modestly seek to hold power to account. It did him no good during the reign of Alexander I, who turned against him as he had turned against Speransky.

The Soviet Union was a revolutionary socialist state from the beginning to the end. During the Brezhnev era, however, conservatism re-entered the fringes of Russian political life. The Soviet government permitted the creation of some organizations which drew obliquely on older conservative traditions, such as the All-Russian Society for the Preservation of Monuments of History and Culture (VOOPIiK). Cultural trends emerged, exemplified by the novels and stories of the so-called rural writers, as well as journals like *Moskva*, that were part of the same tendency. Contemporary Russian conservatism has partly emerged from this sometimes wistful, sometimes authoritarian approach. In the 1990s, Alexander Solzhenitsyn was, informally, its most famous spokesman, arguing that the state was not simply a collection of economic and military interests, but a spiritual entity, expressing Russia's uniqueness and its Christian heritage.[62] Putin honoured Solzhenitsyn with the State Prize of the Russian Federation in 2007. In a private conversation with the US ambassador shortly after, and just months before Solzhenitsyn's death, the writer offered qualified praise for Putin's government.[63]

This type of conservatism emerged from the Soviet Union and reacted against the circumstances of its collapse. (Its tendencies to explain Russia as a 'Eurasian' civilization is something we'll come back to in chapter 7.) Like most of its predecessors, this form of conservatism existed to promote the state, not to hold it in check. President Putin has used some of its symbols, but he's not really of the Left or of the Right, let alone of the far Right; he's a person of the state, a *gosudarstvennik*, drawing on instincts of authority, imperatives of international statecraft and consolations of nationhood, adapted for the age of politics as business and business as politics.

Yet Russian political culture has generated different conservative traditions that are independent of the state and even exist to keep its excesses in check. Contemporary politics, not Russian history, have made the independent centre-right weak. There were the great thinkers, like Pyotr Struve, who moved from left to right between late-nineteenth-century St Petersburg and 1930s exile, always being guided by the same humane commitment to liberty. And there were the politicians who formed a centre-right that could be an active opposition. Between the Third Duma, elected in 1907, and the Revolution, the Octobrists played a major role under the leadership of Alexander Guchkov. They were an independent centre-right party, not of the state but capable of criticizing it. Other centre-right groups emerged that could dynamically represent particular interests, such as the Progressist Party, which spoke on behalf of sectional groups in business and industry during the First World War. Their post-Soviet successors included the Union of Right Forces and the People's Freedom Party, and such politicians as Boris Nemtsov and Irina Khakamada. There were politicians of the centre-right who resigned from Putin's government, such as the former finance minister Alexei Kudrin, who occasionally spoke critically and productively from the edge of power before returning to office in a less central post in 2018. Yet the position of a centre-right opposition became very weak during Putin's third term, its parties unable to get properly registered with the authorities, let alone elected to the Duma. In early 2015, Nemtsov, the charismatic rebel whom Yeltsin had made a deputy prime minister nearly two decades before, and who had recently become an anti-corruption, pro-democracy campaigner of national importance when his party was squeezed out of parliament, was killed by assassins outside the Kremlin walls in an international *cause célèbre*. Mikhail Kasyanov, Putin's former prime minister who came back to lead the People's Freedom Party, fell victim to a compromising scandal and polled disastrously in the 2016 Duma election. Khakamada had long since returned to private life.

For many Russians, these liberal-conservative politicians could be difficult to stomach. When Mikhail Kasyanov had been prime minister, he was nicknamed 'Misha Two Per Cent', for his alleged attachment to bribe-taking. Was he really now a democrat? Boris Nemtsov was in the end a hero to many, and a tragic figure to almost all, but he was just a 'Soviet playboy' to one of my Russian teachers in the early 2000s. Russians are quick to call hypocrisy out. Like most people, they find lectures from outsiders difficult to take. And when the teaching from on high concerns democracy, they are quick to respond, having lived through the economic and moral disaster of 'democracy' in the 1990s. But democracy flourishes best when illusions about it are most secure. Calling out hypocrisy can have the most unintended of consequences. As we'll see in the last section of this chapter, the relationship between Russia and the outside world has achieved precisely this, shattering the country's democratic illusions. The Russia Anxiety requires its proponents to look down on questions of democratic development from the moral high ground, when a more revealing perspective might start from within.

## THE HYPOCRISY RADAR

Russian political culture possesses a sensitive radar that detects hypocrisy. It's always switched on, and it makes plenty of false readings. But not all the readings are false. False or true, the radar's readings are calibrated in moral equivalences. A questionable action by Russia looks more normal when compared in moral terms with a stupid, thoughtless or malicious policy pursued by a Western government. Some comparisons, especially about empire or invasions, carry more obvious moral weight than others. Ben Rhodes, one of President Obama's speechwriters and a deputy National Security Adviser in his White House, pointed out in early 2017 that the moral equivalences might be misjudged, but the United States does indeed have a record of intervening in other countries and changing regimes – and also of taking advantage of Russian weakness so that NATO expansion could be facilitated. Speaking of Putin, Rhodes concluded: 'There is just enough rope for him to hang us.'[64]

Western journalists coined the term 'whataboutism' to define the principle on which the radar works.[65] Never was there more whataboutism that during the Cold War, when the actions of the United States provided a natural foil for the rhetoric of the Soviet Union. The KGB? What about the CIA? Human rights? What about Southern

Blacks? Shortages of goods? What about unemployment? Housing queues? Homelessness. Afghanistan? Vietnam. As a principle of international political debate, it is now back with a vengeance. Ukraine? Iraq. Crimea? Kosovo. Democracy? Trump.

Critics point out that 'whataboutism' merely constructs false moral equivalences by drawing comparisons between quite different phenomena; it's nothing more than a debating ploy to distract from violations of international law and human rights. 'Whataboutism' has a long if not very distinguished record in the history of rhetoric, though the Cold War was a particularly natural environment in which it could prosper. Take John le Carré's fifth novel, *A Small Town in Germany*, published in 1968. The action unfolds in Bonn at a fictional moment when the far Right was once more gaining in popularity and making the political weather. 'The Nazis had persecuted the Jews: and that was wrong,' le Carré writes, glossing the speech that the would-be fascist leader makes at the culmination of the novel. 'He wished to go on record as saying it was wrong. Just as he condemned Oliver Cromwell for his treatment of the Irish, the United States for their treatment of the blacks and for their campaigns of genocide against the Red Indians and the yellow peril of South East Asia; just as he condemned the Church for its persecution of heretics, and the British for the bombing of Dresden, so he condemned Hitler for what he had done to the Jews; and for importing that British invention, so successful in the Boer War: the concentration camp.'[66]

Whataboutism might sometimes be crass, making it easy for the Russia Anxiety to dismiss it out of hand. Yet the history of democracy across Europe is an unlikely story full of cynical subplots rather than an inspiring fairy tale based on the triumph of values. Never does the hypocrisy radar twitch more vigorously than when democracy is up for debate.

Democracy is an emotional subject, discussed in terms of moral values. For Aristotle, democracy was not a morally good form of government; like tyranny or oligarchy, it was a perversion of politics that was based on self-interest and extremism. He heard the stormy applause and imagined mob rule. His lessons were influential. Moral anxieties about democracy have been a staple of modern European politics since at least the eighteenth century. They have diminished with time, but became respectable again in the age of Trump and Brexit, with their assumptions that the people might not know best after all.

Since the 1940s, though, democracy has almost always been described as a moral force for good. During the Second World War, the Allies were 'making the world safe for democracy'; the language of democracy accompanied the foundation of the United Nations and then the reform of the defeated powers, Germany, Italy and Japan; ever since, democracy became an approximate synonym for human rights and the rule of law. Those countries which seem to fall short in democratic qualities don't simply have political weaknesses that might be treated, but deep-seated moral failures. They deserve ritualistic condemnation at best, and the 'shock and awe' of invasion and occupation at worst.

In the Soviet Union, democracy was also described as a moral good. After 1945, its zone of enforced influence in Eastern Europe was made up of countries called 'People's Democracies'. In everyday life, behaving 'democratically' was a good thing. Soviet people recognized when the rhetoric rang hollow, but they also valued some of the real consequences of 'Soviet democracy'. By the Brezhnev era, some of those things for which there was consensus support, notably universal social rights and the rhetoric of international peace, fitted easily inside a framework of notional democracy. Later, Soviet ideology could label Gorbachev's democratization policies as morally right. Describing democracy in primary moral colours made sense to many citizens, partly because Soviet political culture had given them the words, and partly too because democratic reform offered self-evident remedies to the abuses of late-Soviet politics and bureaucracy. The speeches of Anatoly Sobchak and others were not tin-eared.

This was a narrow window of hope. By 1993, democracy looked very different. Now it was associated not with things of universal value, or aspirations for a better world, but with the likes of Anatoly Chubais and Yegor Gaidar, Boris Yeltsin's deputy prime ministers in the early 1990s. Such men proudly called themselves democrats. The label was widely used and unfortunately it stuck. Unelected themselves, and working for a president whose election predated the break-up of the Soviet Union, they had the feeblest of mandates for their headline reform. Beginning on 1 January 1992, they initiated the economic policy of 'shock therapy', which unleashed market forces overnight. Eschewing the possibility of more gradual reform, and ignoring the fact that they were leaving tens of millions of their fellow citizens in conditions of utmost peril, they brought about unpaid wages and runaway inflation. Those citizens who did have jobs often found themselves unpaid for months on end. Crime soared. Savings were lost. Corruption was rampant. Pensioners sold their possessions in the street. Some people were lucky and earned tremendous success, but most people's lives were irretrievably spoiled. This was the most difficult time for Russian people since the aftermath of the Second World War. Meanwhile, at the end of 1993, Yeltsin's forces fired heavy weapons at parliament.

For Russians in the early 1990s, this was democracy. Those who most self-consciously labelled themselves as democrats and used a high-sounding language of democracy were those who were most impoverishing the population and enriching themselves. There was nothing more Soviet than describing politics in moral terms. Just two years after the red flag came down from the Kremlin, the habit was ingrained in the post-Soviet population. But the language of the reformers was an American language. In post-Soviet Russia, it sounded false. For many Russians, democracy scarcely looked virtuous. As the 1990s went on, the people's trust in politicians and political institutions was at extraordinary low levels; in one major survey, under 10 per cent of the population expressed trust in parliament between 1993 and 1998, while trust in the president fell to 6 per cent in 1995.[67]

Meanwhile, in Western capitals, Yeltsin was seen as the best hope for a stable transition out of Soviet power, and the reforms of Chubais and Gaidar were considered appropriate. For the Washington Consensus, pain is something that is worth enduring if it's happening to other people. Unsurprisingly, a deficit in sympathy led to a disjunction in communication. If democracy is always a good thing, then there must have been something wrong with Russians for not seeing its virtues. In the 1990s, talk of democracy in the abstract generated hollow laughter among Russians who were living with what they assumed were its concrete effects. Since 2000, years after Chubais and Gaidar had left the Kremlin – Chubais to make a fortune as a top energy executive, while Gaidar died young from a heart attack – the hollow laughter became the established backdrop of political culture.

The hypocrisy radar went into overdrive whenever Western politicians waxed lyrical about the moral case for democracy. Not only had these foreign leaders never cared about the fate of ordinary Russians, but many of them were elected into power on a minority of the vote, sometimes when actually coming second. And it was never difficult to find examples of how they also abused power, denied people their rights and looked after their own, all the time maintaining a fixed grin and talking about the power of the people.

The case for democracy might be made in three ways. First, democracy is a universal value. Evidence suggests that democracy can take root in all kinds of cultures, not just the stereotypical 'Western'. Witness the story of Indian democracy, which has had a continuous history since the end of colonial rule in 1947, and has facilitated changes of government and the protection of freedom of expression (while less successfully securing universal rights and combating corruption). Democracy allows a political community to understand what it has in common and to shape its political values accordingly. It enables people to participate politically, to demand responsiveness from their government, and to maximize the dignity of citizenship. All of these things might work weakly in practice in any democratic state. But democracy can still facilitate the shaping of a minimum level of consensus and respect.

Second, democracy has useful practical consequences. Above all, the government can be replaced, and there's an established way of doing it peacefully, even in win-win ways, so that the defeated party can recharge its batteries and come back stronger. The rule of law is more likely to work effectively in a democracy. This is not a universal truth. Courts and lawyers can sometimes operate plausibly in the subject territories of empires or in modern authoritarian states. But it's much easier for them to work without too much fear or favour in democracies. The range of practical rights that people depend on – to walk about freely without being arrested, or to own property securely, or to return faulty purchases, or to have defensible access to social goods like healthcare and education – are also more robustly protected in a democracy. But there are many exceptions to this rule: take internment without trial in Northern Ireland during the Troubles, or the relative sanctity of property in right-wing authoritarian regimes, or the elevation of social rights in socialist dictatorships. Meanwhile, government in democracies is usually more transparent than in dictatorships. This in turn reduces corruption (though not so much in democratic Greece and Brazil).[68]

Plainly, these two justifications for democracy are subject to detection by the hypocrisy radar. A third, however, which Winston Churchill famously put forward, is less easy for the radar to pick up. This is the truism that of all systems of government, democracy is the worst, apart from all the others. It's best able to control the worst instincts of elites, gives people something to believe in if they wish to close their eyes, is unlikely to unleash arbitrary violence against its own population, or to start wars against other democracies. No one can really be inspired by the least-worst argument, but they might appreciate its effects; it seems honest rather than hypocritical, and it seems interested in a practical goal: clearing the minimum hurdle of a satisfactory politics.

Ultimately, though, it's a weak defence, given the democratic deficits of many Western democracies. Without some appeal to political morality, democracy can look enfeebled. What about, a critic might ask, the representative credentials of governments? Democracies look pointless when people are disenfranchised. Donald Trump won a majority in the electoral college – but nearly 3 million fewer votes than Hillary Clinton. In Britain's first-past-the-post system, hundreds of constituencies are not competitive, making it pointless to vote if you live in the heartlands of one of the major parties – in other words, in most of the country. Cynical self-interest makes the problem worse.

Gerrymandering has fundamentally weakened the democratic credentials of the US House of Representatives. This is an historic challenge that has got much worse with time. By taking control of a raft of state legislatures and governors' mansions in 2010, Republicans were able to execute their REDMAP strategy, by which they could redraw the borders of swing districts to make them safe for their own party. The process was openly cynical; the resulting districts, connecting pockets of supporters in different parts of the states, were so bent out of any rational shape that their purpose was clear. 'It means basically that the whole constitutional notion of the House as a mirror of popular views comes into jeopardy,' argued one expert from the non-partisan American Enterprise Institute.[69] Awareness in Russia of such democratic failures merely solidifies a sense of American hypocrisy.

But the result of presidential elections, and also British general elections, is almost always in question. Although the value of many people's votes is discounted, the election overall is competitive. More representative voting systems can actually make it impossible to change the government. Coalitions that nobody voted for are the common consequence of proportional vote-counting. Meanwhile, in the history of Swedish government, the Social Democrats were immoveable between 1932 and 1976. Japan's Liberal Democrats ran the country without interruption between 1955 and 1993. Democratic elections without real choice can reflect a national consensus, in favour of social welfare and an interventionist state in Sweden, or the prioritizing of economic success in Japan.[70] But the system is still stacked against the basic function of democratic elections: making possible a change of government.

Keeping incumbents in power for long stretches, whether as United States Congressmen or as ministers in Sweden or Japan, is still different from the way that dictatorships perpetuate the grip of a party or a small clique in power. It's true that in nearly all district elections to the House of Representatives, the incumbent will win. But incumbents still have to face the voters; there is a chance they can lose, both in the primary election among their own party supporters and in the general election across the electorate as a whole, even if the chance is remote. One political theorist claims that this is the ideal outcome. Unlike the 'charade' elections of dictatorships, the House elections allow voters to express their will and ensure that their choice is respected. So the politicians are kept on their toes, a bit, and by staying in office, they build up expertise and potentially become better politicians. The aim of the election is therefore to make elected officials do their jobs better, and it achieves this by ensuring the election is as uncompetitive as possible without being completely uncompetitive.[71]

Given all this, it's unsurprising that the success of democracies requires the voters to undertake a leap of faith. Modern democracies look utterly unlike their predecessors in ancient Greece. Citizens no longer participate in government. Some of them – usually between half and two-thirds – go out to vote once every few years, sometimes with barely a choice before them or an opportunity to be heard. They might be free to say or read what they like, but they cannot *but* keep in power an elite which is rich and strong, and which bets on democracy as the best way to maintain its privileges.[72] Any solution to this problem – such as selecting citizens at random, in a process called 'sortition', to take part in lawmaking for a few weeks at a time – is probably unpopular and anyway coercive.[73] Unable to formulate policies to deal with medium- or long-term threats, incapable of perceiving how serious any given crisis might be, hysterical and complacent in turn, democracies survive because the voters refuse to reject the shaky theoretical premises on which their politics works. Up on the high wire, the voters don't look down. The political scientist who makes this argument calls democracy's predicament a 'confidence trap' of a particular kind. 'People have to believe in democracy for it to work,' he writes. 'The better it works, the more they believe in it. But the more they believe in it, the less likely they are to know when something is wrong.'[74]

The total system shock of the early 1990s destroyed Russians' capacity to take this leap of political faith. Democracy's advantages have seemed illusory. The claims made on its behalf have looked obviously hypocritical. Western commentators scoff at Russians' hypocrisy radar, ignoring those of its results which are obviously true, and refusing to see the stubborn reasons for its existence. But twenty years on from the 1990s, with living standards relatively high, society more stable than it has been for decades and metropolitan life ever more liveable, why take a punt on a political experiment? It is not the campaigners from abroad who are taking the risk with their children's futures. Russian politics sometimes acknowledges the link between a democratic deficit and the failure of everyday life, such as after the avoidable catastrophe in the Winter Cherry shopping centre in Kemerevo in March 2018, when a fire killed sixty people, including children trapped in a cinema: the governor of this region of Siberia, Aman Tuleyev, was forced to resign. Failures of oversight, regulation and policy increased the risk of disaster, and he took responsibility. But there was a cynicism about this; he reappeared as Speaker of the region's duma shortly after.

The nightmarish failures of public accountability are one thing, but some commentators have come to link them to a more outlandish picture, comparing Russia's current political culture to those which feature concentration camps, civil wars and the exclusion of women. In the Freedom House survey for 2016, which ranks a country's political rights and civil liberties out of 7, with 1 representing the freest, Russia was given scores of 7 and 6 respectively. Hardly any countries did worse; North Korea, which forbids its citizens from travelling abroad, and Syria, engaged in a civil war, both got 7 and 7. Russia's rating was the same as Libya, Yemen and the Democratic Republic of Congo. Afghanistan and Iraq were scored significantly better.[75] (Freedom House is a non-governmental organization almost completely funded by the American government.)

When it comes to democracy, we know deep down we're up on the high wire, but for good reasons we cannot admit it openly to ourselves. If we could, we would understand Russia's predicament more clearly. But that might come at a cost to ourselves. A democratic country is probably more likely to remain so if it does not spend too long weighing up its own democratic weaknesses. It's much easier to keep going if you don't look down. In Britain, the intense introspection of two constitutional referendums in two years, over Scottish independence and Brexit, created a crisis of legitimacy; the country's political culture seemed no longer sure of what it really was. Being able to point or jeer at apparently undemocratic others – the European Parliament, Hungary, above all, Russia – was a helpful if limited safety valve. Wherever democracy seemed most vulnerable, not least in the United States, Russia was talked up as a dictatorial enemy, and was imagined as culpable for democracy's failings, thanks to hacking and other electoral interference. As the foil for the West's own insecurities over several centuries, Russia probably needs precisely the kind of moral support that Western governments might be least able to give.

And so the Russia Anxiety not only misinterprets Russia's democratic experiences, it has stopped the outside world from giving Russia the support it has needed. Western governments missed the chance to redesign international institutions in 1991 in such a way as to incorporate Russia as a natural democratic member. Instead they sent highly paid advisers to help deliver the crushing burden of economic reform, while maintaining the external institutional architecture of the Cold War. And by keeping Russia as their foil, they failed even to provide the rhetorical support that might have made democracy seem right for the Russian people. The great danger of the Russia Anxiety is that it is a self-fulfilling prophecy; Russia's natural proclivity to dictatorship is a deception, unless enough people believe otherwise.

# 5

# The Terror Moment

*Is Russia Built on a History of Violence?*

Dressed in the black robes of a monk, Ivan the Terrible fell to contemplation, atoning for his sins and imagining his future. It was May 1567. He had come as a pilgrim to the monastery of Belo'ozero, or White Lake, an isolated religious settlement in the far north of Muscovy. The abbot offered him consolation. 'I had found a divine bridle for my ungoverned heart and a refuge for my salvation,' Ivan is recorded as saying.

Ivan IV (1533–84) was Russia's cruellest Tsar. His wicked acts were probably shaped by mental illness, though retrospective diagnosis is impossible.[1] He was periodically gripped by extreme suspiciousness and unlimited rage. With his own hands, he carried out acts of extreme violence. In November 1581, he murdered his own son. Time and again, when the fury abated, a sense of vulnerability seems to have enveloped him, as he came to terms with his own weakness and sinfulness.

One such moment was prompted by the events of summer 1566, when the nobles' fears about Ivan's rule got the better of them. Gathered together in an Assembly of the Land, or *Zemsky sobor*, they were discussing how best to support Ivan in the war against Livonia. But it was they who were under siege. Eighteen months earlier, unstable and unpredictable, Ivan had left Moscow, apparently forever, promising to abdicate. Abdication could be catastrophic, a prelude to anarchy. Back in the capital, the nobles pleaded for him to return. Ivan accepted the petition. But he had a big proviso. The nobles had to agree that he could set up a state-within-the-state, a territory that would be his own private domain, run and policed by his own private security force. They agreed, as did the other groups in the *Zemsky sobor*.

The state-within-the-state was called the *oprichnina*, and the private 'policemen' were known as the *oprichniki*. Between 1565 and 1572, when it was disbanded, the *oprichnina* became Ivan's zone of terror. Located to the north of Moscow, it was a substantial area with major towns and economic activity, many of whose nobles and townsmen were recruited as *oprichniki*. It was the centre of cruel exploitation and mass violence. So much so that in their gathering of July 1566 the nobles exhaled a collective shout of protest: 'Our Lord, most illustrious master, why do you order the deaths of innocent brothers?' The *oprichniki* were, for them, agents of terror. 'They kidnap our brothers and relatives, insult, harass, ill treat, ruin and finally kill us.'

Ivan could not tolerate such a statement of opposition, however loyally it was couched. Confused about how to respond, he ended up at Belo'ozero. He soon returned to the heartlands of his *oprichnina*, where he turned the *oprichniki* into a sinister monastic movement, clad in black monks' robes. They sometimes hung a dog's severed head from their horse's neck; the image of the dog's head and a broom symbolized the hunting down of enemies and the removal of filth.[2] Their songs of repentance and the monastic routine were only the prelude to violence.

This violence was the result of Ivan's uniquely dreadful interpretation of Muscovy's geopolitical circumstances. Like the Russian Empire that emerged in the eighteenth century, though on a smaller scale, sixteenth-century Muscovy had long borders that were difficult to defend. Relations with neighbours, especially the emerging Commonwealth of Poland-Lithuania, were not easy; Sweden (which also possessed today's Finland) was another source of worry. For Ivan, the borderlands might be full of treachery. The bigger towns too, away from the borders, might be seedbeds of opposition to Moscow. His rage grew, and it focused on distinguished old towns to the north-west of Moscow: Tver, Pskov and Novgorod. They felt the force of his wrath.

In December 1569, *oprichniki* blocked the route towards Novgorod. Marching onwards, they killed people on the way. When they reached Tver, they located Filipp, who had been removed as metropolitan for his opposition to the *oprichnina*. He refused to change his stance, and was suffocated. In only five days, the city was devastated, its inhabitants killed in terrible ways. One chronicle claims that 9,000 people were executed, with many others dying soon after the violence, not least of starvation. A similar fate came to the other cities in Ivan's sights. He seems especially to have feared and detested Novgorod, a city with a record of stubborn independent attitudes. Here the great buildings were looted, hundreds of homes were destroyed, thousands executed. Amid an epidemic of plague and cholera and an encroaching famine, cannibalism spread. Pskov was hit next. But this was only one sequence in the much longer narrative of Ivan the Terrible's violence.

On 25 July 1570, Ivan oversaw the construction of a killing ground in Moscow. At the city's Poganaya meadow, the *oprichniki* built a massive wooden framework for multiple gallows. They dragged in cauldrons, which would be filled with either cold water or boiling water for torture. Ivan himself wore black clothes. He was armed with a bow and arrows, held an axe and observed events from the back of a horse. Ivan's enemies were brought in for torture and execution. He imagined how they had conspired against him as he conducted their terrifying demise.[3]

These are just episodes in the terrible story of the *oprichnina*. Given what we know of Russian history – the merciless reforms of Peter the Great, the prison camps of nineteenth-century Siberia, above all, the terror of Stalin – it might seem obvious that Ivan the Terrible was only one act in a continuous history of violence which continues to define Russia today. Such a narrative is a foundation of the Russia Anxiety.

But is it true?

## THE DAY OF THE *OPRICHNIK*

Faced with the awful human consequences of the industrial revolution in Britain and Germany, Marx and Engels concluded that any state which could make this possible must ultimately be founded on violence. Generations of Soviet historians followed their lead, looking for sources of violence in the long history of the Russian state. But the pre-modern East Slavic state lacked the capacity or will to rule by violence alone. Kievan Rus was not really a recognizable state at all, lacking fixed administrative structures, but it was built on compromises. It was a compact between the grand prince of Kiev, who was often politically weak, and other princes who had power over their own demesnes. During the Mongol period, between the thirteenth and fifteenth centuries, an external power deployed violence and accommodation to oversee its alien and complicated Eurasian territory. As Muscovy emerged and flourished from the late fourteenth century through to the end of the sixteenth century, the grand prince, then tsar, became an increasingly powerful figure – but he neither owned his subjects nor everything within his realm, and did not possess the tools of violence to enforce such ownership. If he had, Ivan IV would not have had to invent the *oprichnina*, which stands as an exception rather than a rule in early Russian history.

Ivan devised the *oprichnina* because he was afraid of enemies. It allowed him to live in a physically separate zone from many of his fellow countrymen. From this base he eliminated alternative sources of power that seemed to be a threat: strong noblemen, different-thinking churchmen, robust towns. The method was terror. Suffering and fear spread across different parts of Muscovite society. Power was exercised in an arbitrary way. Autocracy as a functioning and sustainable system of power, rooted in legitimacy, was in abeyance. One prominent historian wrote a book drawing a straight line between the *oprichniki* and the agents of the NKVD.[4]

It's a bold claim: that Russian history is a predictable structure defined by state violence. But the *oprichnina* belonged to its time and place. It was the consequence of Ivan's worldview and personality. The particular connection between domestic and foreign threats, and Ivan's perception of them, facilitated its creation: the conflict in Livonia was unresolved, Poland and Sweden seemed endemic threats, and nobles were either reluctant or not competent to prosecute war effectively. The consequences of the *oprichnina* were likewise fairly clearly defined rather than open-ended. It contributed to the disintegration of the Muscovite political order, a miserable process that reached its apogee during the Time of Troubles. And it made subsequent Muscovite political culture more risk-averse, less willing to innovate and embrace reform (because in a perverse way, the *oprichnina* was a kind of reform, and no one wanted to repeat it).[5] But as the decades wore on, the imperative of reform returned, and Muscovy-Russia pursued it again in the seventeenth century under the new Romanov dynasty, though this time it was reform unaccompanied by mass terror.

The *oprichnina* did not set up a historic highway to Stalin, let alone Putin. It was a dead end.

And while it was Russian, it was also early-modern, a recognizable fragment of Europe's sixteenth century. Ivan the Terrible had famous contemporaries, especially in the early part of his life: Martin Luther, Henry VIII and the Holy Roman Emperor, Charles V. Such men made a world of violence whose logic and savagery gripped Western and Central Europe far longer than the *oprichnina* disabled Muscovy.

Martin Luther, the German monk whose Theses of 1517 promised a more democratic Christianity based on popular involvement, comprehensible language and the primacy of an individual's faith, did not hesitate to embrace violence when it seemed right. In 1525, he spoke out against rebellious peasants, whom he compared to mad dogs that must be killed, calling on the faithful to 'smite, slay and stab, secretly or openly, remembering that nothing can be more poisonous, hurtful or devilish than a rebel.'[6] Henry VIII destroyed England's established links with Rome, dissolved the monasteries, quelled rebellions and crushed dissent. He might have believed that his actions were the manifestation of divine will and self-evident law rather than egoism and arbitrariness, but some of his subjects disagreed. For a priest from Middlesex, Henry was 'a great tyrant rather than a king'; he was the worst 'robber' and 'pillager' ever to have been the English monarch.[7] Charles V, Holy Roman Emperor (1521–55), held talks with Luther and toyed with the compromises that could have preserved his Central European empire in peace, but when the time came, he used great force to defeat the heretics and preserve Catholicism.

Muscovy was not directly touched by the religious struggles of the sixteenth century, a fact which is sometimes regretted: another Western rite of passage missed. But the Protestant Reformation and Catholic Counter-Reformation were very violent processes. They were given force by a language of purification and elimination. Clergymen released the lethal energy of crowds which performed 'rites of violence' against their enemies – dwellers of the same town who now practised their religion slightly differently. Local authorities followed centralized orders and carried out mass executions, such as the Paris-directed killings of Protestants in Provence in the 1540s; unleashing the violence of the crowd, officials accepted orders to torture and even to desecrate the bodies of the dead.[8] In Geneva, the home of John Calvin, torture defined the symbolic and practical pursuit of justice: a study of the early 1560s shows that more than one-third of all judicial investigations made use of torture, and that torture was used in 84 per cent of cases that led to capital punishment.[9]

In places like Geneva, the aim was to use violence to systematize power and enforce purity. The *oprichnina* was part of a more personalized and perhaps more arbitrary form of political violence, whose very peculiarity lent it scant possibilities of becoming a system that could be passed on down the ages. By contrast, the ethics of Reformation violence were part of a historic approach to politics that has shaped the modern period, including, perhaps ironically, in the Stalinist USSR. Take the language of Henry's Act of Supremacy of 1534, which made him head of the Church of England. The Act granted the King and his successors 'full power and authority from time to time to visit, repress, redress, reform, order, correct, restrain and amend all such errors, heresies, abuses, offences, contempts and enormities', and in so doing, to ensure 'the conservation of the peace, unity and tranquillity of the realm'.[10]

The foundations of Stalinism were as generally European as they were specifically Russian. In England, the state used violence against the people in a systematic and brutal way. Historians of Tudor and Stuart England estimate that 75,000 people were executed between 1530 and 1630; adjusted to early twenty-first-century United States population size, so that the comparison is meaningful, this would be the same as today's US executing 46,000 people per year for the next hundred years. In sixteenth-century England, the number of capital crimes increased, the clergy lost their immunity from certain prosecutions, vicious forms of corporal punishment were increasingly common, and martial law was introduced in 1589. Political rebels and those suspected of thinking differently were crushed with extreme prejudice: hanged, quartered, burned. The extent of the violence suggests that Tudor politics was not merely legitimated by laws and culture, or by organic compromises between people and power, but by arbitrary coercion.[11] The Tudors colonized Ireland, whose inhabitants they considered barbarous and savage, and where brutality had few limits. The numbers killed in the pacification of Munster – up to one-third of the population, or 48,000 – and perhaps 9.2 per cent of the population of Ireland as a whole[12] – outstrip the work of the *oprichniki*, and the violence was probably more embedded, and ordinary, than it was in the time of the *oprichnina*.

The devastation that swept across Muscovy at the start of the seventeenth century during the 'Time of Troubles' (1598–1613) took place amidst dynastic crisis, foreign invasion and economic disaster. Awful as it was, it was not a wilful episode of state-driven political violence. But it fitted its European context. Compare the Thirty Years War, which ravaged Western Europe between 1618 and 1648. By its end, 20 per cent of the population of the Holy Roman Empire – at their core, the German lands – was lost, more than three times the percentage killed during the First or Second World Wars.[13] Magdeburg, for example, was destroyed in 1631, when 80 per cent of its population of 25,000 was killed. Christian II, prince of nearby Anhalt, wrote in his diary on 11 May: 'News that yesterday morning at eight o'clock Magdeburg was captured, plundered, set ablaze, men, women and children cut down.' He went on: 'Prisoners brought here from Magdeburg repeat that the slaughter continued this morning and the city is completely burnt down, that no building remains but the cathedral which burnt down this morning.'[14] Meanwhile, the death rate in the British Civil Wars of the 1640s was greater than during the First World War.[15] Functional violence was embedded into the society of the British Isles as much as it was anywhere. And the Spanish had been laying waste to the Americas for more than a century.

In 2006, the novelist Vladimir Sorokin published *The Day of the Oprichnik*, a fictional blend of killing, rape, drug-taking – and politics. It describes Moscow in 2028, when 'Rus' is brutally governed by a new *oprichnina*, with the old symbols of broom and dog's head moulded onto the futuristic technologies of a new age. This small-minded world of nationalism, surveillance, conspiracy, beatings and murder updates Ivan the Terrible's reign as science fiction. The novel apparently gives a warning for contemporary Russia about the dreadful tendencies of violent dictatorship. Critics of government violence have always been quick to look back to the precedent of the *oprichnina*. One Socialist Revolutionary leaflet that was distributed in the provinces during the height of the early twentieth-century terrorist campaign called for 'Death to the soulless *oprichniki* shooting the defenceless people!'[16] The message is: the *oprichnina* might be encoded into Russia's DNA, and so it might happen again.

Vladimir Sorokin was part of the large crowd on Lubyanka Square, outside the yellow-and-red headquarters of the KGB, in August 1991. It was the end of the putsch against Gorbachev. The KGB looked as if it had played its last card and lost. Unbelievably, the most formidable intelligence agency in the world seemed vulnerable. The crowd wanted to pull down the massive statue of Felix Dzerzhinsky that dominated the square. 'Iron Felix' was the Polish revolutionary and founding chairman of the Cheka. If anyone had a claim to being the Soviet Union's prototypical secret policeman, the first boss of the security organs, the chekist *nonpareil*, it was Dzerzhinsky. The crowd's hatred and frustration, and also its caprice, and its wilful, hazy judgement, focused on the statue.

Sorokin remembers what happened next. The crowd was gearing up to tear the statue down with its bare hands. But a leading supporter of Boris Yeltsin appeared on the scene and warned that the massive statue might crash into the underground pipes and cables beneath the tarmac and cause severe damage to surrounding infrastructure. Instead, he'd called for a crane to remove the object in a more orderly fashion. It took two hours, but the crane arrived and the statue was taken down safely. 'Doubts about the success of the coming anti-Soviet revolution first stirred in me during those two hours,' wrote Sorokin in May 2014. The moment to take control from the KGB seemed to dissipate; something primeval in the Russian-Soviet state was not snuffed out, but went into safe hibernation. The statue was stored for safe-keeping in a museum of Soviet antiquities, not ripped to pieces. Perhaps the statue will come back. And why? Because of something deep in Russian history, 'the vicious nature and archaic underpinnings of the Russian state's "vertical power" structure'.[17]

A different lesson from history, and one that takes more account of the clash between structures and contingencies that marks the Chernomoyrdin Dictum, would be to imagine a modern Russian state that is apparently built on a 'power vertical' but is really characterized by overlapping institutions like all states are. It is strong in some ways – it has a big police force, and a powerful presidency – and weak in others, with an uncertain reach into the most distant periphery, and an excessive reliance on things beyond its control, like foreign trade or the price of oil. Agencies of the state inevitably channel imperfect information up to decision-makers, who in turn misperceive some threats, are excessively worried about the stability of their ruling order, and take precipitate action as a result. This was the context of the Great Terror of the 1930s.[18] That scale of Terror never came back, but the complexities of ruling Russia, where state violence is a possibility, though usually a remote one, have never gone away.

The form of the *oprichnina* was a bizarre aberration, but the extent of its violence was the European norm. Whether in peacetime or wartime, whether targeting outsiders or one's own people, state and popular violence engulfed Europe from Ireland to the Urals in the early-modern period. Meanwhile, Ivan's reign combined violence and reform. Despite the elemental catastrophe of the *oprichnina*, Ivan the Terrible set in train processes that led eventually to modern life in Russia. Most significant was the introduction of a law code (*sudebnik*) in 1550 that rationalized and codified court practices. The Church was better organized in theological and administrative life alike after the 'Stoglav' church council, held a year later. Administration in the provinces was bolstered by the local appointment of elders. The conquest of Kazan took place amid army reforms that removed numerous inefficient traditions.

Even the reign of Ivan the Terrible – the stand-out cruellest tsar – suggests no cultural disposition to state violence in Russia. Most Russians for most of history were not troubled by such barbarity. Many Russian rulers were not terrifying. Some were so banal that there is no folk memory of them at all. The Russia Anxiety is right that violence has marked Russian history, but wrong to neglect the wider European violence of which Russia is a 'normal' part. And it does not see that Russia's history of violence is sporadic and not continuous, and is, above all, a modern tragedy, not an ancient, eternal or inescapable one.

## THE DANGER OF MODERNIZATION

Count Aleksei Arakcheyev, who exercised power at the apex of Alexander I's government, was one of the great pantomime villains of imperial Russia. Contemporaries swapped stories about his capacity to bite off a man's nose or rip off his moustache.[19] As a man whose 'name should be written not in ink but in blood',[20] he seemed to have a sense of the potential of total power. For Joseph de Maistre, philosopher, ambassador to Alexander's court, and no gentle soul himself, Arakcheyev was 'evil, and even very evil', but there was a design behind the wickedness: 'it is probably true that at present only such a man can restore order'.[21] From 1808, Arakcheyev served as Minister of War and from 1810 as chairman of the military committee of the newly founded State Council. A traditionalist in his political and cultural commitment to autocracy, Arakcheyev was nevertheless a socio-economic modernizer *avant la lettre*. Like many other modernizers, his work combined creation and destruction.

Having risen from obscurity to become a favourite of both Paul and then Alexander, Arakcheyev was gifted 2,000 serfs and the village of Gruzino in the province of Novgorod. As yet unburdened by high office and still only in his thirties, he developed the estate and built a model rural community. He constructed functional roads, bridges and farm buildings, drained the land, and aimed for symmetry, uniformity and cleanliness throughout the estate. The measures seemed to exemplify his precise and rational approach. Obsessed with detail and improvement, he tutored the peasants on good farming and child-rearing, and launched a bank that dispensed credit to those who sought to buy livestock or build a house. Ascetic and unsmiling, Arakcheyev was a man who knew best. He even designed the gardens that lay between the peasants' huts.[22]

In 1810, two years after Arakcheyev's elevation to high office, the tsar visited him at Gruzino. Alexander greatly admired the 'order' and 'neatness' of the settlement, and reflected on how a social reform might simultaneously improve standards of living and enhance popular discipline. This was a time when Alexander was considering new ideas for recruiting troops in the most efficient way. He had resolved on the idea of military colonies in the first part of 1809.[23] Perhaps this famous visit crystallized in the tsar's mind what the military colonies, the new self-sustaining, prosperous and hygienic settlements of a caste of army recruits and their families, should look like. Drawing on seventeenth- and eighteenth-century precedents, with roots in the Roman Empire, these colonies were to be model villages. The men would be away for part of the year with the army, and be at home for part of the year on the land; they should later form a military reserve. This promised to solve the financial burden of the army draft and the social dislocation that arose when recruits were indefinitely extracted from their home villages. Such a scheme offered the possibility of building the prototype of a rational universe of work, welfare and service. Since Peter the Great, the monarchy had adapted, reformed and modernized the autocracy. Peter and his successors were fascinated by the capacity of the state to engineer people's souls for secular ends, a fascination only increased by the arrival of Enlightenment ideas in the Russia of Catherine the Great.

But when you cut wood, chips fly. Even while the Napoleonic Wars were still being fought, in 1810, a colony was established in Mogilev province: peasants owned by the crown were removed, and settlers brought in from Novorossiya.[24] Colonies were developed on a larger scale from 1816, after the war was over. Arakcheyev, unfazed by cruelty, coordinated the programme. New villages were to be built by soldiers and peasants, and locals moved from their homes to inhabit them, in what amounted to coercive resettlement. Force and ruthlessness underwrote Alexander's practical and ideal goals. The military colonists were supposed to be equals before the law. Their environment should not be backward or poor. The settlers were required to make the most of their land. They would enjoy decent primary education, limited care for the elderly and medical assistance. Resources were focused on the construction of hospitals (in 1820, every colony for the infantry had its own hospital), together with provision of medical orderlies and midwives. All of this was run by a major military bureaucracy.[25] Up to a million people lived in the colonies by 1823, which Alexander visited on a number of occasions and for which he expressed enthusiasm.

Yet the settlers' former communities, many of which were centuries old, were eliminated. Arakcheyev was obsessed with the tiniest details of these welfare schemes, considering the appointment of particular midwives and tormenting schoolteachers who were insufficiently obsequious.[26] He oversaw arrangements that came close to forcing soldiers to marry particular women. Most brutally, Arakcheyev put down uprisings in the colonies, at one point forcing court-martialled rebels repeatedly to run the gauntlet of 1,000 of their peers. Alexander Herzen called the colonies 'the greatest crime of the reign of Alexander I'.[27] Even Charlotte, the wife of the future Nicholas I, who observed the colonies during Alexander's reign, wrote in her memoir: 'The emperor had the idea, but the execution was entrusted to Arakcheyev, who did not do it gently but on the contrary with hard and cruel measures that made the poor peasants discontented.' The picture was bleak: 'Going about, we found here and there the residents of some villages on their knees, imploring us that their traditional way of life not be changed.'[28] On top of all this, the finances of the colonies did not add up. The grandiose project was perhaps doomed on those grounds alone by the end of Alexander's reign. But the colonists themselves protested on a mass scale, too, at Slobodskaya Ukraina in 1819, Staraya Rusa in 1831 and at numerous other locations in the 1820s and 1830s,[29] before the experiment came to a close in the 1850s.

One might argue that it failed for the reason that utopian projects always fail: because they fail to take account of the humanity of their subjects. A British doctor with extensive experience of the Russian Empire, Robert Lyall, wrote in 1823 of 'how bitterly' the peasants 'regret their fate in being forced to become colonists; and how warmly they talk of [the colonies'] utter ruin'. Even serfdom was better. 'Their former state of *civil slavery*,' concluded Lyall, 'seems perfect freedom in comparison of the new military arrangement of their affairs.'[30] The peasants did not seek this aggressive interference, even if its aim was their improvement. They wanted to run their own lives, in line with the rhythms and the mutual responsibilities – the basic peasant justice – of the village commune.

Arakcheyev knew better. He sets the scene of modernity's

dangerous potential. But the point about modernity is that it is a universal: it is a set of practices that have been applied across the globe, sometimes with less violence than in Russia, sometimes with more violence. What the Russia Anxiety often misses is that Russia's history of violence is a history of modernity. The encounter between Russia and modernity can be pivoted on two dates, one a century before Arakcheyev, one a century later. First, Peter the Great set about the construction of his new capital city, St Petersburg, on 16 May 1703. Second, an awful massacre disfigured the centre of that city on 9 January 1905.

# 16 MAY AND 9 JANUARY

Towering above his subjects, driven by massive ambition, playful and cruel by turn, Peter the Great wanted to build a perfect city. Quixotically he chose Russia's empty north-west marshlands, by the Neva river and the Baltic Sea. This was a defensive zone on the edge of Russian lands, from which the main enemy of the day, Sweden, could be faced down. But it also looked out of the Russian interior and down onto the heartlands of Europe. Two hundred and forty-nine years later, Vladimir Putin was born there.

On 16 May 1703, according to tradition, the city of St Petersburg began. The fortress of Saints Peter and Paul was its foundation, and was dedicated on 29 June. Surrounding buildings were hewn roughly out of earth and wood, but star architects were brought in, palaces and cathedrals were imagined, and, within a year, Peter was writing to Prince Menshikov, one of his right-hand men, about this new 'capital'. Peter moved there properly in 1710.

The scale of the project was vast. In the summer of 1703, 20,000 soldiers were at work constructing the Peter and Paul Fortress. Thousands more workers supplied the site with building materials, cutting down trees and lifting the trunks so that they would float downriver towards the would-be city. From 1704, the authorities demanded the employment of 44,000 workers for up to half a year at a time. This was a press-ganging operation. Those with specific skills were especially vulnerable to being uprooted and drafted to the wasteland in the north. At any one time in the twenty-two years between the foundation of the city and Peter's death, up to 30,000 labourers worked on the city's building sites.[31]

Building paradise was a project of both biblical and all-Russian dimensions. In May 1706, Peter wrote to Menshikov about how pleased he was to be in Petersburg, because 'in God's heaven there can be no evil'; four years later, he wrote to him of 'the beauty of this Paradise'.[32] Although Peter in some ways continued the reforms of the late Muscovite period, and brought his modernizing energies to the city of Moscow as well as his new capital, St Petersburg took on a novel and even dangerous form. It brought into focus themes that would feature again in Russia's modern period: imperial ambition, rooted in the inheritances of ancient Rome, Byzantium, Rus and Muscovy, but reshaped into a modern European state; colonial force, pushing back frontiers and developing territory; the harnessing of large numbers of people in vast peacetime construction projects; and the elevation of an ideology.

But it came at a terrible cost. The labourers who built the city had no proper housing or nutrition and quickly succumbed to cholera and other diseases. Often lacking tools in the early days, many were reduced to digging with their hands. Vasily Klyuchevsky, whose seminal historical account appeared nearly two centuries later, wrote that the construction project of St Petersburg 'turned out to be a huge graveyard'.[33]

Peter's construction of St Petersburg was the prototypical act of urban modernization in Russia. It was not deliberate state violence; it had nothing in common with the *oprichnina*, and there was no cultural or political line of continuity between the two. But its epic disregard for the wellbeing of its subjects – its self-conscious sense of sacrificing life in the mundane here and now for the good of the future – had its analogues in the industrial revolutions and imperialism that dominated Western Europe's experience of modernity. New cities in the Americas, constructed at the same time, bore similar material and human costs. Peter's reign came in Russia's early-modern era, a short post-medieval forcing house that prefigured modern life. His life's work was Russia's 'modernization', on permanent display in the architecture of his new capital.

The reign of Peter the Great does not belong to the modern period. Traditional life, the world we have lost, began to give way to modernity, a world marked by glimmers of things we might recognize, later in the eighteenth century. It was the ideas of the Enlightenment, the politics of the French Revolution and the economics of industrialization that made the fundamental changes that led to modern life. Russia started to become deliberately modern during the reign of Catherine the Great (1762–96), at least in government policies and the worldview of those who fashioned them. Peter lacked the language of modernity. But he and the men who surrounded him were, nonetheless, according to one of their leading historians, 'self-conscious modernizers'.[34] They wilfully set about creating a new world that aggressively discounted tradition. Aspects of this world would soon have more in common with our own times than with the medieval past. State violence was built into modernity from the start, whether it was in the Terror of the French Revolution or the perfect prisons dreamed up by Jeremy Bentham in England. Sadly, Russia later encountered the state violence of the modern period in dreadful ways, thanks not to the predispositions of its people or the failure of its cultural 'system', but to the decisions of its rulers.

On 4 January 1905, radical Petersburg workers struck for better working conditions. They were led by Father Gapon, a charismatic political organizer with shadowy connections to the security services. It was a mass event, bringing out 100,000 workers within three days. Gapon collected a petition and planned a march to the tsar for 9 January. The petition professed loyalty and begged for protection, though its specific demands, such as the eight-hour day, were radical. The procession to the Winter Palace included women and children, together with male workers; they carried icons and pictures of the tsar. Even in this single event, tens of thousands marched. It seems that, in response, the authorities lacked precise orders and plans, and that the soldiers who guarded the approaches to the Winter Palace panicked. They opened fire. The government itself admitted to killing 130 people and causing serious injury to a further 299; presumably there were many more.[35]

Thus began the Revolution of 1905, finally defeated in Moscow in December. At that point, Muscovites rose up, their organization and energy focused on the radical working-class Presnya district. The governor-general of Moscow directed the fury of the autocracy against them, giving orders to 'exterminate the gangs of insurgents'. The best estimate was that 1,059 Muscovites were killed, including 137 women and 86 children. Much of the state's violence was indiscriminate; it seems that the majority of the dead were innocent of involvement in the uprising. They were collateral damage, the cost of the state expressing its power.[36] For comparison, think of what the French government did to its own people when crushing the Paris Commune in 1871, killing perhaps 10,000 and executing the same number out of hand.[37]

Socialist Revolutionary terrorists responded with their own exterminatory political violence. Between 1905 and 1908, the SRs' Combat Organization and their even more extremist offshoot, the Maximalists, conducted the terrorist operations and assassinations that caused the deaths of 2,563 government officials; a further 2,954 were wounded.[38] These are official figures, and they might well be underestimates. The Grand Duke Sergei Aleksandrovich, younger brother of Alexander III and governor-general of Moscow under Nicholas II, was one of the most famous victims, killed by a bomb thrown by an assassin called Ivan Kalyaev in 1905. A few days earlier, Kalyaev had deliberately foregone his first chance to carry out the assassination because there were children in the grand duke's carriage. In the revolutionary movement, this decision first to spare and then to murder became a legendary narrative that could justify crime and honour alike. Virtue and violence became indistinguishable. In any case, the lines of guilt and innocence ran through both state and terrorists, rather than dividing them.[39]

The government replied in turn. Military courts were given the authority quickly to execute civilians charged with political crimes. In the six months between the publication of the October Manifesto and the convening of the Duma in April 1906, as many as 15,000 people were executed, and 45,000 sent to Siberia. Perhaps another 20,000 were killed or wounded in such events as the crushing of the Moscow Uprising. There were multiple accounts of soldiers firing into crowds in different parts of the country. In the three years after that, the courts passed death sentences on 5,000 political prisoners, and the 'Stolypin wagons', named after the prime minister who oversaw the repression, continued to trundle to Siberia.[40]

This polarization set the scene for the Russian Revolution of 1917. It did not make revolution inevitable. Nor did it make Russia unique. Political extremism had its limits, and people of conscience in government, Duma and wider society continued to work on sensible social reforms – but it brought a brutal quality to political and social life, which would soon be magnified horribly during the First World War. The intelligentsia was infected by the symbols of apocalypse, while some members of the government became prematurely fatalistic about the monarchy and empire. The violence went on, and revolution – the force that would increase the killing a thousandfold – became more plausible. By 1914, Russian society was divided, unable to generate a consensus, tense, accustomed to violence. Yet political collapse and unlimited violence required the First World War to activate them. They did not derive from the imaginary Russian tendency to violence that turns the country into a phantasmogoria.

Russia's modern age began twice in St Petersburg – first on 16 May 1703, then on 9 January 1905 – and it did so both times in a context of violence. But violence was a malfunction of modern Russian politics, not its purpose. Violence was made by political leaders: by their bad judgement, or personal choice of utilitarian ethics, or malice. In the first fifty years of the twentieth century, Russia's leaders created violence without limits; their successors ended the violence, or most of it. What we understand by modern Russian political violence was largely limited to the years between 1904, when Russia went to war with Japan, and 1953, when Stalin died. During that time, the Russian political machine broke down, generating a catastrophic sequence, which had no obvious precursor in Russian history, and was not thereafter repeated. That's no consolation to the tens of millions of victims, but this chronological exactitude is an important truth to set against the fictions of the Russia Anxiety.

## TEARS WITHOUT END, 1904–53

Alexander Askoldov directed only one film. Made in 1967, *The Commissar* was about the Russian Civil War. This conflict took place more than a decade before Askoldov was born, but the heart of his film, the moral of the tale, was probably autobiographical.

Askoldov was five years old in 1937. This was the most infamous year in Russian history, the core of the Great Terror of 1936–8. During that brief time, 692,000 innocent citizens were shot on trumped-up charges as enemies of the people. To some it was a 'meat grinder', to others a 'whirlwind' of unlimited state violence.

Alexander was born in Moscow, but the family moved to Kiev when he was small. His father was a factory director. No professional people were more important in Stalin's industrial revolution than the industrial bosses. Since the start of the first five-year plan of 1928, the country had been turned upside down by record-busting industrial expansion, mass migration, and 'cultural revolution'. The industrial achievements were unmistakable: new cities, massive factories, catapulting growth. But mistakes were made. Targets were missed. Machinery was damaged. Foolish things were said. The political culture of the Bolshevik Party and the logic of the Russian Revolution had always amounted to a project of purification, a purging of enemies in the pursuit of utopia. In 1936, in the context of Stalinist politics and foreign threats, this visceral fear of enemies was unleashed across society. It was easy to imagine that any factory worker, not least the boss, was a saboteur or a wrecker.

As the terror gathered pace, it was no surprise that Alexander's father was arrested. Soon after that, in the middle of the night, the secret police came back. They hammered on the door. The boy woke up to find that they had come back, this time for his mother. Spouses were often implicated in the grotesque imaginary conspiracies and denunciations that fed the Great Terror. Alexander's mother was a doctor, acquainted with many people. No doubt she was unsurprised that the NKVD had come for her. But she still asked the policemen to look away while she got dressed. They laughed in her face. You'd better get used to it, they said; no one will give you a second's privacy where you're going.

The five-year-old boy watched them leer. Decades later, he said that this was the instant of the whole tragic story that he remembered most piercingly. The arrest was in itself a much greater violation, but the policemen's refusal to turn away their gaze summed up for him, and always did thereafter, the power of the Stalinist state to destroy people in an arbitrary way, to deny their individuality and humanity, and to create a hierarchy of power that demeaned every member of it.

'We'll come back for the boy,' they said, pushing the mother out of the flat and clicking the door behind them. Alexander remembered how he felt at this moment of eerie silence: he knew that his home was now a place of utter peril. He had to leave. Telling the story decades later, he said that there were two insuperable obstacles on his path. The first was that he could not tie up his shoelaces. The second was that he could not work out how to unlock the door. Adults had shown him many times how to lace up his boots, and yet he'd never managed it. This time, though, he put the boots on and the bow somehow formed. He stood on a chair and stared at the mechanism of the lock. Somehow it clicked open in his hand.

It was dark outside. The pavements were menacing. He walked on and on, deciding eventually to walk down the middle of the traffic-less roads, where the lighting was better. By now he was in the very centre of the city, in Kiev's main thoroughfare, the Kreshchatyk. Bit by bit, or almost automatically, he was making his way towards some friends of his parents. They were a Jewish family, more modest in material circumstances than his own, with several children. He found his way to their front door, and kicked at it gently.

They opened it straight away, fell upon him and brought him inside. Their pity and affection was as unlimited as the violence of the secret police. They knew straight away what had happened. They hid him away, kept him quiet and helped him mend, until his grandmother came to collect him some time later. She took him back to Moscow, where she worked as a cleaner in a tram depot, and brought him up.

As a young man, after the end of the Stalin era, Alexander Askoldov visited Kiev. He went to try to find the Jewish family that had saved him. But they had long gone, he told an interviewer much later: to Babyi Yar, the ridge above Kiev where the Nazis killed the city's Jews in 1941.[41]

*The Commissar* was Askoldov's vision of the violence that created Soviet society. It told a story of the Civil War, drew obliquely on his childish experience of the Great Terror and made connections with the Holocaust. There are hints of redemption and hope in *The Commissar*, but they're the consequence of common humanity, not Soviet ideology.

Between 1918 and 1920, the Russian lands were devastated by civil war as the Bolsheviks secured their revolution by force. The Revolution of October 1917 was a *coup d'état* that possessed some democratic credentials: the country unmistakably turned socialist during 1917, even if there was no national majority for the extremist variant of socialism put forward by Lenin's party. For many of its proponents, the October Revolution promised a democracy of liberation and dignity, but events showed that its democracy was that of implied violence: of the loudest shouts in the crowd, and the elimination of opposing points of view.

The Russian Civil War, during which both sides terrorized opponents, murdered innocent bystanders, and requisitioned grain, always without limits, anticipated the mass destructiveness of Stalinism fifteen years hence, and learned from the political violence of fifteen years earlier. It magnified the assassinations, uprisings and state reaction that surrounded the Revolution of 1905, as well as the mass violence of the First World War and the murderous rhetoric of the revolutionary year of 1917. One historian describes a 'continuum of violence' that stretches across the period from 1905 to 1921. Some of its features looked Russian, others had a Marxist tint, but above all it was a modern phenomenon.[42] It gathered momentum thanks to the technologies of food requisitioning that the tsarist state used during the First World War, as well as its methods of cataloguing the population by such criteria as name, gender, ethnicity, tax status and address, which made possible the labelling and rounding-up of 'enemies' and their easier transfer to refugee camps.[43] These were wartime phenomena, owing something to modern developments elsewhere, such as the Defence of the Realm Act in Britain, which in 1916 greatly increased the power of the UK state, and the formation of the FBI in the USA. Government in Russia learned from foreign examples, and made its own contribution to the universal trend. As a result, the violence of the Russian Civil War was nothing if not the ugly side of modernity. But it could not have happened without Lenin and Trotsky, and the White leaders, such as Kolchak. This was not an explosion of ancient Russian hatreds or a magnification of the barba-rism of the Russian village writ large. Neither of these existed in a measure greater than anywhere else in Europe. Proponents of the Russia Anxiety should remember how quickly any society can disin-tegrate when processes that take place in all modern societies combine with a contingent crisis, and a particular collection of personalities have the gifts and skills to take advantage.

Askoldov wanted to make a film about the violence in which Soviet power was forged. A female commissar, Vavilova, has served in the Russian Civil War with courage and strength at the head of a detach-ment of Red soldiers. They have taken the town of Berdichev. But she is heavily pregnant. She is billeted with a Jewish family, who are angry at the huge reduction in their living space: young mother, grandmother and blacksmith father now sleep in one room with their many children, while the commissar takes the other. Yet they come to protect Vavilova when they discover her pregnancy. They cherish the little boy when he is born, and the commissar herself begins to imag-ine a life of motherhood alongside them, beyond the Red Army. But the Whites are still nearby. The news comes that they are about to launch an attack to retake the city. Residents spend the day before the onslaught hunkering down. While they are doing so, the children play at enacting a pogrom.

Meanwhile, Yefim, the blacksmith, is putting up makeshift barri-cades around his modest property. 'I must tell you, Madame Vavilova,' he says, 'this is the best time for the people. One power has gone and the next hasn't yet arrived. No contributions, no pogroms.'

Modern violence in the twentieth century was unleashed most unstoppably in Germany and Russia. Yefim and his family faced the results of both. He carried on talking to the commissar, as he ham-mered planks of wood across the gate: 'I tell you, when a new power comes, first it says that everything will be fine, then it says that things have got worse, then it says we've got to find those who are guilty. And' – he asks in the Russian way – 'who's guilty in this life? Who?'

There are two great Russian questions: who is guilty, and what is to be done. Although the mass violence of the Stalin period was a Soviet phenomenon, and had no direct causes in the deep history of Russia, it was still shaped by Russian people and their culture. When the secret policemen denied Alexander Askoldov's mother her dignity by watching her undress in front of them, they did so because she was an enemy of the people, a label which they viewed through a Russian lens. She was one of the guilty ones. As the fate of the Askoldov family showed, however, guilt was nearly always something ascribed to the innocent.

During the Civil War, Reds and Whites alike ran their own programmes of terror, sweeping up potential opponents, torturing known enemies, razing villages. Hundreds of thousands were killed in atrocities that were fired by ideology, racial prejudice, class hatred, military exigency and specific contexts of the Civil War rather than some kind of Russian national character. The Bolsheviks continued after the Civil War had ended. Political violence flowed naturally out of the Revolution. Laws of 1921 and 1922 targeted non-Bolshevik socialists for arrest and extended detention before trial. In January 1922, the Cheka was repackaged as the OGPU, the 'political administration' arm of the People's Commissariat of Internal Affairs (or NKVD). The aim of the organizational change was to promote more thorough and effective surveillance and coercion. When the Soviet Union formally came into being in 1922, its Criminal Code included Article 58, defining political and counter-revolutionary crimes. Article 58 was the legal basis of much of the Great Terror and the dramatic expansion of the Gulag in the 1930s.[44]

Yet the 1920s also indicated that a different path was possible, and that the Russian Revolution contained within it multiple possible futures. The atrocities of the Civil War were largely coterminous with the fighting itself. When the Party purged itself, as it did, for example, in August 1921, the aim was not to eliminate and kill, but to systematize membership rolls that had got out of control during the Civil War, to cut out double counting and to deprive of Party cards those opportunists who had joined during chaotic times, despite demonstrably lacking a commitment to Bolshevik principles. More generally, the period of the New Economic Policy was not unmarked by diversity and pluralism. This was evident in the overlapping Soviet worlds of urban trade, high and popular culture, village life and the exchange of ideas, all of which unfolded in part beyond the Bolshevik gaze. Between 1922 and 1927, the annual number of people who received custodial sentences for political crimes ranged from 2,336 to 7,547, whereas in the 1930s it was usually above 100,000 and sometimes above 400,000.[45]

Even in the middle of the most terrible half-century, therefore, there were peaks and troughs of violence. For quite extended periods, it seemed that the direction of Russian or Soviet life had changed. Between 1904 and 1953, violence was not consistently encoded into Russian and Soviet politics; even at this time, it was not an inevitable outgrowth of the Russian experience of modernity. Instead, it took Stalin to write the most terrible chapter yet in the period's chronicle of political violence.

Stalin became increasingly powerful as the 1920s wore on. Among all his contemporaries, he was the most effective politician, the most charismatic patron, the toughest enforcer, the clearest communicator. He was not the grey nonentity of Trotskyite legend. Instead, he accrued power in a brilliantly systematic way. By the late 1920s, he was the most powerful figure in Soviet politics, impossible to remove, and the subject of a growing cult of personality. He used this position to articulate a far-Left interpretation of revolutionary progress. Out went the compromises of the New Economic Policy; in came the five-year plans, with their collectivization of agriculture and breakneck industrialization. At the end of the 1920s, the Soviet Union was upended by mass mobility, as the migration of millions of peasants to cities began, and by social mobility at a pace that was unprecedented perhaps anywhere in history, as the most modest factory workers and just-migrated former peasants raced up the career ladder. Thanks to the explosion of new factories and jobs, many became managers and technical professionals. This 'Stalin revolution' was administered by a growing state apparatus, animated by ideological enthusiasm, typified, on the ground, by chaos and misery, and bolstered, increasingly, by the demands of political conformity. It was the 'great break' in Soviet life.

The Stalinist order engaged in the most dramatic process of creation and destruction. Its vision of a communist utopia was given energy not by harmony but by violence. The collectivization of agriculture was a 'civil war against the peasantry'. The peasants' consistent wish to be autonomous was violated. Their traditions, embodied in the self-governing commune, were liquidated. The very slightly more prosperous among them (the so-called 'kulaks') were arrested, shot or exiled. Grain was ripped from children's hands, and famine spread across parts of the Ukrainian, Kazakh and Russian republics. In the Ukrainian republic alone, 3.9 million people died in a process labelled the *Holodomor* (terror-famine). (Some historians call the Ukrainian famine a genocide, arguing that Stalin deliberately sought to destroy an ethnic group in whole or part, but the evidence for this motive, unlike for the numbers of victims, is disputed, and it remains one of the most politicized issues in the historiography of Soviet life; more of this in chapter 7.)[46] Meanwhile, cities grew at a rapid pace, some springing out of nothing. Migrant workers slept in barracks, tents and on factory floors; bunks might be time-shared by shift. New factories were put together so quickly that industrial accidents were an epidemic.

Agricultural and industrial modernization caused millions of casualties in the 1930s. The process illustrated the ethics and mood of Stalinism, prefiguring the great political violence that was about to break out. It also explains its likely cause, and why people like Askoldov's father, a factory boss, were victims.

When Sergei Kirov, the Leningrad Party leader, was shot dead by a lone assassin in December 1934, Stalin took full advantage. He explained the shocking event with reference to an imaginary conspiracy, which he then crushed without mercy. The middle 1930s were characterized by a growing emphasis on purity – of belief, expression, behaviour – in Soviet life. Past events in one's biography could come back to haunt one. There were Party purges, whose expellees were not yet shot, and show trials. Between 1936 and 1938, the process escalated. Party functionaries, industrial managers and professional people were targeted; ordinary citizens were swept up; orders were sent out to arrest members of particular ethnic groups, such as Poles and Koreans; local branches of the NKVD were given targets and invited to exceed them. In all, 692,000 people were shot, typically on trumped-up charges of espionage, industrial wrecking, ideological transgression or orchestrating far-fetched conspiracies.

The Great Terror of 1936–8 – to Russian people, 'the repressions', or '1937' – seems to defy explanation. Why, for example, execute hundreds of senior army officers if you are worried about a Nazi invasion? Historians have argued that the Terror might have had different causes.[47] Perhaps it was the work of a deranged Stalin, making use of unlimited power; perhaps it was driven from below, by denouncers and collaborators robbed of moral sensibility by totalitarianism, driven to ideological frenzy by the promises of the extreme Left, or pushed on by fear or ambition; perhaps it showed that Nazi Germany and the Soviet Union were really the same place, not least because ethnic identity became an important factor as the Terror went on; perhaps it was the latest chapter in a political history of violent cabals.

None of these explanations is wholly correct. The Great Terror started and stopped because Stalin ordered the NKVD to get on with and then desist from its work, and in that sense it was never out of control, but was personally directed from the top. Stalin was driven by ideology, politics and the brutal logic of administration, not to mention great personal cruelty – but not by madness.[48] Terror gained force because ordinary people denounced their neighbours or bosses, but such behaviour was sporadic and not the Terror's origin. The repressions were a strike against the body politic, an act of vicious self-harm. They were not an aggressive push outwards, of the type that Europe's fascists aspired to. And they came out of a unique political system, the world's first socialist state.

Stalin stood at the apex of this system, uneasily calculating how to preserve the revolutionary state that the Bolsheviks had been building since 1917 against any reasonable odds. By 1936, the top Bolsheviks knew two things. First, the achievements of collectivization and industrialization were self-evident. Second, these achievements were self-evidently vulnerable. They could still not believe their luck in rising to power; their sense of the world was shaped by chance and risk. For one leading historian of the Terror with an eye for a paradox, Stalin was in command of a strong state, capable of turning society on its head, but a state which to him looked weak, beset by enemies on the borders, in the Party, and in the heartlands. Capitalists and fascists were waiting to invade. After all, Franco's conspirators had just risen up against Spain's progressive republican government and started the Civil War, and Hitler's hatred of Bolsheviks and Slavs was clear for everyone to see. Meanwhile, any shortfalls in the economic plans – so carefully designed, so well informed by Marx – could surely only be caused by conspiracy, so there must be spies and wreckers in the factories. Enemies of the people were everywhere. The NKVD gathered intelligence about all this. Their agents' training and ideological sympathies – their basic *raison d'être* – required them to expose the existence of enemies. Stalin read their reports. His conclusions made sense in the context of his worldview and the flawed information that was presented to him. In the strange world of the Soviet 1930s, but not before or after, unrestrained judicial killing, whose causes looked incomprehensible to outsiders, possessed their own logic to the executioners, especially the dictator who oversaw the process.[49]

While the Great Terror would never be repeated, the population of the Gulag continued to grow. At the time of the Terror, the great majority of people convicted for political crimes under Article 58 were shot, and the population of the Gulag was relatively stable, around three-quarters of a million in total, mostly made up of apparently ordinary criminals. By 1941, however, it had doubled in size, with nearly one-third of the inmates 'politicals'. It contracted during the war, until its population was little more than half a million in 1946. In line with old Russian traditions, the authorities called an amnesty at the time of victory: many were released, and the judiciary was apparently more lenient – though the flow into the Gulag did not stop. Thereafter the number of convicts rose relentlessly, reaching a peak of almost 1.75 million in 1953, when Stalin died. At this point, one-quarter were inside for counter-revolutionary crimes; in 1947, of a population of just over 600,000, half had been politicals.[50] Meanwhile, by 1953, a further 750,000 arrestees were trapped in so-called special settlements: brutal townships which they had been forced to build themselves.[51]

Not separate from Soviet society but deeply intertwined within it, the camps conformed to many of the system's ideological precepts. They had the same functions as society as a whole: to create a secure, future-facing workers' state driven by an industrial economy, where all right-thinking people were convinced communists, and enemies had been eliminated. Even though death rates in the camps were very high, many prisoners were given a chance to recant. The Stalinist project destroyed while it created, killed while it redeemed. While the Gulag was at the sharp edge of this destructiveness, and was often characterized by the most extreme brutality, this double ambition was its mission too.[52] In such ways it differed from the concentration camps of Nazi Germany, where the possibility of redemption and reforging did not exist. It also differed from its forerunners. The Siberian incarceration system of nineteenth-century Russia, cruel for sure, bore little resemblance to the Gulag. Locations could be the same, and sometimes the extent of brutality was similar. But in imperial Russia the numbers were much smaller, the economy was different, the ideological coercion was absent.

Although one can draw out the origins and consequences of Stalinist violence, it was strikingly of its time. It had no forerunners in Russian history and it never recurred. Even in the late Stalinist period, the post-war years of 1945–53, political killings were much reduced. While political terror was still arbitrary, and the moral value of each individual case was the same as before, the overall scope of violence was now precisely controlled and carefully limited. The 'Leningrad Affair' of 1948–50 was the stand-out post-war case: a terrifying purge that ripped through the political elite of the second Soviet city. It led to about 200 executions, vastly fewer than during the Great Terror. Stalin's Terror must remain a warning, a set of lessons. But misreading these lessons, and constantly imagining that the past is about to repeat itself, is also risky. After all, the 1930s were not even a precedent for the 1940s. It is almost impossible to see how Stalinism's combination of extremist ideology, police power, state-building, social flux, long-term brutalization, popular mobilization, and personal dictatorship in a closed-off society could have any explanatory power for twenty-first century Russia, which is not to say that bad things won't or don't happen. Recognizing this might damp down the Russia Anxiety a bit.

Huddling in the cellar as the Whites bombard the town, Yefim and the other adults comfort the children. In a lull, Vavilova points out that the Reds are fighting for the future, for the destruction of the old ways. For her, religion and tradition are fairy tales, supporting repressive property relations and class injustice. But Yefim is bemused and angry too. 'If you take fairy tales away from people,' he asks her, 'how would you tell them what to live for?'

'People don't need fairy tales,' she replies. 'People need the truth, for which they wouldn't complain about dying!'

'To die?' asks Yefim. 'And when will they live?'

Yefim's story seems born out of centuries of Eurasian suffering: Russian, Ukrainian and Jewish. But it took place at a very specific moment, in the heart of the Russian lands' most terrible half-century. This violence emerged from 'modernity' more than it did from Russia itself: it belonged in the modern spectrum of administrative and technological 'practices', though it took on a Russian form. But political leaders designed the policies, built up the forces, and made the ideological weather that could make the storm of violence happen.

There are two facts about Stalinism. First, it was one of the most terrible phenomena in human history. Second, it ended. There was a dreadful continuation of Stalinism in some parts of Soviet-dominated Eastern Europe – it never ceased in communist Romania, for example – but in the Soviet Union, Stalinism effectively ended on 5 March 1953, when Stalin died, and the half-century of unlimited violence came to a close. Askoldov probably didn't mean it like this, but the answer to Yefim's question – 'when will they live?' – would be: after Stalin had gone.

# THE END OF THE WORST HALF-CENTURY

Stalin's demise was a life-and-death moment not only for the dictator himself, but for tens of millions of people. Take the story of another little boy – Pasha.[53]

His family's great fear unfolded during their longest day and night. It was the post-war Stalinist period. Pasha was six years old and at kindergarten in Moscow (where children start school at six or seven). One morning, invited by his teacher to utter some pleasantry about

Stalin, he refused. He stood on his chair so that his voice would carry better. 'Lenin is better than Stalin!' he declared, having little idea why he said it. Then he said it again.

The children around showed only passing interest, but the teacher turned ashen. She looked at Pasha, first mournfully, then with fear, then with resentment. She spoke to the director of the kindergarten. The child's parents were called. When they eventually arrived, having made feeble excuses to their bosses, they took their son home early. They were as terrified and exhausted as the kindergarten staff.

In the main room of their flat in central Moscow – they had their own apartment, and enjoyed a decent standard of living – the young parents sat in silence with their small child. The clock ticked. Nobody was hungry, apart from the boy. Of course he sensed their fear and could still feel it decades later. But he still went to the kitchen with his mother and ate a bowl of buckwheat. He went to bed, and his mother tossed and turned in the same room.

His father sat up all night. He didn't even remove his coat. The curtains did not quite meet in the middle of the window. A small bag with a change of clothes and a bar of soap was at his feet. No doubt he rehearsed his explanation in his mind. How could it have been that his son came up with such a form of words, his interrogators would ask him. What have you been saying? Who've you been saying it to? Is it because you're a Jew? All night he waited for a knock on the door.

But the knock on the door never came. Scattered light started to shine through the gap in the curtains. It showed up the dust on the floor. Pasha came in, yawning. It was 6 March 1953. The world was about to hear that Stalin had died the day before. So perhaps the secret police never heard about the incident. They certainly had other priorities. The Soviet Union was about to change for ever. Its Stalinist chapter was over. A new Soviet Union was coming into being. The prospects for Pasha's family, like those of families across the USSR, were changed out of recognition by Stalin's demise. Their family would not be ripped in two by a stray childish comment in a kinder-garten, repeated from a whispered kitchen conversation, overheard when the boy woke up the night before and wanted a drink of water. No longer would political violence define the Soviet Union.

Vladimir Putin was not yet five months old. This was the world he was born into: the aftermath of violence, when Soviet society attempted to come to terms with what had happened.

Immediately after Stalin died, the Bolsheviks dismantled their system of violence. Not completely: many camps remained, and some prisoners, such as the dissident Anatoly Marchenko, endured experiences that replicated those of the Stalin period. But the system was dramatically reduced in size and transformed in function. Many people were released. For those who remained, most of whom were regular criminal convicts, conditions usually improved considerably. Outside, the experience of arbitrary arrest became rare. People were now pretty sure that if they didn't talk out of turn they could live to some extent as they pleased – though they were very unlikely to be able to travel abroad, and had to put up with censored media and economic shortages. Still, the rules of how to live were clearer. Arbitrary rule, and Stalin-style political violence, had gone.

No one expressed the transformation more dramatically than Lavrenty Beria. Beria had been Stalin's secret police chief for nearly fifteen years, since the Terror had consumed his predecessor, Nikolai Yezhov. He had built a massive empire, running the Gulag, managing the nuclear weapons programme and eliminating enemies. He knew where all the bodies were buried. He was personally cruel, too, kidnapping and raping young women.[54] No wonder his colleagues were so afraid of what he might know about them and of what he could do to them.

Beria understood the limits of Soviet power and his ability to shape them for his own benefit. The Gulag was probably still economically viable, and Beria had not become a man of peace, so it was the perception of political advantages that made him press so quickly for reform. He argued in spring 1953 in favour of a Gulag amnesty, and also for a more conciliatory attitude in Cold War diplomacy. Within less than a year, from 1 July 1953 to 1 April 1954, the population of the Gulag and special settlements fell by half, to 1.27 million. Big Gulag projects, such as a major railway line in north-western Siberia, were immediately suspended.[55] But on 26 June 1953, Beria's two rivals for power, Georgyi Malenkov and Nikita Khrushchev, struck, theatrically arresting him during a Presidium (Politburo) meeting. He was executed in secret at the end of the year.

Beria's demise was the last major act of Stalinist political violence. The reforms he cynically proposed were amplified over the next two years. They were given ideological clarity and political direction by the most dramatic moment of the post-Stalin years, the Secret Speech of February 1956, when Khrushchev, now dominant, confirmed the course of de-Stalinization. The Secret Speech, which we will return to in more detail in chapter 9, transformed the Soviet Union. The Communist Party still gripped power and controlled a police state. But for the vast majority of the population – and there were exceptions, not least in the western borderlands – a kind of normal life began, though one that continued to be shaped in part by economic shortages and relative isolation from the outside world.

Alexander Askoldov made *The Commissar* in 1967, three years after Khrushchev had been deposed by Brezhnev's clique. In those early Brezhnev years, there was scope for artistic experimentation, but the artist had to know how to work with the authorities.

Askoldov refused to do that. His film was uncompromising. It did not even pay lip service to the aesthetic of socialist realism, which, officially at least, still governed Soviet cultural production. There was no trajectory from loss to hope, mediated by class triumph and social-ist power. Askoldov made the Civil War seem pointlessly barbaric, and he implied certain equivalences between the Whites and the Reds. At the end of the film, while the family is holding out in the cellar, there is a fantasy sequence in which Vavilova looks on while Yefim and his family, and all the other Jews of the town, are rounded up. Dressed in prison clothes and Jewish stars, they are herded towards a camp. What to make of this foretelling of the Holocaust by a Civil War commissar? At the very least, it raised problematic ques-tions about Jewish life in the USSR that by the late 1960s were better ignored.

And there was a final twist. When morning came, Vavilova let her-self out of the cellar. She understood that the Reds were evacuating the town. It was a moment of agony for her. She had to choose between joining them, so that she would get the chance to fight another day, and staying with her baby. If she left, she might also help her protectors: under the impending White occupation, sheltering a Red commissar was an obvious capital crime. But if she stayed, she had a chance to raise her boy. She pulled on the remnants of her uniform and her commissar's overcoat, placed the baby on the ground, shouted out to Maria, Yefim's wife, and ran off. Emerging into the morning light, cradling the Bolshevik child, the Jewish couple wondered – with curiosity, not condemnation – what sort of person would do that. What kind of alien force were these Bolsheviks?

It was an open-and-shut case for the State Cinema Authority. *The Commissar* could not be salvaged. There was no chance it could ever be shown. The censors said that the film portrayed the Bolshevik Revolution as 'a force that opposes the very essence of human existence, a phenomenon that destroys personal ties by causing alienation, despair, and uncertainty about the future'.[56] Askoldov was prevented from working as a film director, exiled from Moscow, removed from Party membership. It was a career catastrophe and a personal disaster. But it was a different fate from his father's: no arrest in the middle of the night, no bullet in the back of the head. In 1967, it had been possible to make *The Commissar*, with all its personal vision and subversive potential, using the facilities of one of the country's most famous film institutions, the Maxim Gorky Studios, and employing some of the country's greatest actors and actresses, imagining that it might be shown in some form in cinemas. In retrospect, it seems less important that the film was banned than that it was made. Stalinism had plainly gone.

The Russian Revolution would have contrasting futures ahead of it. It was born in violence, and its first goal was the elimination of its enemies with extreme prejudice. Yet it promised liberation. It turned the world upside down, creating winners and losers. In time it gave Pasha and millions of others the chance to live in a kind of peace and normality, at least without fear of arrest. There was not even much need to conform: just to keep quiet. Askoldov, of course, crossed the wrong line. When the film was banned, he protested, appealed to the authorities, 'knocked at all sorts of doors'. But it was only during the Gorbachev era that he got the chance to stand up for his film in public. In the context of reform and openness, *perestroika* and *glasnost*, books by the likes of Boris Pasternak and Vasily Grossman were emerging from the hidden archives of the KGB. Askoldov had to fight for it, even in 1987, but *The Commissar* was finally shown at home and abroad, to rapturous acclaim.

The searing experience of his mother's arrest gave Aksoldov his personal insight, at full magnification, into the Stalinist dictatorship. But that terrible night, when he learned to lace up his boots and make his own way to safety, was not the last time he saw her. Unlike his father, she was not shot. Instead, she was sent to a camp.

Her medical qualifications, at a premium during the wartime emergency, saved her. Four years after her arrest, she was freed, and was given the opportunity to redeem herself by serving the country in the army. She came back to Moscow, and mother and son were briefly reunited. Now she abandoned him in a different way. 'My own mother, a military doctor, left me alone to go to the front,' he told an interviewer in 1988.[57]

What was the difference between Comrade Vavilova and Comrade Askoldova, the commissar and the physician? They both left their sons. Vavilova chose to. Askoldova had no choice. Vavilova participated in building the Soviet dictatorship. Askoldova was victimized by it. Vavilova was a true believer who thought that destruction could lead to creation. Askoldova, whatever her beliefs, can scarcely have thought that. They both wore the uniform of Soviet power during its most violent incarnations, in the Civil War and the Stalin period respectively. Who was the victim and who was the perpetrator? They were fighting for different things. But how do you tell the difference so many decades later?

The question is more important than the answer. There is no answer. If you've asked the question seriously, if you've paused, looked away, and really thought about it – if you've removed yourself from the equation and treated these people on their own terms – then you're free of the Russia Anxiety.

# 6

# The Europe Question

## Has Russia Ever Been Part of the West?

On 12 May 1914, Natalia Goncharova caught a train out of Moscow for Warsaw, ultimate destination Paris. She took a berth in a second-class carriage with her companion, Mikhail Larionov. On arrival, they stayed in the Hotel Helder. They were in Paris to work on the sets and costumes of Sergei Diaghilev's popular *Ballets russes*.[1] Goncharova was perhaps even more distinguished than her partner. Fêted at home and abroad, no artist was more insistently Russian, and yet so emphatically European. It is a logically consistent identity – not twin-tracks of a double life – that the Russia Anxiety cannot understand.

Goncharova and Larionov stayed together for the rest of their lives, and were two of the greatest Russian artists of the day. Despite the usual constraints imposed by her gender, Goncharova had already enjoyed formidable success: only in her early thirties, she had displayed her work in some of the most famous exhibitions of the day, *The Donkey's Tail* in 1912, *The Target* in 1913 and *No. 4* in 1914. She had been the subject of two major exhibitions in her own right, in 1913 in Moscow and in 1914 in St Petersburg. Together with such artists as Liubov Popova and Varvara Stepanova, she was part of a self-conscious group of 'amazons' that made the Russian avant-garde so distinctive in all senses.[2] In the few years before the First World War, Russia's avant-garde swept across Europe, accumulating brilliant reviews and astonished audiences, and shifting the continent's cultural centre of gravity due east. No wonder that France's leading poet, Apollinaire, was so interested in her, recognizing her cultural dominance. 'Madame Goncharova, it seems, is the head of the Russian school of futurists,' noted the mercurial and ebullient Apollinaire, ever on the look-out for the curious and the exciting, and a partisan for international futurist art.[3] It was no mean feat for this female artist to be seen at the top of her profession.

Kazimir Malevich – famous, despite the brilliant variety of his vision and gifts, for his dull, eponymous *Black Square* of 1915 – defined the quest of Goncharova and her fellow avant-garde artists when he wrote that 'the art of naturalism is the savage's idea'; art 'derives not from the interrelation of form and colour, and not on the basis of aesthetic taste . . . but on the basis of weight, speed and direction of movement'.[4] Like other masters of abstraction, Goncharova harnessed these forces, deploying colours, lines and shapes in vivid ways that made audiences gasp, in such compositions as *Yellow and Green Forest*, *Cats* and *Emptiness* (all three painted in 1913). Such paintings depicted the essence of a subject without representing it in an immediately recognizable way. They were universally modern, equally available to all modern consumers of art, regardless of national origin, and were not limited by the references of a particular national culture. Goncharova's subjects deliberately looked to the future: *The Cyclist*, *Electric Lamp*, *Aeroplane over a Train*. Deliberately throwing off the backward-looking and the local, the avant-garde from Russia was, by definition, European.

But Goncharova was not satisfied with exclusively abstract forms or a deracinated vision. Ever since the turn of the twentieth century, she had brought together Russian traditions with universal motifs and techniques. She and others like her, not least Larionov, borrowed from the universal 'visual language' of modernism in its fauvist, expressionist and cubist forms, while going back to Russian traditions such as the *lubok* (the painted signboard), the decorations and designs of village life and, above all, icons.[5] 'Hitherto I have studied all that the West could give me, but in fact, my country has created everything that derives from the West,' she wrote in the catalogue to her Moscow exhibition of 1913. 'Now I shake the dust from my feet and leave the West, considering its vulgarizing significance trivial and insignificant – my path is toward the source of all arts, the East.' This eastward orientation was both a national and artistic statement. 'The art of my country is incomparably more profound and important than anything I know in the West,' she went on.[6]

Brought up in a prosperous home deep in the countryside, she was drawing on her intuitive interaction with peasant culture, her knowledge of folklore and her immersion in icon painting.[7] Her madonnas and angels came in different forms, but they sought to convey spiritual energy and holy beauty in a Russian key.[8] Meanwhile, she and others made a parallel set of assumptions about Russia's Asian hinterland and empire. Alexander Shevchenko's *Neoprimitivism* manifesto of 1913, a product of this artist's Ukrainian, Russian and 'Eastern' heritage, influenced Goncharova. For him, Western art and Russian culture alike derived from the East. Byzantines, Armenians, Georgians and Tartars had shaped the process. The ultimate source lay in an abstracted 'Asia'.

And yet for all the Russian, Eurasian and Eastern dimensions of Goncharova's work, it is unmistakably part of the single European currency of the avant-garde. The most Russian of Russia's modern artists was European.

Like an elephant viewed from a few feet away, Russia is not seen clearly by its neighbours, whether those in the Baltic and the middle of Europe, or those in the West. Like a massive elephant, it seems frightening and alien, unattractive and undignified, even if it hints at something exotic. It's not like them (the Poles, the Balts); and not quite like 'us' (the Germans, the British) either. Countries that are more distant and more likely to disrupt the status quo, such as India, or perhaps more threatening, such as China, are often perceived in an entirely different way, judged according to a different index. The first might be a tiger, and the second a dragon, but, however you try, you can't really worry about them. This problem of perspective is a feature of the Russia Anxiety.

Yet it is possible to place Russia inside its European heritage while also acknowledging it has some Asian roots. This chapter looks at the lives of those who, like Goncharova, stand at the apex of Europe and Eurasia, of West and East. And it challenges the assumption that 'the West', for all its significance, can ever be a unitary set of values and interests that exist in contradistinction to Russia. True enough, there have been many Russians, like Goncharova, who have revelled in their identity as Europe's other, denying their European identity when it suited them. Yet while Russia might be Eurasian and Eastern, it's nothing if not Western, too, with a sensibility that is unmistakably European.

But like the English judge who pointed out that income tax is a tax on income, we should begin by remembering that Russia is Russian.

## UNIQUELY BASIL

Stand in the middle of Red Square, and stare straight at St Basil's Cathedral.

St Basil's is an obvious signifier of Russia and its traditions, so famous that it symbolically substitutes for Russia in the world's imagination. Yet it's not only familiar: it's exotic. Dating from the reign of Ivan the Terrible, it hints at fear. It was built as the Kazan Cathedral, offering thanks for Ivan's conquest of the great Muslim city, and named after Vasily – Basil – the Blessed, a 'holy fool' to whom the victory was symbolically owed. St Basil's has nine tent roofs topped with onion domes; the roofs are not organized symmetrically and the domes are decorated with multi-coloured swirls, studs, and other devices. But you know this: a written description of St Basil's is an otiose thing.

For all the familiarity of the St Basil's ensemble, there are two specific things about it that are distinctively Russian, or rather Muscovite, and which show that it could not belong to anywhere else. The first is the tents, and the second is the domes. These two architectural forms emerged in the 'Russian north' in the late medieval period after the fall of Kievan Rus. They have their analogues elsewhere. They derive in part from interactions with other civilizations. Together, though, they made for a unique way of imagining Church architecture. This was a different way from their Byzantine predecessors, with their heavy domes, and it was different, too, from the spires of Western European churches. The tent tower was a wooden structure defined by its vertical orientation, pointing towards heaven, and by its practical utility, preventing snow from piling up anywhere on the building. Onion domes, thick around the middle, had the same advantage, and they added a dramatic and prayerful intervention on the horizon.[9]

This civilization of the tent and the onion dome was shaped in

Muscovy's powerful monastic foundations. The most famous monastery was that of St Sergius of Radonezh, founded in remote forests to the north-east of Moscow in 1337 and dedicated to the Holy Trinity. It was in such monasteries, located in isolated surroundings, on the tough frontiers of Muscovy, amid a harsh climate, that the doctrine of Hesychasm became dominant.[10] This approach to the Christian life was ascetic and autonomous. It fostered direct communication with God, out of the reach of those higher up the religious hierarchy, not least those Orthodox superiors far away from Muscovy, and had few foundations – or barriers between believer and God – in classical learning. Muscovite monasticism was practical and political, too, as these monks pushed back the frontiers of Muscovy, 'colonizing' their surroundings for economic advantage, and thereby contributing to the expulsion of the Mongols in the fifteenth century. This was a particularly Muscovite version of Orthodoxy. It drew on the example of monks who in the fourteenth century were fleeing the encroachment of Islam into the Balkan heartlands of the Orthodox faith; Christian Byzantium's final collapse was not far off, in 1453. But its specific qualities, and its role in making the political future, were particularly Muscovite, even forming the basis of a specific proto-Russian ideology. Leading monks mediated between the monasteries and the centre of political power in Moscow. As we've seen, Ivan the Terrible understood power partly in monastic, or perhaps pseudo-monastic, ways. He searched for consolation at the Belo'ozero monastery, founded twenty years after St Sergius's, and further to the north. He conceived of the separateness of the *oprichnina*, and even the dress of the *oprichniki*, after a monastic example. In the end, the influence of the Muscovite church was challenged by Tsar Alexei Mikhailovich (or Alexis), and secular power triumphed over the patriarch in 1667. But the Orthodoxy that defined itself in distinction to Catholicism after the Schism of 1054 developed its own form in Muscovy between then and 1667. It is impossible to detect specific connections between that religious history and today's Russian society outside of Church life itself. But that doesn't matter: the tent and the onion dome show that a *sui generis* Russia exists.

The 'uniquely Basil' institutions that determined people's lives on a day-by-day basis, however, were more local than monasteries. They were not directly touched by the dialogue between high-flying monks and the grand prince (later the tsar). In fact, to some extent, they existed in contradistinction to 'power', though the Speransky Conundrum periodically found ways of moderating the demands of the autocracy. The village *mir* in particular was an incubator of a multiplicity of local Russian ways of understanding the world. Orthodoxy was at the heart of this world view, though one that resulted more from a dialogue between peasant and priest than cosmopolitan monk and national ruler. Yet both these dialogues were, in effect, discussions about the specific content of a Russian mentality.

And one could go back thousands of years to speculate on the root of this mentality. Further back than the tent and the onion dome were the forest and the steppe. Tribes – ultimately, the Slavs themselves – crossed the steppe lands in the south over perhaps 1,500 years, in a process that was sometimes one of violent colonization. This shadowy history has been explained by cultural symbols: the *bogatyr* is the knightly hero on horseback who emerged from the forest to face down invaders, and the flying serpent is the inexorable force that spread across the steppes. The steppe was the location in which early tribes, from Scythians to Cimmerians and others, came to the future Russian lands, bringing both violence and a contribution to the ethnic melting pot. If they were symbolic birds of prey, the forest of the north was filled with elks, on the defensive, and the incubator of an older and more local heritage. Forests were also filled with berries, mushrooms and bears, and were a place of resilience. The steppe offered dynamism but was beset by sudden violence. People and their allies in nature endured in the freezing, sometimes frightening forest.[11]

Russia has special claims to fame. As the biggest country in the world, its sum of unique characteristics is vast – from landscape to culture, from cuisine to customs, from sayings to habits – but might be summarized by an assumption in favour of taking one's interlocutor disarmingly seriously (an outlook otherwise known as the Russian soul). But every country and every civilization is unique. Russia is uniquely itself not just because of traditions or ways of thinking, of which St Basil's Cathedral symbolizes only the most high-blown and historically particular, and the forest and the steppe the most lyrical and allusive. Russia is also defined by its transnational qualities. Many

Russians explain Russia to themselves not by putting their backs to the frontier and staring towards the interior, but by facing outwards, looking beyond the border, and by being part of the world. This is not only a matter of borrowing or learning from others, and it goes far beyond trade and diplomacy. Deeply rooted in culture, it's a state of mind. But does this make Russia a European country, or is it just another way of saying that Russia is Russia, prone to be itself, and a natural subject of anxiety for outsiders?

## EUROPE'S RUSSIA

Why ask this question? Because Russia is European, but it looks like an exception. For instance, 'the West' and 'Europe' are not quite the same place, but they have sometimes seemed like that in the Russian historical imagination. Some countries – one thinks of the Netherlands – are unmistakably Western and European. Others, however, like Britain, might imagine themselves to be of the West but not of Europe; some places, especially on the southern or south-eastern periphery, are sure they are in Europe but have not always felt themselves entirely Western; while one or two, not least Turkey, have aspired at times to both identities without consistently assuming either. Russia sometimes seems the most complicated case of all. Its European identity has two halves. There is 'Europe's Russia', that we consider in this section, in which Russia owes its Europeannness to borrowing, openness and integration, to absorption or osmosis, affecting many aspects of life, from culture to finance. And there is 'Russia's Europe', the subject of the next section, which shows that Russia gives to Europe (and the West) and does not only receive, and that many of its European features are not borrowed, but are grown naturally from within.

Despite its political and cultural ubiquity, 'Europe' is not an obvious geographical entity. In his bestselling 'history of humankind', which takes its captivating view of the human past as if from a circling satellite, Yuval Noah Harari does not even much consider Europe, over millennia, as a separate continent, folding it instead within 'Asia-Africa'.[12] Europe is a modern concept, though it has a medieval forerunner – Christendom. Both of them have enjoyed credentials that derive from ancient Greece and Rome, in terms of values (law, democracy) and geopolitics (marking out the borders of civilization). For centuries, there have been quarrels about where civilization began and where it ended. It was not just an academic discussion. After all, barbarism teemed beyond the edges of 'Europe'. [13]

The problem with defining Europe, then, is firstly a matter of where to draw the boundaries. But the boundaries are not only external. There are internal borders too, which divide Europe up, both in hard politics and in our imaginations. These are often focused on the words 'East' and 'West'. During the Cold War, for instance, this division ran broadly down the middle of the continent, separating capitalist NATO from the communist Warsaw Pact. In the early twenty-first century, the lines of exclusion were more subtle. An idea of 'Eastern' Europe persisted in the imaginations of people in the 'West', while membership of 'Europe' became conflated with its big supranational institutions, especially the European Union.

Milan Kundera felt this controversy sharply and bitterly. Kundera is perhaps the greatest novelist from Czechoslovakia, a European country that no longer exists. Despite being a member of the Communist Party in the 1960s, he managed to satirize and condemn it, but after the Prague Spring of 1968, he was expelled from it. His books were banned, and he was eventually allowed to leave the country. He settled in France in 1975. For Kundera, his motherland and his adopted country were part of the same place: Western Europe. True, the ancient lands of the Germans, Czechs, Slovaks, Poles and Hungarians were geographically in the middle of Europe, but in a more profound sense they were entirely Western. This was because, he argued, they traced their shared history through ancient Rome and the Catholic Church, whereas the truly Eastern parts of Europe had their origins in Byzantium and Orthodoxy. In a literal and formally geographical sense, then, Russia might be a part of Europe, but only of a shadow-Europe. Russia's Europeanness was no more than an historical technicality, a mere accident of classification. '[N]othing could be more foreign to Central Europe and its passion for variety,' he wrote in 1986, 'than Russia: uniform, standardizing, centralizing.'[14]

Kundera, like all of us, should have the last word on his own experiences. His judgement of Soviet power in Czechoslovakia should stand on its own terms. Historians should not start to second-guess it. But we should challenge his understanding of Europe, his classification of Russia and his explanation of European history. Kundera offers only one incarnation of a much longer historic prejudice.

Imagine Europe as a sequence of slopes which have changed their position and direction over time, shifting the location of peaks and low-lying plains. Sometimes the biggest slope has been north–south, sometimes west–east, and sometimes a complicated combination of both. In every case, though, civilization lies in the upper reaches, and falls away with the gradient. It is as if Europeans can't imagine themselves without looking down on their barbaric neighbours or staring up at their more civilized betters.

As the Russian avant-garde reminded their audiences, the ultimate source of world civilization lay in the East. But it's the West that came to claim civilization for itself. The division between a 'civilized' West and a 'barbarous' East – the rhetorical fix that Kundera articulated – had distant forerunners, even underlying the ancient Greek cause in their Persian Wars during the fifth century BC. Later, membership of the Roman Empire came to mark the dividing lines of civilization: its enemies were literally known as barbarians. The Empire's boundaries, or *limes*, were far from a straightforward Iron Curtain down the middle of Europe, but they were still used in the twenty-first century as a very vague proxy for where 'European values' really belonged. When Rome came under intolerable strain in the fourth century AD, and the Empire was divided into western and eastern parts, the centre of civilizational gravity shifted east, to Byzantium, which soon became the sole successor to Roman power. Its wealth and cultural magnificence astonished visitors. But it was still of the East, a different type of civilization, Greek not Latin. Its Orthodoxy was viewed by the West as an inferior Christianity. In 988, it was Byzantine culture and Orthodox Christianity that came to Kievan Rus, placing the future Russia, Ukraine and Belarus in the cultural as well as the geographical East. As power shifted west again, 'Christendom' became the label for 'Europe', with many of its component states following the spiritual instructions of the pope in Rome, which had a powerful influence on politics. In the eleventh century, knights and soldiers from across Christendom came together to launch the first Crusade on the Holy Land, regardless of the kingdom of which they were a citizen. It was Catholicism versus Islam, but it was also a West–East strike. By the time of the Renaissance, the great civilizational divide seemed to run north–south. Italy was the focus of classical learning, new art and the wealthy networks that connected Europe with the outside world. The lands to the north still seemed barbarous, just as they had done when they had threatened Rome a millennium before. But by 1683, with the Turks at the gates of Vienna, the geographically long and enduring fighting frontier in Central and South-eastern Europe between the Christian Habsburgs and the Muslim Ottomans was another axis of civilization.

Europe's metaphorical slopes of imaginary civilization are not neat and tidy, then, or always easy to label, but they are suggestive of a mentally constructed 'East' and 'West' in Europe. It was during the Enlightenment that these mental constructions became clearly visible in people's minds and durable in politics. North-west Europe, not least Paris and London, was now the driving force of history. Travellers would reach the borderlands of Prussia and Poland, and take the next step eastwards – back into the past – with deep trepidation. For all their fascination with these places, writers like Rousseau, Diderot, and Voltaire marked them out as 'other', at best exotic. 'Eastern Europe', then, was an idea not made by Eastern Europeans – Kundera, after all, resented the idea that he might be such a person – nor was it a label that Russians invented to pin on their 'near abroad'. Instead, 'Eastern Europe' was a coinage created in Western Europe. Even then, though, the place of Russia was complicated, 'backward' and yet powerful, the combination which drove the contempt and fear of the Russia Anxiety.

Yet the division of Europe into an 'East' and a 'West' by the eighteenth century was not only a matter of imagination. The science and power of the West during the nineteenth century really did deepen the division, as industrial revolutions came first to some Western cities, though the East was often not that far behind. Empire and racism further put the East in its place, in practice and in theory. And then the Cold War provided the most brute demonstration of the real existence of an East and a West in Europe. Even as the European Union expanded eastwards from the early twenty-first century, Western Europeans found new ways to express their anti-Eastern prejudices against 'Polish plumbers', 'Balkan gypsies', let alone the new Russians.[15]

A single Europe stretches geographically from Ireland to Russia. But 'the West' goes as far as the political point that one wants to make. In a certain imagination, it stretches further, to Vladivostok, Melbourne, New York and Buenos Aires. 'The East', meanwhile, remains a source of danger to 'the West' in ways that transcend Europe. Russia is often a problem case. In *Orientalism*, Edward W. Said's influential book about the West's cultural and political subordination of the East, Russia seems to fit both sides: in cultural terms, it sometimes acted like the Western empires, imagining its Eastern territories in its own way and using the subjective knowledge it created to repress them; and yet it has also been 'orientalized' itself by the West, made 'other' and alien by Western policymakers with their own agendas.[16]

From the earliest times, the lands from which Russia grew were part of Europe, directly plugged into its institutions, power politics, trade and culture. In 1051, the daughter of Yaroslav the Wise of Kievan Rus married Henri I of France. True enough, many of the strongest connections went southwards rather than westwards. Kievan Rus had many links to Byzantium. But these ties were still European ones. Rus might not have been part of the Roman Empire, and it might have lurked, exposed, beyond the *limes*, but its encounter with the Roman Empire in Byzantium strengthened its European reach.

Rus existed in the 'Commonwealth' of Byzantium; it was part of Eastern Europe, with the religion of the region, many of its political rituals and an embedded place in trade and cultural exchange. But Rus also had a tangle of relationships across the whole of Europe. Vladimir Monomakh, one of the great rulers of Rus, was the grandson of Constantine IX, emperor of Byzantium. Around 1074, when he was in his early twenties, Vladimir married Gytha, who was the daughter of the doomed King Harold of England. He had been killed at the Battle of Hastings in 1066, after which the Normans took over the Anglo-Saxon kingdom. By a roundabout route, Gytha fled with other members of the family to Denmark. King Sweyn, who was her cousin, had relations with the court in Kiev and arranged Gytha's marriage to Vladimir, whose career generally made him a European figure. Not yet on the throne himself – his uncle Sviatoslav was grand prince of Kiev – Vladimir was sent to support the Polish king in his conflict with the Duke of Bohemia. The Rus forces did not fight, but Rus was involved, however marginally, in much bigger contests, which were ultimately wrapped up in Papal politics. After a long and bitter career of dynastic intrigue, family violence and rulership of one or other of the cities of Rus, Vladimir was eventually crowned as grand prince in Kiev in 1113. Later in his reign, frescoes were painted on the walls of the largest church in Kiev, St Sophia, that depicted Constantinople, and emphasized the influence and example of the Byzantine emperor in Rus, a point that Vladimir wanted to make clear. His life showed that Rus was a modest principality, but it was wired into the circuit of Christendom – European, before the term came much into use.[17]

In the middle ages, lands which would soon come under Muscovite control – many of which would later consider themselves heartlands of Russia to the west and south-west of the future capital – had been part of the Polish-Lithuanian Commonwealth at the same time that Moscow itself was under Mongol domination, so parts of the future Russia possessed non-Mongol European credentials. Meanwhile, towns in the north retained their links to the Hanseatic League and to the German lands, and were in a sense Baltic outposts. Hundreds of years before Peter the Great built westward-looking St Petersburg, parts of Rus had major westward ties. Novgorod was an *entrepôt*, a centre of imports from different parts of Europe (metals), not least the Baltic territories (amber), as well as the Caucasus (woods) and the Urals and further east (precious stones). In return, it exported fish, honey, wax and furs.[18] With the retreat of the Mongols, Muscovy took control of Novgorod in 1478. Trade through the Baltic was fundamental to its plans for the city. From the end of the fifteenth century, thanks to diplomatic exchanges between Muscovy and Sweden, Western European as well as Byzantine practices inflected the territory's coronation ceremony.[19] Meanwhile, Lithuania in the fourteenth century and then Poland-Lithuania from the end of the fourteenth until the start of the seventeenth century governed parts of western and south-western 'Russia'. This territory, including that of the future Ukraine, in a sense made Muscovy and then the Russian Empire more European, though in practice people's lives either side of any of these borders were not dissimilar.

From the middle of the sixteenth century, Muscovy was trading with England via a new White Sea route. The tsar granted the 'Muscovy Company' special tax status in 1555, a deal that was lucrative for both sides. The Dutch soon caught up, as trade with Western Europe became increasingly vigorous. In 1584, northern trade routes were more firmly secured with the foundation of the port city of Arkhangelsk. Visitors from Western Europe left physical and cultural traces, too. Italian architects contributed to the extension of the Moscow Kremlin during the reign of Ivan the Terrible. War also drove the interaction between Muscovy and its neighbours, increasing the circle of Muscovy's European relations, especially with Sweden and Poland-Lithuania. Towards the end of the Time of Troubles, around 1612, the King of England, James I, even considered intervening in the Muscovite civil wars.[20]

When it came to East–West ties, sixteenth-century outsiders saw Muscovy as a special case just as their descendants labelled Russia and the Soviet Union. Migrants tended to live in particular settlements, such as Moscow's Nemetskaya sloboda. This could be the result of a deliberate choice by Western expatriates, just as migrants often cluster today in communities; but the term *sloboda* referred to a settlement that was subject to a particular tax regime (and the adjective *nemetskaya*, which today refers to Germans, then simply meant 'for foreigners'). In terms of international comparisons, though, Muscovy was not an outlier in the way these living arrangements were designed. Take the example of the Massachusetts Bay Colony, which placed tougher limits on outsiders. When it came to taxation and trade, Muscovy was not exactly xenophobic. It was engaged. And it was not a case of Muscovite brutality versus Western civility. England and the Netherlands, its principal partners, were aggressively business-minded centres of ruthless merchantry rather than gentle proponents of transnational exchange. As Muscovy went about accumulating specie and developing mercantilist policies, it did so by dominating contiguous lands, which looked expansionist and aggressive to observers; England and Holland were maritime powers, exploiting territory that was far away, and exerting violence far from home that it was easier for such observers never to notice or conveniently to forget.[21]

The range of interaction, influence and exchange between Muscovy and its Western neighbours expanded greatly in the long seventeenth century between the end of Ivan's reign and the rule of Peter the Great. Muscovites learned from the example of Polish education and from their encounter with the manners of the Polish court.[22] They studied the technological achievements of the Prussians and the Dutch. And they learned too from rivals, enemies and invaders, borrowing from Sweden's governmental structures and military formations, as well as from Polish high culture. In the latter case, Kiev was an important point of transmission, with its Rus heritage but colonial position inside the Polish-Lithuanian Commonwealth.

During Peter's reign, these existing realities became the centre of the state's ideology. 'Westernization' was the most characteristic strategy of Peter's rule. Begun in 1703, St Petersburg was conceived in Western terms, in design more Venetian and neoclassical than Muscovite and Eurasian. Peter's 'embassy' to Western Europe during his youth was a time of practical absorption and 'technology transfer'. Later, during his reign, opening up to the West was also a matter of exposing a gap; Muscovite educational and scholarly life had been bleak, and Peter could not tolerate this. 'Learning is beneficial and basic for every good, as of the fatherland, as also of the Church,' insisted his Ecclesiastical Regulation of 1721, 'just like the root and the seed and the foundation.'[23] Peter's reforms were related to a vision of administration and law that he had learned about in Prussia, although he was also developing practices that already existed in Muscovy. Peter was supreme, but his very supremacy required that the new 'colleges' he introduced, a forerunner of ministries, should be governed by the rule of law. The Table of Ranks was a way of rationalizing and explaining the service that nobles owed to the state. Their required adoption of 'European' dress, and the razing of the Orthodox beards, was mere decoration by comparison. Meanwhile, he followed and even anticipated the example of some Western powers in subordinating, in law, the Church to the State. These were processes that were deepened and expanded throughout the eighteenth century, not least by Catherine the Great.

Russia's rulers and elites therefore stood on the edge of Europe and worked out how to become more European. Peter the Great borrowed technologies and practices from Western European countries to enhance the power of the Russian monarchy and to establish Russia as a great European power. But even when he was making use of European ways for Russian ends, the result was to make Russia more like other parts of Europe. Perceiving this 'narrowing of the gap' is bound to reduce the Russia Anxiety.

But it suggests too a slope of superiority, along which those near the bottom try to imitate those near the top. It is in some ways a variant of 'us' and 'them', of copyists and learners in the struggle to be more like an imaginary West. Such a way of thinking about Russia and Europe is unstable. There are bound to be moments when Russia seems to be learning badly or reverting to type. At such moments the Russia Anxiety will increase, with all its harmful effects.

The relationship between Russia and the West was not simply a matter of Russia borrowing from its neighbours and becoming more European. 'Russia' was within Europe from the times of Rus through the Muscovite period and beyond. It contributed to the shaping of Europe. And more: even when Russia looked like it was borrowing from other European countries, it was sometimes simply finding a new way of expressing things that its own civilization, with its European dimensions, had already created for itself.

## RUSSIA'S EUROPE

If Russia's westward ties and borrowings meant that Europe transmitted itself to Russia, then Russia also transmitted itself to Europe. The West is more Western because Russia has done this for centuries. Europe is more European because Russia is part of it. Many of Russia's characteristics are European and Western because they are Russian. This is the second half of Russia's European identity, and is the subject of this section.

The Golitsyn name is one of the grandest in Russian history. In the late eighteenth century, one of the family's princes eschewed the chance to serve Russia and perhaps enjoy a brilliant career – he was destined for a life in the military – and instead went off to see the world, travelling to the United States. His companion was a priest. Under his influence, Golitsyn went to Baltimore and trained for the priesthood. He went on to work as a missionary elsewhere in Maryland, as well as in Pennsylvania and Virginia.

Golitsyn built a church in 1799. His name was Americanized to Gallitzin. He founded the colony of Loretto in Pennsylvania; later, the town of Gallitzin was incorporated nearby. He put all his money into the colony, forewent his inheritance by refusing to return home to claim it and gathered financial support from sources high and low, from the king of Holland to the local community. At Loretto they erected houses, fenced off farms, built mills and constructed basic infrastructure. Prince Golitsyn spent forty-five years in this isolated part of Pennsylvania in the service of God and the local people.[24] It was a vocation that was at once Russian and American; had he stayed at home, he would have looked like Prince Levin in *Anna Karenina*. By going to America, he created an American dream.

Russian civilization has projected itself outwards for hundreds of years – not just in Europe, but also in America. In so doing, it has shown that it is recognizably of the 'West', in part if not in whole. It possesses a similar grammar to the rest of the West, even if its stock of vocabulary is sometimes quite different. For example, over hundreds of years, Russians developed a sense of themselves as a chosen people, something which they share with, among others, the French, British, Americans and Jews. As it came and went, the Russian sense of chosenness, their Messianic mission, was a European one.

'Two Romes have fallen,' wrote a Pskov-based monk, Filofei, to Grand Prince Vasily III in 1511, 'and the third stands, and a fourth shall never be.' His sentiment became a cornerstone of Russian identity. Almost sixty years earlier, in 1453, the Turks had captured Constantinople. Byzantium, the long-surviving eastern wing of the Roman Empire, was thus brought to an end. If the first Rome fell to the barbarian invasions in the fifth century, and the second Rome fell a millennium later, then it was up to Moscow to take on the mantle of the world's third Rome. The link was clear: only Muscovy possessed the moral and religious resources to be the heart of a new Christian empire.[25] Filofei's was the great statement of Muscovite messianism, of the chosenness and special status of the Russian people. Elected by God for the purpose of leading Christians towards the imminent end of the world, the people of Muscovy were in a unique position. As the Orthodox, they had stood apart from Catholic Europe since the Great Schism of 1054, and more recently had rejected the terms of the Council of Florence in 1439, whose aim had been to reconcile the two branches of Christianity. Under the weight of self-serving theology, populist sermons and the accumulation of political chance, the Orthodox flock could be convinced of the Third Rome message.

Muscovy was making the claim, at least in spiritual terms, to be the successor state of Byzantium. This was a statement that it aspired to be a major power in Christendom. Or in Europe, to use the term anachronistically. Yet this was *Eastern* Europe, the world of Orthodox Christianity. In 1472, Ivan III married Zoe (Sophia) Palaeologina. She was the niece of the Byzantine emperor who had been deposed in 1453. This was another symbolic revivification of Constantinople within Moscow. Ivan started to call himself tsar, a word for 'emperor' that was related to 'Caesar' and to the Greek *basileus*, and his grandson, Ivan the Terrible, used the title formally from 1547. Embedded in the title was a sense of quasi-theocratic power that was similar to the ideology which underwrote the Byzantine emperor. Ivan III used the two-headed eagle in his official seal, another inheritance from Byzantium. But Ivan and his successors did not make much of the claim to be the new Byzantium, and the symbolic legacies they employed had other roots too. Nor did they make any active attempt to unite with other Orthodox principalities in the Balkans, instead focusing their diplomatic and military efforts on Kiev and its surrounding lands from Poland-Lithuania.[26] So the history of the Third Rome was a symbolic projection of Muscovy into Europe, but not one that was politically or militarily expansionist.

The world did not end in 1492 as the Muscovite messianists predicted (this was precisely 7,000 years after the creation of the world according to Byzantine teaching). Instead, the concept of Moscow as the Third Rome renewed and reinvented itself many times. Peter the Great took the title Imperator, whose Latinate form implied the Roman virtues; the influential Slavophiles in the nineteenth century placed the Russians at the head of the Slavic peoples, who in turn had a unique destiny; under communist rule, Moscow became the capital of half the world and in its Soviet guise Russia again possessed a messianic mission. In 1933, when he was experimenting with scenes and ideas that would become part of his masterpiece of ten years later, *Ivan the Terrible*, the great film director Sergei Eisenstein reflected on Filofei's words about the Third Rome. 'This pronouncement by Filofei comes across to us from medieval times through tsarist Muscovy and autocratic Moscow,' he wrote. 'Moscow as a concept is the concentration of the socialist future of the entire world.'[27] Moscow was now, in effect, the *Fourth* Rome; it incarnated the proletarian revolution of 1917, which was the destiny of the human race. After 1945, as a superpower capital, Moscow dominated half of Europe. Its influence filtered into revolutions across the globe. Moscow's people really were the chosen ones of the socialist dream. In all senses – socialist, superpower, messianist – this was a European mission.

Back in the first half of the nineteenth century, such a future was as inconceivable as it was undesirable. But the messianism question was live. Among educated Russians, the issue of their chosenness or otherwise, and, by extension, whether their civilization tilted westwards or eastwards, became a matter for self-defining debate. Between 1807 and 1814, Russia had played a central role in Europe's struggle against Napoleon. The Russians emerged victorious because of the skill of their generals, the sacrifice and 'patriotism' of their peasant soldiers, their industrial production, the suppleness of their logistics and their brute determination both to evict Napoleon from Moscow and then to chase him back to Paris.[28] Alexander I found himself a celebrity in Paris, the saviour of Europe. When he visited London in May, thousands of people thronged the streets, and Oxford honoured him with its highest degree. Unlike the other crowned heads of Europe, he took an active role in the Congress of Vienna, which, with its 20,000 visitors, established the diplomatic shape of post-Napoleonic Europe in early 1815. Russia was at the peak of European politics, unmistakably one of the leading powers.

And yet even at this moment there was a paradox. Russia's most famous military leader in 1812 was Marshal Kutuzov, who seemed to combine all the Russian virtues. Tolstoy would soon publish *War and*

*Peace*, which describes Kutuzov's heroism, courage and patience in the same terms as his peasant soldiers. But Kutuzov's military leadership was supported by Marshal Barclay de Tolly, whose origins were in the German-speaking Baltic nobility (with some Scottish blood mixed in). Both men were central to the campaign, and indispensable to the form it took. Meanwhile, writing in his diary during the Congress of Vienna, Alexander Mikhailovsky-Danilevsky pointed out that 'Russia presents the unique example of a country whose diplomatic corps is composed in large part of foreigners. Some of them do not even know our language, some have seen of Russia only the city of St Petersburg.' Mikhailovsky-Danilevsky was a general who was about to start writing a history of the war. He spotted that only sixteen out of thirty-seven imperial personnel recorded in a diplomatic directory had Russian names. But for him this was not a weakness. He was not seeking greater insularity. Russia was strong because it was European. 'Does this not testify to the true grandeur of a country, so sure of its strength that it is completely indifferent about who represents it outside!'[29]

Yet this was a controversial position. In the 1830s, an intellectual contest opened up between the Slavophiles, who celebrated the uniquely Russian nature of their society, and the Westerners, who thought that Russia drew strength by engaging with the rest of Europe. Led by such thinkers as Ivan Kireyevsky, the Slavophiles argued that Russian culture had been nourished by Byzantium and Orthodoxy. Kireyevsky emphasized the *sobornost* to which this had given rise: the collective congregationalism, which defined not just religious experience, but also everyday life, especially in peasant communities. This true spirituality was absent in the West, which was obsessed instead with the individual. The Slavophiles harked back to a golden age, hated the Westernizing reforms of Peter the Great, deplored the unRussian qualities of serfdom. For them, the free peasant commune was one of the heights of civilization. 'A commune thus represents a moral choir,' wrote the leading Slavophile, Konstantin Aksakov, 'and, just as in a choir one voice is not lost but is heard in the harmony of all voices, so in the commune the individual is not lost, but renounces his exclusivity in favour of the common accord.'[30]

In the same decade of the 1830s, the Westerners, by contrast, drew on models from outside Russia. The historian Timofei Granovsky of Moscow University argued that the inefficiencies and evils of Russian life, notably serfdom, were temporary blips on the empire's general progress: a progress broadly in line with that of the countries of the West. According to Boris Chicherin, who articulated this position for a wider educated audience, Russia too would share in the institutions and ideas of the Enlightenment. Its future depended on constitutional monarchy and the rule of law.[31] Above all, the common experience with the rest of Europe was a social and economic one, the consequence of a shared 'modernization'.[32]

Chicherin and his followers made an assumption that is still familiar in the twenty-first century: that if Russia is to embrace individual rights, it must renounce its own traditions and become more like the West. Thanks to its traditions of Christianity and then of secularism, the story of the West has been, for one of its leading British historians, about the 'slow, uneven and difficult steps' that led to the primacy of 'individual moral agency being publicly acknowledged and protected, with equality before the law and enforceable "basic" rights'.[33] The assumption of the Russian Westerners was that Russia had to drink of this Western draught in order for individuals to gain rights.

Many in the West have made the same assumption, marking out Russians as collective beings with little sense of what it means to be an individual in any legal or moral sense. Such assumptions drove the political culture of the Cold War. In the 1940s, influential but bogus research by Geoffrey Gorer, picked up by Margaret Mead, purported to show that the apparent tendency of Russian mothers to swaddle their infants, severely restricting their movement, accounted for their grown-up Soviet personalities. As adults, they were characterized by guilt, fear, 'undifferentiated collectivity', passivity, depression, rage, over-emotional mood swings and the inclination to subordinate themselves to power. Many academic colleagues pointed out the absurdity of the thesis. First, no one was sure how common swaddling actually was. Second, no sane scholar could make the empirical leaps between a method of child rearing and an entire national character.[34] But the damage had been done, as versions of these ideas seeped into public debate. As late as May 1985, the *Financial Times* warned its readers who were thinking about visiting Moscow:

'Russians have a fearful preoccupation with keeping things under control – showing individuality simply disturbs them.'[35]

And if that was true, then Soviet citizens, especially those of Russian extraction, couldn't possibly have a sense of human rights. Some historians came to argue that after the Helsinki Accords of 1975, and especially during *perestroika*, Western ideas about human rights destabilized Soviet rule, precisely because the term entered the Soviet lexicon. Dissidents, ordinary people and finally Gorbachev himself started talking about them. The assumption was that if a discourse of rights, especially of human rights, did indeed contribute to the collapse of the Soviet Union, it must have been imported from outside.[36] If Marxism had failed, then human rights were 'the last utopia' that people across the world, including in the USSR, could believe in.[37] And it was therefore by definition not a Russian or a Soviet utopia.

By 1990, Gorbachev had come to talk the language of human rights fluently. It made for comfortable conversations with President Bush. Human rights had in fact only recently become a common concept in European and global politics, largely thanks to the Helsinki Accords of 1975, but thereafter they exerted an influence on the language of international politics and the development of legal systems. Human rights were one of the frameworks in which the Eastern bloc collapsed in 1989, and also shaped the way that the claims of the Soviet nationalities were then being formed.

In other words, they contributed to *perestroika*. But while human rights had a Western flavour, the deeper sense of rights that occupied the imaginations of Gorbachev and many other Soviet people actually derived from the staples of Russian culture, as well as some of the norms of Marxism. Deepest of all, perhaps, was the concept of *pravda*. Embedded into East Slavic peasant culture, long predating serfdom, was the balance of rights and obligations that defined the individual's relationship to the community. Each village community was a separate, self-regulating unit, and was sometimes known as the *mir*, which means 'world', signifying its scope to those who lived inside it. Justice was dispensed inside this world. The justice that regulated these communities was captured by the concept of *pravda*, which means 'truth' in a broad sense, encompassing moral correctness, divine law, and therefore justice. It was the basis of the mutual obligations (the Russian term is *krugovaya poruka*) that operated inside the community and which made possible the reasonably equitable collection of taxes and rents, and the fair raising of army recruits, without unduly disadvantaging any particular household in the village. By the same token, *pravda* regulated the entitlements which the community as a whole owed to its individual members: appropriate land to till, social protection when falling on hard times, and punishment of transgressors who caused harm. The peasant uprisings which helped to shape national politics over hundreds of years were often driven by the sense that *pravda* had been infringed. It was no coincidence that by 1917 many Russians were attracted to socialism, on the professed basis that it was about justice, rights, liberation and security. In turn, these concepts were written into the Soviet Union's constitutions, however little the authorities respected them.

What Soviet dissidents usually demanded was not that the USSR live up to the West, but that it honour its own laws.[38] They were not awestuck students of the Western teaching, though they adopted some of its language. To understand this process better, we should go back to the 1830s.

However you look at Russia's twentieth century, it was all about socialism. You might agree with Trotsky, and think that the socialism that emerged under Stalin was socialism in name only. But even when state violence was at its peak, Stalin and the men around him really believed that they were implementing a socialist programme. Across all of the Russian twentieth century, socialism was the thing. First it was the focus of a revolutionary movement. Then it became the governing ideology. And finally it was a massive object to be dismantled.

Where did this socialism come from? If you rewind to the 1830s, you can see that it came from the same place as human rights talk in the 1980s: from both Western words and indigenous traditions. Even during the reign of Nicholas I, Germans exerted a powerful reach into the imaginations of Russia's Westernizing intellectuals, first with their idealist philosophy in general, and then via the works of Marx and Engels in particular. The precise models of dialectical materialism that drove the Bolsheviks towards their understanding of revolution and their pursuit of would-be scientific planning emerged from this intellectual encounter. Marx offered, too, a 'romantic' side, a model of mass mobilization and the whipping up of enthusiasm that would drive the Soviet experiment.[39] But the ethical content of Russian socialism was provided by local traditions. Writing in the 1840s, Alexander Herzen drew out all kinds of proto-socialism from Russia's ancient traditions, often in fanciful ways; the peasant commune was actually much more about rational risk calculations than, as Herzen liked to think, brotherly love. Still, the communal dimensions of the Russian experience were striking, and they flowed through the works of other leading socialists, such as Nikolai Lavrov, and into the Populist movement of the later nineteenth century. Socialism was an indigenous phenomenon as well as a foreign import, and it was the blend of these things that gave it particular force.[40]

It was the same story with rights. The reason why Mikhail Gorbachev could talk so fluently about rights was because he combined the grammar of an indigenous tradition with the vocabulary of a Western model. The 'grammar' was the traditions of Russian culture, reshaped by Soviet life. Meanwhile, the phrases and cadences of his human-rights talk had two sources: the new discourse that came out of the Helsinki Accords, which was a Western import, and an older language of rights associated with Marxism-Leninism, whose original source was also the West, though it had been reshaped for seventy years in Soviet conditions. It was crucial that he grew to professional maturity during the Thaw, as a Komsomol official in Stavropol Region, where one of his early tasks was to explain the Secret Speech to local Party members. He observed at first hand how some of those rights laid down in the Constitution of 1936, which had been notional or nonsensical under Stalin, assumed meaning under Khrushchev. Most people came to live as if they had the right to a job, healthcare and a pension, as well as to more abstract things such as inviolability of the home.[41] Gorbachev's Russian rights inheritance derived more deeply from the flexibility of the old Russian autocracy, with its ability to incorporate a limited form of rights into Russian life: the pursuit of the Speransky Conundrum. Legal reforms in the nineteenth century – notably Alexander II's introduction of trial by jury, an independent judiciary and an impressive network of district courts – plainly depended on a sense of rights. And the operations of the Russian economy over the long-term, from the organization of the peasant commune, to the outsize role of state enter-prises, to vestiges of welfare reform, all implied the existence of a version of social and economic rights.

When it came to human rights, then, the USSR and Russia drew on their own legal and cultural resources as well as those from outside, in a combination familiar to other countries. The process did not suggest Russia was different, but actually that it possessed a fundamentally European sensibility. Russia was not the obverse of the West, as hardline proponents of the Russia Anxiety would have it, and it was not a pale imitation of the West, ever ready to fade completely, as gentler Russia critics, who had never really lost the Anxiety themselves, hinted. Never-theless, the border between Russia and 'the West' was a complicated place. At no time was that truer than when the country was apparently sealed off from the West, when the Iron Curtain was in place.

## THE BORDER

Vladimir Putin was part of the 'Sputnik' generation, born just five years before the start of the Soviet conquest of space. For him, the Cold War – the arms race, the space race, the great superpower rivalry with the United States – was a daily reality until he was almost forty. But Putin was also a Leningrader with a taste for German culture. Leningrad had a self-conscious Western style that it inherited from St Petersburg. It can also be a spiky place whose citizens see their cul-tural accomplishments as superior to those of less refined Muscovites, let alone the rest of the country. It was not entirely inappropriate that Putin would end up as a spy in dainty Dresden.

Putin can't remember when the Soviet Union was hermetically sealed off from the West. He was not quite five months old when Stalin died in March 1953 and Soviet life began its transformation. Those last eight years of Stalin's rule, when the Cold War began and reached its height, were marked by the closing of the Soviet Union to the outside world. The wartime alliance fractured. Rumours of impending war with the former allies spread: the Soviet population was fearful. The search for enemies marked out domestic politics. Andrei Zhdanov, the Party's ideology chief, who had been the boss of

Leningrad during the siege, vilified artists and writers suspected of 'cosmopolitan' sympathies. Outside the USSR, the Berlin blockade gave way to the Korean conflict. When the new state of Israel tilted towards the United States, Soviet Jews became objects of suspicion. At the time of Stalin's death, the press was running an anti-Semitic campaign called the Doctors' Plot, which briefly looked like a prelude to the mass arrest of Jews. Such a wave of violence did not take place. But tensions were very high, and the Doctors' Plot was the symbol of the Soviet Union's sharp separation from 'the West'. This was the Europe of Churchill's Iron Curtain at the time of Putin's birth.

He only knew this closed world, heavy with expected violence, at second hand. For all the sudden crises, high risk, and relative isolation that continued to mark the Cold War, the Soviet Union in which Putin grew up was not a solitary planet. It was connected first to a socialist universe (an empire of a type) behind the Iron Curtain. And it forged new links with Western Europe, the United States, and other places too. Khrushchev was aiming for 'peaceful coexistence' with capitalism. He travelled widely, for example visiting the United Kingdom in 1956. On this trip he toured the country together with the head of government, Nikolai Bulganin (Khrushchev was first secretary of the Party and formally part of a leadership collective, though he was already the dominant figure). He had lengthy talks with the prime minister, Anthony Eden, and other leading politicians, making a big impression in the process. Although the *Daily Sketch* had Khrushchev and Bulganin down as 'Russia's terrible twins', *The Times* was effusively impressed, pointing out that Khrushchev could 'present a case at a moment's notice with an almost Churchillian ease'.[42]

A year later, the world came to Moscow for a temporary inoculation against the Russia Anxiety. For two weeks in the summer of 1957, the city hosted the World Festival of Youth and Students. Organized by the World Federation of Democratic Youth, which had been founded on a basis sympathetic to socialism in November 1945 in London, the festival turned the capital of communism into a global meeting place. For these two weeks, more than 34,000 young people from 131 countries converged on Moscow.[43] This was big news. By comparison, the Melbourne Olympic Games in 1956 hosted 3,314 athletes from 72 countries, and the organizers sold 56,000 tickets to overseas spectators.[44]

On 29 July, the opening ceremony unfolded in the Central Lenin Stadium at Luzhniki. Participants marched from the centre of the city towards the stadium in the south-west, while 3.5 million Muscovites lined the route. Thereafter, sporting, cultural and work-exchange events took place in numerous venues, from the 'Paris Commune' footwear factory to the House of Architects, from a cycle race on Leningradskoe Chaussée to a display of 1,500 books at the Central House of Literature. All sorts of people mingled at mass concerts on Pushkin Square and Manezh Square, and on the penultimate day of the festival, 'tens of thousands' gathered on Red Square. On 11 August, the festival closed with a night-time extravaganza at the Lenin Stadium.[45]

Kliment Voroshilov was at that time chairman of the Presidium of the Supreme Soviet: the ceremonial head of state. He said at the opening ceremony: 'you have come to the Festival in order to strengthen, through friendly meetings and exchange of opinion, the ties of fraternal friendship and mutual understanding which are cementing ever stronger the youth of diverse countries of the world'.[46] The words fitted a formula, but it was a quite different formula from five years before. Now, in what had recently been a deeply suspicious place, Muscovites and foreign delegates mingled, often unsupervised, sometimes – as historians have not been slow to investigate – with riotous joy.[47] Writers in the USSR's *Literaturnaya gazeta* invoked the images of freedom. One mentioned 'dancing in the squares and singing in the streets', while another wrote of the omnipresence of the word 'festival' in the city: 'A happy word, it weaves and flutters above the town, like the song of a lark.'[48] The correspondent of the *New Statesman* might have exaggerated in detail if not in spirit when he wrote: 'People discussed at impromptu street meetings fundamental questions of civil liberties, not only with foreigners, but – and this is more important – among themselves. Few foreign participants left Moscow without seeing the inside of a Moscow home.'[49] *The Times* of London made a similar point: 'it was not these planned events which were most impressive and most instructive but rather it was the spontaneous outpouring of eager curiosity and warm friendliness on the part of the Russian populace.'

During the Thaw, the Soviet intelligentsia became newly fascinated with 'the West'. The effects were complicated, 'ideological and neurotic' according to one historian, who points out that some intellectuals used these encounters to reinforce their sense of inferiority to the West, others to enhance their sense of being trapped behind the Iron Curtain.[50] Most of the encounters took place on Soviet soil, such as during the exhibition of Picasso's works at Moscow's Pushkin Museum of Fine Arts, which opened on 25 October 1956. By contrast, it was a rare privilege to travel abroad to the West, usually on scientific or industrial exchanges. But tourists travelled, too, almost 400 of them on a cruise ship called *Victory* for a one-month European trip in autumn 1961. Only two of them were factory workers.[51]

In May 1967, the decision was taken to found a new United States Institute within the Academy of Sciences (renamed to incorporate Canada in 1975). Georgy Arbatov was appointed the first director. Arbatov was a creature of the Soviet system with alleged links to the security services. And yet he had an intellectual commitment to see America afresh. 'From the first steps, we tried to avoid ideological stereotypes,' Arbatov wrote in his memoirs.[52] Was this a contradiction? In one sense, the Soviet Union in the Brezhnev era had become sclerotic. Following the failure of the Kosygin economic reforms in the late 1960s, which would have decentralized the economy, increased the autonomy of industrial enterprises and cut back obsessive central planning, the Soviet bureaucracy reverted to excessive caution. New ideas, let alone criticism, had few opportunities for expression or fulfilment.[53] Yet the Soviet Union in the 1970s was also dynamic, with a complex culture of 'permitted dissent', an inventive second economy, underground sub-cultures and a welfare deal that was one factor that brought acceptance of the system.

Still, it was a tense time. In the year after the Institute was created, the Warsaw Pact had suppressed the Prague Spring (much less violently than in Budapest twelve years before) while the Americans continued to fight in Vietnam. In April, months before the culmination of events in Prague, the Soviets cancelled their involvement in a music and dance festival that was being planned in New York. 'Soviet people simply could not allow themselves to sing and dance in a carefree way in a country that was carrying out an aggressive war in Vietnam,' the authorities declared.[54] But this was the storm before the calm. It was a time for imaginative diplomacy. Détente followed.

*

Putin did not exactly spend his childhood at the 1957 Festival of Youth, any more than he was a child of the intelligentsia. But he did grow up in a country influenced by its effects, and especially those of the Secret Speech. In Leningrad's School Number 281, he could not have avoided the notion that the Soviet Union was part of the world. His school focused on the natural sciences, but Putin's interests lay in the humanities. Under the careful attention of his teacher, Mina Yuditskaya, he learned German enthusiastically. Like other schools during the Thaw, his teachers grappled with the problem of how to talk to their pupils about Stalin and the outside world. Some of them passed round banned literary texts or openly discussed the ongoing implications of the Secret Speech.[55]

Notwithstanding the opening of his mind, Putin wanted from a young age to be part of the state's repressive apparatus. He perhaps thought that the KGB promised foreign glamour. A career as an intelligence officer might give the opportunity to travel to the West, live abroad, learn foreign languages and observe foreign cultures. For a time, spies basked in the reflected glory of Stirlitz, the charismatic and much-loved hero of the wildly popular seventies TV drama *Seventeen Moments of Spring*. Stirlitz was a deep-cover agent in Berlin at the end of the Second World War, so accomplished in language, manner and culture that he passed for an elite German officer. But *Seventeen Moments of Spring* was also a patriotic show, a brilliantly produced image of Soviet victory.

So if the Soviet Union offered Putin a particular kind of exposure to the outside world – on its own terms, and with severe reservations – it also pointed the way towards Soviet and Russian patriotism. Likewise, the KGB offered Putin a window on the outside world, but from within the Eastern bloc, and from inside an organization with its own sense of Russian nationhood. Putin joined the KGB during a 'rebirth of Russia'. But what was Russia during Soviet times? The Soviet Union was a multinational enterprise made up of fifteen national republics. By far the biggest was the RSFSR, the Russian Soviet Federated Socialist Republic, but there were fourteen others, ranging across Eastern Europe (Estonia), the Caucasus (Georgia) and Central Asia (Uzbekistan). But like they did for England in the United Kingdom, outsiders constantly said 'Russia' when they meant 'the USSR'.

Russia's capital, Moscow, was the capital of the USSR, and Russia was the engine of Soviet power. But living standards were higher in the Baltic republics; Russians ran the Union, but only alongside men and women from the republics (after all, Stalin was a Georgian); many of the repositories of Russian national culture, from the peasant commune to the Orthodox Church, had been destroyed or mangled by Soviet rule. It was not only a technical point that Russia lacked many of the institutions that other republics possessed, from its own republic-level Communist Party to an Academy of Sciences, relying instead on the all-union equivalents. During the 1970s, it became polite again to talk about 'Russia', to seek the protection of its cultural monuments and natural ecology, as if it had interests slightly separate from those of the USSR.[56] Less benignly, there was a national Russian 'clan', whose members extended into the KGB, competing for influence within the Soviet political machine.[57]

As a young KGB field officer, then, Putin was exposed to overlapping and deeply felt expressions of Soviet and Russian power. It was normal to assume that the USSR had a long global reach, while Russian ethnicity, culture and landscape offered other consolations of identity.

The Soviet Union identified itself as the antonym of the West in the politics of the Cold War: 'West' had become a label with a newly specific meaning. Beyond the surface of politics, though, many Russians occupied a mental space that went across the Iron Curtain. Their daily lives were shaped too by practices common across Europe, for example in social policies and urban planning. This was the context in which the Soviet position on the world stage was shifting. Brezhnev met successive American presidents – Nixon, Ford, Carter – and set the parameters for arms controls. This era of détente replaced Khrushchev's turbulent diplomacy, though it grew out of one of Khrushchev's insights: that NATO and the Warsaw Pact had no choice but to coexist peacefully, and that they might on occasion quite enjoy doing so. Yet in December 1979, the Politburo made one of its greatest errors, ordering the invasion of Afghanistan, supporting a local communist regime against what would in time be defined as Islamist insurgents. The Cold War had reverted to crisis management. When Ronald Reagan entered the White House just over a year later, promising to pursue a hard line, the tension grew.

Putin eventually got his chance to be a cold warrior on the international stage, but in the communist bloc rather than the capitalist world. In August 1985, he arrived in Dresden for the major posting of his KGB career. His wife Lyudmila arrived a few weeks later, together with baby Masha, born that April. By all accounts, Putin was an effective intelligence officer in a town that was hardly a Cold War hotspot. He got on well with his colleagues, made effective ties with his East German equivalents in the Stasi and recruited and ran agents. He joked later that all this made him 'an expert in human relations'.

He lived in East Germany with his family for nearly five years, rounding out his interests in German life and culture. Photographs show him playing table tennis in swimming trunks. He drank the local beer and put on weight. Lyudmila learned German and found her place in the community. His children grew through infancy. Spy or not, he fitted a European mould.

The Soviet Union was a closed society, but closure was relative, and the Iron Curtain was far from fixed. Russia became increasingly open to foreigners from the 1980s on. But openness to the outside increased dramatically with the end of the Cold War. Contact between Russians and foreigners usually diminished the Russia Anxiety, spectacularly so during the World Cup of 2018, though many expatriates always wore their scepticism about Russia on their sleeves. Russia's tourism sector expanded. In 1995, there were 10.3 million tourist arrivals in Russia; by 2011, this had grown to 24.9 million. Russia was a minority destination: in the same period, tourist arrivals in the rest of Europe grew from 333.3 million to 469.1 million, and across the rest of the world from 531.4 to just over a billion. The great majority of visitors to Russia came by land, however (many by train), and were visiting relatives or friends. Russia remained tied to its 'near abroad'. In 2010, 31 per cent of tourist trips were to Ukraine, and 5 per cent to Kazakhstan. (Turkey and Egypt were the most popular destinations for Russian package holidays.) Tourists coming into Russia spent relatively modest amounts, showing again that Russia occupied only the edge of the big-spending international tourist circuit. But the amount of money that Russians spent on foreign tourism (capital flight was a separate phenomenon) almost doubled between 2006 and 2011, from

552.8 to 919.6 billion rubles.[58] Events such as the Winter Olympics of 2014, held at Sochi, and the World Cup of 2018, had an ambiguous status: partly a moment in which Russia seemed unique and exposed, but partly too an unmistakable integration of Russia into the deeper structures of the global economy, when Russia seemed Western. Even as tensions with the West increased in the second decade of the twenty-first century, Russia's big centres became more liveable and 'normal'.

Even bureaucracy became more accessible, importing more manners from 'the West', with Moscow's local authority offices given the friendly name 'My Documents', and offering free coffee if your appointment started more than fifteen minutes late. Stepping out of Starbuck's, avoiding a bike in the cycle lane and looking up at a renovated Orthodox church, Muscovites would reflect on the border between Russia and the West. It was seldom a line that separated them from the outside world, though at times it continued to divide Russians from each other, some of whom looked to another place: not Europe, but 'Eurasia'.

Russia has borrowed from non-Russian Europe and the West more generally. But it has also been *of* Europe and *of* the West. It has helped to shape these places from within. Those concepts it has apparently borrowed from the West, such as human rights, often turn out to have a native lineage in their Russian form, suggesting again that Russia is of the West rather than separate from it. There are many Russias, including those in distant and poor locations, and those where obscurantism and parochialism have triumphed. But even during the Soviet Union's Cold War isolation, the imaginative and practical engagement with the West went on. And yet Russia is clearly not only of the West. It is also of the East, which is why the term 'Eurasia' has not only come back into fashion, but has become a new source for the Russia Anxiety.

## EURASIA'S RUSSIA

Deep in the East, in the heart of Mongolia, a group of powerful tribal chiefs gathered in the year 1206. Their task was to declare their support for a new ruler: Chinggis Khan. Within a few years, he had transformed global politics, creating one of the great empires of world history. In 1206, the peoples over whom Chinggis ruled were nomads, capable of gliding on horseback across the steppe, sheep and cattle in tow, trading with those passing along the silk route. Gathered in strong family units but looking outwards for opportunities, they became a militarized civilization. In the Mongol lands, Chinggis was their charismatic and ambitious ruler. He moulded his disparate followers into a terrorizing force of tens of thousands of horse-riding warriors. His vision was brilliantly fulfilled in the north of China between 1210 and 1215. The Mongols smashed their way through Central Asia in 1219 and into today's Iran and Afghanistan in 1221.

By 1223, western detachments had defeated the Polovtsy (the Turkic nomads who dominated the southern steppe). They were now an imminent threat to Rus. The following year, the Mongols defeated a divided force of surviving Polovtsy troops and men from some of the principalities of Rus. This was the limit of Chinggis's reach. He died in 1227. Chinggis's sons then continued the Mongol expansion. In the West, on the other side of the Volga river, it was his grandson Batu who pushed across the Urals and attacked Eastern and Central Europe between 1236 and 1241.

Eurasia – a linked-up political whole that ran across Europe and Asia, animated by a dominant civilization yet drawing strength from ethnic and cultural diversity – was coming into being, thanks to a 100,000-strong army from the East that targeted the East Slavic lands and captured Kiev. The descent of the Mongols on Muscovy was brutal and terrifying. Many thousands of subjects of Muscovy and the other territories of Rus were killed. The period of Mongol domination lasted for about 250 years, during which the terrible bloodthirstiness of the initial invasion was sporadically repeated. To take just one example: in 1408, the Tatar emir Edigai besieged Moscow, extorting thousands of rubles, and causing famine and plague. The 'Golden Horde' itself, as Mongol or Tatar overlordship is sometimes described, had its headquarters in Sarai in the south, was prone to division and civil war and was defeated by Tamerlane at the end of the fourteenth century. But the Mongols hung on, until their final defeat and expulsion in 1480.

We should not minimize the plight of those who suffered because of the Mongols: ignoring the victims breaks one of the first laws of studying history. But Mongol violence was not more barbaric than European violence; if anything, the real breakthrough in medieval barbarism came with the Christian attacks on the Holy Land in the First Crusade,[59] which is no consolation to those who were violated and killed by a detachment of Mongol horsemen. Crucially, though, most of the 250 years of Mongol rule was a matter of diplomacy and governance rather than brute force.

During these centuries, the Mongols inevitably left their imprint on Muscovite institutions and culture. In so doing, they provided a stock of arguments to back up the Russia Anxiety. Some of these are fair, but many are mendacious. For some later observers, the Mongols marked the start of the long night of Russian exceptionalism, mired in the mindless violence of the East, which merely continues today under new rulership. For others, led by the Orthodox Church since the seventeenth century, the civilization of the East Slavs in Rus-Muscovy-Russia was a pure and precious thing which could admit of no Mongol contamination; the invaders' effect was transient, their existence in the area best described as a 'Tatar yoke', something separate that was eventually thrown off.

But it seems fairer to stake out an argument somewhere between these two positions. The impact of the Mongols was substantial, but sometimes positive. It was a solvent in which legacies of Europe and Rus blended into a hybrid culture, not a pure one, with powerful possibilities. The blend was literal and genetic; the incoming Mongols lacked a sense of ethnic exclusivity and promoted intermarriage, facilitated by their ability to have many wives. And the blend was stirred by cultural and economic exchange, whose aim was to bolster Mongol power. The Mongols were ever keen to learn from their subject peoples and to enrich themselves at their expense, but these exchanges had a continental, mutually beneficial scope which was almost an end in itself.

A redesigned and much more effective civil administration probably emerged from Mongol overlordship. Muscovite princes made extended visits to Sarai, during which they observed the efficacy of Mongol administrative practices, in particular the division between structures of military and civil government. The introduction of the *pomest'e* system to Muscovy was at the heart of this transfer of the arts of government. It involved granting land to leading cavalrymen who then owed military and other service to the grand prince, and helped him raise tax. Adapting Mongol approaches to tax-raising allowed Dmitry Donskoi and his successors to devise a more confident fiscal system that could do more than pay off tribute.[60] (And Donskoi then inflicted a major reverse on the Tatars at the Battle of Kulikovoye Polye in 1380.) Servitor-cavalrymen also learned new military techniques, with better weapons, a more imaginative strategy and a greater variety of tactics. The techniques of diplomacy and the culture of collective responsibility in local communities were shaped by Mongol influence. All of these practices made possible Muscovy's rapid development after Mongol rule, and the principality's expansion thereafter into a full-fledged empire. Meanwhile, new trade routes and expanding commerce began to pay off from the middle of the fourteenth century; Muscovy was richer at the end of its Mongol dominance than at the start. Byzantium continued to shape the Church, showing the limits of Mongol power, while the Mongol practice of secluding women in the *terem*, and assumptions about the powers of the autocrat, probably had darker consequences for Muscovy's social and political culture.[61] These interpretations rest on medieval historians' learned readings of challenging documents and their immensely nuanced interpretations of them. But the weight of evidence shows that Russia's Asian heritage might, paradoxically, generate a European future.

This paradox deepened in the nineteenth century. By then, the Russian Empire was extending far into Asia and east to the Pacific Ocean. All of this was a contiguous space; there was no physical gap between the Russian nation and its imperial possessions. Where did the European core end and the Asian possessions begin? And were not some of the imperial territories, such as eastern Poland, European anyway, and further west than St Petersburg? The fading in and out of Russia's European and Asian identities was a complicated process with unresolved consequences.

There had been two moments in the history of Rus and then Muscovy when the rulers of the Russian lands had entertained a possible Asian future. The first took place just before Grand Prince Vladimir opted for the Christianization of Rus in 988. He briefly toyed with the possibility of choosing Islam instead. This would have opened up a different future, with the central Eurasian landmass cut off from the influence of Byzantium in particular and Christendom in general. The contours of culture and the shape of international conflict would have been unimaginably different. Second was the moment when Muscovy really did become an Islamic civilization, though not a majority one: in 1552, Ivan the Terrible annexed Muslim Kazan, and four years later he conquered Astrakhan.[62] This time the country did turn east, as the gates were now open to Siberia, the Caucasus and Central Asia. But the centre of the empire remained in Moscow, the dominant culture was still European, and foreign policy looked westward for inspiration.

For centuries, Christendom had counterposed itself to barbarism, a superiority complex whose violent logic was revealed in the Crusades. By the eighteenth century, Europe saw itself in a similar relationship to Asia: its rationality and power counterposed to the other's superstition, effeminacy, childishness and backwardness. The obverse of this attitude was the desire to study, depict and objectify the East, in ways that seemed 'orientalizing' to Edward Said, but were also born of scholarly and cultural passions. Russians shared this common European impulse. In the nineteenth century, Pushkin, Lermontov and Tolstoy all wrote affectionate portraits of the Caucasus. This exotic zone, all of which was under Russian control by 1864, was treated as imperial Russia's 'Asiatic' periphery.

The Slavophiles joined in. They began to develop an idea whose effects have come back to haunt Russia time and again: that Russia was unique. It was the Eurasian civilization. We have had a sense of the Slavophiles already, but the idea of Eurasia found a famous new proponent a century later.

When Lev Gumilev was eight years old, in 1921, his father, Nikolai, was arrested by the Cheka. The secret police accused him of taking part in a pro-monarchy plot, and he was executed. Nikolai was an important poet, but Lev's mother, Anna Akhmatova, became a world-famous one. She spent the 1920s as a literary figure in Leningrad, while he grew up in poverty with his grandparents deep in the provinces, victimized because of his class origins; it was a separation that haunted mother and son alike. He came to Leningrad as a young adult, by which time Akhmatova had married again; his stepfather was unfriendly, confining him to a camp bed in the hallway of the communal apartment where they lived. Thanks to affirmative action and outright class exclusion, Gumilev was prevented from going to university until 1934, when he began to study history. He did not graduate until twelve years later, following his arrest and incarceration in the Gulag, which took place in two interrupted spells and covered the first half of the war. Tormented by the authorities, Anna Akhmatova queued up to send him food parcels, but he thought that his fate was her fault. And after a few years of freedom in miserable post-war Leningrad, he was arrested again, in 1949. Meanwhile, the authorities tormented his mother during the *Zhdanovshchina* campaign against selected cultural figures who were Jewish or from Leningrad or both. Gumilev spent seven more long years in the camp. It was only in 1956 that he was freed and cleared of the fictional crimes for which he had been imprisoned.

Like many former convicts, Gumilev experienced a traumatic homecoming. His personal relationships, especially with his mother, were badly damaged. But unlike many others, he was quickly able to find work that was appropriate to his qualifications and fitted with his interests. He worked first in the Hermitage Museum and then as a researcher in the Faculty of Geography at Leningrad State University. Still, he felt that he'd been shunted into an appointment that lacked prestige or prospects. He sensed that the authorities were still on his tail.

Over the next decades, Gumilev pursued his scholarly interests in the early Russian lands and their contiguous territories, using archaeological and many other sources. He tried to prove both the special uniqueness of the Russian ethnos as well as the capacity of the many ethnicities that inhabited this European and Asian space to coexist productively. He was a product of Eurasia himself: Anna Akhmatova, who lived until 1966, made a lot of her own family origins, a combination of all the points of the imperial-Eurasian compass. She had Ukrainian-Cossack roots on her father's side and was born near Odessa. Her mother was Russian, and the family moved to St Petersburg where she attended the elite Marinsky Gymnasium, receiving the most high-imperial of schooling. Later, she took the Tatar pen name Akhmatova, apparently borrowed from her maternal great-grandmother, descended from Chinggis Khan.[63]

Gumilev worked on a large body of scholarship on the Soviet lands, establishing neologisms ('passionarity', 'complementarity'), forging long-term chronological explanations for ethnic and historical development and ranging geographically across the whole of the Soviet space. This was the basis of a new theory of Eurasianism. Gumilev himself did not enjoy conventional academic success in the Soviet Union but he was a success all the same. Despite what he felt was his place in the institutional margins, he became an influential voice at home and abroad. The publication of his work in some sense testified to a level of pluralism in pre-*perestroika* Soviet life, and he was read by specialists in the West as well as in the USSR. In the closing years of the Soviet Union and ever since, Gumilev's vision of Eurasia has compelled different audiences. Gumilev himself was not a Russian nationalist, arguing (usually) that the different ethnic nations of Eurasia were equal. But Russian nationalists found his theories useful nonetheless, and he sometimes collaborated with them despite the professional risk, at the cost of only belated recognition from the Academy of Sciences.[64] Gumilev became prominent during *perestroika*. At a time when the country was gripped by debates about what a reformed Soviet Union could become, his vision of Eurasia was an antipode to Gorbachev's 'common European home'. It rejected the idea that 'Western values' should become the global norm; they had no more right to universality than any other system of values, such as Islam and Orthodox Christianity. Instead, he offered a vision that was conservative and more specific to the Soviet Union, combining Russian nationhood with a wider Eurasian sensibility. It appealed to nationalists, who were a significant anti-Gorbachev minority, but it did not capture the mood of the time.

In the 1990s, Gumilev's work was taken up by Alexander Dugin, a controversial and well-known nationalist writer who was linked – and also not linked – with the Kremlin. Gumilev influenced Putin personally; the president mentioned him from time to time in public meetings, for example when addressing students and older schoolchildren at the start of the academic year in September 2017. But Gumilev's writings were rich and varied, and one could take from them what one wanted. In 2012, Putin announced his support for a Eurasian union, apparently as a counterbalance to the European Union. It seemed unlikely that this was really a matter of ideology or of historical destiny, though. It was more a geopolitical rebalancing, keeping open the option of a pivot towards China. As Halford Mackinder, the famous turn-of-the-twentieth-century geographer, had pointed out more than a hundred years before, Eurasia is all about geopolitics. The thing about geopolitics is that they change, and sometimes quickly, even if the geographical faultlines remain eternal.

Eurasia has come to mean different things. It has meant the landmass of Europe and Asia together, a kind of greater China-and-Russia, taking in Poland, Ukraine, the Balkans, Turkey, the Caucasus, Iran, Central Asia, sweeping over the Hindu Kush and the Gobi Desert.[65] When applied as a political label, it excludes Europe further west, which shows the term's flexible and subjective qualities. It has been a handy substitute for 'post-Soviet' when academics had to relabel their research institutes, journals and professional clubs after 1991. It has meant a way of studying the history of the Russian lands and their neighbours that emphasizes interactions, exchanges, empires and the long-term ability of cultural and political institutions to have impacts across borders.[66]

And as Lev Gumilev showed, Eurasia, like Europe, could be a state of mind. During the confrontations of the 2010s, when some Russians despaired of – or welcomed – the impossibility of Russia being Western, Eurasia offered a consoling alternative, one that might remind them of the Russian Empire and the Soviet Union. But, as Putin himself pointed out more than once, reimagining the Soviet space was a process that owed more to emotion than intellect.

In various speeches, years later, Putin would regret the passing of the Soviet Union, but not as a country, or an empire, or as an economic system, or as a closed political entity: more as a way of organizing an international worldview, with a sense of identity and a basis of security. Above all, he regretted the humiliating manner of the Soviet collapse. His public regrets about the end of the USSR were specific, drawing on particular rhetorical tropes that acknowledged a strong desire for Russia to be accepted among the great powers, or the community of leading countries, with their self-consciously stated values.

As Putin began to increase the scope of Russia's foreign policy, and its willingness to use force, many Russians could explain events with reference to such a worldview. In other words: it was time for Russia to take its rightful place in world affairs and to be respected accordingly. Some Russians were susceptible to it, and some of them were not. But even those who quite liked the sound of Russian exceptionalism very seldom rejected the West. It was true that for some political figures on the Eurasian fringe, including powerful ones, like Putin's former Svengali, Vladislav Surkov, the time had come to take up the old Slavophile mantle. Surkov outlined a value-laden approach to history, according to which Peter the Great had made a big mistake, because Russia's tradition lay outside European civilization. By spring 2018, shortly after Putin's fourth presidential election, Sergei Kurginyan, the leader of the nationalist Essence of Time movement, claimed that Russia's attempts to integrate with the West had led only to insecurity and even impending war with the United States.[67] Although such voices were loud in political debates on the big Russian TV networks, they went against Russia's own stated aims, and seemed outlandish to many, though of course not all, Russians. 'It seems,' drily editorialized *Nezavisimaya gazeta*, in response to Kurginyan, 'that neither influential segments of the Russian elite nor the middle class are prepared to be a motor of change towards the rejection of European values.' By contrast, the paper went on, anti-Western voices offered 'an apologia for barbarousness, an unwillingness to learn lessons from the past, a mercenary interest in forcing a confrontation with the West', things which 'carry within themselves an anti-national character'. Interestingly, one of the Russian words for 'barbarous' is *aziatichesky*.

And yet there is a further puzzle. Those Russians who distrust the idea of Eurasia still express themselves in the language of 'Russia and the West', in which the two quantities are quite separate. They don't want to fight the West, but to work closely with it, just as they might go on holiday *to* the West or trade *with* a Western firm. And yet while Russia is not a subset of the West in the way that Denmark or Luxembourg is, whose citizens presumably never take a trip *to* the West, it overlaps with the West. It is of the West but not only of the West: it is European and Eurasian. Russia is the biggest country in Europe as well as the biggest country in the world. In the end, *Nezavisimaya gazeta* made the point clear. Russia's mission statement was its Constitution, which expressed norms which were simultaneously Western and Russian. 'Political and civil society must stand up for the functioning Constitution,' the editors wrote.[68]

Russia is itself[69] – but this does not make it anti-Western. It is *of* the West – and it *borrows* from the West. It is European – and it is Eurasian. But far from opening up Russia in the imaginations of outsiders, this combination of identities has come to be seen as the driver of Muscovy's unstoppable empire. For the Anxiety-prone, as we will see in the next chapter, the myths and realities of expansionism would be encoded into the DNA of the future Russia.

# 7

## The Empire Relationship

*Is Expansionism in Russia's DNA?*

On the evening of 29 October 1939, a sixteen-year-old Polish Jew and his parents pulled into Innsbruck railway station, last stop inside the Third Reich. They shared a forged passport given to them by a South American honorary consul, stamped with a counterfeit consular seal by a Jewish engraver in Warsaw. Their chances of escape rested on the slender prospects of this unlikely document – after all, none of them spoke Spanish – and the encounter that was about to unfold on their train.

They were on the run for their lives. Two months earlier, Germany had invaded their country, causing Britain and France to declare war. Within four weeks, German forces were encircling Warsaw, and the boy's resourceful parents were completing their escape plan. While the family sheltered from German fire, the Red Army invaded Poland from the east. Polish resistance was considerable, but it was ultimately futile. The country was dismembered. Most of it became part of Greater Germany. Austria, somewhat more willingly, had already been part of the Third Reich for two years. So for this family, Innsbruck was the final hostile frontier. Next stop: the relative safety of fascist Italy, which was still a non-belligerent.

At Innsbruck station, a Gestapo officer entered the train. The Polish family waited. They had a compartment to themselves. Eventually, he came in and inspected their passport. He told them to leave the train: their papers were not in order. There was no exit stamp. They could get one in Berlin.

It was late evening and the Alps were barely visible, though travellers with skis clustered on the platform. The boy and his father pulled their suitcases off the train. This was it. In Berlin, their passport would be exposed as a fake and their story would unravel. The father of the family was sufficiently clear-headed to admit that there would be no escape from that. So he went off to roll the dice one final time.

He headed down the platform, disappearing in the night-time Alpine air. The boy and his mother guarded their things. Everyone around, clutching their skis, was red-faced, noisy and jolly. It was time for the train to leave.

Suddenly, the father returned. The stationmaster had told him to get back on the train. They piled their bags on board, jumping back into their compartment. The train set off, passing the Alps, rolling towards the border. Italy was minutes away.

But the same Gestapo man was still on board the train. He came back to their compartment and took their passport. They were still in Greater Germany. Eventually, the officer returned. OK, he said, handing the document back: you can leave but you will never be allowed to return.

In a fog of tears and cigarette smoke, they passed across to Italian territory. Many of their relatives would be destroyed in Auschwitz.[1] Eight months later, the family would reach the United States, where the boy would learn English, serve in the Army, go to Harvard and become the most naturally gifted of his adoptive country's historians of Russia. Americanizing his name to Richard Pipes, he went on to write one of the most remarkable collections of works that an outsider has ever assembled on the history of Russia: he wrote on the nationality question in the early Soviet Union, the historian Nikolai Karamzin, the liberal Pyotr Struve, the reformer Alexander Yakovlev, the Russian Revolution, property relations, conservatism, late-imperial terrorism, the paintings of the 1860s – not to mention the history of Russia from the beginning to the present, and much else in between. In every case, the research was formidable, the argument exemplary, the pace and style enticing.

But Pipes wilfully gave up the one advantage held by outsiders who specialize in the history of Russia. The Russians themselves hold the trump cards of native-language skills and instinctive cultural knowledge, the practical benefits of living and working alongside all of their sources, and the enduring commitment that comes from studying the past of one's own place and people. But the outsiders have distance, and the fresh angles and perspectives it brings. Even outsider-historians can never stand apart from their subject, but Pipes was determined to engage 'morally' as well as 'scientifically'.

Although his family had fled the Germans, and although it was the Holocaust that killed their relatives, Pipes and his parents were only one step ahead of the Red Army, too, which had invaded the eastern zone of Poland on 17 September 1939. He grew up in a part of the country where Polish, German and Czech were spoken, but where the historical memory of the Russian Empire and the 1920 war with the Bolsheviks was still strong. It made him an insider-outsider, and when Soviet scholars read his early works and excoriated 'Meester Paips', they were in a sense quarrelling with a former neighbour, even an estranged relative. Decades on and thousands of miles away from Warsaw 1939, Pipes still chose to forego the possibility of distance. His understandable anger about the Soviet invasion of his country was always consistent with his scholarly conclusions. He ignored the scholarship of 'Sovietologists' and revisionist historians with whom he disagreed, whose vituperative responses were scarcely less appealing. His pre-judged sense of Russia circulated far beyond Harvard and all the way to the White House, at the most dangerous moment of the Cold War since the Cuban Missile Crisis.

Thanks not least to the brilliance of Richard Pipes, and the crystal clarity of his bestselling, heavyweight books, the 'Cold War' interpretation of Russian history hardened and was rehearsed in the White House Situation Room. Drawing on deep research and engaging exposition, Pipes argued that Russia's authoritarian past was the inevitable prologue to its totalitarian future; that totalitarianism consisted in monolithic, top-down repression, brain-washing and uniformity, and nothing else, inside the USSR and in its satellite states alike; and that the Soviet Union was an expansionist threat not just because of communism, but because of a deeper Russian history, characterized by a tsar or a political elite which ruled 'patrimonially', owning everything within their realm, and pushing back borders to satisfy their need for resources.

Pipes was a warrior-scholar. This was the scholarly armed wing of the Russia Anxiety. We might call it the Pipes Protocol.

## THE PIPES PROTOCOL

'In the history of Russia,' Pipes wrote in the early 1980s, 'expansionism is not a phase but a constant.' No wonder, he argued, that the Soviet Union had ended up the biggest country in the world. The long-term expansionism of Russia had three recurring causes: as a means of escaping the poverty of the heartland; as a way of maximizing an existing geographical advantage, hitting the multiple targets – to the west, south, east, north – that Russia's Eurasian core made available; and as a method of enriching elites. What expansionism precisely did not result from was 'anxieties' about invasion, Russia's uniquely long borders, or its complex geopolitical situation. 'Those who make this point,' Pipes insisted, 'usually have but the scantiest familiarity with Russian history.'[2]

During the second half of the 1970s, Pipes nurtured contacts in the most anti-communist wing of the foreign policy establishment, with men such as Paul Wolfowitz. He made high-level but temporary contributions to policy development during and after the presidency of Gerald Ford. This put him on the radar of Ronald Reagan. In 1981, Reagan had just been elected president of the United States. Leonid Brezhnev, sick and unresponsive, was soon to enter his last year. Soviet troops were in Afghanistan. Martial law was about to be declared in Poland. The United States had boycotted the 1980 Olympics, held in Moscow. Détente was finished: Reagan had a straightforward ideological commitment to fighting communism, at least diplomatically. The Cold War really did look like the Cold War, and the Soviet Union really did look like a dictatorship.

Following Reagan's election, Richard Pipes was appointed to the National Security Council (NSC), the body that outlines for the president his foreign policy options. For two years, on leave from Harvard, he helped to develop the Reagan White House's hardline attitude to the Soviet Union. Pipes was convinced that the centuries of Russian imperial expansion had left an indelible mark on the mentality of the country's current rulers. More than this, he thought, the Soviets' interventionist foreign policy derived from communist principle. They pursued a grand strategy for extending Soviet power beyond

Soviet borders; they were not simply diplomatic dealmakers looking for peaceful coexistence. Seeking to explain why this had not led to more outright conflict or an encroachment on Western Europe, Pipes pointed to the aim of achieving global hegemony through a range of methods that need not be military.

Cosying up to the Reds as a means of avoiding war, as many specialists and politicians in the United States were advocating, was no good. 'That objectives of life other than physical survival, objectives which enabled our ancestors to bequeath to us the benefits of the [sic] civilization – among them, personal freedom, the rule of law, and human rights – must in our age take second place to "good relations with the Soviet Union"?' he asked rhetorically, tearing into a Congressman who had suggested that this might be the best aim of American foreign policy. 'That,' he asked further, 'we must give the Soviet government carte blanche to perpetrate inside its country and abroad any barbarity as long as it refrains from firing nuclear weapons at us?' In the book he wrote straight after stepping down from the NSC, he came close to saying that a large collection of otherwise disparate groups – government employees, trade unionists, intellectuals, even businessmen – conspired together to minimize the threat from the USSR, precisely so that they could more easily pursue their own vested interests. What was needed was a policy that transcended the famous division between hawks and doves. 'The key to peace,' Pipes concluded, 'lies in an internal transformation of the Soviet system in the direction of economic decentralization, greater scope for contractual work and free enterprise, national self-determination, human rights and legality.' Making this point a year or so before Gorbachev was appointed general secretary of the Communist Party, when such a transformation seemed vanishingly unlikely, Pipes believed the only way to achieve change in the USSR was through the strongest American measures: 'a combination of active resistance to Soviet expansion and political-military blackmail and the denial of economic and other forms of aid.'[3] (By 'aid', he broadly meant the normal exchanges of international relations.) When the time came, Pipes argued that Gorbachev had succumbed to external pressure rather than made his own radical diagnosis based on internal evidence.

In any case, this was a high-risk strategy, though it was plain to Pipes that the risks were worth taking. President Reagan increased the tempo of his rhetoric, famously calling the Soviet Union 'the evil empire'. His administration stepped up the arms race with its proposed Strategic Defense Initiative, which promised to militarize space itself, and threats to transfer new ballistic and cruise missiles – the Pershing II and Gryphon – to Western Europe if the Soviet side did not remove its SS-20 missiles from the Eastern bloc. Just as the Soviet Union was developing a new strategy to avoid a nuclear escalation – if war broke out in Europe, their response would be to destroy Western nuclear emplacements with conventionally armed aircraft strikes – the Americans seemed to be risking the finely balanced structure of peace. Between 2 and 11 November 1983, when Pipes was already back at Harvard, NATO ran a series of command-and-control exercises in West Germany codenamed Able Archer. It was a prime moment when misunderstandings and fears could have made the Soviets trigger-happy. But the Soviet response suggested they were rational actors rather than desperate expansionists.[4] The paradox was that a hardline NATO response to the USSR in the age of mutually assured destruction depended on the assumption that the Politburo would respond calmly and realistically, which was not quite the message of the Pipes Protocol.

Pipes's experience in the White House, where everyday politics was about as far from the result of deep historical structures as one could imagine, might also have challenged his long-term view of Soviet and Russian history. He saw close-up how specific personalities could shape high politics, sometimes in irrational or absurd ways. His first boss on the NSC, Richard V. Allen, was crowded out of top-table influence by Reagan's closest lieutenants, and ultimately brought down by a manufactured scandal: he was entirely innocent of the corruption with which he was unfairly tainted.[5] Everywhere Pipes looked, a chaotic blend of anger, envy and amiability seemed to play an outsize role in shaping America's response to global events.

No doubt this helped clarify his own approach to the past. He had an ongoing dispute with Marxism, with its overarching historical theories about class struggle. 'I believe that various events are propelled by diverse forces,' he wrote, 'sometimes it is by accident, sometimes individuals make all the difference, on other occasions it is economic factors or ideology.' He underscored the basic point that every historian knows, but which was not always clear from his long-range explanations of Russian development: 'No one cause ever explains everything.'

Pipes wrote the toughest of historical polemics about how the authoritarian tendency in Russian political culture caused one of the most sustained national expansions in human history. But his general view of history seems to have been quite different. 'I have learned that human beings are utterly unpredictable,' Pipes wrote at the end of his memoirs, 'that one can neither anticipate what they will do nor understand why they will do it.'[6] This points to the central paradox of Pipes's work. Even after spending decades describing a relentless authoritarian path for Russian history and its expansionist dynamic, he also saw the possibility of mere historical chaos. Even as he described a Soviet grand strategy masterminded by ideological clarity and fuelled by history, he also saw the Soviet government as a rational actor, capable of responding quickly to events. Had he not, he could not have advocated probing, testing and pushing the adversary. The stakes were just too high.

His might have been the most brilliant voice arguing for the long-term continuity of Russian history. But Pipes was a man whose whole life depended on an episode of blind courage and sheer chance at Innsbruck railway station on a terrifying night in October 1939, and he saw that contingency and personality can undermine the structures of historical explanation, though he held fast to a single main cause – the basic violence of patrimonial rule – to explain the *longue durée* of Russian history. Possessing all the gifts of scholarship and rhetoric in abundance, he convinced many of his readers. The 'Pipes Protocol' therefore leaves a mixed legacy: it was a successful attempt to apply a powerful but rigid interpretation of the past to present policy; it represented a body of historical research marked by both brilliance and wilful omission; and it leaves a model that can be applied to post-Soviet and Putin-era contexts too, with equal risk. Pipes was prepared to test his view of history against the future, sometimes with success. He was one of the few scholars to anticipate that the Soviet Union might plausibly soon fall, though in the end it fell by accident rather than logic, diminishing the force of his prediction. And he was one of even fewer to imagine (correctly, it turned out) that a fault line with Ukraine could be a proximate cause of Soviet collapse.

The Pipes Protocol contributed to the Russia Anxiety; it still does. This was one of its author's intentions. But there are at least three good reasons to give us pause. First is the comparative perspective. Muscovy was not the original territorial aggrandizer in the region, or the only combative state seeking competitive advantage, which at least relativizes our understanding of the original sins of colonization. Second is the way the Muscovites and Russians ran their territory. The method was exploitative, for sure, but it was a collaborative exercise, too. This combination applies to all empires, but it is highly unlikely that the Russian Empire was a more violent and 'extractive' place than, say, the still larger British Empire. (Remember that the period 1904–53, the age of 'tears without end', is an exception in Russian history.) Third is the convoluted history of relations between the different national groups in the Soviet Union, featuring Stalinist violence against specific ethnicities as well as affirmative action to support ethnic minorities in general. In the end, Russian nationhood might even have been weakened by its imperial and Soviet heritage, and for all the drama of events in the 2010s, especially in Ukraine, it is likely that only a very small proportion of Russians have the slightest appetite for invasions and expansionism.

## IN THE BEGINNING, WHO COLONIZED WHOM?

Moscow was founded in 1147. Its early history shows that it was far from the only grabber of land in the region.

The early expansion of an East Slavic 'state' emanated from Kiev, not Moscow. By 912, Kievan Rus had extended its reach to the Baltic coast, as well as to the west, east and south, taking in the area of what would become St Petersburg, Moscow and Minsk, stretching down to the Black Sea coast, and making Crimea a dependency. In every case the lines of its authority were loose, and it possessed nothing like a central state to administer its periphery, or even its home city. Even though the Kievan patrimony was splintering at the start of the eleventh century, Kiev continued to exercise hard and soft power across the region. Vladimir the Great, who reigned between 980 and 1015, sent out his sons to take control over what would become neighbouring principalities: Vyacheslav, for example, became prince of Novgorod, and Yaroslav took Rostov. The princes brought with them the Kievan principle of *kormlenie*, of 'feeding off' the locality by right of raising tribute from it.[7] Even more importantly, Vladimir the Great secured Kiev's relations with Byzantium in 988 with the conversion of the Rus people to Christianity. This was not only of spiritual and strategic importance, but it provided a unified religious mentality that could animate and justify territorial expansion.

Kiev became the elder sister of East Slavic civilization. Later in the eleventh century and after, the city dominated the region without controlling it directly. The Rus went beyond Kiev. Other Rus principalities were formed. The Houses of Galicia, Suzdalia, Volyn, Smolensk and Chernigov came into being. They competed for power and space. To the north was the capacious, prosperous and outward-looking 'Republic' of Novgorod, a large territory with a more 'democratic' political culture that governed itself from 1136, and was fully capable of coercive expansionism. Medieval Novgorod had trade connections to the West, and its political system hinted at the promise of rights, representation and responsiveness. But its wealth rested on the ill treatment of another place. Novgorodians colonized the 'land of darkness' to the east and north, up towards the Arctic, to capture the fur that made them wealthy. They exploited the indigenous people who helped them in their quest. This was the European way for centuries, and the people of Novgorod were typical of this wider trend. Their desire for the skins of squirrel, otter and sable was insatiable.[8]

Only at this point, with Kievan Rus losing momentum, and other versions of Rus, in adjacent territories, becoming more powerful and distinctive in their own right, did one of their rulers, Yuri Dolgoruky, the founder of the Suzdalia dynasty, establish or at least fortify a number of settlements to the north-east of Kiev. One of these was Moscow, in 1147.[9]

So it was not that the new Moscow possessed unique expansionist genes. The expansionist genes were European, and other polities in the region shared them. Meanwhile, the urge to expand stretched across Europe. On Christmas Day 800 AD, Charlemagne, King of the Franks, was crowned emperor of Catholic Christendom by Pope Leo III in

Rome. On 27 November 1095, Pope Urban II preached the sermon that launched the First Crusade.

The rise of Moscow did not imply the fall of Kiev. All the way through to 1918, Russia's was only one of the empires seeking power over the territory that had once been dominated by Kievan Rus.

It was the Mongols who finished off Kievan Rus, defeating Kiev in 1240. For more than 400 years, Kiev was subordinate to other empires: to Mongols, Poles and Lithuanians, while the Ottomans occupied nearby territory in what would also become modern Ukraine. In 1569, following the Union of Lublin, large parts of the Ukrainian lands were subsumed in the new Polish-Lithuanian Commonwealth. Only in 1667 did Moscow gain control of part of this territory.

Moscow became an expansionary power in its own right during this period, thanks to favourable political circumstances. For a start, it had emerged stronger from its encounter with the Golden Horde, eventually inflicting a major defeat on the Mongol-Tatars in 1380. Within a century, it threw off Tatar oversight completely and became a major regional power. Like other would-be superpowers – like China before it, or Spain and Portugal, colonizers of the Americas, at the same time – it spread its wings. It was keen to secure the ideological legacy of Kievan Rus: to have access to its founding legends and its uninterrupted history of Christianity since the tenth century. Not only did this history offer the promise of salvation, but it was a way of binding local people together, Slavs as well as other tribes, giving them something in common and a set of symbolic reasons to support the 'tsar' (Ivan III was the first ruler of Muscovy to use the title). But in annexing such former Rus heartlands as Novgorod and Smolensk, Muscovy was not fixated on Kiev in particular, and did not have a specific strategy to absorb Ukrainians. Instead, it wanted access to a shared history. Symbolism was more important than annexation; after all, Moscow would not rule Kiev until the seventeenth century.

Meanwhile, Moscow itself was subject to the attentions of neighbouring empires. The Commonwealth of Poland-Lithuania was the regional great power, a large and effective empire. Political circumstances gave it a brief chance to conquer Moscow, just as Russia would later take a more lasting opportunity to defeat Warsaw almost

200 years later. When Muscovy was on the ropes during the Time of Troubles (1598–1613), the Poles seized their moment, offering a candidate for the vacant throne. In 1610, Polish forces occupied Moscow. They torched the city and battened down in the Kremlin. Meanwhile, another Polish army captured Smolensk, while Sweden took control of Novgorod. In November of 1612, Muscovite forces relieved their own capital and expelled the Poles.

The Muscovite 'conquest' of Ukraine took place in this context of clashing East European empires rather than its own *sui generis*, uniquely malevolent expansionism. In 1648, Cossacks rose up against Polish rule, releasing the anger of the Ukrainian peasantry at the Polish lords who had enserfed them. It was a time of bitter anti-Semitism, as many of the stewards who managed the lands were Jews, and they too were now targeted by local 'Ukrainian' peasants. A Cossack state, the Hetmanate, emerged. Six years later, Cossack leaders accepted the overlordship of Muscovy. There were clashes between Muscovy and Poland, and the Ottoman Empire took advantage, extending its own control up the western side of the Dnieper (what has come to be known as 'right-bank Ukraine'). But in 1667, the Poles and Muscovites came to terms, agreeing to their spheres of influence in the Ukrainian lands. Naturally enough, the Cossacks struck back at them both.

'Ukraine' – the term is unhistorical for the seventeenth century, though the basis of a Ukrainian consciousness had come out of Polish rule, even if it was not yet much of a priority for most Ukrainian peasants – became part of Muscovy, soon to be part of Russia, and then the Soviet Union. It was formally tied to Moscow for 324 years. Yet the story is not as simple as that. The western part of today's Ukraine, even as it was subsumed within other empires, was clearly Polish. It did not have another identity. In the eighteenth century, Poland would be partitioned between the rival powers of Romanov Russia, Hohenzollern Prussia and Habsburg Austria. Until 1918, the Habsburgs governed large parts of 'Ukraine' and 'Moldova', such as Bukovina. They ruled over the Ruthenians (as they called the inhabitants of modern western Ukraine) thinking of them as part of their Polish patrimony. From 1918, this zone became part of independent Poland. It took the Nazis to eliminate the Poles and Jews in western Ukraine before the zone was taken over by the Soviet Union with their defeat of the Nazis and joined to its Ukrainian republic. Polish-Ukrainian relations warmed in the twenty-first century thanks to their common opposition to Russia, but for many years their relationship in the western borderlands was extremely hostile.

Crimea entered the Russian Empire in the eighteenth century after a long contest between Ottomans and Cossacks. Much of the historic territory of later Belarus, the 'White Russian' lands which are the third element of East Slavic civilization, also came under Russian rule at this time. The medieval city of Minsk (Mensk) is originally traced to Polatsk, on the edge of the Galicia-Volhynia principality that was one of the leading Rus power-centres in the eleventh century. After this, part of what would become modern-day Belarus lay in medieval Lithuania. The 'Belarusian' territory was ruled by the Polish-Lithuanian Commonwealth from its formal inception in the Union of Lublin of 1569. Many of the local peasants belonged to the Uniate Church, practising a version of Catholicism. From the middle of the seventeenth century, they faced plunder by the Cossacks. But as the Kingdom of Poland emerged from the Polish-Lithuanian Commonwealth, Minsk continued to be governed from Warsaw. The Partitions of Poland from 1772 brought 'Belarus' within the Russian Empire. This was a belated 'reunification of Rus'; the tsar was now monarch of Great, Little and White Russia, the meaning of which became central to the evolution of Russia's imperial and national identity over the nineteenth century.[10] But while history was rewritten and deployed to best advantage by all sides during that period, and while St Petersburg came to 'Russify' the region culturally from the 1860s, as we will see below, this was a contingent outcome. It was not the latest chapter in an age-old process of Russian expansionism in the region.

Who colonized whom? Who has the deeds of ownership across the East Slavic lands? The state that would soon become Russia was no more expansionist when it came to Ukraine and Belarus than its rivals, Lithuania, Poland and the Ottoman Empire, while, earlier, Kievan Rus possessed its own expansionist dynamic. Before this, expansionist Varangians had come from Scandinavia to create Kievan Rus in the first place, and before that, the region was home to many competing tribal groups – jostling, fighting, scattering, spreading and naturally 'expansionary' like all such early human groups – of whom the Slavs won out. All these peoples and polities fought over the East Slavic lands. Moscow was only one of several expansionist powers in the region.

In the last decades of imperial Russia, by which time Kiev had been part of the Empire for two centuries, a Ukrainian-speaking intelligentsia, made up of poets, historians and educators, was codifying the basis of a language and culture that for the first time could make a coherent sense of Ukrainian nationhood. The various groups in St Petersburg's governing and intelligentsia circles, from Slavophiles to Westerners to hard-nosed administrators, acknowledged its significance. A common response from St Petersburg elites was to regard the western borderlands, where Ukrainian was spoken, with affection, celebrating the wealth of their harvests, the security of their strategic location, and the cultural consolations of their twee peasant customs. These Russians increasingly constructed their own sense of what it meant to be Russian with some reference to this place.[11] The idea that Ukraine could be a sovereign territory, which in a sense it had never been, even at the time of Kievan Rus, was, though, incredible. Even when Ukraine voted for independence from the Soviet Union in 1991, this sense of incredulity among many members of the political elite in Moscow persisted. Arguably, it persists, exacerbating the tensions and conflict between Kiev and Moscow that developed from the early 2000s. For the leading Ukrainian historian, Harvard's Serhii Plokhy, overcoming the problem of how Russian elites perceive Ukraine is the defining crisis of modern Russian nationhood,[12] though this surely risks reducing a complex phenomenon to a single cause.

In any case, when future historians look to explain relations between Russia and Ukraine in the age of Putin, they would be wise to start not with Kievan Rus but with the twenty-five years since *perestroika* and the end of the Cold War: the circumstances of the collapse of the Soviet Union, its impact on domestic Ukrainian and Russian politics, together with the role of NATO, the EU and Washington. It is not that the rest is just ancient history, but that this older past has not made Russia into a uniquely rapacious colonizer that can't help itself, despite the assumptions of the Russia Anxiety.

# MANAGING DIFFERENCE OR COLONIZING ONESELF?

Russia became one of the great empires of world history. It was a contiguous empire. Expanding outwards over land and into different peripheries from its metropolitan centre, it was the same type of empire as its great rivals, the Austro-Hungarian and Ottoman. To an extent – especially in the imaginations of some of its rulers, such as Peter the Great – it had something in common with the Roman Empire. But it was quite different from the overseas, maritime empires of modern Britain and France, or the intercontinental conquest machines that took the Spanish and Portuguese to the Americas, and the Mongols across Eurasia. Russian rule, like Turkish and Austrian, was based on the steady accumulation of territory, often populated by peoples of related ethnicity, and requiring not just coercion but a collaborative strategy of rulership. Historians Jane Burbank and Frederick Cooper call this approach to empire the 'management of difference'. As they show, it's an essential way of understanding the operation of the Russian Empire.[13] The Anxiety, of course, puts forward opposite conclusions about Russian imperial rule.

And yet empires exist because of military conquest. They use force or its implicit threat to maintain their rule. Taking leave of the empire is not usually an option for subject peoples. The expansion of Russia over many centuries seemed inexorable. Violence was central to conquest and security, just as in every empire that's ever been in human history. No wonder, you might think, that the Russia Anxiety set in.

Facing mightier towns, such as Tver and Novgorod to the north, the earliest princes of Moscow gradually pushed out their borders through guile and toughness. Dmitry Donskoi (1359–89) captured Vladimir in the east and increased the area of Muscovy twofold, pushing northwards to the monastic settlement of Belo'ozero, and close to the major northern lakes of Ladoga and Onega, not far from the space that would later become St Petersburg. Vasily II (1425–62) annexed such important towns as Vologda in the north and Nizhnyi Novgorod in the east. Muscovy prepared for a future without the Mongols.

It was during the reign of Ivan III – Ivan the Great, from 1462 to 1505 – that Muscovy greatly increased in size, becoming a serious power, thanks to the so-called 'gathering of the lands'. Most importantly, Novgorod was defeated and its territory – and fur trade – entered Muscovite control. But Muscovy pushed out too to the south as well as the north, closing in on the Black Sea and brushing up against the Crimean Khanate, and taking Chernigov, not far from Kiev. Ivan the Great's grandson, Ivan the Terrible, took miles of open territory and fought wars to win contested zones. The great gains were Kazan, the homeland of the Tatars, in 1552, and Astrakhan, near the shores of the Caspian Sea, in 1554. It was these victories that signalled two of the future Russian Empire's most important characteristics. One was its multinational character, and especially its ability to reign over Muslims as well as Christians. The other was the drive to the south, towards the Black Sea, the Caucasus and Central Asia, and, in time, to war with the Turks. Meanwhile, at the end of Ivan's reign and during the rule of his son Fedor, the route into Siberia was opened up, with the conquest of such staging posts as Tyumen in 1586 and Tobolsk in 1587.

Between the reign of Ivan the Terrible and the Revolution of 1917, the Russian Empire grew, on average, at the rate of 50 square miles per day.[14] Despite the Anxiety's assumptions, most of this was the exploration of virgin territory, big forests and uninhabitable land, and was not military in nature. Other empires challenged them, not least the Swedes and the Turks, fighting time and again over Russia's southern conquests. But it was expansion to the west that both guaranteed Russia's great-power status and most raised the heat of the Russia Anxiety. During the reign of Catherine the Great, Prussia, Austria-Hungary and Russia carved up Poland between them in three partitions. In 1772, the Russian border was pushed less than 100 miles westwards, in a curve that followed the line of the Dnieper river. The next partition was in 1783, when a much larger slice of Poland entered Russian rule, including big parts of what would later be Belarus and Ukraine – Minsk, the Pripet marshes and land further to the south. Then, in 1795, the final land-grab went as far as the Baltic, taking Lithuania from Polish rule. After the Napoleonic Wars, when the Congress of Vienna adjusted Europe's borders, Warsaw itself entered into the Russian Empire, and the Grand Duchy of Warsaw, which had been controlled by Prussia, was no more. Poland was off the map until 1918. Countless Polish exiles, scattered across Western Europe, understandably gave dark accounts of the destruction of their homeland; if they had a kind of moral immunity to the irrational syndrome of the Russia Anxiety – their country had, after all, been partitioned by Russia, Prussia and Austria – they helped to disseminate the Anxiety to those who did not.

Peter the Great had declared himself Imperator, a deliberately European title. From the turn of the nineteenth century especially, the Russian Empire developed a deadlier edge that gave it more in common with other modern European empires. A new wave of expansion in the Caucasus caused bitter colonial wars, not least the struggle over Chechnya. Georgia (southern Caucasus) entered the Empire in 1801, and Dagestan (northern Caucasus) as late as 1881. In Central Asia, the Russians found themselves face to face in a colonial confrontation with the similarly expansionist and strikingly risk-taking British. The bulk of today's Kazakhstan had been incorporated by 1855, and the Russians peered at Afghanistan. In all these territories, it was difficult for the government to understand its new subjects and to keep accurate information about them. The style of campaigning and governance seemed to select from the crueller repertoires employed in the overseas empires of the Western Europeans. This was the world from which Stalin emerged later in the century. But the Russians were only the latest imperial visitors to Central Asia – Tamerlane and then the Qing Empire were there first – and the Persians had swept through the Caucasus long before them.

Tsarist Russia was distinctively part of Europe and its great-power politics in the nineteenth century; it had (or was) a European empire with a Eurasian reach. If it did not resort to the exterminatory policies of Belgium in the Congo, or the concentration camps of Britain during the Boer War, it made use of some familiar methods of violence. Nationalist uprisings were crushed in Poland, the most reluctant corner of the empire, in 1831, 1846 and 1863, though the British destruction of the Indian Mutiny was more violent. Life began to change very quickly across the western parts of the Russian Empire in the last third of the nineteenth century thanks to the urban and industrial development, and especially the expansion of the railways, that were common to other modern empires. Crucially, Ukraine was no longer a sleepy backwater. The population of Kiev was 25,000 in the 1830s; in 1900, it was ten times as many.[15] Such unrestrained growth was both necessary and threatening for the tsarist government, ensuring industrial development and international security while loosening control over the population. Migration from the countryside brought more Ukrainian speakers to the cities. Cultural nationalism among the intelligentsia deepened and spread. The government responded with 'russification' policies, aggressively limiting the opportunities to teach, learn and publish in Ukrainian. In Poland, too, russification measures had a sharp edge. Now only Russian was spoken in law courts and government offices, while members of the Uniate Church were required to convert to Orthodoxy.[16] Meanwhile, across the empire, ethnic Russians themselves continued to be exploited in the name of imperial development, as the motor of 'internal colonization' ticked over.

And so the bottom line of this centuries-long expansion was force. It could not be otherwise; this was an empire, after all. But force was only part of the story. Unlike some empires, Russia's did not systematically eliminate those who were different, but 'managed' the differences between contrasting groups. Its form of governance required limits on violence, and it made use of multiculturalism and toleration.

Take the example of Finland. Never a sovereign nation, it was annexed from Sweden in 1809. Under Russian control, it became a grand duchy, where Alexander I and his successors ruled not as tsar of all the Russias but as grand duke of Finland. 'In determining conditions in Finland,' wrote Alexander, 'my intention has been to give the people of that country a political existence, so that they would not even consider themselves conquered by Russia, but joined to it by their own self-evident interests.'[17] Helsinki, the capital from 1819, took on the look of St Petersburg, but this only emphasized its cosmopolitan and European features. A national Finnish intelligentsia and cultural tradition emerged. The *Kalevala*, Finland's literary masterpiece, and the music of Sibelius were central achievements. Towards the end of the nineteenth century, concerns about the security of the

Finnish–Swedish border and about the extent of Finnish separateness led to tentative russification measures, such as proposals of 1890 to align criminal law and postal practices with imperial norms. But the Finnish Diet was scandalized, and protests set in.[18] The last twenty years of Russia's rule in Finland, through to independence in 1918, were marked by unrest. This took place in the context of the revolutionary changes that were gripping St Petersburg and other parts of the Empire rather than representing self-starting decolonization.

Or take the example of Mathilde Kshesinskaya, the most famous ballet dancer in the Marinsky Theatre, even in the Empire, and the favourite of Nicholas II. She was Polish, brought up in a Polish family that had a long record of making a living in the world of dance and music. And yet she was born in St Petersburg, where she found great artistic and professional success, and formed connections across the city's nobility. Far from being an obstacle, her Polishness was an asset. After all, the nobility itself was cosmopolitan by language and sometimes ethnicity; Baltic Germans, for example, held prominent positions at court and in the country's civil administration. Kshesinskaya spent part of her childhood in Poland, where the family had a country house, and her early career depended on a Polish network in St Petersburg. She played up a rumour that she herself had noble blood – though of Polish heritage, which gave her added exotic appeal. She seemed to make choices about her national identity. She was Catholic, but her son was baptized Orthodox. When she fled Petersburg during the Revolution – Lenin famously made a speech from the balcony of her house – she did not end up in Poland, but in France. According to one historian, nationality was 'a costume that Kshesinskaya either put on herself or had placed upon her by others'.[19] But the dressing-up seems to have been strategic and opportunistic – and successful – rather than to have been forced upon her.

Over the centuries, pushing the borders back had required the ability to rule over a disparate and diverse set of peoples. Rulers of the empire and the men who worked on their behalf – the soldiers, merchants and nobles – mastered a repertoire of soft power with a hard edge. They devised cultural exchanges, initiated trade on favourable terms, exploited local resources, allied with newly conquered elites who then managed the territory on behalf of Moscow: they demanded oaths and taxes, alternated between gifts and violence. Moscow, and later St Petersburg, ruled a hugely varied contiguous territory. It was a European project, but one which lacked the obsessions with racial hierarchy and racial exclusion that were built into many of the other European empires, and which found their ultimate expression in the Third Reich.

By the nineteenth century, the Russian Empire offered a Eurasian perspective. When Ilya Repin completed his famous canvas of 1886 which showed Alexander III meeting village elders at the Kremlin, he was showing the tsar as he wanted to be seen: in Moscow, at the heart of his realm, with his European-styled family standing behind him, and the Eurasian diversity of the Empire around him. This was a stylized image, a reflection of awe. Repin also painted *The Zaporozhe Cossacks Write a Mocking Letter to the Sultan* during the 1880s. The message about Russia's comfortable and comforting diversity was the same, though the tone was comic. Repin's painting showed how the Cossacks, who had long been a dominant force in what is today's southern Ukraine, gleefully thumbed their noses at the Ottoman Sultan's 1676 ultimatum against them, turning instead to the protection of the emerging Russian Empire. It was an open celebration of one of the Empire's most famous cultures, one that was strong and rough-edged, but whose martial tradition was not a threat to St Petersburg. Repin combined different intelligentsia traditions: the urge for social criticism, and an openness to the West, a feel for nationhood and a curiosity about empire, and the attitudes that cut across these viewpoints: the serious-minded and the joyous, the career-minded and the heartfelt.[20] The reviews of the painting were mixed, because while critics agreed on the colour-filled life it gave to part of 'Russia', they could make it serve either conservative or liberal agendas.[21]

Diversity supported various political ends, and was encoded into the different political visions of the Russian Empire. The Empire could not have worked as it did without toleration. Catherine the Great, in her epochal *Nakaz* (her monarchical manifesto) of 1767, promised 'wise toleration' of other faiths, and followed it up with a decree of 1773. Orthodoxy remained the state religion, but higher-ups in the state administration debated ways of extending toleration throughout the nineteenth century, for example with limited experiments on the validity of mixed marriages in the western provinces, where they were most common. Such men as Konstantin Pobedonostsev were bitterly opposed, but toleration did have friends in high places, such as Pyotr Valuyev, who became minister of the interior in 1861. Four years later, he recorded the following diary entry: 'Since 1861, I have been fighting for freedom of conscience.' As these ideas became increasingly commonplace for educated Russians, the language of toleration became more familiar. In 1905, it was a serious aspect of the October Manifesto, Nicholas's programme of concessions designed to secure the monarchy in the face of revolution. Thereafter the Department of Religious Affairs of Foreign Confessions pushed forward its commitment to the principle.[22]

It bears repeating that this was an empire, not a Sunday school. The picture was mixed, and there were many exceptions. Elite Russia was fascinated and entranced by the peoples and places that made up its changing hinterlands, but a tendency to racism among some officials – for whom nomadic Kazakhs, Kalmyks and Bashkirs were 'wild, untamed horses'[23] – persisted. Muslims played a fundamental part in imperial life, and members of other leading religions, including Buddhists, went about their lives, but the authorities were much less sure of the Jews. Many Jews had become subjects of the Empire following the partitions of Poland. Most of them were confined to the 'Pale of Settlement' in this region, which effectively institutionalized anti-Semitism, though the pogroms that took place from time to time, famously at Kishinev in 1903, were the work of local anti-Semites, not the government. But official and elite attitudes were inconsistent – Prime Minister Witte was married to a Jew – and were driven by the usual modern imperative of identifying and cataloguing the population so that it could be taxed, supervised and regulated.[24]

And what about Pyotr Valuyev? He might have argued with Alexander II in favour of toleration, but he also supported the prototype of russification in the western borderlands.

An opposite imperial process stood out in distinction to toleration and violence alike. This was the tendency to standardize. Take the example of the currency. All the parts of a contiguous land empire should really use the same money. In Hungary, for example, Austrian currency became the standard legal tender following the great compromise that established the Austro-Hungarian dual monarchy. But in the western borderlands of the Russian Empire, the process took much longer, beset by technical complications. For decades, the new Polish lands in the Russian Empire continued to use their own currency (alongside others, including the ruble), and the territory operated its own financial system. It was only in 1866 that Poland became an official user of the Russian currency.[25] Before then, the persistence of the zloty was just one example of the patchwork of imperial life. The desire to standardize, to make the economy more efficient and administration more rational, was a modernizing instinct, a universal tendency shared by the other modern empires.

But the Russians were not the most expansionary people in modern history, and they did not administer the cruellest empire, far from it. Was the conquest of Eurasia as coercive as the rollback of the continental United States? The latter process rested on the enslavement of black Africans. It was coterminous with the removal of land and political rights from native Americans, formalized, for example, in the Indian Appropriations Act of 1851. And it caused war with neighbours – Mexico, in 1846 – and, as expansion went inter-continental, with rival empires such as Spain. Was Russia an empire where America was a republic? Hardly, if the most recent historian of this topic, in his clearly titled and massive book *American Empire*, is to be believed.[26] Could the Russians not keep away from their post-imperial 'near abroad', whereas the Western Europeans beat a dignified retreat from empire? The war in Chechnya was as traumatic as France's Algerian War or Britain's rage in 1950s Kenya, but at no stage of Russia's imperial disengagement, either after the Russian Revolution or the collapse of the Soviet Union, was there violence on the scale of August 1947, when the British washed their hands of India. (By contrast, the fighting in Ukraine in the 2010s looked more like a conflict over border security and national integrity that had something in common with the territorial crises over redrawn borders after the First World War.) To some extent, all this takes us back to the 'hypocrisy radar' that we discussed in chapter 4. With their genius for rhetoric, the Americans could talk of an 'Empire of Liberty'. The French made *la gloire* sound like a virtue, and the chutzpah of the British made for warm words about the rule of law over subject peoples. By contrast, the Russians scratched their heads and told it as it was. 'Equality had nothing to do with it, and neither did the rights of man,' write Burbank and Cooper. 'But men, women and children of lesser and greater gods could be brought under the multicoloured wing of the Russian empire.'[27]

Russia was a Eurasian empire, but it was a European power. Naturally enough, Russian empire-building was not a compassionate process. It was driven by the need to control resources, secure borders, act out national and masculine identities and stand up to foreign powers. Geography, ideology and great power politics merged together – just as they did in the other leading European monarchies. Muscovy-Russia was hardly unique. But it was not a more violent and insatiable empire than its rivals, though it was certainly ready to crush movements that sought independence.[28] Comparative history, then, deflates the Russia Anxiety. As George Kennan taught us in chapter 1, the process of confronting Russia's realities must come through scrutinizing our own societies. And when it came to the Russian Empire, Russia's people themselves were colonized too.

Some Russians were victims of their own empire, just as some Americans were, but most Britons, whose empire was far away, were not. How did this start? As the Muscovite realm expanded eastwards, especially in the sixteenth century, soldiers and traders targeted fur on an ever-greater scale. Local people, most of whom had had little interest in working with fur, were required to operate the everyday business of the fur trade, while the big profits that they generated were quickly transferred back to the capital. The process was even more exploitative thanks to the taxes that were levied and the corruption that sprang up. This system brought thousands of square miles under the exploitation of the imperial centre. It has been called 'internal colonization'. The social organization of local people south of the Arctic was changed to exploit them better. Whole ethnic groups incidentally vanished in the process, while the animals themselves experienced a miserable state of permanent massacre. Even later, the process went on: in the eighteenth- and nineteenth centuries, for example, the Kamchadal population fell by 90 per cent, and the Vogules by 50 per cent.[29]

One of the drivers of Russian economic development was, therefore, the exploitation of its own peoples. The Russian Empire grew and grew between the reign of Ivan the Terrible and the period of Soviet power (though it faced an upset with the destruction of the Tsarist order at the end of the First World War). This process – expansion, enrichment, extermination – was one of the repertoires of the great world empires. The Spanish and Portuguese conquest of Central and South America unfolded in an even more violent way, together with greater force of arms and the onset of catastrophic epidemics. It made possible, though, the seizure of extraordinary riches, especially in the accumulation of massive silver reserves from such places as the Potosi mines.[30] Three hundred years later, in Australia, the British rollback of territory, securing the interior, came at terrible cost to the Aboriginal peoples. The British gained the resource of land on a massive scale, increasing the Empire's agricultural capacity, opening new zones of colonial settlement and expanding the scope of the global economy of the Anglosphere.[31]

Yet the Spanish, Portuguese and British were engaged in mass destruction thousands of miles from home. The violence of imperial conquest not only did not threaten the personal security of people in the homeland, it did not trouble their consciences. Distance lends enchantment. By contrast, in Russia, the territory that was being gathered up was contiguous country. It was the homeland itself – the native soil of the motherland and the domestic state institutions of the fatherland – that were increasing in size and reach. The metropole (the native heart of the empire) was immediately adjacent to the periphery (the conquered imperial territory). Aside from some long-standing conquests that were recognizable civilizations in their own right, such as Georgia and Armenia, and other conquests that did not reconcile themselves to Russian rule, not least Chechnya and Poland, the whole place was 'Russia', nation and empire, rolled into one – and even the exceptions were still viewed as Russia by some.

So the exploitation of the Russian peoples by their own government was inseparable from a still wider historical problem: the impossible-to-disentangle relationship between the Russian nation and the Russian Empire. But this was not uniquely a Russian problem. It was similar to the United States. Starting with the English in Virginia and Massachusetts in the seventeenth century, the native American population became embroiled with the newcomers in a zero-sum game that they were bound to lose. Progress, modernization and enrichment coincided with destroying the locals. From the early nineteenth century, under President Andrew Jackson, the expansion of the United States into the territory of indigenous peoples was a matter of seizing natural resources (gold in Cherokee Georgia in 1829, for example), taking and fencing off land, evicting natives, repressing them, cheating them, using violence against them, and involuntarily but conveniently spreading disease to which they were vulnerable. 'The waves of population and civilization are rolling to the westward,' said Jackson in December 1830, 'and we now propose to acquire the countries occupied by the red men of the South and West in a fair exchange.'[32]

If America and Russia had something in common, then a difference was the extent to which the politically dominant ethnic group – the Russians themselves – suffered in the process of Russia's 'internal colonization'. In the United States, there was a pretty clear hierarchy of social advantage, based on racial identity, with whites at the top, especially those of Anglo-Saxon descent and Protestant religion. The men who ruled were from the ethnic group that enjoyed the most economic advantages. By contrast, the tsar and his government could scarcely be accused of looking after their own. The Russian interior was not opened up for free farmers to populate the land. Instead, migration there was often forced, and economic advantage was focused on the landowning class. The men and women who might have been farmers in their own right in the United States were enserfed in Russia, and made to work under the ultimate threat of corporal punishment. True enough, serfs developed robust systems of mutual protection based on customary laws, and could enjoy a basic standard of living that was similar to that of agricultural workers in some other parts of Europe. They were not exploited in the way that American slaves were exploited, and in 1861 they were emancipated. But for many years, Russians still extracted profit from their fellow countrymen without paying for it in return. Meanwhile, there were non-Russian zones of the Empire where serfdom did not extend, in the Western borderlands, for example, and in parts of Siberia. The standard of living in some of these places was relatively high. Nowhere did the imperial project do less for the Russians themselves than in its penal system. Like other empires – like the British sending convicts to Australia – Russia created a zone of incarceration. Even here, though, the ruling principle was the 'management of difference'.

Nineteenth-century Siberia was the Russian government's 'prison of peoples'. Thousands of convicts were transported there. They left an historic mark not just on Siberia's landscapes, cities and inhabitants, but on the world's imagination too. Over three centuries, soldiers, adventurers and merchants had gathered the Siberian lands under Tsarist control. Bit by bit, hundreds of small ethnic groups were caught in an alien empire.

This was Vasily Surikov's homeland. He was born in 1848 in Krasnoyarsk, in a two-storey wooden house with decorative, Siberian eaves. His home was full of history. The family observed traditions, told folk tales and put the women in their place. They were Cossacks. It was his father's job in the local administration of justice that took the family to a distant Siberian village when Vasily was five. His childhood was filled with the deep Siberian forest – the *taiga* – and its mushrooms and berries, with horses and hunting, birch trees and meadows, and, in time, with schooling back in Krasnoyarsk, where he lived with his godmother. It was a tough education, with beatings and little praise. When he was eleven his father died. The family came back to Krasnoyarsk, and Vasily lived with them again. They were reduced to one floor of their house while another family lived upstairs. The pension that came from his father's service was not enough to live on, so his mother and sister Katya took in sewing.

It was a solemn time. One of the few sparks of fun came from his uncle, another Vasily, on leave from the army, who told stories and drew pictures for him. He pointed a way out, unexpectedly focusing his nephew's interest in drawing. At school he had an art teacher called Nikolai Grebnev. He helped to channel Vasily's talent in a town without art galleries. Grebnev took Vasily under his wing, buying him paints, telling him he would become an artist.

But life got worse. Vasily's sister Katya married, moved out, then died. The teenager had to earn money. His mother appealed to her husband's former colleagues. Vasily was levered into an undemanding job in the provincial administration. At least he could keep the remnants of their household secure, though Grebnev's prediction about his future now seemed more unlikely than ever. Still, he got another break. First he was invited to give drawing lessons to the governor's daughter, Vera. Then, in the middle of a lesson, the governor brought him a letter from the Academy of Arts in St Petersburg. The governor had sent them some of Vasily's pictures, and now the Academy wanted to meet him. Thanks to a gift from a local art-loving businessman, Vasily had the funds to make the trip. It took him two months to get there. He arrived on 19 February 1869. Vasily was only twenty, but he had the improbable chance to become the greatest history painter of his time.[33] He made use in part of his own history.

Cossacks, including the ancestors of the Surikov family, had fought to make Siberia part of Russia. Vasily Surikov would paint some of the pictures that celebrated and humanized their role in Russian history, most famously in *Yermak's Conquest of Siberia*, which he completed in 1895.

Yermak might have been the conqueror of Siberia, but the band of soldiers and adventurers that he led had many Cossacks in it. Although much of his life is shrouded in mystery, and he became the subject of nationalist myths in the decades before 1917, it seems that he crossed the Irtysh river and defeated Khan Kuchum's army of Siberian Tatars in October 1582. He was bankrolled by the Stroganov family to the tune of 20,000 rubles, which paid for muskets, cannon and 800 mercenaries. The Khan had no chance with his bows and arrows. Of course, Yermak didn't capture the whole of Siberia, and his expedition was a private one, but he declared his victory in the name of Ivan the Terrible, and sent him the tribute that the conquest extracted. Yet soon his army began to disintegrate under the devastating pressures of the frontier. Ivan sent Yermak a back-up force which arrived just in time. Now the path across Eurasia beckoned.[34]

By the turn of the 1890s, Vasily Surikov the Siberian-Cossack was already one of the most celebrated painters in Moscow and St Petersburg, able to command fantastic sums for his monumental canvases of historical scenes. He decided to tackle Yermak's triumph, the great event that fused his family's and country's destinies. On a visit to Krasnoyarsk in 1889, he went to his old family house and communed with its Cossack past; he explored the Irtysh, and returned to live in Siberia for a time in 1892. He wanted to get to know Cossack faces, and studied them on location in the Don, and in his Moscow studio.[35] And he had a good knowledge of historical sources.

Meanwhile, in 1891, the future Nicholas II – still crown prince, imagining it would be decades yet before he ascended to the throne – led the dedication ceremony for the Trans-Siberian railway.[36] This was nothing if not Yermak for the modern age. The locomotive had displaced the musket, but it was the latest chapter in the tsarist state's assertion of real and symbolic control beyond the Urals. Sergei Witte, who as minister of finance raised the investment, wrote to Alexander III about what the railway meant. Russia, he claimed, 'has long since appeared among Asiatic peoples as the bearer of the Christian ideal, striving to spread among them the principles of Christian enlightenment, not under the standard of Europeanization, but under her own special standard'.[37] The Imperial Geographic Society had been founded earlier in the century, dedicated to exploration and ethnographic study: the aim was to show how the Russian lands made up a cohesive and special territory. Its members made discoveries, constructed knowledge, and fired imaginations. By the 1890s, this work was popularized by exotic adventurers such as Nikolai Przhevalsky and Esper Ukhtomsky.[38]

Surikov's painting of *Yermak's Conquest of Siberia* shows the battle at the Irtysh river and the defeat of Khan Kochum. Cossack soldiers loom out of the visually dominant left of the picture, larger than their opponents. One of them wears a red coat, catching your eye. They are Surikov's stock. He loved them, just as Tsarevich Nicholas and Tsar Alexander III did; as crown princes, they had taken great pleasure in their investitures as ataman of the Don Cossacks at Novocherkassk, Alexander in 1869, Nicholas in 1887. The ceremony went with being heir to the throne.[39] In the painting, the Cossacks massacre their opponents with their muskets, while the arrows of the Siberian Tatars fall short, in the river. But they hold their ground on the right of the picture despite the terror. The Cossacks' hats and helmets, and the even more ornate and traditional clothing of the Siberians, are authentic. Their faces reflected Surikov's study of Cossack and Siberian features and the hours of sketching in his studio and on his travels, while the depiction of costumes derived from his research. The canvas brings together the ancestors of different groups inside the late Russian Empire, and different parts of Surikov's own life, in an image that celebrated Russia's geographical destiny. It's a violent picture.

But like the leaders of other durable empires, not least their neighbours in the middle of Europe, the Habsburgs, Russia's imperial rulers could not only be violent and exclusive.[40] Far from it. They had to use ethnic and religious diversity productively if their imperial project was to be stable and successful. And so they employed local soldiers: in one Siberian expedition of 1659, 150 Yukagirs served alongside nineteen Russians. The tsars' lack of administrative reach required them to make political compromises, collecting little or no tribute in some places, conscripting few or no army recruits in others. Meanwhile, local groups were often allowed to exercise their own customary laws and administer their own forms of justice. So in the small transactions of Siberian life, exploitation might come from faces more familiar than those of the imperial centre and its agents, be they Yermak's troops, greedy fur traders or aristocratic governors. Russian expansionism assumed an organic and multi-ethnic aspect, less artificial than the overseas global empires of Western Europe, and sometimes less deadly than America's westward drive.

And so it was no wonder that the newly crowned Nicholas II loved Surikov's picture. A year after his accession, he bought it for 40,000 rubles. But even at the height of the painting's success, when Surikov was presented to Grand Princes Pavel and Vladimir, in an atmosphere of extravagant praise and great excitement, Vladimir's wife, Maria, expressed her abundant enthusiasm to Surikov in French, so often the language of the elite in the last century and a half.[41] Imperial Russia looked west and east, to Europe and Eurasia. Its expansionary identity was precisely what made it a great power like France and Britain, and even what defined its European status.

Expansionism isn't an indispensable part of Russia's historic political culture. It isn't an especially Russian phenomenon. But it is a reality of European and then global politics. The question is, then, whether Russia has taken a 'normal' geopolitical process to extremes, and whether the charge against it – that it's the bad actor of world politics, that it has expanded in ways that lie outside international norms – is really a fair one.

When the Russian Revolution came in 1917, the Bolsheviks were emphatic anti-imperialists. They were committed to ending the Russian Empire, though they were also committed to defending the Revolution. The Russian Empire survived as a collection of territories. Some of the repressive qualities of empire persisted, while other qualities – the management of difference – continued to be required.

And in an important way, the Soviet Union was also something other than an empire: it was the Eurasian experiment in communism. All of these factors knock down the two-dimensional cut-out monster image, on which the Russia Anxiety depends, of an exceptionally aggressive expansionist power, one that has probably even today not got the bug out of its system. As the historian Geoffrey Hosking has pointed out, Russians were the rulers of the union that resulted, but also, perversely, its victims.[42]

## A FRATERNAL UNION OF PEOPLES OR A SOVIET EMPIRE?

Stalin was the Bolsheviks' resident expert on issues of nationality and empire. Before the First World War, he had found himself trapped in lengthy Siberian exile following his arrest for revolutionary crimes. Lacking opportunities to impress Lenin and the other leading Bolsheviks, and feeling the self-conscious worries of the autodictat, it became important for him to establish an area of expertise, flex his theoretical muscles and perhaps also transcend his origins in the Caucasus. In his tract of 1912, *Marxism and the National Question*, Stalin argued that to be a nation, a people must possess defined historical roots, a dominant language and a shared culture and mentality. Crucially, though, a nation must also have its own territory and economy. Anything less, and the group in question might be little more than a tribe. This meant, for instance, that – in contradistinction to Russian tradition, later Soviet law and the usual definitions that were prevalent in Eastern Europe – the Jews were not a nation. Nation-states were a capitalist phenomenon, and they were not permanent, but nor were they, as Lenin maintained, merely transient.

This arcane disagreement between two politicos on the fringe of the fringe became, amazingly enough, the fulcrum of twentieth-century nationalities policy in Eurasia. The dispute levered between visions of multiculturalism and Russian domination, accommodation and exclusion, and compromise and violence. It was not that Lenin took one position and Stalin the other, let alone that Lenin was a compromiser. The Leninist ideal – propounded by the multilingual exile on the run from country to country – was one of internationalism. Focusing on cultural differences and national separateness risked undermining the cross-border alliance among the proletariat. Class trumped nation every time. Yet many in the Bolshevik Party, and more widely in the Russian radical Left, took a different view, and not simply one based on theoretical posturing, but on practical politics. Take the 'Bund', an autonomous Jewish socialist organization. Many of its members were drawn to Bolshevik or Menshevik politics because of late-imperial anti-Semitism, especially the pogroms, which they connected to economic grievances and came to explain in class terms. In time, the Caucasian nationalities would also have specific representation in the predecessor organizations of the Communist Party of the Soviet Union, such as the Armenians' group in 1907. Lenin came to see that a purist position was not going to work. Strategy trumped principle. He thought that the far Left had to ally with national minorities, and accept that the same groups could campaign for both national sovereignty and working-class liberation.[43] Lenin came to recognize Stalin's point that nations had a part to play in the coming collapse of capitalism.

As a result, the Russian Revolution also made possible a period of national liberation. On the day that the Bolsheviks came to power, the second All-Russian Congress of Soviets promised to 'provide all the nations that inhabit Russia with the genuine right to self-determination'. Yet this was a revolution from which it was not really possible to opt out. It quickly became apparent that the tension between an overarching Russian identity and the status of the smaller nationalities was as difficult to resolve as the other tensions that beset the revolution: between individual and collective, liberation and coercion, class and gender.

The solution: Lenin and Stalin would build the nations which would equip the inhabitants of those territories with the language and culture to become revolutionary socialists. In debate, they saw off those who retained their idealist attachment to internationalism, the likes of Nikolai Bukharin. Yet while they built nations, they also built something that looked a bit like the old empire. Lenin and Stalin fell out in the process.

On 30 December 1922, the Union of Soviet Socialist Republics came into being. It replaced the Revolution's original Russian Soviet Federative Socialist Republic, whose constitution was approved in July 1918. Some of the old territories, notably Finland and Poland, had gained independence, while Ukraine and Belarus, Transcaucasia and Central Asia, were incorporated during the Revolution and the Civil War, making the RSFSR a kind of successor of the old Russian Empire, centrally driven and strong enough in the centre to defeat the Whites. It was the formulation that Stalin had favoured. But in his last political actions before suffering a disabling stroke, Lenin prepared for the Party Congress that would approve the new, more 'democratic' solution to the nationalities issue, the USSR. In the new USSR, some of the constituent nationalities within the Russian republic itself retained a certain level of autonomy, but now those nations that were larger and more distinctive, including Ukraine, gained their own status as republics, formally on the same level as Russia, though Moscow was the capital of the union as a whole. This was where Stalin and Lenin diverted from each other again. Even though he himself was a Georgian, Stalin had preferred that the revolutionary state continue to be called Soviet Russia, rather than have the label of a multinational union, which caused Lenin to say he was a national 'chauvinist'.

Still, Stalin oversaw the introduction of an extraordinary experiment, before he moved on from the Commissariat of Nationalities and became general secretary of the Communist Party in 1924. The experiment ran into the 1930s (in some places it slowed down sooner), when it was replaced by a more Russia-dominated model of Soviet life; but even after that, Soviet nationalities policy was still a revolutionary phenomenon. What the Bolsheviks did was this. They turned languages that had only before been spoken into *written* texts, making possible literacy, complex local administration and a published literature. The Bolsheviks opened new schools in which the status of the local language was privileged. Venerable languages, such as Armenian, or those threatened by russification during the late imperial period, such as Ukrainian, were both promoted. All the infrastructure of mass publishing and culture, from newspapers to movies, was put in place. Local people, conversing in local languages, became new elites. Small and large nations experienced an accelerated development or were more or less created from scratch through a sequence of policies that amounted to positive discrimination. And yet the Russians were still clearly in charge. Moscow ruled. For one of its leading historians, this was the 'affirmative action empire'.[44]

Bolshevik nationalities policy in the 1920s and early 1930s was called *korenizatsiya*, from the word *koren'*, or root, and often translated as 'indigenization'. The idea was that the Bolsheviks were deeply planting the roots of democratic nations in the soil of the old empire. This also applied to the Jews. Trotsky and many other Jews had played a pivotal part in the Bolshevik Revolution. Notwithstanding Trotsky's own exile, they became central in the Bolshevik state, from the Politburo on down. In 1931, an autonomous Jewish republic was created inside the Russian republic. Called Birobidzhan, it was a Janus-faced place, weirdly located in the middle of nowhere, near the border with China. The policy of indigenization made it possible. It emerged at a time when Jews were doing well in Soviet society, but Birobidzhan hinted at Jewish separateness, even at the old Pale. Most Jews stayed where they were, though a few sought a better future in the East. Never popular, Birobidzhan survived.[45]

The Russian republic contained within its borders a number of other 'autonomous republics' like Birobidzhan. In Tatarstan, for example, the percentage of Tatars in local government rose from 7.8 in 1921 to 35.4 in 1930. In Udmurtia, where the Udmurts were 59 per cent of the population, they occupied 68.7 per cent of leadership posts in government in 1935.[46] There were unforeseen consequences, such as when Muslims in Central Asia responded to enforced secularization by discovering an attachment to the veiling of women that they had not hitherto possessed.[47] Still, even sympathetic outsiders looked on the most incontrovertible examples of post-imperial modernization with an Orientalizing gaze. Jahon Obidova, who was born in 1900, grew up in a poor peasant family in a village north of Tashkent. She was forced to marry a brutal sixty-five-year-old when she was thirteen, enduring her torment until she ran away to the city, worked in domestic service and joined the Bolshevik Revolution. By the middle of the 1930s, she was the senior official in the city's government. Even so, a German socialist, Fannina Halle, who had come to Tashkent to write about feminism, saw her not as the product of modernity and communism, let alone of her own personal qualities, but of history, empire and the East. 'Such burning, flashing eyes,' she wrote, 'reflecting . . . the hardship and despair of past centuries, and the succeeding revolt, rebellion, struggle, and readiness to die of an Eastern woman.'[48] Even when the Soviet Union constituted itself in ways quite unlike the old empire, it was difficult for observers to escape an older perspective upon it.

Nevertheless, if the new Soviet Union could liberate national groups, it could also find new ways to coerce and harm them. As part of the Great Terror, 'special operations' were conducted against those national minorities which seemed especially threatening, such as Germans and Koreans. Such people either were inhabitants of borderlands or might conceivably owe allegiance to a foreign power, even if their ancestors had lived in Russia for centuries. The most notorious such order was number 00485, introduced on 9 August 1937. On its basis, lists of potential enemies of the people who were of Polish nationality were drawn up. In total, as many as 247,157 people were shot as a consequence of the orders against nationalities. Nearly all of these people were entirely innocent of any possible conspiracy; on the contrary, they were probably broadly in favour of Soviet power. They were lost resources in the fight that was coming against Germany, rather than a fifth column.[49]

Nation-building was an exercise in social engineering, though it probably went more closely with the grain of people's lives than other Bolshevik programmes. Despite the appalling violence of the Terror, nation-building was usually a peaceful process, avoiding ethnic bloodshed. Indigenization might come with long-term risks of regional violence, some of which were realized after 1991, but in its early stages, it was more inclusive and harmonizing than many other Bolshevik policies.

If the early history of nationalities policy and 'empire' in the Soviet Union undermines the assumptions of the Russia Anxiety, does Ukraine fit into the same picture? By the time of the Russian Revolution was Ukraine ripe for independence, or was it ready to embrace a shared communist experiment with Russia? The answer was both. The Ukrainians effectively claimed independence during the revolution with the establishment of the parliamentary 'Rada' in Kiev. But these lands were of such strategic importance and cultural sensitivity that Ukrainian independence was unthinkable for the Bolsheviks. Ukrainians were themselves divided about the Revolution. Some of the bitterest fighting of the Civil War, worst barbarism – on both sides – and most terrible anti-Jewish pogroms took place on Ukrainian land. When they were secure in power, however, the Bolsheviks introduced national policies that promoted a genuine Ukrainian nationhood. These were political concessions and so were vulnerable to reversal, but they also made ideological sense to Lenin and many of his supporters.

In the 1920s, a programme of 'Ukrainianization' took place as part of the USSR's wider nationalities policy. It had major consequences. In 1923, 12.5 per cent of newspaper circulation was of Ukrainian-language titles; in 1932, it was 91.7 per cent. As a result, by 1932, the coal miners' trade union arranged 61.9 per cent of its 'cultural circles' and 75 per cent of its lectures and discussion groups in Ukrainian; in the agricultural sector, almost all these events were in the local language.[50] Of course, this expanded the sense of Ukrainian nationhood. But people often did not express that sense of nationhood in political ways. This was because the Soviet Union was a dictatorship. Dictatorial control allowed the rapid introduction of a nationalities policy which assuaged many Ukrainian concerns; it also made the organization of a separatist movement impossible.

The essence of the Soviet dictatorship in the time of Stalin was suspicion, not least of national minorities. If peasants – that awkward class whose work had to pay for Stalin's industrial revolution – were often distrusted, peasants of certain nationalities were seen as the most likely traitors or saboteurs. In 1932, following agricultural collectivization, the grain yield in the Ukrainian republic was very low, as it was in the Kuban region of the North Caucasus. One of the reasons for this really was popular resistance, which was not just a figment of the government's imagination, but there were other causes too. It was not difficult for a conspiracy-minded Kremlin to explain the failure of collectivization in terms of a beneficent nationalities policy gone wrong, which needed radical and vicious correction. The grain requisitions that usually accompanied collectivization were especially extreme in these regions. This was terror, because it deprived people of the food they had grown themselves and desperately needed in order to survive. It took place in Russian regions, too, especially but not only in the lower Volga, and also in the Kazakh lands but in Ukraine and the Kuban it became a 'nationalities terror'. In Ukraine alone, as many as 3.9 million people died during what became known as the *Holodomor*, or extermination-famine. The most deaths were in Ukrainian-speaking areas.[51] Aside from the deaths of Ukrainian-speaking peasants, the police took action against certain Ukrainian elites: members of the Communist Party, especially those who were prominent supporters of Ukrainianization, and writers, intellectuals, teachers and administrators who worked in Ukrainian programmes. Emigrés who had come into Soviet Ukraine from what would later be west Ukraine, which was still in Polish hands, were also targeted.[52] All these groups were made up of likely 'conspirators'. This was mass murder on an epic scale. Calling it 'genocide' has become more of a political than an historical label, often designed to push political change rather than to describe or explain what happened.[53] The judgement of the leading American historian of early Soviet nationalities policy avoids talk of genocide, because the intention of the Stalinist authorities was to root out opposition of all kinds, rather than to exterminate a nationality as such.[54] The consequences of grain requisition and famine in the Russian Volga region, especially near Penza, and on Kazakh territory, were also devastating. No major scholar doubts the extent of the Ukrainian tragedy. The crime was not perpetrated by Russians against Ukrainians, but by a multinational Soviet government led by a Georgian.

But in the end the argument might be splitting hairs. Let Nikita Khrushchev have the last words, ones taken from the Secret Speech. Here he condemned many of the crimes of Stalin. He drew attention to the forced deportation of some ethnic groups, especially the Chechens and Ingush from the North Caucasus. 'The Ukrainians avoided meeting this fate only because there were too many of them and there was no place to which to deport them,' he said wryly.[55]

For the rest of Soviet history, and in a reversal of their national origins, Russia acted like an elder brother to Ukraine – often patronizing, sometimes implicitly regretful for past wrongs, sometimes keen to help, sometimes aloof, sometimes didactic, occasionally vindictive. But

Moscow was not Kiev's enemy. The worst of what happened next took place in western Ukraine after its annexation from Poland in 1939 during a brief Sovietizing occupation that soon gave way to Nazi control. The city of Lviv – Lwow, Lvov – had been part of the Polish-Lithuanian Commonwealth, the Kingdom of Poland, then the Habsburg Empire, finally modern Poland; it had not really been a Ukrainian city before. For three years during the Second World War, it was occupied by the Germans. They killed the Jews. Poles suffered disproportionately. To a limited extent and in a very dangerous context, Ukrainian nationhood developed.[56] Later, when it was part of the USSR, Ukrainian identity there began to coalesce – the city became more and more Ukrainian – in quiet or outright opposition to Soviet policy. The USSR deplored Ukrainian nationalism for its backward and bourgeois qualities, and accordingly acted against it. From being a mixed borderland, without a dominant ethnic identity, western Ukraine became one of the few genuine centres of opposition to Soviet power, together with the Baltic states, whose Soviet roots were similarly shallow.

But other futures were possible for Ukraine in the Soviet Union, as the federation's 'second republic', and a member state of the United Nations in its own right. One was the consequence of well-meaning if patronizing direction from Moscow, which assumed an unshakeable logic of fraternal union under Soviet leadership. Dmitry Shelepin, a senior official who worked closely with Khrushchev on ideological questions and became a bitter critic of his boss, noted that after Khrushchev moved from Kiev to Moscow 'he was vain enough to want the Ukrainian people to regard him as their generous "chief" and "patron"'. Shepilov argued that, time and again, Khrushchev took the side of Ukraine or simply worked hard to gain support there. The most famous example was his proposal to transfer sovereignty of Crimea to Kiev. Shepilov did not like this: it was 'senseless and a gross violation of historical tradition and the Leninist nationalities policy'. According to his figures, 71.4 per cent of the Crimean region was Russian at that time. Only Molotov spoke against the policy in the Presidium, and the decree was approved on 19 February 1954. Shepilov so disliked Khrushchev that he could never see a positive motive for any of his actions. 'Khrushchev wanted to hand Ukraine an anniversary present and thus polish what he fancied was his already glorious image in that land,' he concluded.[57] The transfer was part of a wider post-war celebration of Ukraine-Russia ties, prompted by the 300th anniversary of the Pereiaslav Council of 1654 that had brought the Cossack Hetmanate within Muscovite protection. Khrushchev witnessed poverty and devastation in post-Nazi-occupation Crimea and argued that direct administration from Kiev would more quickly solve its problems.[58] However one explains the Crimean handover, it can't be interpreted as oppression. It was not about equality – it seemed to be more about paternalism, goodwill and gift-giving than national rights and an ineffable statement of sovereignty.

An extension of this approach was associated with Petro Shelest, the first secretary of the Ukrainian Communist Party between 1963 and 1972. He was also a member of the Politburo in Moscow. Shelest restored the vision of 'national communism' that had been put forward by Mykola Skrypnyk after the Revolution. Skrypnyk was a long-standing Bolshevik, a passionate revolutionary, who saw a Soviet and national vision for Ukraine. He put the 'indigenization' policy of Ukrainianization into practice as commissar of enlightenment, or education, in the republic. Skrypnyk committed suicide in 1933, during the violent repression that accompanied the famine. But during Khrushchev's Thaw, he was rehabilitated, and life was breathed into some of his ideas. The point was that a person could be both Ukrainian and Soviet, that both identities could prosper simultaneously, and that the advantages of being Soviet – the fruits of domestic communism and international security – offered the best possible chance for the Ukrainian people.[59] A version of this approach, stripped of illusions, was probably the instinctive assumption of many people who lived in the Ukrainian republic, including Ukrainian-speakers, through to the late 1980s.

In Kiev State University and other places of learning, this new approach to nationhood was consolidated during the Khrushchev era. It was a time of communist idealism among significant numbers of people, including in Ukraine. But a complementary notion also probably gathered support: cultural distinctness and practical autonomy as part of a shared Soviet drive to a modernized and better future. This was a revised national communism or a particular Soviet nationalism with poles of attachment: the Soviet Union and the

Ukrainian nation. Kiev State University was allowed to conduct more of its work in Ukrainian. There was an inner logic in this way of understanding Soviet-Ukrainian identity.[60]

But Soviet-Ukrainian identity in the years after Stalin also possessed a destructive tension. In Lvov/Lviv, whose Jewish-Polish-Ukrainian composition had been shattered by German occupation, and whose Ukrainian majority had been targeted by the 'pacification' campaign of the post-war era, the sense of Ukrainian nationhood was quite different. The city developed a youth culture and a counter-culture that rejected Soviet norms; there was an established hippie scene in the city in the 1970s, as well as a taste for nationally inspired pop music. In 1969, the success of the city's football club, the Carpathians (Karpaty), in the USSR championship prompted some Ukrainian nationalist celebrations. The public culture of Poland seeped across the border, helping to give focus to calls for independence from 1990,[61] placing western Ukraine and especially Lviv, together with the Baltic states, at the vanguard of this movement.

Brezhnev, who was himself from east Ukraine, feared that what was happening in Lvov (as he called it) could ultimately lead to the same thing happening in Kiev. He ran the Soviet Union and Ukraine from the vantage point of his 'Dnepropetrovsk' mafia, which was culturally and economically closer to Russia and distrusted a more national vision of Ukraine. In a sense he was right to be cautious. But most of the time it seemed certain that the Ukrainian republic was a fundamental part of the Soviet Union, that its separation was unimaginable, and that the voices off-stage in Lviv were of no relevance to anyone.

By 1991, ethnic differences placed the USSR at mortal risk. The Soviet collapse was not inevitable until just before it happened; and calls for national sovereignty were an unlikely precipitant until they were the very factor that brought the union to an end.

Remember that the post-war USSR consisted of fifteen republics, of which the Russian republic was the largest, and the Ukrainian republic an indispensable junior partner. The others stretched across Eastern Europe, the Caucasus and Central Asia. This multinational project carried risks. With time, the ethnic structure of the USSR had destabilized the coherence of the Soviet project. In 1989, ethnic

Russians made up 50.8 per cent of the total population of the USSR. They were a majority, and they controlled the union, but their position was not quite secure. Even in the Russian republic itself, they were only 82 per cent of the total population (and probably less), a reminder of Russia's heterogeneity. In some republics, the dominant ethnicity was under strain because of many years of Russian immigration. Kazakhstan was the most striking example. In 1989, only 40 per cent of the population belonged to the titular nationality, and 38 per cent were Russian. More politically consequential was the composition of Latvia, which was 52 per cent Latvian, and 34 per cent Russian, the result of migration to fill factory jobs. This created instability, compounding the Baltic grievances that strained the union.

Other ethnic stresses resulted from rapid population growth in the Caucasus and especially in Central Asia. The population of Uzbekistan grew by 26.4 per cent in the 1970s, when Russia's population grew by 4.9 per cent; in the 1980s, Uzbek growth had risen slightly to 27 per cent, while the extent of Russian increase had gone down, to 3.9 per cent. The Russian republic benefited in terms of security and superpower status from its relationship with the smaller republics that surrounded it, but it paid for the privilege, transferring 67 billion rubles in subsidies in 1989 according to one calculation, and perhaps gaining fewer advantages than any other republic from trade within the union.[62]

But others had paid, too. The 'small peoples of the north' – such ethnic groups as the Nenets and Dolgan, who live around the Arctic Circle and who traditionally make a living from reindeer hunting and other native occupations – were researched, catalogued and given written cultures and 'freedom' by Soviet power. But the collision with Soviet modernity brought increasing risks to native culture. Between 1959 and 1979, the percentage of native people who worked in the old, traditional ways fell from 70 to 43. Yet by the late 1980s, many of the basic advantages of modern life had not penetrated far into their homelands, as only 0.4 per cent of their overcrowded homes had running water, and only 0.1 per cent were equipped with central heating. Thanks especially to alcohol, the mortality rate was six times higher in this geographical zone than in the Soviet Union as a whole.[63] In the end, Soviet life had brought its own sharp twist on the fate of the

Aborigines in Australia or to the troubled communities of native Americans.

In 1991, the collapse of the Soviet Union brought into being fifteen independent nation states, many of which were historically recognizable but had never existed as unitary states before, like Ukraine or Belarus, or could have possessed no imaginable existence a few decades earlier, like Kazakhstan. The Russian Federation itself was an enigma. On the one hand, it was the logical successor state of the Soviet Union, inheriting its capital city, many of its central institutions, its seat at the United Nations Security Council, the lion's share of its armed forces and its nuclear arsenal. Many outsiders didn't notice much difference: it was 'Russia' before and 'Russia' now. But this was actually the first time that 'Russia' had been a nation state rather than an empire or the centre of a Communist federation. Even now, with hundreds of ethnic minorities, a complex structure of local 'autonomous' republics and provinces, and many languages, the ancestral cultural centre of Russianness possessed both a national identity and an imperial inheritance. What else could one imagine in the biggest country in the world? Yet for all the dominance of Moscow, and notwithstanding the catastrophe of war in separatist Chechnya in the 1990s, this has been an unusually peaceful decolonization, and a plausible transition from an imperial to a communist to a national identity.[64] Russians have had to come to terms with a Russianness that defines their territory and their state (using the adjective *rossiisky*) and a complementary Russianness that describes their ethnicity, language and culture (*russky*). For all the complexity and apparent contradiction, the linguistic explicitness of these labels has perhaps helped them to achieve a clearer and more stable identity than the English in the United Kingdom.

If Western Europeans ever reflect more carefully about their own imperial pasts, they will find it more difficult to think of Russia's history of expansionism as unusual. They might think about the similar challenges that their own countries have faced, and the more violent and harmful ways that their own countries have sometimes tried to solve them. Self-awareness is one of the antidotes to the Russia Anxiety. But this is not always easy, if all the time you are thinking about war.

# 8

# The Invader Obsession

*Does History Make Russians Seek Peace or War?*

'The Russians are bent on world dominance,' argued the Leader of Her Majesty's Opposition in January 1976. 'And the Russians are playing to win.' A few days later, the Soviet press called Margaret Thatcher 'the Iron Lady'. Her uncompromising message reached far and wide. When a minor gas explosion woke up my neighbourhood not long after Thatcher's subsequent election, the lady across the road had a common reaction. 'I thought the Russians were coming!' she told us. More persistent than any other aspect of the Russia Anxiety is her age-old fear: the Russians are coming. Speculation that Russia was going to invade its NATO neighbours, or the conviction that it was already engaged in 'hybrid war' with the United States itself, drove the international crisis of the 2010s. 'Putin's attack on the US is our Pearl Harbor,' wrote two American journalists in a widely read piece of July 2018, as if a military assault had already taken place and thousands were dead.[1]

The Russia Anxiety is a syndrome with three sets of symptoms: fear, contempt and disregard. Disregard and contempt join with fear in a destructive cycle of relations with Russia. A crisis produces fear; the crisis is resolved, and disregard sets in; disregard causes a crisis; fear returns. 'We won't be hearing from them again,' says 'the West', seeing Russia as a busted flush following a military or economic disaster. It forgets about Russia, reconfiguring Europe's security, even changing its map, while Russia is in no position to voice objections. At such times of disregard, 'the West' does not really accept that Russia might have legitimate interests of its own. And when Russia eventually responds, rhetorically, defensively or pre-emptively, the West again fears

Russia, misreading it, overestimating it, expressing itself with extravagant bombast.

There are no laws in history: the cycle of international relations that derives from the Russia Anxiety is a suggestive explanation, not a definitive one. But interpreting the cycle takes us towards the right questions, about how 'great powers' relate to each other and cause war or peace. It diverts us from the wrong assumptions, about guilt or innocence, fault and blame, and empty moral outrage. The great powers always misbehave, now and in the past, America and Britain, Germany and France, China and Japan – and, not least, Russia. They invade other countries, topple foreign governments while pretending not to, take sides in civil wars while claiming to look the other way, prepare for war while misleading their own populations. Too often for its own good, though, Russia has misbehaved from a position of weakness, when other powers have misbehaved from a position of strength.

Talk of Russia versus 'the West', meanwhile, is always overblown, because 'the West' has never been a cohesive category (and Russia has anyway been an element inside it). Even in the 2010s, when 'the West' was in theory fairly tightly aligned and recognizable within international organizations like NATO, there were major divisions, caused by such things as the euro crisis, energy supplies, Brexit and the election of Trump. And notwithstanding the noisy talk in much of the media, opinion on Russia was split across 'the West'. Social media indicated that scepticism about the Russia Anxiety was rife, if unfocused; common sense suggested the same. Very many people doubted that the Russians really were coming, or that a wider war was a good idea. This was crucially the case in Germany, where eastern areas were partly 'russified' in their assumptions, the Left was sceptical about anti-Russian reactions, the energy industry was open for big business with Moscow, and the government was trying to keep it all together. There was nothing new about this. Fractures of class, ethnicity, gender, region and empire, not to mention arguments between governments, have always counterbalanced a fundamental Western unity associated with individual rights. After all, in the long centuries when the European powers were either divided by clashing alliances or at war with one another, there was no single 'Western' power bloc at all. Russia simply took its place in a wider landscape of European power politics.

These provisos remind us that the cycle of the Russia Anxiety is a simplification. But it is a helpful one. Let's take two examples, from the 1850s and the 1990s.

Fear of Russia and an epidemic of Russophobia was the context in which the Crimean War broke out in 1853. By 1856, the alliance of Britain, France and the Ottoman Empire had defeated the Russian army. The Russians licked their wounds, retreating from European affairs and beginning a process of modernization. With Russia off the scene, the centre of Europe was completely transformed. First Italy was unified within a few years, then Germany was unified in little more than a decade, in both cases without reference to Russia's legitimate interests in the European balance of power. As Russia recovered, the disdain of the other powers – especially Germany – gave way to fear again. As we will see in detail later in this chapter (and as was mentioned at the start of chapter 1) these German fears of Russia contributed to the outbreak of the First World War.

In the 1990s, Cold-War fear of the Soviet Union gave way to disregard for the wrecked new Russia. Following the collapse of the USSR and 'defeat' in the Cold War, and grappling with a devastated economy, the new Russian Federation was in no condition to play a role in international affairs that was appropriate to its size, history and nuclear arsenal. Russia was irrelevant: we won't be hearing from them again. American and other Western politicians comfortably talked about the end of the Cold War as a *victory*, even though this was probably meaningless and certainly tactless. If Russia was a defeated power, as the rhetoric suggested, what were its people to make of the Americans who were promoting the economic reforms that were causing such great pain to so many of them? This was the time of Washington's full-spectrum dominance, the new American Century, when democracy was a synonym for American power, and Russians feared that their country was disappearing demographically. It was during the 1990s and 2000s, in disregard of Russia's interests, that NATO extended itself as far as Russia's borders. Such a redrawing of the security map of Europe was bound to be destabilizing; it could only happen when Russia was too weak to say or do much about it. Given the logic of the Russia Anxiety's cycle, though, Russia was bound eventually to respond, and Western disregard would give way to fear.

When Russia is out of synch with the international system, Europe as a whole is vulnerable. Europe is much more secure when Russia is at the centre of international affairs, an indispensable partner, given its due. The most spectacular examples of that were during the Napoleonic Wars and the Second World War. But the willingness to take advantage of moments of Russian weakness has often made this impossible. Instead, 'the West' has been foxed by the feedback loop of the Russia Anxiety. Unwilling to plan for the medium term, makers of foreign policy in Western capitals have tended to assume that moments of Russian weakness will last indefinitely. Thinking that 'now' is forever, policymakers don't imagine the world of tomorrow, when Russia recovers and exploits their own weaknesses mercilessly. Too often they fall instead for the diplomacy of 'instant history', the flawed concept of how past and present are connected that we debated in chapter 1.

In this chapter, we'll look at three things: the *legitimacy* of Russia's international interests, disregarded by the Russia Anxiety; the *cycle* of the Russia Anxiety; and the *normality* of Russia's international relationships and diplomatic conduct, which of course the Russia Anxiety cannot see.

What can 'normal' mean? Russia is one of history's exceptions: it is the world's largest country with some extreme experiences in its past. Risk-averse, defensive, prickly, fearful, Russia has had to deal with the reality of overstretch brought on by the world's longest borders. It has faced uncertainty and danger, and has been prone to reimagine plausible threats as existential crises. Such themes have run through centuries of Russian history. And yet Russia's responses have usually been predictable. It has behaved in the 'normal' way associated with great-power politics and the diplomatic norms of the day. Russian invasions and foreign occupations have been the exception rather than the rule and can't be explained as an historical tendency.

And what about legitimacy? We might think of a cardinal example. 'Russia' – actually the Soviet Union – was a country with ordinary and legitimate international interests even at the peak of its ideological distinctiveness and historical weirdness in the two decades that followed the Russian Revolution. With Germany unmistakably a 'bad actor' in the international arena by the 1930s, the inability of Britain and France to recognize Soviet interests, even when they aligned with their own, was ultimately devastating. Alexandra Kollontai was the Soviet diplomatic celebrity of the time. This situation was her purgatory. What follows is a case study of the need to recognize Russia's legitimate interests in European affairs, and not to disregard them.

## LEGITIMACY: ORDINARY INTERESTS IN EXTRAORDINARY TIMES

Alexandra Kollontai lived for the Russian Revolution and suffered for its place in the world. Born into the noble Domontovich family in St Petersburg in 1872, when Alexander II was on the throne and Marx's First International was eight years old, she grew up in a progressive and modern household. Her mother, for whom she was named, dressed her for comfort and hygiene, and her father, Mikhail, was gentle and scholarly. In 1877, when the Russian and Ottoman Empires went to war with each other, Mikhail served as a staff colonel. It seemed a just cause. The Bulgarians, who were Slavic and Orthodox kin of the Russians within the Ottoman Empire, rose up – quixotically – in 1876. A year later, Russia and Turkey were at war over the matter. The Russian victory led to the creation of an independent Bulgaria, granted statehood at the Congress of Berlin in 1878. Mikhail Domontovich was promoted to general and given the post of Russian vice-consul in Sofia. The six-year-old Alexandra Kollontai went to live in the new Bulgarian capital, but the family were back in St Petersburg just over a year later, and were there when Alexander II was assassinated in March 1881. Mikhail, moderate and open-minded, was briefly arrested on the basis of a personal connection with an alleged terrorist. The fact that two of the six people hanged for the crime were women captured the girl's imagination, though not yet her sympathy.[2]

These two themes – the projection of Russian power and the projection of Russian socialism – ran through Kollontai's life. She had to face the questions of war and peace that dominated her time. No retiring daughter of the nobility, she had a rigorous schooling, learned history and literature with professors from St Petersburg University, trained as a teacher and married a Marxist called Vladimir Kollontai. She learned about the revolutionary cause. What concerned her most was what it could do for women. As a young mother – her son Mikhail was born in 1894 – this had a practical dimension, born of experience. But it was about sex, too. She praised the fulfilling possibilities of open marriages based on 'free love', just as she deplored the sexual harassment that such licence could give to men. The key was revolution. Without it, real liberation of any kind was impossible. An end to property would mean an end to prostitution; the opening up of marriage would eliminate women's double burden of paid and domestic labour. She had affairs herself. 'The question arises whether in the midst of all these exciting labours and Party assignments I could find time for intimate experiences, for the pangs and joys of love,' she wrote, looking back, after the Revolution. 'Unfortunately, yes!'[3]

She stepped onto the international revolutionary circuit, learning economics in Zurich, writing about workers in Finland, joining the Bolsheviks, standing on the barricades in 1905, joining the Mensheviks, going to Germany to learn from socialist women, fleeing Russia when the police put out a warrant for her arrest, ending up in Berlin, befriending Klara Zetkin, travelling on to Brussels, Paris and London, and writing about feminism in the reading room of the British Museum. She agitated for Marxism and the 'woman question' in Scandinavia and the United States. Then she came back to Petrograd in early 1917 to play the fullest possible role in the revolution. Her son was grown up. She was forty-five. Kollontai had led a revolutionary life across the Western hemisphere, given form by her gender and her conviction that the revolution could transform sexuality for the happiness and liberation of all. 'It was not sexual relations that defined the moral profile of a woman,' she later wrote, 'but her value in the sphere of labour, of socially useful labour.'[4] Sex was something women had a right to as much as men did; it was not a moral category to divide them. This made her a controversial choice to talk about questions of Soviet war and peace on the European stage. When she later became ambassador to Sweden, her hosts lost no opportunity to dismiss her as an oversexed harridan, before she won them round.

*

Kollontai had a distinguished career in Soviet government during the Revolution and Civil War, blending the skills of publicist, intellectual, organizer, ideologist, writer, campaigner, and administrator. When the Bolsheviks seized power in October 1917, Kollontai was elected Commissar of Social Welfare. She liked to recount that when she showed up at the old ministry building, the commissionaire, still in tsarist regalia, told her to come back during visiting hours. Still, she immediately organized a conference of female workers. Hundreds of delegates attended, mostly from the capital, but also from Moscow and surrounding towns. On the basis of such meetings, Kollontai used her authority to prepare legislation to support mothers and children. She also had Party roles, famously leading the new Women's Department, or *Zhenotdel*. But she sided with the Workers' Opposition in protest against the narrowing of Party democracy at the end of the Civil War. Marginalized and underemployed, she was given a way out. The Soviet Union did not have proper diplomatic recognition in the early 1920s, but it did conduct informal diplomacy and trade negotiations. Kollontai was sent to Norway as a member of the Soviet trade delegation in 1922. When her head of mission was transferred to Ankara, and diplomatic relations with Norway were formalized, she found herself promoted to ambassador. Transferred to Sweden in 1930, she continued to represent the Soviet Union in Scandinavia for more than twenty years, notwithstanding an unhappy nine-month spell in Mexico.

She could be technocrat, revolutionary and old-style *intelligent*. A master of detail, she learned the facts about commodities and local politics alike. In October 1923, for example, she caught the train to Berlin to conduct trade negotiations with the Soviet Union's main diplomatic interlocutor, Weimar Germany, a role which required her to know all about a range of goods from bread to oil.[5] She conformed to the needs of court protocol, but remained a revolutionary. In December 1922, addressing trade unionists in The Hague, she attracted support and admiration for her promise that the Bolsheviks would not cease to pursue the struggle for women's equality.[6] But despite her Bolshevism, she remained her parents' daughter, balancing a commitment to people and ideas with the requirements of power and revolution. 'Alexandra Kollontai simply could not fail, situated as she was in her visible diplomatic post, *but* become the centre of gravity of a significant part of the Left-inclined Swedish intelligentsia,' remembered an awe-struck junior colleague who was later an adviser to Brezhnev and Gorbachev. 'And that's what she became.'[7]

This was the combination of values which in other contexts could be mutually exclusive – Bolshevism tempered by warmth, revolutionism alongside humanity – that she brought to the conduct of Soviet foreign policy. In the 1930s, Scandinavia was far from a backwater, and together with a couple of other old survivors, her friends Ivan Maisky, ambassador to London, and Maxim Litvinov, long-time commissar for foreign affairs until Molotov replaced him in 1939, she remained a venerable diplomatic voice, strangely indispensable. Against the odds, she was not consumed by the Terror. Kollontai stayed in Sweden until 1945, when she came home to a busy working retirement. She died of a heart attack seven years later, a few months before Stalin succumbed to a stroke.

On 18 September 1934, the Soviet Union joined the League of Nations. The application process had been a long one. 'Only now,' wrote Litvinov to Kollontai, 'can we properly take our place in the international arena.'[8] One year on, Kollontai was invited to join the Soviet delegation to the XVI Assembly of the League. She arrived in Geneva on 5 September and checked in at the Richmond Hotel. The Soviet delegation took up all of the second floor and had access to a miserable dining room, though Litvinov had a two-room corner suite. Kollontai was there to talk about women's rights, relating to the recent Montevideo Convention on gender equality. The backdrop to the Assembly, though, was the League's response to Italy's looming war on Abyssinia: yet another colonial war by a Western European power on an African people, but one of particular ferocity. In the wider context of the 1930s it warranted sanctions, and seemed part of an emerging reckoning with fascism. In the same year, 1935, the Soviet Union concluded a defensive pact with France. Both countries were alarmed by the rise of Germany, as well as the militarization of Italy.

For Kollontai, being in Geneva reminded her of revolutionary exile before the First World War. Yet coming to the League of Nations demonstrated the different set of international questions that Europe faced twenty years on, and the new style of diplomacy that now existed to confront them. No longer were secret negotiations and *ad hoc* conferences of statesmen the norm. Half the players in European diplomacy had changed, with the post-war disappearance of four European empires. The new format was structured and institutional. 'In the League, and especially in the commissions, they don't like verbosity on issues of principle,' Kollontai recorded in her diary while she was in Geneva. 'It is, probably, just the way it is, but for us the League is a world arena and we have to be able to use it for the USSR and in the matter of women's rights.'[9]

This was a revolutionary diplomacy. It took place in a transformed environment, one which was unable to prevent the outbreak of another European war, but which offered a precedent for the United Nations a decade later. If the USSR had long given up on using foreign policy to export revolution, its diplomacy still had an ideological dimension. After all, the Commissariat of Foreign Affairs had brought Kollontai, one of the world's leading feminists and also one of their busiest ambassadors, from Stockholm to Geneva to talk about women's rights. Stalin would soon insist on greater ideological purity in the conduct of foreign affairs, describing, for instance, the non-communists in left-wing Popular Front governments in Spain or France as 'social fascists'. Soviet diplomacy was revolutionary in another sense. It was committed to defending the Revolution. This was its *raison d'être*. This meant ditching the 'social fascist' rhetoric when a higher purpose, of national defence, conflicted with it. After all, Stalin had declared during the First Five-Year Plan that industrialization and agricultural collectivization had to proceed at such a breakneck speed precisely because the Soviet Union had ten years to prepare itself for invasion from the West.

Defending the Revolution meant avoiding risks, seeking allies where one could find them, and preparing for the ultimate conflict with Germany. In 1936, the Soviet Union sent military support to the Republican side – a whole ragbag of Leftists – in the Spanish Civil War, where they fought against Germans and Italians as well as Franco's fascists. Britain and France declined to support the Republic, contributing thereby to the Fascist victory. Kollontai and others worked to gain capitalist allies, ultimately fruitlessly. She was as worried as anyone when the Nazi–Soviet Pact was agreed in the absence of an alliance with Britain and France. But she helped secure Swedish neutrality when the Germans invaded Denmark and Norway in the spring of 1940.

Adapting to the manners of the Swedish royal court one day, and expounding on international feminism the next, Kollontai was the face of a radically new Bolshevik foreign policy as much as a traditional Russian diplomacy. It was a matter of Soviet Russia's legitimate interests. Defending the Revolution had become a legitimate thing for the Soviets to do, and even the Swedish king understood it.

Few questions in European history seem easier to answer than why the Second World War broke out. It was a result of German aggression. Prefigured in Nazi ideology, built into the logic of Nazi economic, foreign and racial policy, and clarified beyond doubt by its annexations of Austria and Czechoslovakia, Germany's aggressive intentions were there for all to see. When the Wehrmacht invaded Poland in 1939, France in 1940 and the Soviet Union in 1941 – not to mention their attacks on Scandinavia, the Balkans, the Low Countries, Central Europe, North Africa, their aerial bombardment of Britain and their destruction of Jews everywhere – they were prosecuting a war of extermination for a Greater Germany. They were driven in part by an economic need to annex land in the East; by its nature, as long as Nazi Germany existed, it could not be contained. Their task was made easier by the repertoire of violent practices which Europe's global empires had developed, and which the Germans now deployed within Europe itself. The ultimate aim of racial purity required violence against Jews (and Slavs) not just inside Germany's 1933 borders but also beyond them.

Yet the clarity of this reasoning is obscured by the Nazi–Soviet pact of August 1939 to June 1941, the short-lived non-aggression treaty whose secret clauses permitted Soviet control of eastern Poland and the Baltic states. Was the pact a legitimate measure to delay a very probable war, a fair strategy on Stalin's part in the age of great-power imperialism? Stalin thought so. Meanwhile, despite her incomprehension at the agreement with the Nazis, Alexandra Kollontai was only one major Soviet diplomat apparently pursuing legitimate means, of talks with all possible interlocutors, and legitimate ends, of frantic war-avoidance at all costs. Or does the pact show that Soviet policy in the run-up to war was opportunistic and unlawful, facilitating German aggression for the sake of a Soviet agenda that was itself expansionary and conspiratorial? This is, after all, the long-running assumption of the Russia Anxiety, and it continues to shape European politics. In 2018, one former Polish foreign minister compared work on the Nord-Stream 2 gas pipeline between Germany and Russia to the Nazi–Soviet pact.[10]

Seen in these terms, the historical question has become a moral problem. Some historians think of Hitler and Stalin as two profiles on either side of the same totalitarian coin; the Nazi-Soviet pact was the moment of truth, and the Soviet occupation of part of Poland and the Baltic states its ultimate reality. 'Hitler and Stalin were birds of the same totalitarian feather,' writes a recent historian of these matters. '[F]ar from being anomalous, the Nazi–Soviet pact might be seen as symptomatic of their shared misanthropy.' Another historian writes: 'German policies of mass killing came to rival Soviet ones between 1939 and 1941, after Stalin allowed Hitler to begin a war.'[11] The notion of Nazi–Soviet equivalence is, understandably enough, toxic in contemporary Russia, and it troubles many historians from other countries. In the age of Trump and Putin, the argument has come into vogue. It seems to possess a logic of its own: that Hitler is equivalent to Stalin, who is equivalent to Putin, who is equivalent to Trump, who has something of Hitler about him, while Ukraine is equivalent to Czechoslovakia, and the two locations of peace negotiations – Minsk (2014–15) and Munich (1938) – are really the same place. A. J. P. Taylor, the great historian-provocateur of the last century, had no truck with this kind of reasoning. Writing about the origins of the Second World War twenty years after the events in question, he worried that historians were fighting contemporary, not historical, battles, especially about 'appeasing' the dictators of their own day, not those of the 1930s. 'Historians often dislike what happened or wish that it had happened differently,' he wrote. 'There is nothing they can do about it.'[12]

*

A. J. P. Taylor was responding to criticism of his infamous book *The Origins of the Second World War*, which was published in 1961. A famous troublemaker, Taylor, as usual, wanted to overturn conventional wisdom, and he pushed the envelope with his argument that Hitler was a rational statesman in the Bismarckian mould.[13] But Taylor stuck close to the documents, was a master of old-fashioned diplomatic history, and some of his other conclusions have withstood decades of scrutiny. For Taylor, the Nazi–Soviet pact was a diplomatic deal of the kind that had been common in Europe since the eighteenth century. The Soviet Union was a great power facing a devastating threat from another great power, Germany. It was conducting a normal great-power foreign policy: seeking national security and allies, while avoiding invasion and war. Even though Stalin's domestic policies were extraordinarily bloodthirsty, his foreign policy was quite ordinary. It was as legitimate as that of the other great powers, not least Britain and France.

In this light, Alexandra Kollontai's diplomacy makes sense. She was committed to defending the Revolution: a 'communist' aim that required 'normal' diplomacy. Within her own arenas, in Scandinavia, the League of Nations, and in other international meetings, her methods were usually conventional, even if her ultimate goals were radical. Viewed from Stalin's office, too, the immediate purpose of Soviet foreign policy was a traditional one: to prevent the Western powers, which wanted to put a stop to the construction of socialism, from invading Soviet territory. This was not an irrational fear. After all, if a revolution had taken place in Russia before 1914, the Western powers would probably have invaded, invoking monarchical solidarity, in order to strangle the first socialist state at birth. When it came in 1917, though, the revolution was saved by the great powers, by their actions and omissions. The armies of Britain and France could barely advance beyond their own trenches, let alone stop a revolution more than a thousand miles to the east, while the Germans, fighting the Russians, were only too pleased to help the anti-war Bolsheviks and allowed Lenin to travel back to Petrograd from his exile in Zurich. Following the German defeat, Britain and other capitalist powers faced no obstacle to intervene during the Civil War against the Bolsheviks. Throughout the 1920s and 1930s, Soviet intelligence services informed the Kremlin of constant Western threats. Objectively speaking, these threats only became urgent or even realistic as late as 1938, but the barbed language and mixed signals of the Western powers always made the threat seem real in the minds of the Bolsheviks. As we'll see again in chapter 10, Stalin himself made the point at a famous speech to industrial bosses in February 1931. 'We are fifty or a hundred years behind the advanced countries,' he said. 'We must catch up in ten years. Either we do it, or we shall be crushed.' The task of Soviet foreign policy was, therefore, to ensure that the Soviet Union was not attacked during that decade, that it had the chance to fulfil the promise of the Revolution. When the Germans invaded in June 1941, Stalin's disbelieving and despairing response was that he and his team had squandered their inheritance from Lenin.

This does not mean that Stalin pursued *Realpolitik* abroad and conspiratorial, ideology-soaked violence at home, that he was simultaneously modern statesman and totalitarian dictator. For Stalin's most recent biographer, the same worldview ran through Stalin's foreign and domestic policies: the tendency to divide the world into two camps, of friends and enemies. Britain, France, and Germany were all potential enemies, capitalist destroyers of one type or another, and a nimble policy should find the moments of shared interest that allowed deals to be struck with whichever partner was most willing, delaying international conflict and enabling domestic revolutionary change to keep unfolding.[14] The greatest threat came from Germany. France was the most likely anti-German ally. But why, if the political weather changed and made it more likely in the short term, should the Kremlin rule out a temporary pact with the Germans? The aim, after all, was to delay a German invasion for as long as possible. It was not to expand beyond existing borders. The strategy was cautious, not reckless.

In May 1935, the French foreign minister (within weeks, prime minister), Pierre Laval, came to Moscow and agreed a mutual assistance pact with the Soviet Union. It was not uncontroversial in France, but the agreement was ratified in February and March 1936. Franco–Soviet cooperation was not easy, thanks to residual suspicion, especially among military leaders, the opposition of the British, and Stalin's 'two camps' worldview. The predicament was made worse by the Spanish Civil War, which broke out in 1936. Spain's tragedy was precipitated by the polarization of Left and Right. It was a Spanish war with Spanish causes, but for many outsiders it seemed to reflect the troubled politics of Europe as a whole. The Spanish split took on a continental scale with the interventions of the USSR and Nazi Germany in the conflict. Germany and Italy, prefiguring their alliance, joined the fascist side; Soviet involvement, anticipating the lack of an anti-Nazi coalition before 1941, scared off the British and the French from offering any assistance to the Spanish Republic. As a result, Franco's victory became more likely. The experience worried the Soviet government. It demonstrated the growing power of Germany, confirmed that Nazi ideological obsessions were focused on foreign as much as domestic policy, and exposed again the difficulty of forging an anti-Nazi agreement with the Western powers of Britain and France. Meanwhile, the British government sought to undermine military cooperation between the French and Soviet armies, seeing the Soviets as an unreliable anti-German force. But this was not a universal view in London. Lord Vansittart, permanent undersecretary at the Foreign Office, and Winston Churchill, loose cannon, repeatedly met the Soviet ambassador, Ivan Maisky, to pursue the alternative of a British–Soviet accord.[15]

Churchill illustrated the pragmatism that ran through the minds of those from Moscow and London who favoured an agreement. No one had hated communism more. From the War Office in 1919, he had ordered British troops to intervene on the side of the Whites in the Russian Civil War. As chancellor of the exchequer between 1924 and 1929, he always had the domestic red menace in his sights. He spoke of 'the baboonery of Bolshevism'. But during the 1930s, Churchill was convinced that it was Germany, not the Soviet Union, that was the danger to Britain and her Empire. In the run-up to the Czechoslovak crisis in 1938, Churchill wanted a 'grand alliance' of 'England', France and 'Russia' against Germany just as show trials were taking place in Moscow.[16] He had the capacity to weigh up the national interest without succumbing to the Russia Anxiety. But the decision-maker was Neville Chamberlain, not Winston Churchill, and time was running out.

The problem was Czechoslovakia. Germany had already started expanding in Europe. Reoccupying the Rhineland (March 1936) could be justified as the return of German territory that was unfairly removed at Versailles. Annexing Austria (March 1938) could be explained away as a Germanic union based on substantial Austrian support; it was only after 1945 that the Austrians rewrote themselves as 'Hitler's first victim'. Yet Czechoslovakia was another matter.

In the autumn of 1938, the Germans were threatening to enter the Sudetenland, that part of Czechoslovakia with a majority of German inhabitants. This was a first-rate European crisis. If the French intervened to defend Czechoslovakia, the Soviet Union would be obliged to support them, according to the terms of the Franco-Soviet treaty. This raised logistical questions for the Soviets as they did not share a border with the Czechs. They seemed to be readying themselves nonetheless. But it became an academic question. The French made it clear that they would not get involved.

British non-involvement was still more ostentatious. Britain's prime minister went all the way to Munich to avoid war, his famous flight lit up for posterity by the flashbulbs of the world's newspapermen. The Munich summit of September 1938 between the German chancellor and the British prime minister was the third of three 'appeasement' meetings. Chamberlain stepped back from confrontation, accepting Hitler's promises about German intentions in Czechoslovakia, and claiming that he had secured 'peace in our time'. Of course, the Germans invaded anyway shortly after. The chance to nip Nazi expansionism in the bud and avoid global war had been missed. Interpreted ever after as the failure to stand up to a tyrant, 'Munich' is eternal shorthand for weak, short-termist, counterproductive diplomacy. Churchill himself came to dispute this reading of Munich, in a generous tribute when Chamberlain died in 1940.[17] Tony Blair, as determined as Churchill never to be an appeaser, said similar things in his autobiography.[18] And A. J. P. Taylor saw the 'appeasers' as men who were simply doing their best to avoid another terrible European war, who acted within the political culture of their time and according to the expectations of their electorate. Few thought that Britain was guilty for the outbreak of the Second World War, but 'Munich' still became a codeword for diplomatic guilt by omission.

*

For some people, Neville Chamberlain and Adolf Hitler are never far away. 'We run the risks of repeating the mistakes made in Munich in 1938,' David Cameron was reported to have said – about Ukraine – in September 2014. In the same month, an EU official who was present at EU–Russia–Ukraine talks warned from Brussels 2014 that 'it is Munich 1938'. Five months earlier, Garry Kasparov, the chess grandmaster and democracy campaigner, wrote a *Time* article on Ukraine under the headline 'Obama's Munich moment', citing the words of John Kerry, the United States secretary of state, who had called the Syrian crisis 'our Munich moment' in September 2013.[19]

For seventy-five years, almost every diplomatic crisis has been compared to Munich 1938. It is as if thousands of years of international history have yielded only a single reference point to guide those who make and report on foreign affairs. For Anthony Eden during the Suez Crisis of 1956, Nasser was Hitler; for George H. W. Bush after the Iraqi invasion of Kuwait in 1990, Saddam Hussein was Hitler. The problem derived in part from the need to dress up a foreign policy that is understandably and always interest-driven – such as the need to reset the equilibrium of oil distribution in the Middle East after Iraq invaded Kuwait – in the moral language of standing up to the schoolyard bully, personified by Hitler. 'The "we must stand up to Putin as we did to Hitler" line is pure schoolboy politics,' wrote the senior diplomat Tony Brenton at the height of the Ukraine–Russia crisis of 2014. 'Putin, of whom I saw a fair amount as UK ambassador to Moscow, is not an ideologically driven fanatic, but much closer to Talleyrand – the calculating, pragmatic rebuilder of his country's status in the world.'[20]

Talleyrand was Napoleon's leading diplomat; he was still in office during the July Monarchy in the 1830s. As foreign minister, he led the French delegation at the Congress of Vienna in 1815, the peace conference that marked the end of the Napoleonic Wars, complete with a diplomatic stellar cast: not just Talleyrand, but also Metternich, Castlereagh, and Alexander I. After pushing Napoleon all the way back from Moscow to Paris, Alexander was keen to accept the garlands of victory at the Congress, and to project Russia's undisputed status as a top-table powerbroker. The aim of the Congress of Vienna, though, was not to advance Russia's interests, or any other single power's interests, at the expense of wider security; the goal was to prevent the outbreak of another major war. It was important to control France, to strip it of its Napoleonic territorial gains, and to impose reparations, but not to eliminate France's place in European diplomacy. France had been defeated, but she still possessed legitimate interests. Europe was made less safe by disregarding these. Russia could not be allowed to push its borders much further westwards, but it was indispensable to the diplomatic process. And Britain had to be included in the system, not allowed to go its own way.[21]

Instead, a Concert of Europe should maintain a balance of power, securing the interests of the victorious and the defeated alike, and keeping peace between them as these interests changed and their relationships waxed and waned. As Talleyrand pointed out, in Europe's complex map of large empires and small states, the balance was not secure, and peace would always be vulnerable. 'Such a situation only admits of a very artificial and precarious equilibrium which' – he wrote – 'can only last for as long as some large states continue to be animated by a spirit of moderation and justice that will preserve it.'[22] As we saw in chapter 1, the Congress of Vienna opened the way to a revival of the Russia Anxiety, especially in France, as fear of Russia's military prowess, and shame of defeat at its hands, set in. But Nicholas I, who was tsar at the height of this post-Napoleonic outbreak of the Russia Anxiety, was charming in company and keen to secure ties with the other great powers, notwithstanding his reactionary reputation. He visited Britain twice. The balance held until the outbreak of the Crimean War in 1853.

At its core, the Concert of Europe assumed that peace could be maintained when each power respected the basic interests of each other power, and responded to crises in a fluid and pragmatic way. Peace would not come by generating ambitious shared interests, of the type to which the United Nations is, in theory, committed. From the Russian perspective in the twenty-first century, it can seem that international organizations – the complicated and institutionalized successors of the Concert of Europe – simply do not accept Russian interests as legitimate. Combining hard power with a rhetoric of freedom, NATO has extended itself as far as Russia's borders. A European Concert that was charged with protecting states' most basic interests and rebalancing international relationships might have found a better compromise than this.[23] It might also have done a better job of protecting the interests of Ukraine. Few approaches seem less in the spirit of pan-European values or less designed to promote durable security than the suggestion in 2013 that Ukraine now had to choose between the EU and Russia.

Far from being demolished in 1991, when the Soviet Union collapsed, the Cold War framework for international relations survives, both in the institution of NATO and in the mentalities of policymakers and observers everywhere, from Moscow to Brussels to Washington (via London). In such a framework, it becomes difficult to recognize that Russia has any legitimate interests in European affairs at all. It would seem impossible to explain the crisis in Ukraine without taking account of this major structural failure of international politics.[24]

In February 2007, when Russia and America were still cooperating in many areas of foreign policy, Vladimir Putin went to Munich to make a robust speech about Russia's place in the world. By sharply criticizing American 'unipolar' domination, he was seen as bringing a chill into foreign affairs, and his comments have become notorious. But much of the speech was a plea for Russia to be respected and for its interests to be taken seriously. Putin's speech in Munich 2007 suddenly seemed a more useful reference point for explaining international affairs in the twenty-first century than Chamberlain's umbrella in Munich 1938.

In August 2008, the south Caucasian country of Georgia, formerly a republic of the Soviet Union and before that a territory of the Russian Empire, attacked Russian forces on its border. Russia had long supported autonony for Abkhazia and South Ossetia, which were sovereign Georgian territory but pro-Russia separatist enclaves. Georgia had finally succumbed to what it saw as a provocation. A major Russian incursion into Georgian territory followed. The war lasted five days. Russia succeeded, at least temporarily, in postponing the accession of Georgia into NATO. The brief conflict, played out while the Olympic Games were taking place in Beijing, was a shocking moment: terrifying and tragic for those seeking shelter from the onslaught in Tbilisi and elsewhere, but shocking because Russian foreign policy has historically been more measured.

Moscow's complaint was that NATO was wilfully expanding into zones which exposed Russia to undue risk, with its long borders, diverse neighbours and complex security dilemmas. In 1990, a reunified Germany stayed in NATO, rather than becoming a neutral power, and in 1999, the pass was sold when Poland, Hungary and the Czech Republic became members. Seven more countries in East-Central Europe, including Estonia and Latvia on Russia's border, joined in 2004. NATO's strategy was to continue to enlarge, projecting American power, the reach of global financial institutions based in the United States, and the promises of Western values. On 4 April 2008, at the time of a landmark NATO summit in Bucharest, Putin outlined his countervailing point: 'It is obvious that today there is no Soviet Union, no Eastern bloc and no Warsaw Pact. So NATO exists to confront whom?' He talked about the expansion of NATO into former Soviet spheres of influence and territory, and up to the present-day Russian border, disputing the avowedly peaceful intention of this expansion and the argument that it was not an anti-Russian step. 'You know,' he told the assembled journalists, 'I have a great interest in and love for European history, including German history. Bismarck was an important German and European political leader. He said that in such matters what is important is not the intention but the capability.' Putin homed in on the oft-repeated grievance. 'We have withdrawn our troops deployed in Eastern Europe, and withdrawn almost all large and heavy weapons from the European part of Russia. And what happened?' he asked rhetorically. 'A base in Romania, where we are now, one in Bulgaria, an American missile defence area in Poland and the Czech Republic. That all means moving [NATO] military infrastructure to our borders.'[25]

Eight years later, during a sequence of interviews with the American film director Oliver Stone, Putin expanded on this point.[26] He argued that the logic of NATO ('the Atlantic camp', or America writ large) required it to have 'an external enemy' – Russia. There was a constancy about this. When Stone asked what changed when a new American president is elected, at least in Washington's interactions with Russia, Putin replied, 'Almost nothing.' Putin went on, 'Everywhere, especially in the USA, there is a strong bureaucracy which in effect rules the world.' Was this a conspiratorial 'deep state', or just really-existing international institutions like NATO, as well as the top officials who serve long-term in national administrations, regardless of parties or elections? If it was a conspiratorial world view, it has typically been attributed to Putin's early KGB career. But the foreign policy of Putin's third term actually fitted inside a longer heritage, one that was illuminated by the origins of the world wars, with their stories of zero-sum blocs, unreliable would-be allies and Western disregard of Russia's interests. If a weakened, distracted Russia had no option but to respond to NATO expansion between 1990 and 2004 with risk-avoidance and unremitting pragmatism, its embrace of risk thereafter seemed to reflect the cyclical turns of the Russia Anxiety.

But were Russia's reflex kicks into Georgia, Crimea and east Ukraine part of a grand strategy to bring down Western democracy? If they were, they can scarcely have been prompted by legitimate foreign-policy concerns on Russia's part. For Michael McFaul, the US ambassador in Moscow from 2012 to 2014, NATO expansion was irrelevant, Russia's perception of foreign threats was overblown or invented, and foreign policy changes were caused by domestic politics, especially Putin's return from the office of prime minister to the presidency in 2012.[27] According to this explanation, Putin and his team were stung by the Colour Revolutions, not least the uprising in Egypt in early 2011. They were uneasy about the urban protests in Russia that began later that year. If those demonstrations really were supported by Hillary Clinton and the US State Department, as some claimed, then a revolution might even follow. External violence was a way of harnessing internal control by giving a focus for Russian national feeling and thereby bolstering national unity. It was the mood music of a stand-off between Russia and the West.

Nevertheless, this domestic backdrop coincided with NATO's apparent encroachment on Moscow's vital interests. The most prolific and balanced of Anglophone scholars on contemporary Russia concludes in his most recent book: 'Russia's assertion of an independent position in international affairs is justifiable, in the sense of being both reasonable and rational.' For him, global peace was more at risk that at any time since the fall of the Berlin Wall precisely because of a systemic failure of the post-Cold-War order to generate common understandings of security in all parts of Europe.[28] After all, the naval base at Sevastopol in Crimea had been a point of contention when the Soviet Union unravelled, and the government of Ukraine agreed then that it could remain home to Russian vessels. At the same time, they agreed to give up the Soviet nuclear weapons stockpiled on their territory. What were the Russians to make of a Sevastopol that might be controlled by NATO? By 2018, when the Russians raised this question, the American media could only respond in the abstract language of sovereignty and freedom, and seemed bemused by concrete geopolitics, defined in part by which great-power city, Brussels, Washington or Moscow, had the most influence over Crimea's biggest naval base.[29]

For years, NATO enlargement became a consensus among policy specialists on Ukraine, the Baltic states and the countries of the former Warsaw Pact. The Russia specialists who favoured it, not least Condoleezza Rice, George Bush's national security adviser at the time of the invasion of Iraq in 2003, were often those who supported a forward, interventionist and regime-change approach to foreign policy. McFaul himself was often more cautious, but he had long favoured the universal democratic models that we discussed in chapter 4. By the Trump presidency, an enlarged and forward-facing NATO enjoyed support across the floor of Congress, from liberal Democrats to neoconservatives. To raise doubts – as Trump did – was to flirt with treachery. But many commentators had spoken up against NATO enlargement during the 1990s. In 1997, George Kennan argued that it would be 'the most fateful error of American policy in the entire post-cold-war era', that could well 'restore the atmosphere of the cold war to East–West relations' and 'impel Russian foreign policy in directions decidedly not to our liking'.[30]

When Germany captured the rest of Czechoslovakia in March 1939, Britain and France accepted that war was coming. Hitler had unmistakably played his hand. In doing so, he had eliminated the only substantial democratic and anti-Nazi force in Central Europe, improved Germany's strategic position and gained stocks of military equipment which the Wehrmacht would soon make use of. Britain and France now promised to defend Poland's borders. This was unlikely to give Hitler pause; it seemed improbable that the British would really fight for Poland. Instead, the one anti-Nazi partnership that might prevent an attack on Poland and stop further German expansion was a reprise of the old Triple Entente from the era of the First World War, between Britain, France and the USSR. In April, the commissar of foreign affairs, Maxim Litvinov, offered precisely this. But with Neville Chamberlain in Downing Street, the British responses were half-hearted and negative in turn, and always late. The French, with their record of agreement with the Soviets, were keener than the British on a new Triple Entente, but not keen enough. Soviet negotiators pressed the point: it seems clear that they wanted agreement.

It was to no avail.[31] Everyone could hear the clock ticking. Germany was likely to attack Poland within weeks. It would bring the Germans to the Soviet border. Stalin could not face in isolation such an overwhelming threat to Soviet security. Clear reasons existed for Stalin to think the unthinkable and come to terms with the implacable ideological foe that, he knew, would sooner or later attack the USSR anyway. Unlike a Western alliance, it promised immediate territorial security on the border, at the expense of Poland, with its especially despised right-wing authoritarian politics, and perhaps too of the Baltic states and Finland, which only two decades earlier also had been outposts of the Russian Empire. An agreement with the Germans could offer serious trading advantages. There were recent connections that could be revivified, the trading and military ties that had quietly emerged between the Weimar Republic and the USSR when they were international pariahs in the 1920s. And as an old Marxist, Stalin had an underlying sympathy for German civilization, just as he distrusted 'the English' as imperial, class-bound, perfidious relics. But talks with the Nazis represented a huge, counter-intuitive risk. The preference remained for a pact with Britain and France.

On 24 May, the British Cabinet bounced Chamberlain into renewing negotiations before the Soviets sought a defensive agreement with the Germans. By then, frustrated by the inability to enter into mutual protection with the Western powers, and appreciating the imminence of German violence, the Soviet Union was already talking to the Nazis. But even at that point Stalin had not given up on the Anglo-French option, and Molotov, Litvinov's successor, pushed the possibility of the three powers protecting the sovereignty of Poland, Finland, the Baltic states, Belgium, Greece and Turkey.[32] The British claimed not unreasonably that the Soviets had improper designs on the Baltic states, but Stalin did not believe that the imperialist British would halt an alliance on what must surely seem, to them, such flimsy grounds.[33] By August, with the British dragging their feet, and the Germans dangling mendacious territorial guarantees to the Baltic and eastern Poland before the Soviets, the Molotov–Ribbentrop Pact became a reality.

The Second World War was caused by German aggression which Britain, France and the Soviet Union misjudged and failed to stop. An alliance between France, Britain, and the USSR would surely have prevented the Germans from invading Poland. Part of the reason why this alliance was never concluded was the British government's disregard for reasonable and legitimate Soviet defensive interests. In the end, the Soviet government made ice-cold calculations, of an anti-ideological pragmatism that outstripped the Polish goverment's simultaneous non-aggression pacts with Germany and the Soviet Union, both concluded in 1934 and lasting through to the war.

But the Soviet side was also predatory. The Soviet Union took advantage of the secret clauses of the Nazi–Soviet pact and invaded eastern Poland sixteen days after the Nazi invasion from the West. They went to war in Finland and occupied the Baltic states. For the opponents of A. J. P. Taylor, this proved that the pact between Hitler and Stalin was a 'moment of truth', and the dictators were fundamentally the same.

Stalin took advantage of the international constellation in 1939 and 1940 to expand Soviet influence westwards with great brutality. The Katyn massacre of April and May 1940 was only its most notorious episode. But this confuses the means and the ends. During Soviet history from its beginning to its finish, even during the age of 'tears without end' that we discussed in chapter 5, Soviet power was not driven by a logic of expansionism. Socialism was something to be built in one country. When the chance came, in 1939–40, and again with the onset of the Cold War from 1945, the Soviet Union established a zone of socialist influence beyond its borders, underwritten by military force, and, in Stalinist times, characterized by awful violence and dramatic social change (though much of it was 'de-Stalinized' after 1956). But the existence of the Eastern bloc was not built into the logic of the Soviet project; it emerged as a product of particular circumstances in 1939 and 1945. Although Nazi Germany (1933–45) and the Stalinist USSR (1928–53) were defined by extreme violence, they were quite different dictatorships when it came to questions of war and peace. The whole point of Nazi Germany was that it had to go to war: to create living space, to make its autarkic economy work and to eliminate racial impurity. By contrast, the Soviet Union could do everything it wanted to, including collectivization and Terror in the Stalin era, without fighting. As early as 1918, it had decided that exporting revolution was not an option. Much of the Soviet Union's pre-war diplomacy until 17 September 1939, then, involved the pursuit of interests that were ostensibly legitimate in conventional terms of national defence.

The origins of the Second World War are not an analogy of later events, but they illuminate persistent ways of thinking in international affairs that derive from the West's Russia Anxiety and Russia's responses to it. Russia has historically preferred peace to war, and security to risk, and in that way has been a normal great power conducting a legitimate foreign policy. The conflicts and crises of the 2010s were not driven by a grand anti-Western strategy or an inbuilt historical tendency to expansionary violence, but instead followed failures of international and domestic politics that were partly given shape by the Russia Anxiety. When the world looks at Russians remembering the Second World War every 9 May, with a military parade and mass rallies of ordinary people carrying photographs of their relatives who lived during the war, it might be useful to assume the absence of warmongering and cynicism on the part of the people who are marching. Victory Day could be a time to turn down the heat on the Russia Anxiety. After all, the Anxiety tends to follow a cycle.

## THE CYCLE

A defence official in the United States explains the problem with Russia. It's a threat to the free world, a clear and present danger. And in seeking to undermine freedom where it sees it, Russia possesses opportunities that are not in the repertoire of other countries. The implication is that the Russians can do things that the Americans cannot. They have a 'unique ability': they can 'impose tight control over their own domain while destabilizing the enemy's'. Therefore, they 'rely most heavily on political means', including 'military power used for purposes of intimidation'. Their preference is 'to commit to military operations by proxy forces rather than their own'. They espouse hybrid war for the long term. 'This kind of imperialism calls for a protracted, patient and prudent but unremitting war of political attrition,' writes the analyst. 'Its purpose is to undermine the authority of hostile governments and the will of their citizens to resist, while maintaining their own base, solid, impregnable, and in a permanent state of mobilization.'[34]

It sounds like Hillary Clinton during the period of the elections of Trump and Putin that we discussed in chapter 1. But this analysis comes from three decades before Trump's election. It's from the pen of Richard Pipes, just after he had left President Reagan's White House. The Russia Anxiety re-forms itself for every generation, and sometimes it disappears, but in the moments when it is accelerating, it has qualities that stay the same. Russia becomes a phantom: sinister, conspiratorial, combining mighty power with fundamental weakness, malign in intention and strategic in resolve. People think that they have seen Russia take on a new shape, adapting its approach as new technologies emerge and geopolitics change, but really they are repeating what has been said before. 'The Russians don't drive their tanks across borders any more,' said veteran newsman Bob Scheffer on the *Charlie Rose* show, filmed in New York in October 2017. 'They've found out it's much cheaper to use cyber, and to adopt soft power methods.' This was the instant history that we encountered in chapter 1: the assumption of novelty. But Scheffer's insights drew on the experts. The next generation of Washington's Russia hands probed Russia's impact on Ukraine and other parts of Eastern Europe. They used the same analytical framework that Richard Pipes had done thirty years before. 'Russian influence centres on weakening the internal cohesion of societies,' they suggested. 'This is achieved by influencing and eroding democratic governance from within its own institutions.'[35] When it comes to the Russia Anxiety, the point is not whether these commentators are right or wrong, but that they are repeating themselves and each other, and that their assumptions are not neutral in their effects, but contribute to a public discourse that heightens risk.

This way of talking, oft-repeated and raised to the status of unarguable truth, soon enough assumes a unique malice on the part of Russia. No wonder that it generates fear among decision-makers and ordinary people alike. To understand just how much risk is embedded in the cycle, as it switches between fear, disregard, contempt and fear, we should turn to the origins of the First World War.

The outbreak of the First World War was occasioned by the assassination of the heir to the Austro-Hungarian throne and his wife. On 28 June 1914, Archduke Franz Ferdinand arrived in Sarajevo with his wife, Sophie. Sarajevo, the capital of Bosnia-Herzogovina, was ruled from Vienna. It was inside the Austro-Hungarian Empire, a collection of connected territories in Central, Eastern and South-eastern Europe. Bosnia was a Balkan backwater that had become a strategic problem. Long part of the Ottoman Empire, it had slowly slipped from the control of Constantinople while Vienna had steadily taken advantage, until, in 1908, only six years before, the Austrians formally annexed the territory following a major international crisis. The visit of the archduke and archduchess was a celebration of imperial harmony, as well as of the loving couple's wedding anniversary.

By then, Europe's age of nationalism – freedom for peoples, foundation of nation states – was underway, and the old-fashioned empire of Austria-Hungary was struggling to contend with it. There were many among Bosnia's large Serb population who looked to Belgrade, not Vienna, for leadership. Belgrade was the capital of neighbouring Serbia, a principality of the Ottoman Empire for much of the nineteenth century, but a new nation state since 1878. One of the irredentist Bosnian Serbs was Gavrilo Princip. He became a member of a terrorist cell, part of the Serbian Black Hand movement. Sunday 28 June 1914, when Archduke Franz Ferdinand and Sophie came to visit Bosnia, was a day marked not just by their wedding anniversary, but also by a commemoration of Serbian nationhood, the anniversary of defeat in 1389 by the Ottomans in the Battle of the Field of the Blackbirds. In this group which gathered to attack Franz Ferdinand,

Princip was the assassin who held his nerve, and shot the couple as their Graef und Stift sports car went slowly past.

They were killed. Princip was beaten up by the crowd but he survived. It was clear that he was operating on the fringes of an organization that was connected at several removes to elements in the Serbian government. To Vienna this looked like a regicide on Austro-Hungarian soil orchestrated by a rival power. Over the next three weeks the temperature among the great powers rose remorselessly. At 6 p.m. on 23 July, the Austro-Hungarian government sent an ultimatum to Belgrade. It demanded the destruction of the anti-Austrian underground. And it insisted that representatives from the Empire be allowed unlimited access to Serbia to take part in this destruction, as well as in the investigation into the Sarajevo assassination. By then the Serbs were prepared to make concessions to avoid war, but they couldn't accept such humiliating terms. The ultimatum expired forty-eight hours later. On 28 July, one month after the murder of its heir to the throne, Austria-Hungary declared war on Serbia.

And this was something that Russia could not tolerate. Despite the situation in which they found themselves in 1914, Russia and Austria-Hungary might have been friends. They were neighbours: long-lived monarchies that ruled over multinational land-based empires, which meant that they faced the same challenges posed by industrialization, urbanization, democracy and nationalism. Mutual survival was no doubt in each other's interests. But these interests collided in the Balkans. The Sarajevo assassination ripped the Romanovs and the Habsburgs apart for ever.

Russia mobilized its army. Some elements in the government were enthusiastic, though others, and the tsar himself, were fearful, seemingly clear in their minds that this would lead to war across Europe. Now under imminent threat, and prepared to defend its Austrian ally, Germany declared war on Russia on 1 August. German strategy, which was based on a fear of encirclement by the alliance of France and Russia, required first a rapid attack westwards through Belgium before turning to the enemy in the east. When Germany invaded Belgium, Britain asserted her own ambiguously held treaty obligations and declared war on the Germans on 4 August. Europe was now at war, with all the great powers lined up against each other – Russia,

France and Britain on one side, Germany and Austria on the other – with Italy, Turkey and the Balkan states all soon to join in.

On 7 May 1919, six months after signing the Armistice that ended the First World War, the victorious Allies handed their peace terms to the German government at the Trianon Palace Hotel in Paris. Russia did not take part, having withdrawn from the war after the Bolshevik Revolution; it had received its own dictated peace terms from Germany at Brest-Litovsk the previous year, and was in the midst of civil war. The Paris document was the result of complex negotiations among the victors. But its message seemed simple to the Germans. For Max Warburg, the leading banker, it was 'the worst act of world piracy ever perpetrated under the flag of hypocrisy'.[36] Germany would be cut up, with 13 per cent of its land, together with 10 per cent of its population, going to other countries. The Germans would have to pay inflation-proof reparations of 60 billion marks. And why? Because, according to Article 231 of what history came to know as the Treaty of Versailles, Germany was responsible for the damage caused by the war. This was the 'war guilt clause'.

Was Germany guilty? Even in 1919, it was a controversial question, among the Allies as well as in Berlin. John Maynard Keynes thought the judgement was a travesty. A century on, the moral category of guilt seems redundant, helpful neither in explaining why the war broke out nor in allowing us to learn twenty-first-century lessons from it.

Instead, the cycle of the Russia Anxiety helps to explain the outbreak of the First World War, and offers a cautionary tale for the age of Trump and Putin. For a start, one can see the cycle at work in the destabilizing relations between Britain and Russia before 1914. British fear of Russia had been one of the major factors in its foreign and domestic policy over several decades. This fear was often fuelled by misperceptions about Russia's strengths and intentions in Central Asia. In their Convention of 1907, the two countries at last came to a formal understanding with each other. They were both partners of France, and now they were effectively allied to each other. Britain's decision fitted with the cycle of the Anxiety. Fear gave way to disdain following Russia's defeat against Japan in 1905. Now was the moment for the British to 'tether' the fallen power. This alliance did nothing to restrain either country. Nor did it keep the peace. Perhaps it encouraged recklessness in July 1914. It did not help Germany to decode Britain's inscrutable intentions during that final crisis.

The 1907 Convention and its consequences had something in common with the attempt by NATO to 'tether' a weak Russia in the 1990s, during a parallel 'disregarding' stage of the Anxiety's cycle. It did so in a succession of agreements: the Partnership for Peace of 1994, the Founding Act in 1997 and the NATO–Russia Council in 2002.[37] The stated aim of cooperation was to increase familiarity and trust. But rather than enhancing transparency, it did nothing to clarify NATO's agenda of expansion as far as Russia's border, or, after these agreements with Russia had lapsed, to restrain NATO from declaring the ambitions that were almost seen as declarations of war in Moscow: the accession of Ukraine and Georgia to the alliance. For Putin, the prospect of NATO servicemen in Sevastopol was not unreasonable grounds to take control of Crimea.

More important, though, was the feedback loop of misperceptions that powered the cycle of the Russia Anxiety in Berlin during the run-up to 1914. What Germany saw when it looked eastwards was a waking giant. A key index was troop numbers. When the German high command made calculations and estimates about Russian forces, the figures looked terrifying. The Russian industrial economy was growing rapidly and outgoings on the armed forces were ever higher. Army spending was up by a third between 1909 and 1914; naval spending tripled.[38] It seemed that Germany's window of national survival was closing. If the Germans did not go to war at an advantageous moment soon, they would be crushed by the Russians in a few years. All this was hopelessly misunderstood and exaggerated. While Russia's economy was improving, its performance was uneven, and the political system was unstable. Russia had just been defeated by Japan, even if it had begun to learn lessons from the war. True, St Petersburg was increasing the proportion of its economic and human capacity that was available for the armed forces in the thirty years before 1914, overtaking the proportions that Britain and France made available, far outstripping Austria-Hungary, and closing in on Germany. Yet the military numbers did not take into account differences in quality – a raw Siberian recruit had little in common with a hardened Prussian NCO. In the year that war broke out, Berlin was able to boost its defence spending in a way that St Petersburg could not, to more than double that of its rival, before the numbers somewhat evened out in 1915 and 1916.[39]

The danger of the Russia Anxiety was multiplied by the feedback loop of misperception it encouraged. In the run-up to war, the Russians noticed German perceptions of them, confusing themselves in the process. General Sukhomlinov, war minister from 1909, who had an attractive young wife and problematic finances,[40] made the absurd prediction that Russia could defeat Germany, the military superpower of Europe, if it came to it. Meanwhile, the French, who had been allies of Russia for thirty years, were growing alarmed by Russian power. Under the presidency of Poincaré, the feeling grew that Russia was becoming so rich and strong that soon it would no longer need France. It would be able to dictate terms to Europe by itself. Better to take the chance and go to war alongside Russia, Poincaré calculated, than be left out in the cold. Again, the feedback loop closed in: Russia's foreign minister, Sazonov, began to worry that the best moment for ensuring France's support in war was passing, as Poincaré's presidential term would soon end. Better to take a chance to go to war while French support was still available. And the British began to fret that they would lose out in a world dominated by France and Russia after the two powers had defeated Germany.[41]

On 30 July 1914, therefore, the government in St Petersburg mobilized its army. It knowingly made a European war probable. It acted partly for ideological reasons, supporting the Serbs, their fellow Slavs and Orthodox believers. According to pan-Slavist ideas, which influenced some of Russia's leading ministers, peoples such as the Serbs were bound by fraternal interests to Russia, and deserved the benevolent guidance of the Russian monarchy and robust support from Russian power. But Russia had not always been quick to leap to the Serbs' defence – it had backed down, for instance, during the crisis of 1908, when Austria-Hungary took formal control of Bosnia – and it had become decidedly nervous about the growing power of Bulgaria, another Balkan Slav nation, which Alexandra Kollontai's father had gone to war to defend thirty-seven years before. Founded as an independent sovereign state under Russian protection in 1878, and sharing centuries of entangled Slavic history before that, its interests had recently diverged from Russia's, especially during the First Balkan War of 1912, as a result of which it doubled in size and briefly threatened to absorb Constantinople. Russia might have been on Serbia's side in 1914, but the Bulgarians would in fact join the Germans and Austrians during the First World War (just as they would fight alongside the Nazis from 1941). In other words: pan-Slavism might be an instinctive emotion, but it was not enough to make Russia want to go to war.

So Russia's Balkan interests were not only ideological, but strategic. They concerned security and trade. The Russian and Ottoman Empires had frequently gone to war over the centuries, and so Russia was as worried by the prospect of a newly strong Turkey as it was of the growing power of her other Balkan rivals. In 1914, once again, the Russians wanted to ensure that their southern borderlands were safe, from the Turks, historically the power in the region, from the Austrians and Germans, with their Balkan scheming, and even from the Bulgarians, who were getting above themselves. The Russian government was especially worried about the economic consequences of geopolitical changes in the region. Russia depended on access from the Black Sea through the Straits of Constantinople and into the outside world. Without it, its grain exports would be dramatically reduced and its naval strength compromised. Turkey had ordered two dreadnought battleships from Britain, which were due for delivery in the summer of 1914. This force threatened the Russian naval position in the Black Sea region. Meanwhile, in late 1913, a German military mission under the command of General Otto Liman von Sanders came to Turkey. In Russian eyes, this looked like potential German control of Constantinople and the Straits: a catastrophic outcome.[42]

Even reasonable men, such as the foreign minister, Sergei Sazonov, began to sound bellicose. The most powerful restraining voice in Russian policy, the long-time finance minister and then prime minister, Vladimir Kokovtsov, had been removed from office in January. Weakened by geopolitical circumstances and sometimes by pan-Slav fantasies, the Russians stood on the edge of a strategic and national abyss in 1914. They were deafened by the feedback loop of exaggerated perceptions that derived from the Russia Anxiety. The Germans and Austrians were taking over the Balkans; Turkey was reviving its navy; control of the Straits, a Russian worry for centuries, was about to go for good. Economic failure was threatened, and great-power irrelevance would follow. Perhaps revolution would come in its train. The Sarajevo assassination and the July Crisis that followed gave the Russians a last roll of the dice. They gambled recklessly, betting not only their own house but threatening to break the bank of the whole European casino. In backing Serbia so strongly – and perhaps even having a hand in the assassination at Sarajevo, who knows? – they forced war with Austria-Hungary and Germany. The Austrians were entitled to expect that the Russians would not take advantage of regicide, after all; and Russia had indicated repeatedly in the diplomatic crises of recent years that it would not push Austria-Hungary in the Balkans as far as actual war. The response in July 1914 seemed out of proportion, arbitrary and even the result of conspiracy.[43]

There is something of the Russia Anxiety in the framing of this retrospective charge sheet: the claim of recklessness, unpredictability and opacity in Russia's relations with its rivals; the assumption that Russia's interference in neighbouring countries was more heavy-handed and less legitimate than that of other powers; the air of cloak-and-dagger intervention; and the implication that this was the foolish behaviour of a failing power. But if Russia really did see this as the last chance to assert its imperial pretensions, then France, taking its own opportunistic chance to harness itself to Russia and together take on Germany, was quick to back her up. Russia might have been bellicose in its defence of Serbia during July, ultimately mobilizing, but Austria was the one to send the ultimatum designed to provoke war, and then to declare war. If Russia had not always been straightforward or clear in its Balkan dealings, or in signalling how far it would go towards war in its relations with the other powers, then what about Britain? Britain was Russia's ally, but it had sold battleships to Russia's Black Sea rival, Turkey. This really did seem like the actions of perfidious Albion. And Britain seemed to hedge its bets during the July Crisis. In not making its intentions fully clear – would it really defend Belgium, or would it not? – it encouraged Germany to take its chance and attack, thinking that the British might not call them out.[44]

And if Russia looked at times as if it were the country prepared to gamble on war in order to preserve its status as a great power, then that seemed precisely what Austria-Hungary was doing in Serbia: taking the chance, once and for all, to secure its imperial status in the Balkans before it was too late. Germany was the biggest gambler of all, still more openly reckless, alarmed by Russia's growing economy, its capacity for reform and what looked like its unlimited military reserves. Some of its main decision-makers were rendered myopic by the Russia Anxiety. For some in the German high command and civil government, seeing a shortfall of nearly a million soldiers between the two alliances and feeling 'panic' as new French loans stretched Russian rearmament even further,[45] this was the last best chance to stop Russia before it became the star of Europe, outshining Germany for good. By 1917, they feared, Russia would be too strong. July 1914 was too good a crisis to waste. The 'blank cheque' – the unquestioned support that Germany gave to Austria-Hungary over its aggressive ultimatum to Serbia – allowed the Austrians to take their chance to eliminate the Serbian threat without worrying about the consequences. If Russia mobilized, Germany would help the Austrians. There had been crisis after crisis in European affairs in the decade before 1914, and the knowledge among all the continent's statesmen that war would bring universal disaster was enough to act as a final deterrent.[46] But in the summer of 1914, the deterrent failed: for the gamblers, the incentive to go to war was too great.

The Treaty of Versailles would be predicated on the idea of German guilt. German responsibility indeed lies at the heart of the origins of the First World War. It was Germany that set off arms races it could not win, imperial rivalries it could not sustain, tensions it could not defuse. In the final analysis, it was Germany that took the risk that European civilization could not bear. But so much of what happened was caused by the tragedy of the Russia Anxiety.

1914 proves that the international system is only secure when all of its biggest decision-makers can draw on accurate knowledge about Russia. Such knowledge would allow them to make plausible and sober calculations about Russian intentions, and strive to keep Russian power in synch with their own, so that the cycle of fear, contempt and disregard is broken. Yet in the post-Cold-War era, major states cut back on Russia expertise in universities and government, and in some cases even reduced provision for foreign-language instruction in schools. For Henry Kissinger in 2014, a successful American foreign policy rested on two things: America's post-1945 commitment to universal values, plus the unerring focus on balance between the powers that had been a guide to stability since the Peace of Westphalia of 1648. But this combination could not work without 'a recognition of the reality of other regions' histories and cultures'.[47] At that very point, Federal funding for scholarly visits and graduate training in the former Soviet Union was under threat. In February 2015, before the Brexit vote and in the midst of the Ukraine conflict, a report by the British House of Lords noted 'a decline in [European Union] Member States' analytical capacity on Russia'. Echoing (deliberately or not) the title of the bestselling book that had recently been published on the origins of the First World War, it suggested that the EU was found ' "sleepwalking" into the current crisis'.[48] Defining what is legitimate in Russia's interests and overcoming the cycle of the Russia Anxiety will require expertise as well as goodwill. Only an Anxious view of Russia will be possible if the EU's core knowledge of its neighbour is constructed by the ignorant, or if NATO's Russia position is set by vested interests.

And yet the year 1914 is instructive in another way: Russia was no more and no less likely to be at war than the rest of Europe. In the end, the most important counterbalance to the Russia Anxiety is that Russia's history of war is pretty much like everyone else's.

## A BRIEF HISTORY OF NORMALITY

Russia has usually been at peace with the Western powers and enjoyed friendly relations with them. Like the other powers, though, Russia can be provoked; one scholar suggests that Russia has been historically peaceful until the moments when it feels the need to defend its honour.[49] Things have been more complicated with the nearest neighbours, but not to an unusual degree in European history. (The sheer length and complexity of Russia's borderlands can make comparison difficult, though,[50] and we won't return here to the internal conflicts of colonization that were the subject of the previous chapter.) In the three great conflicts that created modern Russia – with the Mongol Horde, Napoleonic France and the Third Reich – the 'homeland' was invaded, and Rus-Russia-USSR was the target, not the instigator. Europe's East Slav region was shaped by repeated violence, but not more than other parts of Europe have been, and only sometimes because of 'Russian' rather than foreign aggression.

In the medieval period, as Rus and Muscovy, its borders were formed by conflicts with, among others, Vikings, Byzantines, Mongols, Teutonic Knights and Lithuanians. The Mongol invasion especially was a crushing and cruel experience. Since early modern times, when Muscovy and then the Russian Empire took on a more recognizably Russian shape, new and old enemies appeared. Ivan the Terrible led wars against Swedes (1554–7) and Livonians, who were supported periodically by Danes and Poles (1558–83). His southwards expansion of Muscovy brought him into conflict with the Ottoman Empire over Astrakhan (1568–70) and Crimea (1570–72); he also faced local powers, such as the Crimean Tatars. Boris Godunov, serving as regent before acceding to the throne, went to war with Sweden (1590–93) before he and then his successors faced the Polish and Swedish invasions that came during and after the Time of Troubles (1609–18). During the seventeenth century, there were more wars with Sweden (1610–17, 1656–61) and with the Commonwealth of Poland-Lithuania (1632–4, 1654–67). Sustained conflict with the Turks set in (1676–81, 1695–1700), though this soon brought the Russians into European alliances with Austria and Poland-Lithuania.[51] None of this quite matches the centuries of warfare between England and France.

Periodic Asian wars began, first with the Persians (1651–3, 1722–3, 1796, 1804–13, 1826–8, and 1909–11). As Muscovy's borders expanded ever further eastwards, skirmishes with the Chinese, especially around the Amur river, took place (1652–89), in whose context were two battles with Koreans (1654 and 1658). Centuries later came the Korean War (1950–53), when Soviet forces unofficially participated alongside the Chinese on behalf of the communist North. Russia played a part alongside all the other powers in humiliating China during the Boxer Rebellion (1899–1901). The catastrophic war against Japan (1904–5) was one conclusion of Russia's risk-driven Asia policy. But Eastern temptations remained. The Soviet Union joined with its Western allies by declaring war on Japan following the defeat of Germany in 1945. It seized territory in Japan's Kuril Islands, which remains a source of strategic tension in East Asia, and took back south Sakhalin, lost forty years before. Russia's military and political leaders are unlikely to repeat the costly mistakes of the war in Afghanistan (1979–89) anytime soon, though Russia's fear of radical Islamism persists, and has contributed to conflict inside the country, notably the two devastating wars in Chechnya in the 1990s, which left a legacy of terrorism, from Beslan to St Petersburg. Still, despite the vast run of its borders, Russia-in-Asia does not have ancient external enmities that endure. The vast, empty spaces on either side of its Asian borders can be burdens but also strategic reserves. On the one hand, Russia is on the back foot in Asia, under pressure from China's economic growth, its patient strategy, and even from Chinese migration into Russia. It would be an even bigger risk than in 1950 to take part in a hypothetical second Korean War. On the other, though, closer relations with China remain one route out of Russia's apparent strategic impasse in the West; combined military exercises in 2018 took place in the context of America's attempt to 'contain' both powers simultaneously.

But Europe is a different matter. In the eighteenth century, Russia became a member of the European system, the shifting alliances of great and minor powers that were periodically at war with each other. The Great Northern War (1700–1721) was a sequence of conflicts between Peter the Great and Charles XII of Sweden, brought about by Charles's massive invasion of Russia, and ended by the Battle of Poltava. Russian armies also went south at this time and fought the Turks with less happy results. The war brought Russia into alliance with Sweden's Scandinavian enemies, as well as Prussia, Hanover and Saxony. Poland-Lithuania and Britain swapped sides. Russia's place in the international order was defined by the multi-state European wars that followed. The War of the Polish Succession (1733–8) brought Russia onto the side of Poland's Augustus III, together with Saxony, Prussia and Austria, against Augustus's challenger, who was backed by Spain, Sardinia and France. And then the War of the Austrian

Succession (1740–48) allied Russia with Austria, together with Britain, Hanover and Sardinia. Their enemies were Prussia, Spain, France, Sweden, Bavaria and Genoa; Saxony swapped sides. In retrospect, the sequence of events seems bewildering. But it was the way that international affairs worked, and imperial Russia was just a normal part of the European system.

During the reign of Elizabeth, the Seven Years' War (1756–63) gave Russia one of the decisive roles in the development of European, even global, affairs, fighting with France, Austria, Spain, Sweden and Saxony against Britain, Portugal, Prussia and several other German states. Franco–Russian relations, and the prestige of France in St Petersburg, were at their height. But this ended, temporarily at least, with the French Revolution and the rise of Napoleon. With Catherine the Great on the throne, Russia joined Austria and Prussia in partitioning Poland (1772), the Russians gaining more land with the second partition that followed their defeat of Poland-Lithuania in 1793. (The complete dismemberment of the long-standing Polish-Lithuanian Commonwealth by these three powers took place with a third partition in 1795.) Catherine's armies also fought over Sweden's Finnish territory (1788–90), a job which Alexander I completed by defeating the Swedes and incorporating Finland into the Empire (1808–9). Looking back, it seems not exactly edifying. But most of this was the normal foreign policy of a European power.

By the turn of the nineteenth century, then, Russia was an indispensable great power, no more aggressive than the others, and less threatening than some. In fact, it became their saviour.[52] The Russian Empire was a member of the coalitions that went to war three times against France (1799–1807), before Alexander I and Napoleon came to terms at Tilsit. Yet when the French invaded in 1812, the Russians endured, halting Napoleon and then pushing him back to Paris (1812–14). At the Congress of Vienna in 1815, all the great powers, including Russia, wanted to prevent France from starting wars on this scale again, and all of them, apart from Russia, were also keen that Russia should not get too big for its boots. It was clear that a strong Russia made Europe secure, though the other great powers were never keen to admit this. This is a useful history lesson. Russia has most obviously posed risks to European security – elevating the chance of war between it and other European powers – when its government has felt exposed, and when it has lacked a face-saving diplomatic exit, such as in the run-up to the Crimean War, in 1914, in the late 1940s, even in the 2010s.

Rus-Muscovy-Russia's geopolitics were for centuries played out in the shadow of Byzantium, even if the shadow lengthened and weakened over time. All the leaders of the East Slavic lands, from Kievan Rus through to the Russian Federation, kept one eye on the south, worried about clashes over trade, religion or contested territory. Military confrontations sporadically resulted. The crucial contests were with the Ottoman Empire. As Muscovy expanded southwards during the reign of Ivan the Terrible, it came face to face with Ottoman forces, first in Astrakhan (1568–70) and then in Crimea (1570–72). A century later, on the back foot, Fedor III's troops withstood military pressure from the Turks (1676–81). From the reign of Peter the Great onwards, Imperial Russia was drawn more deeply into anti-Turkish European alliances. St Petersburg cast a jealous eye on Constantinople – the second Rome to Moscow's third – and in time wanted secure access to the straits that led in and out of the Black Sea. Russia was allied with Austria and Poland-Lithuania (1686–1700) in war with the Ottoman Empire, enjoying a famous victory at Azov, though when the Turks joined the Swedes in the middle part of the Great Northern War (1710–14), they inflicted defeats on the Russians. Anna's armies fought alongside the Austrians (1735–39) to secure some revenge, and when Catherine the Great led her forces against the Ottomans (1768–74, 1787–92) Russia was again victorious, but this time alone. It found common cause with Britain and France during the Greek War of Independence, when the navies of the three powers inflicted losses on the Turks at the Battle of Navarino (1827); Nicholas I continued the conflict alone (1828–9), securing concessions from the Turks in the Treaty of Adrianople. Famously, the Russians fought the Turks during the Crimean War (1853–6) and again over Bulgaria (1877), and Russo-Turkish mutual suspicion exacerbated the July Crisis in 1914. But they were both major European and Eurasian empires, ready to pursue belligerent policies. Over the long term, neither was the victim.

Russia's history of warfare has, therefore, been a *normal* history of warfare. Its wars were usually similar to the wars of other leading countries, and when it went to war with one set of European powers, it usually did so in alliance with another. When it really mattered, Russia was on the same side as 'the West', which was especially important during the world wars. But the Cold War is the big exception to all this. Recent and important, it is understandably a dominant presence in the popular memory of international affairs. Yet this distorts the wider pattern of history, making Russia seem exceptionally aggressive and a default adversary of the United States.

By definition, the Cold War placed the Soviet Union and 'the West' on opposite sides. It was an ideological clash between capitalism and communism whose prehistory went back to the October Revolution;[53] Washington did not send an ambassador to Soviet Moscow until 1933. After 1945, when the Cold War had begun, the Soviet Union retained control over the countries of East-Central Europe, requiring them to implement its Stalinist programme of a centrally planned economy, imposing government through a single socialist-communist party and enforcing consensus through secret-police violence. For all the diverse composition of 'the West', it was quite different from the Eastern bloc. The ideological division underwrote global affairs until 1989. It defined the Soviet Union and its satellites and supporters as adversaries of the West. But while the ideological division was fundamental, the politics of diplomacy were contingent.[54] Much of Soviet foreign policy remained pragmatic, devoted to defence of the Revolution and the borders of the fatherland. After all, the United States fought alongside the Soviet Union during the Second World War. Specific decisions – that could have gone more than one way – created the division of Europe, kept Soviet forces in the Eastern bloc and caused the arms race. Soviet control of the Eastern bloc was not part of a pattern of expansionism. At the end of the Second World War, for example, a putative Soviet intervention in Iran came to nothing, and a quite different consequence of European expansionism, the British Empire in India, was still just across the border. The Cold War was a system of international relations, not a war, though it had casualties. Conflict occurred outside Europe. The Soviet Union fought its major war in Afghanistan – its Vietnam – and intervened in smaller conflicts in the 'Third World'. Moscow's proxy wars in Africa were the strategic equivalents of Washington's armed interventions in Latin America.

But the very term 'Cold War' creates the sense that the Soviet Union was the only villain, and that the United States and the USSR were at war with each other for decades. It helps to explain the loose language of war between them in the 2010s.

This is a long history of warfare. But it is a shorter history than Britain's, thanks not least to its many years of conflict with France, and its permanent involvement in wars great and small across the length of the twentieth century. Is Russia unusually warlike? Despite the Russia Anxiety's constructions of history, it would be difficult to stick to the facts and say that Russia has been *more* warlike than the other great powers.

## BEYOND THE RUSSIA ANXIETY

A. J. P. Taylor spent much of his career studying the great powers as they conducted diplomacy and war in the nineteenth and twentieth centuries. He went to great lengths, for example, to see the world from Bismarck's point of view, writing a biography of him. Taylor was also a member of the Campaign for Nuclear Disarmament, a mass-membership protest group that was founded in 1958. Going on marches and carrying banners, he was convinced that the lesson of 1914 was that the deterrent would fail soon enough. Yet Taylor was no starry-eyed marcher for peace. He saw the dynamics of foreign policy as calculations of interest. 'As a private citizen, I think that all this striving after greatness and domination is idiotic,' he wrote. 'As a historian, I recognize that Powers will be Powers.'[55]

Russia flexed its status as a twenty-first century power with military support for President Assad in Syria. Clear reasons existed for this policy. Like the United States, the Soviet Union had projected a forward position in the Middle East ever since the foundation of the State of Israel. It trained cadres of experts on the region, such as the future prime minister of the Russian Federation in the late 1990s, Yevgeny Primakov, and President Putin's own top specialist, the deputy foreign minister, Mikhail Bogdanov. Through people like Bogdanov, post-Soviet Russia inherited interests in and knowledge of the Middle East, together with connections with particular actors, such as Assad and his father. As a major exporter of arms, like the United States, Russia is tied into regional arms contracts. With historic links to Iran, it is inclined to counterbalance Israel. Worried about Islamist terrorism in the north Caucasus, it has looked for ways to root out international terrorist networks, often by cooperating with the United States. In Syria, the Russians intervened on behalf of a government that was waging a civil war against militants backed by Islamic State. Most important of all, the intervention was a statement about Russia's reach. Under Putin's leadership, it looked like a global power again. But Russia became implicated in Assad's deadly strategy, which included the destruction of Aleppo, the use of chemical weapons and the slaughter of hundreds of thousands of civilians. The assumptions of the Russia Anxiety kicked in: Russia had transgressed norms in a uniquely malicious way. It was the global cowboy. No one else behaved like this.

The same assumption – of a solitary bad actor, stalking on the fringes of the international community and outside the great-power consensus – informed the allegations about Russian interference in the United States presidential election of 2016. American intelligence agencies made the case that Russia-backed hackers penetrated electronic voting databases in four US states and unsuccessfully targeted others. Factories of Russian trolls manipulated social media debate in swing states, spreading fake news and undermining Hillary Clinton's case. Cyber attacks were launched on the Democratic National Committee, with the private emails of leading figures, such as John Podesta, published online. The charge was that Russian hackers used Wikileaks as a conduit for exposing the compromising materials (the so-called *kompromat*), while Russian agents might have penetrated the National Rifle Association as a route into Republican networks. Robert Mueller was appointed to head an inquiry into the collusion question: had the Trump campaign illegally cooperated with representatives of the Russian government? In the two years that followed November 2016, few people wanted to claim that the Russians had changed the course of the election, though speculation about a Trump-Putin conspiracy never ended. Instead, a different claim circulated widely: that the Russians' real goal was to sow seeds of doubt in the national conversation about the integrity and usefulness of US elections. It was only one part of a wider grand strategy against Western democracy. Further claims followed, of Russian interference in elections in France, Germany and Sweden, even in Mexico, as well as in the Brexit referendum in the United Kingdom.

Historians can't add facts to the debate about what happened in 2016, nor can they take sides on the basis of historical judgement. But they can provide a chronological perspective, one which shows there's nothing unusual about one country interfering in the elections of another. In the presidential election of 1996, there was a real chance of the Communists returning to power in Russia. Their candidate, Gennady Zyuganov, offered a determined challenge to the incumbent, Boris Yeltsin. The group of American political consultants who have often been credited with turning Yeltsin's campaign around had close ties to President Clinton. One of those consultants, Richard Dresner, updated the White House on a weekly basis, and advised Bill Clinton on how best to articulate his support for Yeltsin in Moscow. Clinton also helped ensure that an IMF loan of ten billion dollars arrived in time for election day. Four years later, Tony Blair took gentler but still unconventional steps to back Vladimir Putin, signalling respect from the international community to the Russian electorate. One political scientist has found evidence of interventions in sixty-two foreign elections by the American government during the Cold War. Much of this activity was in the form of CIA covert operations. One of the most famously successful of these came in Italy in 1948, when the CIA worked to divert support away from the Communists to make sure that the Christian Democrats would lead the government.[56]

In a sense, this was the thin end of the wedge of political intervention. Stuck between the risk of nuclear war and a distaste for détente-style diplomacy, newly elected President Reagan looked to the CIA to stand out against communism, which meant covert operations against left-wing groups in Latin America. It came at a cost. Military and economic aid flowed, for example, into Honduras, reaching 298 million dollars in 1985, against a background of hundreds of assassinations and 'disappearances'.[57] In the preceding decades, CIA-backed assaults, such as at the Bay of Pigs in Cuba in 1961, were combined with a cultural Cold War. The CIA-funded Congress for Cultural Freedom imported US propaganda into the region.[58] This mixture of approaches would in a later age be described as 'hybrid warfare'. Yet what set America apart was that some of these covert schemes and interventions were exposed and investigated, such as the Iran-Contra affair, a complex conspiracy planned in the White House and famously involving Colonel Oliver North of the National Security Council to divert resources illegally to anti-communist rebels in Nicaragua. North was convicted in 1989, but a year later the convictions were found unsafe and were reversed; in 2018, he was appointed president of the National Rifle Association. Bob Woodward, of Watergate fame, was on hand to document it all, just as he would be thirty years later when it came to the Russia scandal in the Trump White House.[59]

But why make these comparisons? They sound like 'whataboutism'. Or we could go further, and ask a sequence of related questions.

Is external interference in an election more egregious when it happens to the United States? Has Russia's Syria policy done more to destabilize the Middle East than the interventions of the United States in the region? Has Russia's facilitation of the Syrian war done more to kill civilians than the American war in Iraq? Is 'hybrid war' in Eastern Europe and even the United States different from CIA covert action in Nicaragua, El Salvador, Honduras and elsewhere? Is Russia's choice of partners any different from America's selections of friendly dictators? Is the projection of Russian power through social media and the international TV channel Russia Today in the same category as American cultural diplomacy or even the ubiquity of global American brands? Are the human rights interventions of the twenty-first century any different from the imperialism of the nineteenth? Is hacking worse than drone strikes? Are oligarchs worse when they are Russian?

There is no point in answering these questions. They are rhetorical and provocative. You might find them offensive. Any answers to them are meaningless. These questions only exist to be asked. But the act of asking the questions disrupts one's assumptions and destabilizes the Russia Anxiety, because the quickest cure for the Anxiety is self-awareness. Asking these unanswerable questions invites one to experiment with the notion that the leading powers, for all their differences, share moral failures. In turn, this opens up the possibility that the cycle of the Russia Anxiety might be broken.

It will take pragmatists to achieve this, those unwilling to cast the first stone, those uncomfortable with bold moral statements or at least prepared to suspend their preference for them. Such people have taken a lead at important moments. Anxiety-reducing pragmatism has helped solve some of the most dangerous foreign policy crises. Let's look at three examples.

At 10 p.m. on 6 October 1939, Ivan Maisky, the Soviet ambassador to Britain, entered Winston Churchill's office at the Admiralty. It was still nine months until Churchill would become prime minister, but five weeks since the declaration of war against Germany, and six weeks since the signature of the Molotov–Ribbentrop Pact. Churchill was, of course, the great anti-appeaser, who had spent much of the 1930s warning about the German threat. He had been world history's most famous voice in the wilderness since Cassandra. Now he had some power to decide who was Britain's enemy and who was Britain's friend. On that pitch-black evening, it seemed that everyone had gone home. The nightwatchman took an age to open up the gate. Maisky eventually found his way through the dark building and up to the office of the first lord of the Admiralty. Churchill's feelings were clear. 'Better communism than Nazism,' he told Maisky, effectively saying that the non-aggression pact between Germany and the Soviet Union was an understandable insurance policy for the Russians.

For Churchill, the intentions of Nazi Germany were malign, its diplomacy dishonourable, and the word of its leaders untrustworthy. Germany was a true enemy. But what about his stance on the USSR? This seemed less morally clear. He remained a capitalist and a conservative, a willing participant in competitive elections, and the opposite of a Bolshevik. As we've seen, though, his view on foreign affairs migrated from anti-communism in the 1920s to anti-fascism in the 1930s. His language about the Soviet Union lost its vitriol. In facing the Soviet Union, he moved away from moral certainty, from an ideological stance to a pragmatic one. Churchill's conversation with Maisky on the night of 6 October 1939 symbolized the possibility of constructive dialogue at the most unpromising moment. 'We parted "like friends",' Maisky wrote in his diary. 'Churchill asked me to keep in close touch and to turn to him without ceremony whenever the need arose.'[60] This was an essential connection for Churchill. It helped him read the Soviet Union when he became prime minister. A year after that, when geopolitics changed beyond either's control, and the two countries became allies, his connection with Maisky was an important source of insight, facilitating the construction of the Grand Alliance and offering Churchill ways of reading Stalin better, to their mutual benefit.

Not much more than a decade later, Bobby Kennedy was supporting Joe McCarthy in the communist witchhunts of the early 1950s. At his father's request, Kennedy joined William Douglas, a justice of the Supreme Court and friend of the family, in his tour around the Soviet Union in the summer of 1955. Kennedy's display of ill-feeling and distrust towards those Soviet citizens he met was extravagant. He largely refused to eat their food. When he became feverish and ill in Siberia, he turned down medical treatment, until his more senior travelling companion intervened and insisted that he take the help of the doctors, who saved him with penicillin.[61]

Following their return, Kennedy's tone was softer – just. 'We must have peaceful coexistence with Russia,' he declared at Georgetown University in October, echoing Khrushchev, 'but if we and our allies are weak, there will be no peace – there will be no coexistence.'[62] It was tough talk – he was no soft touch for the post-Stalin order – but it held out the glimmer of a more pragmatic understanding of the USSR's role in international affairs. Five years later, as attorney general in his brother's administration, Kennedy was becoming still more flexible in his understanding of policy problems generally. He formed a durable connection with a Soviet diplomat, Georgy Bolshakov, meeting fortnightly and establishing the back channel that made communication possible during the Cuban Missile Crisis of 1962. The two men had their ups and downs, but at the most dangerous moment in the nuclear stand-off, Bobby Kennedy was ready to trust Bolshakov and thereby Khrushchev, and they were ready to trust him.

Two years later, Denis Healey became the defence secretary of the United Kingdom. Born in 1917, he was a twin of the Russian Revolution, but unlike many of his peers, he had no truck with the Russia Anxiety and tried to understand the Soviet Union for himself. Healey was a communist in 1930s Oxford who spent his career at Labour's moderate centre. He was distinguished by a lifetime commitment to politics, huge political skill, deep intellectual seriousness, a certain common touch and great knowledge of policy, which he brought to all the offices he held: defence secretary, chancellor of the exchequer and, had Labour won in 1983 or 1987, would-be foreign secretary.

Healey was a tough-minded defence secretary in the 1960s, serving in that office for six years. Twenty years earlier, he had fought in the Second World War. But he was also a calm diplomat who did not resort to name-calling or obvious bluff. He did not believe that the Soviet Union was ever going to attack NATO. Instead, he recognized that, until the end of the 1980s, Moscow was prepared to use force to keep hold of its Warsaw Pact satellites. This was not just a moral problem: it was the greatest threat to NATO members, because 'once fighting started there, it might conceivably slop over the Iron Curtain and involve the West'. NATO's priority in Europe should be to maintain 'conventional forces at least large enough to control such incidents'. Reducing the nuclear risk was paramount.

Healey travelled widely and frequently, and visited Moscow many times. His repeated snapshots of Soviet life suggested to him that 'ordinary Russians had seen substantial improvements in their standard of living during the Brezhnev years'. Writing some time before the collapse of the Soviet Union, he argued: 'I suspect that Gorbachev may come to regret the record of unrelieved failure he has attributed to his predecessor, particularly if *perestroika* fails to produce similar improvements for the average citizen.'[63] This hit straight to the risk that Gorbachev was taking. Again, Healey forewent an easy moral judgement, instead drawing an independent conclusion based on observation. Eschewing platitudes helps dissolve the Russia Anxiety.

On 28 May 2016, President Obama visited Hiroshima. The American media speculated about whether he would apologize for the atomic bombing of the city. Republicans waited for yet another selling-out of America. But Obama recast the problem. 'We have a shared responsibility to look directly into the eye of history,' he said, 'and ask what we must do differently to curb such suffering again.'[64] Obama was not apologizing, but he was suggesting that modern states of all types can face similar pressures that require the most difficult decisions to be made.

President Truman's decision to use the atomic bomb sprang from the need to defeat an enemy which had attacked the United States. But in justifying the bomb in the name of peace – it would save many more lives than the alternative, which was a costly and bitterly fought invasion of Japan – Truman, and his secretary of war, Henry Stimson, revealed again that all modern states have something in common: they cannot avoid the logic that in extreme situations the ends justify the means.

Stalin could understand that. The Stalinist system was a radical simplification of modern politics, when the ends (communism) never stopped justifying the means (destroying individuals). Dropping an atomic bomb to solve a problem seemed to fit inside a Stalinist mentality.

Thanks to well-placed spies, such as Klaus Fuchs, the Soviet leadership was aware of America's atomic bomb. Stalin's suspicion of potential enemies and cynicism about political life told him why they would use it: not only were the atomic bombings of Hiroshima and Nagasaki a matter of defeating Japan quickly, but of keeping the Soviets from encroaching further into Asia, and of showing them the awesome might of American power. In August 1945, the Red Army was already in China and Korea, and was eyeing up a Soviet-US partition of Japan. The atom bomb put a stop to that. Stalin had no doubt that the bombing of Hiroshima was directed against the Soviet Union.[65]

There were voices in America that made the same point, such as William R. Castle, undersecretary of state under Stimson between 1931 and 1933, who wrote controversially in his diary in February 1947: '[Stimson] knew that Japan was suing for peace, that its economy had been destroyed ... I wonder whether Stimson ... wanted war to continue for long enough to give them a chance to try out the atom bomb on Japanese cities.'[66]

Castle had his own axe to grind. The US Army Air Force set about destroying Japanese cities with conventional bombs as soon as it got within reach; it did not wait. Japan could have surrendered at any point. And, as Churchill pointed out, the atomic bomb was built to be used. But President Truman still made a decision. Other options existed. Half a century on, in August 1995, George F. Kennan, the conscience of American foreign policy, wrote in a private letter of 'our obligation to ourselves – to our sense of what it was suitable and decent for such a country as ours to be doing ... We should have swallowed our militant pride and consented to sound out the Japanese on the possibilities ... of compromise.'[67]

But even if Stalin simplified Truman's mentality, and those without power sniped at him from a safe distance, the American president faced a decision of giant moral complexity and weight at a time of ongoing national danger. Seventy years on, his successor's moral explication was more powerful than an apology. 'We're not bound by genetic code to repeat the mistakes of the past,' Obama claimed in Hiroshima. 'We can tell our children a different story, one that describes a common humanity, one that makes war less likely and cruelty less easily accepted.'[68]

Even if you agree with Obama's words, you can draw different policy prescriptions from them. But at their heart is the assumption that history does not make particular nations predisposed to war. Perhaps every leading politician in Europe and the United States should remember this idea every day. Ordinary Russians, whose history tilts them towards peace, and who have feared war viscerally since 1941, can agree with this statement of pragmatism and war-avoidance. The present day gives them at least as much to lose from war as any of us, and history gives them more to fear from war than most of us. In the twenty-first century, Russia is vastly more open and vastly less ideological than it was before 1991. Its deepest interests in economic, financial and security terms are aligned with the West as a whole, while the way people live, at least in major centres of population, is more similar than ever to other parts of Europe. The World Cup of 2018 convinced people from across the world of this. 'Russia has confounded the expectations of its biggest influx of visitors since the Nazi invasion,' wrote a leading journalist on the London *Times*, an old Russia hand himself. Almost 3 million foreigners came to eleven cities,[69] meaning that they could not but see the rough as well as the smooth. 'In Moscow it was not hard to find an English fan with bad things to say about their hosts,' he went on. 'It was impossible.'[70] The new age is nothing like the Cold War, which also means it is less stable than before: it's unpredictable, the nuclear deterrent is less certain, and rapid change for the worse as well as the better is possible. Russia has no ambitions to invade the European Union and therefore to go to war with America,[71] though the lesson of 1914 is that a crisis can distort perceptions and undermine the deterrent of civilizational destruction. History provides consolations and warnings alike. As we'll see in part III, the materials of history – time and memory – are implicated in the Russia Anxiety, though they might offer a solution.

# PART III

# The Fireglow of History

I'm now absorbing the living pages of history. The world never stagnates, it's always stirring, new forms of life are always appearing. And I love to look back now at the path trodden by humanity, or run forward to the wonderful beautiful future which humanity will inhabit, spreading its wings and saying, 'Happiness! Happiness for everyone!'

*Alexandra Kollontai, 1952*

History, too, depressed him terribly: you learn and read that at a certain date the people were overtaken by all sorts of calamities and were unhappy, then they summoned up their strength, worked, took infinite care, endured great hardships, laboured in preparation for better days. At last they came – one would think history might take a rest, but no, clouds gathered again, the edifice crashed down, and again the people had to toil and labour ... The bright days do not remain, they fly, and life flows on, one crisis follows upon another.

*Ivan Goncharov, Oblomov, 1859*

I am tired of the twentieth century,
Of its blood-filled rivers.

*Vladimir Sokolov, 1988[1]*

This is a history book about a contemporary crisis. As much as it hopes to throw light upon the present day, *history* is its subject. And so in Part I we reflected on the Russia Anxiety as an historic condition, but one that has come and gone, caused by events and personalities as much as by deeper cultural currents. It's a condition, what's more, that history might even be able to cure. In Part II, we saw that the big issues that fuel the Russia Anxiety – the country's apparent predisposition to political violence, for example, or the assumption that aggressive expansionism is encoded into its DNA – are not predetermined by history at all. Instead, history offers alternatives and solutions, and it shows that Russia's story is one of normality as well as exceptionalism.

Yet, as we'll see in Part III, the Russia Anxiety is still made out of history, of ingredients like memory, chronology, narrative and time. After all, if Russians have forgotten how to remember Stalin, are they not doomed to relive him? And haven't Russians throughout the past had a tendency to imagine the wrong kind of futures: of utopias, special paths and force? These two problems – the relationships between history and memory, and history and the future, which are the subject of the next two chapters – seem likely to worsen the Russia Anxiety. But in the following pages we'll see something different. History isn't Russia's problem, but one of its most valuable resources. And the hints of Part I were right, after all: history really does offer one of the best cures for the Russia Anxiety.

# 9

## The Stalin Inheritance

*Should Russians Remember the Past or Forget It?*

One cold night in 2006 I went to the Sovremennik ('Contemporary') in central Moscow to watch that theatre's long-running production of *Krutoi marshrut*. It means 'steep path', but has been translated into English as *Into the Whirlwind*. The play is based on the bestselling memoir of the same name by Evgenia Ginzburg, whose original Russian version was published in Milan in 1967 and then translated and sold across the West. In the 1930s, Ginzburg lived with her husband Pavel and her two sons in Kazan. They were a communist family. Pavel was a senior Soviet official; she was a true-believing *intelligent*, a university teacher and a journalist. They had everything to live for and had done nothing wrong.

On 7 February 1937, the Molotov district Party committee of the city of Kazan stripped Evgenia Ginzburg of her Party card, accusing her of consorting with Trotskyists. The accusation was one of the thousands of invented plots that drove the Great Terror. Nine days later she was summoned to the city offices of the NKVD and arrested. She underwent interrogation in Kazan and Moscow. On 1 August, she was sentenced to ten years without right of correspondence, serving her time first in jails in Moscow and nearby Yarolsavl. Two years later, she endured transit across the whole length of the country, arriving in Vladivostok on 7 July. She entered the notorious Gulag complex of Kolyma. The climate was barely liveable, the conditions hostile, the work heavy and long, the guards were violent, fellow prisoners usually untrusting or untrustworthy, though friendships lightened the load.

She was released on 15 February 1947, ten years after her arrest. She remained in exile, first in a small settlement and then in the city of Magadan. After so long without family news, she was able to start writing again and receiving correspondence. One of her sons travelled out to see her. But she was arrested again on 25 October 1949. This time her incarceration was short, a few weeks, but she had to remain in Magadan, where she adopted the girl she had been raising, and married a doctor, A. P. Walter, whom she had known in the camps. There were new hardships. They both lost their jobs during the anti-Jewish campaigns that marked the last years of Stalin. Meanwhile, it turned out that her first husband, who had been sentenced to death but ended up serving eighteen years in the camps, was alive, but she remained with Dr Walter. At last, after Stalin's death, she was rehabilitated on 25 June 1955. They came to live in Moscow in 1957. Two years later, Walter was dead. Ginzburg threw herself into recording the experiences of herself and her generation, though her work was only published abroad. Still, she was allowed to travel in Western Europe. She died in 1977, a few months short of her seventy-third birthday.[1]

As my wife reminds me, English people are restrained when they go to the theatre. Even after the most momentous of performances, only a handful of the audience will get to their feet, and they are probably foreigners. The most intense applause will only last long enough to get the actors back on stage for another quick curtain call; delirious clapping ends as quickly as it started. Or at least it seems like this in comparison to Russia, where the applause goes on and on, the company comes back time and again, people stride out from the audience to hand over flowers, the shouted compliments lack all restraint. The audience displays its heartfelt gratitude to the actors, the wall between them breaks down, and together they celebrate the power of the performance.

This was something with which I was familiar. But on that occasion back in 2006, joining in with the standing ovation, when there was not a dry eye – including my own – in the house, one saw that tears were streaming down the faces of the people on the stage as well. And these actors did this performance several times a month; some of them had been playing their roles for many years. Was it like this every time? It was as if audience, actors, auditorium, stage, text, past and present had all merged into a single arena of unrestrained emotion, where all the people in the theatre had come to understand the limits of their own lives through their evening's encounter with the worst of Russia's past.

As I walked back to the metro, I wondered what all this had meant. By the time I got to the train, I thought I had never more egregiously trespassed on this other country's history. Whose tears had I been crying? But if what had happened in that theatre was nothing to do with my own past, what did it have to do with the pasts of the weeping Muscovites in the stalls and on the stage? Were they crying for their long-gone relatives or for humanity in general? For the Soviet past or the Russian present? Or were they letting history stand in for some other private grief? Even in 2006, but especially a decade and more later, this seemed like a mystery, because a major cause of the Russia Anxiety was its claims about Russians' historical amnesia. Instead of processing the Stalinist past, they were keen to celebrate their history's patriotic episodes, especially the Second World War, perhaps a little like British citizens forgetting the Empire and remembering the poppies. As a way of explaining the tears of 2006, and reducing the Anxiety that so escalated in the decade that followed, we will turn in a moment to the greatest of the late Soviet novelists. After all, it remains a conceit of Russian culture that a book can solve a problem.

This chapter addresses the Russia Anxiety's fear that relates explicitly to history: that Russians have failed to process the memory of the past, and in particular of the terrible events of the age of 'tears without end' in the first half of the twentieth century. For the Anxious, this not only says something about Russians' attitude to human life, but it might well doom them and the world to relive the horrors of Stalinism. This chapter focuses on how the public came to remember and misremember the Great Terror – the blood-letting of almost 700,000 innocent victims between 1936 and 1938 – during the eras of Khrushchev, Gorbachev and Putin. If shows how people found out about the violence of the Stalinist past, how they memorialized it and came to terms with it. On the one hand, there has been no thorough reckoning with the demons of the past; on the other, there has been enough to reduce the concerns of reasonable sufferers from the Russia Anxiety. And as so often, perhaps deliberately, the Anxiety sets a test that Russia is bound to fail.

# THE URGENCY OF HISTORY

Yuri Trifonov seemed to be built out of history. All of us are shaped by the past: our own, our family's and those of the communities and environments we inhabit. Russians, whose past is always wide awake, display the impact of the past sharply. But even among them, Yuri Trifonov was an outlier. His life and writing were like that performance at the Sovremennik Theatre: past, present and place merged into a single reality. He suggested that history explained the present – and also that the present was the place where the damage done by history could be treated. If people were to live normal lives, and the Revolution was to go on, nothing was more urgent than facing history and learning from it. 'Every person lies in the glow of history,' Trifonov wrote in 1965. 'The glow singes some of them with its heat and threatening light, on others it can scarcely be noticed, it barely warms them. But the glow exists on everyone.' The fireglow of history was a living force that defined the present. In turn, the present defined the fire. 'History blazes like a colossal bonfire, and each of us throws our own brushwood into it,' he went on.[2]

He was born in August 1925, and his first address was house 17, apartment 3 on Tverskoi Boulevard in Moscow. This was a prestigious building on Moscow's Boulevard Ring. The Trifonovs' apartment was on the third floor, Russian-style (where the ground floor is the first floor), and overlooked the boulevard.[3] It was a house of privilege. Yuri's father, Valentin, was an Old Bolshevik who spent time in tsarist jails. He helped to make the Revolution in Moscow, fought in the Civil War in the south of Russia and became a leading official in the 1920s, working for some time in China. Yuri's mother was an economist; she held a post at the People's Commissariat of Agriculture. His sister, Tatyana, was born in 1927. Notwithstanding the dramatic social levelling of the time, this was the kind of comfortable home such men and women could make for their families. Yuri, who would write so much about the interconnectivity of past and present, always placed his own timeline in its geographical coordinates. He was magnetically attracted to history and to the places in which it unfolded. As a toddler, looking out of the window, he stared down at the

Boulevard Ring, the road that encircles the centre of Moscow. 'The strange power of the Ring!' he wrote in an an article of 1980, the year before his death. 'You find yourself in some kind of mystical dependence on it: you go out from here to Kaluzhskaya [District], then still further to Sokol [another district that is also beyond the Boulevard Ring], and then to God knows where, but the Ring doesn't let you go. And the whole city belongs to the Ring.'[4]

The family stayed at Tverskoi Boulevard for five years, before moving to a vast apartment block of sinister luxury, the House of Government, located directly across the Moscow river from the Kremlin and known to all as the House on the Embankment. In his final, sometimes autobiographical novel *Disappearance*, he called the complex 'a city within itself with a population of ten thousand'.[5] The building was home to the families of many senior members of Party and government. Trifonov reconstructed it in another novel, *The House on the Embankment*, a book of 1976 in which the contrasting worlds of the Soviet 1930s and 1970s are placed in dialogue. He depicts the destruction of his family's world of large rooms and soft furnishings, often discreetly but unmistakably tagged with the marks of government ownership. Theirs was apartment 137, on staircase 7; the apartment had four good rooms as well as the kitchen and the bathroom. The parents and two children lived together with Yuri's maternal grandmother and the Chuvash teenager she had adopted a decade before. They had a maid, Anya.[6] At the same time, the Trifonovs also had another government-owned residence, a dacha at Serebryannyi Bor, just outside the city. Here, too, past and present merged: this was a new cooperative settlement of country residences, occupied by leading revolutionaries who were building the future during working hours but spending their leisure in a timeless Russian landscape of silver birch glades, smooth lakes, big skies and endless summer evenings.

They were at the dacha when their lives fell apart for the first time. On 22 June 1937, when Yuri was eleven, he had the great encounter with history that would change his life. The secret police came there to take his father. He found out years later that his father had been shot. Then, on 3 April 1938, they came back for his mother, who would survive the camps. Yuri was then twelve. This most articulate and well-read of children – he was then working through *War and*

*Peace* and composing careful stories – wrote in his diary: 'Mummy-y-y-y-y!!!!yy!! I can't stop cr . . .'[7] The elite population of the House on the Embankment was an object of unremitting and deadly hostility from Stalin personally during the Great Terror. The remnants of this revolutionary family, led by grandma, went to live in a room in a communal apartment on Bolshaya Kaluzhskaya Street. Under attack by the forces of the Revolution, they had moved from one classic Soviet abode to another. It was an almost catastrophic decline in living standards and prospects. For all the internal agony it caused, Yuri Trifonov's encounter with history played out on the stage set of instantly recognizable locales, a Soviet dacha and apartment houses. They locked memory into specific places, but always in conflicted ways. Trifonov begins the novel *Disappearance* with the main character, Igor, who is a version of himself, looking at what seems to be the House on the Embankment. 'I once lived in that building. No – *that* building died, disappeared, a long time ago. I lived in another building, but within those same enormous dark-grey fortress-like concrete walls.'[8]

Yuri was evacuated to Tashkent at the start of the war, together with many other civilians. When the time came to join the army he was prevented from doing so because of a problem with his eyes. Later in life, as a successful novelist, thick spectacles were one of his signatures. But in 1942, that lay in the future; he returned to Moscow to work in an aircraft production factory. Following the victory against Nazi Germany, he began studying at the Gorky Institute of World Literature, no small matter for the son of an enemy of the people. His admission to the institute, and then his great success after graduating – the award of a Stalin Prize in 1950 for his novel *The Students* – was, in a way, an astonishing reconciliation between his personal history and the history of the Revolution. But even though he learned to operate very effectively as a person and a writer during the late Stalinist period, he did not reconcile himself to Stalinism. Quite the contrary. Personally devastated by what Stalinism could inflict on a family, he came to write in the 1960s and 1970s in a way that helped himself and his readers begin to come to terms with the worst of the Soviet past.

The life's work of Yuri Trifonov was to memorialize the fate of his parents and the rest of the 1937 generation by exploring the historical links between the 'developed socialism' of the Brezhnev era, when he wrote his greatest works, and the violence of the 1930s. These were different worlds, but the same families lived in them. Were they bound by a unity or rent by a fissure? Could history unite the Soviet epochs in a way that helped people to remember the past in ways that ameliorated their traumas? Trifonov's interest in history went both ways: the past could help to explain the present, and the present could help to explain the past. By the 1960s, Trifonov seemed to be convinced that history was the key to interpreting the current Soviet reality. Sometimes the key could be found in the pre-Soviet past. In 1973, he published an historical novel called *The Impatient Ones*, set among the revolutionaries of the 1870s. Even in his reconstruction of a very different world, nearly a century before, the focus of the novel was the Revolution. Whatever historical wounds he was presenting to his readership, the Revolution was the phenomenon that ultimately explained them.

Trifonov spent much of his adult life living in a top-floor apartment on Georghe Dhe Street (named after the Romanian leader of the 1950s and 1960s), by Peschanaya (Sandy) Square. He was visited by a German journalist in 1975, who commented that the apartment was 'small' and a little knocked about. 'The mailbox has rusted through and doesn't have a lock,' he wrote. 'At the front door is a broken chair. There's a bag of shopping on it. Trifonov is planning to go to the hospital to see his mother.'[9] This was not the House on the Embankment, but it was still a place of high relative privilege. After all, Trifonov's dacha, at Krasnaya Pakhra at Peredelkino, the country settlement near Moscow that was favoured by the creative intelligentsia, was a substantial and well-appointed dwelling.[10] Here Alexander Tvardovsky was a near neighbour.[11] Until 1970, Tvardovsky was the editor at *Novyi mir* (*New World*) the 'liberal' literary journal in which Trifonov first published many of his most important works.

Much of Trifonov's fiction went back and forth in time, between this world of the Brezhnev era and his characters' early lives during the Revolution and especially the 1930s. In a number of works, the characters physically inhabit the 1970s, but their inner world is locked into the traumas of the Stalin years. The most famous and daring of these works was *The House on the Embankment*. It tells the story of Vadim Glebov, a successful Soviet person of the 1970s, whose biggest concern is his mildly wayward grown-up daughter. But one day he runs into a friend of his youth – a fellow occupant of the House on the Embankment, though Glebov lived in a modest annex – and he's forced to remember the past. The state violence of the 1930s, when he'd been a child, was one thing to contend with, but the late Stalinist era, when he'd been an adult and a student, was another. His passive and active experiences of Stalinism have made him what he is. Even as a child, during the Terror, when his uncle is arrested and his parents try to step gingerly around the 'meat grinder', he learns to make compromises in order to survive. After the war, as a student, he applies these lessons in a harsher way. This part of the novel returns to the same time and place of Trifonov's 1950 novel *The Students*. In the earlier book, moral dilemmas are easily soluble thanks to the work's socialist realist aesthetic, the natural trajectory towards an ideal future. Here, the privileges of some students are taken for granted, and public criticism of a professor is part of the round of institute life.[12] In *The House on the Embankment*, though, Trifonov explicitly depicts these small-scale purges of 1948 to 1953, which seldom ended in arrest, but destroyed people's lives and careers (and where Jews were disproportionately targeted). Bit by bit, switching from the Brezhnev era to the 1930s to the late Stalinist period, we find out that Glebov denounced the supervisor who had brought him into his home, destroying his career and shattering the personality of his daughter – who is also Glebov's fiancée.

Glebov goes on to enjoy great success and relative prosperity as an academic. Trifonov shows that a Soviet success story in the 1970s can be based on Stalin-era duplicity and present-day moral equivalence, avoiding decisions or making them only with reference to personal interest. Dealing with the past offers Glebov the chance to live properly in the present, not that the lessons are easy to learn. It does not give the ending away to say that this dialogue between past and present can't be resolved. Its lessons are ambiguous. 'Several minutes later, as he crossed the river by the bridge, he looked up at the long, squat, ugly house on the embankment and out of habit located the windows of his old apartment, in which he had spent his happiest years,'

Trifonov writes, 'and wondered whether some miracle might happen and another change might take place in his life.'[13]

How could it be that these complex works which engaged in such useful ways with Stalinist history were published in the Soviet dictatorship, even forty years later? This was partly because of a truth that has recurred throughout this book: there were several Soviet Unions. The Soviet Union of the Brezhnev era was a quite different place from that of the Stalin years. But it was also because of the particular gifts of Trifonov and comparable writers and artists, men and women who were fêted by the dictatorship even though they presented it in their works in, at best, an ambiguous light. Their works were 'permitted dissent'.[14] On his fiftieth birthday, in August 1975, Trifonov was commended by the Soviet system with a 'mark of honour'.[15] Yet ten months later, at the 6th Congress of the Writers' Union of the Russian Republic, he was formally criticized for not offering the characters of *The House on the Embankment* the consolations of communist ideology, which might have lightened their desperate psychological and spiritual burdens.[16] The first secretary of the Union, Georgy Markov, failed to find 'the presence of forces capable of alleviating the hopelessness of some lives and situations. In cases like these not only the question of form and genre, but also the philosophical outlook of the author, are open to question.'[17] Socialist realism was still the official aesthetic of Soviet culture. It was predicated on the forward movement of time, and the idea of socialist redemption. It seemed that Trifonov had moved beyond socialist realism, with a different understanding of communist time and a different sense of communist redemption – above all, a different understanding of the relationship between history and the present.

But what did it matter what Markov thought? Trifonov had Mikhail Suslov, the grand high guardian of Soviet ideology, on his side. Suslov read *The House on the Embankment* after it had been submitted to the authorities, and personally approved its publication. He argued that it was truthful.[18] How could this be so, if there were questions about Trifonov's 'philosophical outlook'? Some claimed that Suslov's concession was a sop to a restive intelligentsia, but this perhaps overstated the fear that the intelligentsia could arouse in the organs of power. Suslov's apparent acknowledgement of the novel's truthfulness might just as well have resulted from recognizing the intense concern with socialist ethics that underpins this novel and Trifonov's work more generally. Georgy Markov was right about some things: that Trifonov painted everyday life in shades of grey, debated negative character traits and set up universally applicable moral dilemmas. (In 1981, Trifonov would be considered for the Nobel Prize, and Heinrich Böll argued that his work was 'real literature, humane realism', 'broad and capacious in its transmission of human perception': in other words, it had universal qualities.)[19] But the morality, though recognizable to a foreign readership, derived from the Revolution. Time and again in his fiction, his characters emerge from the same milieu as his – the original revolutionary intelligentsia – and are capable of moral actions in the context of their family origins. When redemption comes, it often emerges from the Revolution itself, though it does so by the most winding and difficult of historical and personal routes.

Amazingly, perhaps, Yuri Trifonov was not a Party member. He stayed an outsider-insider, an echo of the old Russian intelligentsia in action, contriving somehow to hold power to account in improbable circumstances. Still, he enjoyed the rewards of a successful literary career: the comfortable apartment in the good location, the evocative dacha, the dining table at the Writers' Union, the foreign trips. He spent June and July 1980 with his wife in Paris and the south of France, and then went on to West Germany. It was the year before he died unexpectedly, following an operation. In France he was received by the Soviet ambassador, and in West Germany he was fêted by the literary establishment, but he was hardly engaged on literary business all the time.[20] He had the chance to enjoy the consolations of travel.

In Paris, he met up with his old friend Vasily Aksyonov. Aksyonov was an uncomfortable fit for the Soviet system. He was a novelist who had written coming-of-age novels such as *Ticket to the Stars* during Khrushchev's Thaw, but he couldn't reconcile himself to Soviet life. When the chance came – it was only a few weeks before their meeting – he emigrated from the Soviet Union for ever.

Aksyonov was the son of Evgenia Ginzburg, the author of *Into the Whirlwind*, adapted into the play that I saw performed in Moscow decades later. Ginzburg had hoped that her writing could be published in the Soviet Union, and when it became clear that it could not, it was smuggled out for publication abroad, becoming more sharply political in its tone. Aksyonov's writing, too, moved out of the official line, becoming more dissident in focus. Eventually he, too, would write about the Stalinist past. Like Trifonov, Aksyonov was caught in the fireglow of history. Unlike Trifonov, he was unable to reconcile his critique of the past with the demands of the Soviet system. He lacked the temperament or style for 'permitted dissent', the writing that was at once morally coherent, independent and acceptably Soviet. And so he scrutinized Soviet life of previous decades from outside the Soviet Union, in books that could not be read by his fellow countrymen and women. By contrast, it became Trifonov's mission to come to terms with the Stalinist past on pages that were freely available to a Soviet readership. In so doing, he revealed the unexpected ability of the Soviet Union to save itself, at least for a while, by facing up in partial ways to its terrible history.

Yuri Trifonov's whole life was spent in the glow of the Revolution. Stalin had thrown so many bodies on the revolutionary blaze that it got out of control and burned Trifonov badly; but thanks to Khrushchev, the fire was under control again. Trifonov could look into it, feel its warmth, sense its threats, reflect on how its comforts and destructions were part of a single force and explain it all to his readers.

He showed that it was better for many Soviet citizens to look back at the past rather than refuse to do so. They might rescue themselves as individuals and reclaim the Revolution for their generation if they did. Facing the past was an essential way of salving personal and collective traumas. The sickness was urgent and history might be a treatment.

Trifonov proved that remembering the past could be a therapeutic but painful experience, both for individuals and for Soviet society. It did not heal them, but it clarified their world and restrained its dark side. For him, it was not only better to remember the past; it was impossible not to do so. This was not a universal truth: some individuals survived better by forgetting, and many aspects of post-Stalin Soviet society – from social reform to the space race – were about the future, not the past. Or when they drew on the past, they found inspiration from Leninism and the Revolution, not Stalinism, and were a celebration rather than a coming-to-terms.

The example of Yuri Trifonov proves the living significance of history for modern Russians. It shows how they have faced up to the past and learned from it. But Trifonov does not provide us with a universal template, one that can be slotted over our own times in Russia or elsewhere. The engagement with the past that would most help Putin-era Russians is probably of a quite different and less urgent type than that provoked by Trifonov.

He could not have done this without Khrushchev. Trifonov is a brilliant example of how late Soviet society developed in partial symbiosis with the most difficult part of its past. But it was Khrushchev who created the conditions in which this symbiosis could be possible. By recognizing just how urgent history had become after Stalin died, Khrushchev risked the viability of the whole Soviet experiment by starting a conversation about its past. Khrushchev's transformation of the Soviet Union was nothing less than the twentieth century's most consequential history lesson. It's one that proponents of the Russia Anxiety might listen to, because it is the heart of the Soviet Union's attempt in the 1950s and 1960s to construct a past that was located at the meeting place of honesty and wisdom.

## WASHING A BLACK CAT

On the morning of 25 February 1956, the chairman of the Council of Ministers, Nikolai Bulganin, called to order an extra, closed session of the XX Congress of the Communist Party of the Soviet Union. The Congress had opened eleven days earlier but had formally finished. This was an unexpected coda, and the delegates were restive. As the first Congress since Stalin's death, it had already been a confusing event. Delegates had received conflicting signals on how to think about Stalin and his time in power. Over the previous three years, the Soviet Union had struggled to find a coherent way to move on from Stalinism, though it was obvious that the old ways had gone for good.

Bulganin called Nikita Khrushchev, the first secretary of the Party, to the podium. The people who filled the hall had no idea of what was really happening. They were the senior core of the Party from across the USSR, around 1,300 voting delegates, given a special pass to attend the session, something that was not available to representatives from foreign Communist Parties or the press. But there were some unexpected faces. Around 100 former Gulag prisoners were present in the hall, all of them recently rehabilitated.[21] They were innocent victims of Stalin's Terror, released from the Gulag, their reputations restored, though for many such people, the start of their new lives brought many unanticipated hardships. But these former *zeks*, or camp inmates, had regained their Party membership, and were now again activists in the service of communism.

Khrushchev talked for four hours with a short break in the middle. For the most part, he was received in silence, though the speech was punctuated too with the noise of disbelief and indignation. What he was saying took little decoding by those listening, and its impact on all of their lives would be extraordinary. The consequences of his words could not be predicted. It was plain to everyone that the Soviet Union had irrevocably changed direction, that this was a year zero, that it might mark the onset of a Soviet renaissance or a Soviet collapse. This was the greatest gamble that Khrushchev could have taken. For all his strengths and weaknesses, it was a moment of courage and good judgement, and perhaps of conscience.

The report that he read out was called 'On the Cult of Personality and Its Consequences'. He sometimes departed from the text that he and his aides had carefully assembled, though the whole production sounded like him from start to finish. Unimaginably, it was a condemnation of Stalin. Famously, delegates with weak hearts took extra pills, many gasped, others fainted, some were carried out of the hall. Even so, it was a selective condemnation, a partial encounter with historical truth.

From 1953, and for the eleven years that followed, Nikita Khrushchev was first secretary of the Communist Party of the Soviet Union. He was the country's Party boss. But he was not a supreme leader in the mould of Stalin. For the few years after Stalin's death, a collective leadership governed the Soviet Union. Perhaps surprisingly, the men who had worked alongside Stalin in his Presidium, and who carried his coffin – Beria, Bulganin, Kaganovich, Khrushchev, Malenkov, Mikoyan, Molotov, Voroshilov – continued to rule the country in concert. They got rid of Beria in June 1953, and perhaps he was indeed a deadly threat to them (he certainly deserved little mercy), but aside from that, they remained a 'team' that was capable of working effectively together.[22]

Khrushchev's power base, then, was the Party. Malenkov, who was for some time his leading rival, ran the government (until the weaker figure of Bulganin took his place). In April 1955, Khrushchev suggested that the next Party Congress was about due, and that it might be held in February 1956. Congresses were the highest gathering of Party members, and brought together hundreds of representatives from across the country, for policy discussions and committee votes that lasted for almost two weeks. There had only been nineteen of them before. They had been much smaller and more frequent affairs in the early years of the Party's history, when they had also been less ceremonial and filled with much tougher debate. The previous Congress, number nineteen, had taken place in November 1952, so on the ideal basis of a four-year cycle, the twentieth would be ahead of time. This respectful scheduling would help restore the Party to its proper significance. Since the 1930s, its ranks had been decimated by the Terror, and then it had been sidelined; the eighteenth Congress had been held in March 1939, nearly fourteen years before the nineteenth. Paying proper respect to the Party was good politics, not least for Khrushchev. For one reason or another, his colleagues agreed.

Ever since Stalin's death, the country had not found a consensus about how to move on. The bloodletting of the Great Terror and the exclusion of some national minorities were open wounds. Mass incarceration in the Gulag had created a shadow society across the Soviet Union, and the Great Fatherland War had ripped millions of families in two. Still, many people mourned the dictator's passing. They had been shocked into a collective display of extravagant grief in the first week of March 1953, though not all joined in – we have records of jokes, hatred and anger; there were tears even in the Gulag, but there were also opportunistic uprisings there. Under pressure from Beria, who had done so much to construct the Gulag, the Central Committee declared an amnesty on 27 March 1953, three weeks into the new era. According to its terms, half the population of the camps and labour colonies of the Gulag – 1.2 of 2.4 million prisoners – were released, though this excluded political prisoners, those convicted under Article 58.[23] Immediately, this created a moral ambiguity and lack of clarity about post-Stalin reform. It meant that the true innocents were still inside, and that the returnees were criminals. As they came back to villages and towns, moral panic about them set in, and the old category of Stalinism – of the enemy – was recast and redeployed on a widespread scale in the conversations and letters of ordinary people.[24] It was only in a more gradual and sporadic way that the '58ers' started to come back, complete with their stories, to a Soviet world that only sometimes wanted to listen to them.

In all the institutions of Soviet life, from schools to offices, people in authority wondered what to do with the portraits of Stalin on the wall, or how to answer the questions of their students or employees about the future. It was a febrile time. Messages about how most wisely to express oneself were scrambled. At the Gnesin Music Institute in Moscow's Arbat district, for example, generational tensions rose and student indiscipline grew. There were clashes about what to include and exclude from the works of Stalin in the curriculum, as even music students had compulsory courses in Marxism-Leninism.[25] Soviet power did not have a clear answer to all this. Standing apart from officialdom, as was its historic role, the intelligentsia began to offer some solutions. But this was an uneasy process. The Soviet intelligentsia was co-opted into power much more than its tsarist predecessor had been. It was implicated in Stalinism.

Take the example of Alexander Fadeyev, the chairman of the Writers' Union. Born in 1901, he had spent part of his childhood in Vladivostok, joined the Party and fought in the Civil War. He was the author of the socialist realist classics *The Rout* (1927) and *The Young Guard* (1945), but his métier turned out to be cultural administration – a hazardous profession during the Stalin period. As a survivor of the Terror in a walk of life where many had been arrested and denunciation had been common, he knew where the bodies were buried. It weighed on his conscience. He turned to alcohol. In 1946, as the incoming chairman of the Writers' Union, he led his colleagues through the *Zhdanovshchina*, the late Stalinist campaign of cultural purification that had anti-Semitic dimensions. He would stand up in meetings and write articles for the press denouncing the vicious dangers of cosmopolitanism. Fadeyev remained in post until 1954. Two years later, he killed himself.

On the surface, Fadeyev seems to represent an intelligentsia which betrayed itself by pursuing the mission of Party and government, not holding them to account. What was worse, the mission was a deadly one, involving betrayals and killings, in the service of a project which transcended individual conscience. Yet the intelligentsia recovered. From the first chance they had, many writers sought to shape the post-Stalinist development of society autonomously, in their own way, but from within the Soviet world as they saw it. One famous writer, Ilya Ehrenburg, wrote the novel – *The Thaw*, in 1954 – whose title would give its name to the whole Khrushchev era. This story of sincere personal relationships and individual personhood marked a change from a culture whose purpose was to depict the collective triumph of ideology. A few months before Ehrenburg's novel was published, Vladimir Pomerantsev wrote a piece called 'On Sincerity in Literature'. Widely discussed, and often controversial, it seemed to suggest the re-emergence of an honest, critical but still Party-minded intelligentsia.[26] Thanks to many writers and artists, people had a route to a better and more healing understanding of their own lives. Trifonov became an important figure in this process later. In the 1950s and 1960s, dozens of films, stories, paintings and novels examined the recent past. Consuming them was a lesson in communal life. It revealed that your experiences were not unique, that others too were grappling with what had happened, and that it was possible to explain recent history in ways that were both personally sincere and demonstrably Soviet. Alexander Solzhenitsyn's world-famous novel *One Day in the Life of Ivan Denisovich* was published in the Soviet Union in 1962 and widely read by Soviet people. Their responses were varied – some felt the sting of old wounds, some were incredulous about the main character's plausibility and the Gulag slang, others signalled their flashes of recognition – but the book was part of an ongoing debate about the past, in a much more open and less frightened culture than before.[27]

Soviet society performed one of the most difficult tasks of historical memory that one could imagine. While they were still citizens of the same dictatorship, many people had the chance partly to come to terms with the deepest of social and personal traumas. This is a lesson to remember. Modern Russia once made itself able to think through a difficult past. It was a highly imperfect process, but it was a bold attempt. Many other countries, with less urgent histories, have not had to do such a thing, or have averted their gaze from the bad parts of their histories. Lucky places can live in an eternal present where the past is inspirational and decorative in turn. Still, how did the Soviets do it?

Solzhenitsyn – Gulag victim turned provincial schoolteacher – emerged into the literary dazzle six years after the Secret Speech, and when he did, it was with Khrushchev's personal approval. But he takes us ahead of the story. Back in 1955, Khrushchev was already under pressure from a society whose conversations were becoming plural rather than, in the totalitarian way, crushingly singular. Following the decision to call the twentieth Party Congress for the following February, Khrushchev found the task of confronting the past ever more urgent. He was driven by his own demons, as he himself had signed off death warrants during the Terror, especially when he was the boss of the Ukrainian republic. He was a leading participant, but he did not have an overview of the conduct of the Terror or knowledge of its extent until February 1956. It seems likely that his conscience was troubled by his newly growing knowledge of the precise scale of the violence, data made more poignant by the stories and rumours that came from the men and women who had survived and come back. He was attuning himself too to the politics of the moment, the need to secure the Party's position and his future in the unresolved post-Stalin world. Khrushchev could not have been Stalin had he wanted to. Both of them were shaped by Bolshevism, but they were different in temperament, capability and aims, so Khrushchev had to find a different way of governing. In December 1955, he took action. At his suggestion, the Presidium created a commission to investigate the Stalinist repressions against the Party. Khrushchev wanted especially to know what had happened to the delegates of the seventeenth Party Congress of 1934, the last to convene in the vanished age that came before the Great Terror: a lost generation of communist leaders, ghosts from twenty years before, men and women whose fates would needle those sitting round the Presidium table.

The lead investigator was Pyotr Pospelov. He was a history man himself, the co-author of the *Short Course*, the Party textbook that was released in 1936 under Stalin's official authorship. No work of history was more stripped-down and partial, or more strongly battered into shape by Marxism, or more practically influential. It might have been a sincere reflection of its time, but it was far from an objective analysis. Pospelov was now asked to perform a quite different historical task – one that demanded more facts and greater precision, and much more closely focused attention on the archives. Over the next few weeks, under pressure of time, and subject to the stress and grief of the picture they were assembling, Pospelov and his team gathered paperwork from NKVD depositories.

On 9 February 1956, Pospelov presented his findings to the Presidium. He himself read the report, hesitating, eyes full of tears, despite the fact that he was a tough-minded functionary who had been the editor of *Pravda*. This was the heart of it: 1,920,635 persons were arrested between 1935 and 1940 for political crimes, of whom 688,503 were shot, mostly in 1937 and 1938. Khrushchev had wanted the figures from the 1934 congress: 848 of the 1,966 delegates were judicially murdered (more were arrested). Naturally enough, many of those victims from the 1934 'Congress of Victors' were familiar faces to the men sitting round the table. Pospelov filled in much more detail, explaining how the Terror worked, outlining its impact on national minorities, and telling the story of twelve leading Party members who were lost. Pospelov made it clear that Stalin was at the heart of the repressions, as were several of those in the room, especially Molotov and Kaganovich.[28]

Molotov for one was far from apologetic; he was convinced that the Terror was a necessary act to defend the Revolution. Even as late as 10 January 1956, discussions were underway about a quite different memorial to Stalin: a 'house-museum' at the 'nearby dacha' where he had spent many nights and which had been such an important venue of Stalin-era politics. The director of the Central Lenin Museum,

V. Morozov, wrote to the Central Committee to say that the museum could be open in time for the third anniversary of Stalin's death on 5 March 1956.[29] There was nothing inevitable about the Secret Speech until Khrushchev actually delivered it. But colleagues agreed that he should present a summary of Pospelov's report to the upcoming Congress. The museum did not open. Molotov lost.

Khrushchev himself had a complex relationship with his former patron. Sometimes he seemed to remember him fondly, though his depiction of Stalin in the Secret Speech was a devastating one. He recognized that Stalin was the most capable of the revolutionary generation after Lenin, excluding Trotsky, who was never mentioned. 'He stood head and shoulders above the others,' Khrushchev claimed in his memoirs, in a judgement shared widely among historians, who like to rank by intelligence and capability. Khrushchev thought that Stalin was responsible for extraordinary achievements, as the leading figure in the construction of socialist civilization, but that he had taken a fatal wrong turn away from Leninism. 'In all matters relating to Stalin's personality we encounter both good and correct things,' Khrushchev maintained, 'and savage things that don't fit into any framework.' But the bottom line was that 'Stalin had been a murderer and a monster.' It took three years after Stalin's death to come to terms with such a notion; certainly in 1953, it had been easier to lay the blame at Beria's door, even though 'Beria had come along after the "meat grinder" had already done its main work.' Before the Pospelov Commission and the twentieth Party Congress, the instinct of the Party bosses was still to 'whitewash' Stalin, Khrushchev argued. 'We acted contrary to the Russian proverb that says: "You can't keep washing a black cat till it turns white," ' he remembered. 'There's no doubt he was a black cat, but still we were trying to wash him white.'[30]

As he strode up to the podium on 25 February, Khrushchev had a clear task in mind: to stop washing the cat. In so doing, he believed that he could save the Soviet Union, and with it the memories of his fellow countrymen, his own conscience, his political career and even himself and his family. The key was selectivity. Khrushchev's report concerned 'the cult of personality' and Stalin personally was the target, not the system as a whole, or even a list of scapegoats.

Khrushchev showed that Stalin had departed from the path of the Revolution. He had betrayed Lenin personally, by insulting his wife, Nadezhda Krupskaya, and politically, so that Lenin came to want Stalin's removal from the post of general secretary. But the biggest betrayal came later, when Stalin had constructed his cult of personality. Khrushchev pointed out that Lenin had always avoided such personal and political egotism. Stalin's cult, by contrast, had malformed the shape of Soviet culture and society, departed from Marxism-Leninism, violated 'revolutionary legality' and Party integrity and laid the basis for political violence. The speech gave examples of what happened during the Terror and cited some figures. Khrushchev also sought to reclaim the Great Fatherland War for the Soviet people, condemning Stalin for the chaos that met the German invasion in 1941 and for the terribly excessive cost in Soviet lives that Stalin's leadership of the war incurred. Above all, he argued forcefully that the great victory should be reclaimed by the soldiers and civilians who were responsible for it; it did not belong to Stalin.

What Khrushchev said in the Secret Speech was enough to transform the Soviet Union, but it was far from the whole truth. Khrushchev only focused on particular aspects of the Terror: largely those that were conducted against the Party itself, rather than the special operations against ethnic minority groups in the borderlands, or the sweeping up of ordinary people off the streets. It must have given rise to particular pain and anger among survivors and relatives that he had nothing to say about the famine in Ukraine. More generally, he did not discuss the terrible costs of collectivization, and the collateral damage of the fastest industrialization drive in history.

This was an emphatic condemnation specifically of Stalin, and more generally of Stalinism's spirit and ethics. As the speech was gradually released across the Soviet Union, first of all to Party members, reception was mixed. The extent of Stalinist violence was news to everyone, the holding of Stalin to account was a revelation, and the officially sanctioned opportunity to speak in public about it was a novelty, but people were not learning about the Terror for the first time; they were gaining the chance to mourn, listen, reflect and speak. There were those who thought that it was better not to revisit the past, that dredging this up was bad for everyone. This was not always a wilful insensitivity, or a Stalinist predisposition, or even a reflection of personal guilt; it could also be an understandable response to trauma, when remembering was intolerable. Others embraced the turn to memory, recognizing its cathartic possibilities, and, if they were more politically minded, that it could return the Soviet Union to the liberating promise of its revolutionary origins. And another group adapted the language of Stalinism to the new age: as we've seen, they took the black-and-white, two-camps morality of the Stalin years, with its discourse of enemies, but now sought out enemies among those who had actively pushed forth Stalinist violence, or now sought to cover it up. However one looked at it, the past had become part of the present.

The Speech accelerated a process whereby it became easier to come to terms with what had happened. But the aim was more widely political. The Secret Speech was designed to restore the supremacy of the Party, to reinforce Khrushchev's place within it, and to ensure that its authority could never again be replaced by the caprice of a wayward dictator. By focusing on the Party, Khrushchev might go some way towards winning over the audience in the room, which contained many provincial Party leaders, exactly the sort of people who had been so vulnerable during the Terror, and who were now desperate for stability. The Secret Speech might offer them the professional and personal security they craved. Khrushchev was keen, meanwhile, to harness the power, as he saw it, of the Stalinist economy for a post-Stalinist age. He wanted to use central planning and industrial technology directly to benefit the people, not least in a mass housing campaign and a new welfare system. Rather than sacrificing a generation for the sake of a far-off utopia, Khrushchev believed that the benefits of the Soviet economy had to be distributed to people now, and in a broadly equal way. He admired the economic structures that Stalinism had put in place, but not always the way that these structures had been used, and certainly not the priorities that had been assigned to them.

In other words, the Secret Speech sought to relaunch the Revolution, returning Soviet civilization to its original Leninist path and blocking off the chance of a detour back to the diversion of Stalinism. Not only was this the proper ideological choice, and the best way of improving people's lives, but it could make possible a secure transition out of Stalinism and keep the Soviet Union as a going concern, indefinitely viable. Khrushchev had his own personal ambitions and anxieties as well, of course. But the Speech combined all these causes and allowed Khrushchev to walk a tightrope.

Khrushchev deplored the terror, the fake history and the lies: the cult of personality and its consequences. His motives mixed together conscience, fellow-feeling, self-interest and political necessity. The aim was to save himself and the Soviet Union. It was precisely this combination of beliefs and motives that gave the revelations their particular and partial character. Khrushchev showed courage in rolling the dice but good judgement in confining the risk. The Secret Speech was one of modern history's great exercises in truth-telling, but truth in the Soviet Union had its limits. Perhaps no society can take too much of the truth. The Soviet Union in 1956 took a bigger dose than most.[31]

## TRUTH AND ITS LIMITS

No country is honest about its past. Being a nation, as Ernest Renan famously wrote in the nineteenth century, is to agree about what to forget. Even at the hands of a professional historian, the creation of a historical narrative is a programme of omission. Coherence is simplification; selection is leaving out; and the process is never scientific, but a matter of individual judgement. National stories always seem to be about the journey from darkness to light: from subjection to liberty, from poverty to wealth, from repression to self-assertion, from hierarchy to equality, from slavery to rights. There are heroes and villains. Some national stories are darker, and here the focus might be on historic wrongs. Myths are created and defined in schoolbooks, statues, newspaper articles and television programmes. When a government or national culture seeks to expose historical truth or rewrite history – to tear down statues or remember a new set of heroes – it is again selecting and omitting, though it is possible that it might end up with a more plausible version of the past. The process is always a blunt one, and the thing that is apparently being remembered is all too often a proxy for something else. Witness the strange fate of historic Prussia in communist East Germany, its conservative symbols retained or reshaped to bolster the socialist dictatorship.[32] The fact that other societies, not least Western democracies, sometimes wilfully forget their own difficult pasts ought to be a corrective to the Russia Anxiety, because Russia has sometimes done a better job of facing up to what came before.

Other modern countries also endured traumas, remembered them and collectively found ways of coming to terms with the past. After the Second World War, societies across Europe were constantly and everywhere faced with the overwhelming consequences of the conflict, but all of them only discussed it in very selective ways. One historian writes of 'a consensus of silence' in the first post-war decades, where politicians and people alike chose to remember some things about the war and deliberately to forget many others. Nowhere was the Holocaust memorialized (apart from by survivors) or studied (beyond scholarly specialists). This was especially true in West Germany, but it was true everywhere, not least behind the Iron Curtain. The Nuremberg Trials and half-hearted policies of de-Nazification satisfied the occupiers, but many Germans thought they went too far, and resented what they saw as a lack of justice. A myth rapidly developed in West Germany that the army had not been involved in atrocities during the war. Responsibility for those, where it was assigned at all, might be confined to the SS, the Gestapo, parts of the Nazi Party and particular fanatics. This made it easier for family life to normalize again after the war, because surviving soldiers could return to the home and be quietly admired. It made it easier too for West German politics to normalize and for West Germany to become a trusted member of NATO. Field Marshal Erich von Manstein, who served only a brief sentence after the Nuremberg Trials, and who played his part in all manner of atrocities, was already working for the West German government as a defence advisor in 1956. The pressure to 'whitewash' former Nazis rather than to de-Nazify West German society in a proper way therefore came from above, below and outside.[33] But the German case was only the most poignant and instructive. Take France. In an editorial of 11 January 1948, *Le Monde* described the fate of 280,000 French people sent to death camps, and the 25,000 who somehow returned. But it never mentioned that any of them were Jews.[34]

Anti-fascism rose up the West German political agenda only in the later 1960s and 1970s. Social Democrat (SPD) leaders such as Willi Brandt played a role. Brandt travelled to Warsaw, knelt before the war memorial and apologized. Generational change was important, too. In 1968, young people in their early twenties, born after the war, and even in their thirties, with only childhood memories of the conflict, wanted to confront the actions of their parents and grandparents. Twenty years later, West German historians were quarrelling bitterly about the causes and nature of Nazism. By then, forty years after the war, the work of public memory was becoming more thorough and bold, though it was still selective. Additional important changes were still to come in the next two decades. The point was that this happened long after the event, when it was politically safe to do it. There was little risk. The urgency had gone, and the changed relationship to the past could be a commemorative process rather than an active, desperate dialogue.

Following the collapse of the Eastern bloc in 1989, and then the reunification of Germany in 1990, the old East Germany made a much more systematic attempt to excise former members of the Party or alleged secret police informers from state employment, sometimes with unanticipated consequences. Was it always necessary to fire a cleaner from her job in a government building? 'Lustration', as it was called, was important in some other former communist states, too, such as Czechoslovakia, though not in others. If the Cold War had put history wars into the deep freeze, memory brought them out again in the 1990s. The conflicts that resulted were often zero-sum games.[35] Meanwhile, South Africa formed its Truth and Reconciliation Commission. Thanks partly to the wisdom of Nelson Mandela, the country quickly formed a more comfortable relationship with its past than it might otherwise have done. More generally, though, even if there were fewer limits on recovering the past after 1989 than there had been before, there were both winners and losers, and the desire to remember could not go on for ever.

De-Stalinization was an even more extraordinary and challenging process, because the Soviet Union still existed; it was an era, not a whole political order, that needed to be remembered better, and the subtlety that this required was not easy to achieve. Even so, de-Stalinization was not less thorough than de-Nazification in West Germany. Coming from within society and politics, it set a new course that was not determined by military defeat or the demands of occupying powers. Yet it did not systematically set out to remove from office those who had participated in the Great Terror, though some of them were tried and executed. For instance, one name that recurred in the investigations of January 1956 was Colonel Rodos, who tortured leading Bolsheviks such as Stanislav Kosior, Vlas Chubar and many others, famous and unknown alike. Khrushchev made sure that he was tried by the Military Collegium. He was executed.[36] More often, though, victims and perpetrators continued to live alongside each other. As in other post-traumatic societies, the line between the two groups was not always clear.

After the Thaw, over the course of the 'long 1970s', history was sporadically urgent. Yuri Trifonov and his colleagues made their interventions. Countless kitchen-table conversations behind closed doors kept history alive. The best teachers sustained for their pupils a critical engagement with the recent past (Vladimir Putin himself seems to have benefited from such teaching). But there were areas of Soviet history that remained publicly off limits, such as the Ukrainian famine.[37] When it came to a much earlier history, civil organizations operating on the boundaries of the state had begun during this period to question some official narratives and to campaign for preservation and memorials. Local history enthusiasts, long an important part of Russian culture, were crucial. Much of this reflected a renewed emphasis on ethnic Russianness as an identity within the Soviet Union.[38] But history no longer defined a difficult public debate. Images of 'Grandfather Lenin' and stirring reconstructions of past wars, especially the Second World War, made history a source of gentle comforts rather than difficult challenges. The historical narrative of revolutionary improvement gave shape to Soviet life.

History became urgent again during *perestroika*. Staking out an early claim for the recovery of historical truth, Yegor Yakovlev, the editor of the newspaper *Moskovskiye novosti*, introduced a regular column in January 1987 on 'The Past'.[39] In an age of mass debate, where everything was up for grabs, history could help to set the direction of the country. Yuri Afanasiyev, one of the Soviet Union's leading historians, argued that 'There is not a country in the world whose history has been as falsified as ours.'[40] A flood of publications followed – by Solzhenitsyn, Pasternak, Vasily Grossman, Yuri Dombrovsky, Anatoly Rybakov, all authors of historicized novels about Stalinism and revolution – as long-submerged *samizdat* texts not only reached the surface, but were grabbed by millions of readers. Theatrical productions and films were part of this cultural encounter with the past; it was now, for example, that *The Commissar* came to Soviet screens. Some citizens and leading Party hardliners remained proudly Stalinist, and were opposed to placing Lenin and Stalin on the revisionists' table. But in March 1988, when a teacher called Nina Andreyeva had her pro-Stalin letter published in the newspaper *Sovetskaya Rossiya*, the reformers responded powerfully in print and public speeches, making the case for justice, honesty and clarity in society's encounter with its past.[41] In 1987, Memorial was founded. It was one of the first grassroots initiatives to emerge from the new civil society. Its volunteers started to investigate the fate of victims of repression, to locate the sites of violence, to expose the truth and to memorialize it.

Gorbachev, who had initiated the policy of *glasnost*, or openness, of giving voice to the many different opinions that existed, the government activities that were usually secret or historic truths that had long been taboo, helped to drive the rediscovery of history. But Khrushchev was better at politics than Gorbachev. He was more capable of devising a wily and subtle approach to the conflicts of history and memory. 'There is one truth,' Gorbachev announced in 1988. 'Our history took place, and we must really know and understand it.'[42] For all his good intentions, Gorbachev did not in public recognize that many pasts existed, that understanding them was not straightforward or singular, or free of conflicts or losers.

Still, his single-minded approach allowed real improvements to be made in people's lives. Just as the recovery of history had led to releases and rehabilitations in the 1950s, the revision of history in the 1980s also gave new chances to the victims. In January 1989, the Central Committee passed a resolution 'On additional measures to restore justice with respect to the victims of the repressions that took place in the 1930s, 1940s and early 1950s'. Commissions were established to look after the material interests of the victims, protect their rights under law and to create and maintain public memorials. Just like in the Khrushchev era, getting history right was a matter of simultaneously protecting the Soviet state and helping people come to terms with the past. 'The restoration of historical, legal justice has now taken on immense political significance. Our progress along the path of moulding a socialist state based on the rule of law and the development of social consciousness depend on this to a large extent,' the resolution expounded. It went on: 'The public and the relatives and loved ones of the victims expect full rehabilitation of all the innocent people who were repressed and the perpetuation of their memory.'[43]

The encounters between the innocent and the guilty were recorded and rehearsed on a national stage. Lev Razgon, a former Gulag inmate turned dissident writer, wrote in a newspaper article of November 1988 about a chance meeting of 1977. He was in hospital. In the next bed was a former prison guard who had worked at a notorious facility in 1937, forty years earlier. He described to Razgon the daily process of loading prisoners onto trucks, driving them deep into the country-side and shooting them. The guard, one Grigory Ivanovich Nyazov, showed no remorse. Razgon had been shattered by the conversation. Now, a decade later, he deplored the absence of Gulag memorials. He also wondered what should be done with the men who pulled the triggers, administered the process and signed the death warrants. Many were alive, fifty years on. 'They are sitting in the squares, enjoying the playing children; they go to concerts, we see them at meetings, when we visit people, or sitting at holiday tables with mutual friends,' Razgon wrote, full of bewilderment and anger. 'They are my age and even younger.'[44] But the investigations were now freely taking place. Foreigners as well as Soviets were involved, including the American author Adam Hochschild. He arrived for a long stay in the USSR in January 1991, and travelled widely around the country in order to seek out the 'unquiet ghost' that was haunting the country.[45]

Meanwhile, at the first Congress of People's Deputies in 1989, documents concerning the Molotov–Ribbentrop Pact were published.[46] It all amounted to an historical assault on Stalinism. The historical work of de-Stalinization was being reactivated. Observers of Russian life and Soviet history have sometimes concluded that the Secret Speech effectively marked the beginning of the end of the Soviet Union. By letting some historical truth in; by raising the Iron Curtain a bit; by permitting a kind of pluralism; by improving living standards enough to set up a logic of disappointed expectations; by emphasizing equal treatment of individuals as well as the primacy of the collective, and therefore giving some substance to an idea of Soviet rights – in all these ways, Khrushchev probably stabilized Soviet power more than he destabilized it, in the short and long term alike. He prevented the Soviet Union from reverting to Stalinism, or from collapsing as a result of the accumulated instabilities that Stalinism wrought. It is unlikely that remembering the past in 1956 led to collapse thirty-six years later; more likely, it relaunched the Soviet project, and probably prolonged its existence. By the late 1980s, it was not the discussion of history that destabilized Soviet power. It was Gorbachev's combination of reforms, and the incentive they gave to industrial management and senior administrative personnel to jump ship, that brought about collapse, not an engagement with history, however powerful that was.

By the 1990s, the recovery of the Stalinist past quickened and deepened. Archives across the country became increasingly accessible, allowing readers to obtain the kind of documents that would still have been closed off in many other countries. Historians investigated Stalinism in great detail and from multiple angles; document collections, monographs and bestsellers proliferated. Family members went into the archives as well, in an effort to piece together their own histories. All TV channels, especially the 'independent' NTV and the slow-paced 'Culture' channel, aired regular discussions about Stalinism, and print publications of the whole range of reliability and usefulness became ubiquitous. Monuments and museums were opened, such as Perm-36 in Siberia, commemorating a Gulag camp. Marking the continuity in memory practices from the late 1980s into the early 2000s, Alexander Yakovlev, one of Gorbachev's leading advisers and a member of his Politburo, was appointed to chair the Presidential Commission for the Rehabilitation of Victims of Political Repression. This great burst of activity transformed our understanding of the details of the past, but it was different from the Thaw or *perestroika*. For a start, it was not clear whether this free-for-all with history brought consolations or not; it certainly lacked the intense national purpose of the de-Stalinizing programmes of Khrushchev and Gorbachev. After all, people were so busy desperately trying to make a living that remaking the country's past could not be a priority.

Eventually, as life became more stable in the early 2000s, different vistas of remembering and forgetting opened up. It seemed self-evident that remembering was essential for national life, but like in other countries, shiny distractions made history less urgent than before. The political context of all this was that a new president controlled the Kremlin, and that he possessed a keener understanding of the uses of the past. His historical interests were broad, but when it came to a 'useable' past, one that might help Russians to understand their lives better, as well as their place in a broader national community, nothing was more useful than the Second World War. By the 2010s, the war helped to provide an historical explanation for people's lives, to offer patriotic consolations, and to be the justification for foreign policy, but its memorialization seemed, to the Anxious, to be the prelude to a new war.

## REMEMBERING AND FORGETTING

The dominant politicians of the 1990s disparaged the Soviet past gleefully, even though it had made them who they were and circumscribed their views more surely than they claimed. 'I hate Soviet power,' said Anatoly Chubais many years later. 'In my life there's been nothing more loathsome than Soviet power.'[47] For Chubais, Yegor Gaidar and their colleagues, the emphasis was on the future, problems were caused by the past, and solutions often came from abroad. The 1990s were a period of acute suffering for many Russians, as their old worldview was ridiculed, their salaries went unpaid, their pensions were devoured by inflation, crime and corruption exploded around them, and the universe seemed to be governed by injustice and ill will. Yet many Russians gave the new world a chance and in time benefited from aspects of it. Like Chubais, some Russians were entirely disillusioned with their Soviet experience and remembered nothing good about it. Many, though, came to look back at the recent Soviet past and remember the good things: guaranteed jobs, salaries that were paid, welfare that had not yet malfunctioned, a world that was comprehensible and coherent. They were usually remembering the Brezhnev era. But as the criticisms of the Soviet past grew sharper from politicians who were living lavishly and seemed neither to respect nor comprehend the voters, the fond recall of Soviet times became more generic and less time-specific. For a certain type of post-Soviet Russian, especially members of an older generation, 'Stalin' became less an historical personage than a code for the Soviet past *tout court*. Professing admiration for Stalin, or, more commonly, refusing to condemn him outright, was really an exercise in asserting one's moral support for the disappeared country of one's earlier life. Or it was a cloaked demand that listeners respect the purpose and value of one's existence under communism, which might have taken up most of one's working life. What it wasn't, 99 per cent of the time, was a personal campaign to eliminate today's enemies of the people.

Or this is how it seems to me. After many conversations in Moscow about recent history, I eventually learned to read between the lines of people's forceful claims about the past, and to observe a more complex and coherent worldview than I had imagined might exist.

It was closely related to how people thought about Russia's historic place in the world. One fundamental worldview that was common in the 2010s was already widely apparent in the Yeltsin-era 1990s. In a serious opinion poll of March 2000, conducted as Putin was being elected for the first time, 66 per cent of respondents agreed that 'Russia was always perceived as an adversary by other countries and today nobody wishes us well'. Meanwhile, 60 per cent claimed that Russia had its own 'special Russian destiny', 18 per cent wanted the Soviet Union to return, and only 15 per cent saw a shared Western future for their country.[48]

This was not nostalgia – it was a realistic reading of an unhappy situation – but nostalgia existed too. The question, after all, was curiously self-pitying, and unlikely to be asked in many countries. Yearning for traces of the USSR was often a material phenomenon. When Western chains or cookie-cutter international-style cafés grew dull, people hankered after Soviet ice cream, cafeteria dumplings or seventies movies. For some, nostalgia was more complicated than this. The historian of St Petersburg's 'shadows of the past', who has researched extensively in the city's oral history, cites one respondent who stated aphoristically: 'Petersburg was far more like Petersburg when its name was still Leningrad.'[49] An eternal set of the city's values was inscribed more powerfully into its late Soviet spaces, people, culture, ideas and food, than it was into the more fluid and less distinctive period since 1991. By Putin's third term, soft-focus nostalgia for the late Soviet past extended from those who could remember it to those who were only born after the Soviet collapse. The rapper Timati was just one of many artists and performers to draw on Soviet motifs, often in playful rather than political ways.[50]

Svetlana Alexievich won the Nobel Prize for her writings about the elusive space between the Soviet past and present, which she explored with the help of oral history. When accepting the award in Oslo in December 2015, she said that Russia was 'a space of total amnesia'. Eighteen months later, she claimed that this full-scale forgetting was a wilful exercise on the part of the people of Belarus and Russia, who were rejecting the past because they wanted to and not as a matter of government diktat.[51] She knows how to listen to ordinary people and to liberate their voices on the page. But her complaint about amnesia is a familiar one. As we saw in chapter 1, Pyotr Chaadayev complained in 1836 that Russia lacked history; it was a country without proper monuments or memory.[52] The deep structures of Russian history have from time to time promoted deliberate forgetfulness: when late Muscovite churchmen rejected the Mongol inheritance, or when Peter the Great redefined the Russian Empire and built his new capital on the Neva, or when the Bolsheviks proclaimed a new world and ripped down the old monuments, or when a post-Soviet year zero began on 1 January 1992. What's more, in modern Russia, a bit like in Japan, planners show little preference for protecting old buildings. They have been keen to build anew, often to their financial advantage, and have had little interest in looking after historic ruins so that they might be sustained in recognizable ways.[53]

And thus comes the narrower but more lethal claim: that Russians have forgotten how to remember Stalin. The leading Russian biographer of the dictator ends a recent book with a warning: that the miserable circumstances of the Soviet collapse and the 1990s brought about an atmosphere in which people might seek easy political solutions, and that in the popular imagination these could easily derive from the Stalin period, especially when encouraged by 'unscrupulous commentators and politicians'. 'How great is the danger that a blend of historical ignorance, bitterness, and social discontent will provide fertile ground for pro-Stalinist lies and distortions to take root?' he asks.[54] The single greatest concern has been about school textbooks. Often compiled by teams of writers under the direction of a very senior historian, such as A. V. Torkunov, the rector of the prestigious Moscow State Institute of International Relations, these books provide comprehensive building blocks of knowledge. But commentators have drawn attention to the omission of details, the blurring of edges and a focus on heroic sacrifice. Even the bitterest critics do not usually suggest that this is a matter of fabrication, but of politicized selectivity.[55] The result is that the harsh reality of the Stalin period is only rendered in softer focus.

Does this mean a return to Stalinism? Some say yes. Journalists might confidently mark out a precise 'echo' of Stalin-era show trials in the judicial treatment of Mikhail Khodorkovsky, the billionaire head of the Yukos energy corporation, or Pussy Riot, the controversial avant-garde performance artists. They might see the shadow of a cult of personality in the way that Putin's sixtieth birthday was marked in October 2012.[56] The president of Georgia, Mikheil Saakashvili, claimed that in the run-up to the brief military conflict of August 2008 Putin often talked to him about Stalin – about how he used Stalin's old Kremlin office and a dacha near Moscow.

But Putin did not talk about Stalin in public in such ways, and in 2010, when then-mayor of Moscow, Yuri Luzhkov, who had frequently spoken out against Stalin, wanted to include a portrait of Stalin at the 2010 commemorations of wartime victory, apparently for the sake of historical coherence, President Medvedev made sure this did not happen.[57] Putin's attitude to Stalinism is expressed most by absences, allowing people to fill the gaps as they wish. In 2010, at the Valdai Club, where Russian and international elites mingled, Putin talked of how every country finds ways of incorporating its most dangerous or deadly figures (he liked to mention the statue of Oliver Cromwell outside the British Parliament).[58] But Putin does not praise Stalin, in fact he has little to say about him, apart from by inference and allusive international comparisons. There is no sense available in the public record to suggest that he holds Stalin up as a role model or as someone to be admired, and no unambiguous reason why his background in the KGB, an organization which was more comfortable with its origins as a ruthless builder of the state during the Revolution and Civil War than its chaotic experiences in the Stalin-era Terror, should elicit such a response.

Since Putin succeeded Medvedev as president in 2012, the past has played a greater role in public culture, especially in wartime commemoration. As ever, the Russia Anxiety has ascribed coherence and strategy to Russian policies, lending them ideological significance and malign intention: a masterplan to make a new history. It emphasizes a law of May 2014 that criminalized public falsifications of the events of the Second World War, especially denial of 'the facts' as they were accepted at the Nuremberg trials. Large fines and prison sentences were possible punishments. Only one successful prosecution was brought during the first three years of the memory law, for a post on social media by a man in the Urals city of Perm. But the very historians who had done so much to reconstruct their country's memories could not disregard this, and one of them, Kirill Aleksandrov of the Institute of History at the Russian Academy of Sciences in St Petersburg, faced official pushback for his work on the wartime Vlasov movement of Soviet collaborators which sided with the Nazis.[59] Since 2014, the Memorial Society, which has catalogued Stalin-era crimes and been a focus for public memory, has been threatened with closure. Even statues and monuments to Stalin have re-emerged in some provincial towns. Stalin has periodically scored highly in opinion polls concerning the greatest Russian leader, though as we've seen, it seems likely that he is a proxy for a range of historical emotions. The well-known Gulag museum on the site of the Perm-36 labour camp still exists, but visitors say its exhibits have lost bite and focus, their function of commemoration and exposure diminished. In the far north-western Russian republic of Karelia, near Finland, the local historian Yuri Dmitriyev, who has spent years meticulously uncovering the locations and identities of the region's victims of Stalin-era repressions, was arrested on 13 December 2016, on a charge concerning an unrelated allegation.[60]

Yet much high-quality history work went on. Despite widespread misreporting, which has given weight to the claims of the Russia

Anxiety, Russian state archives remain open to foreign researchers, who continue today to work in significant numbers on all kinds of topics. The archives of the defence ministry and the security services are very hard to access, but this is the same in many Western countries. 'The unsung heroes of all this are the Russian archivists, who with few exceptions are highly trained, dedicated specialists, who go out of their way to help scholars, both Russian and foreign, obtain the sources they need for their research,' writes the veteran researcher who has spent as much time as any Western historian in Russian archives over the last thirty years.[61] At the start of my own lengthy spell in Moscow archives during work for my PhD, when I was immediately stricken by the lonely despair of the solitary researcher, an overworked archivist let me into the reading room after hours to explain to me how the bewildering institution worked, how to find the material I needed and how to fill in all the forms.

When a person like Yuri Dmitriyev feels the weight of the state pressing down on them, the sensation is universal: it must feel equally terrible wherever one is across time or space. Historical reference points become inexact. But for those who observe events dispassionately, this did not look like the 1930s. Drawing direct comparisons between contemporary Russia and the Stalinist past added confusion to an already unclear picture. Nor are these events recognizable as a 'prelude' to the 1930s. Stalinism was a revolutionary phenomenon. It came into being as a consequence of the Russian Revolution and retained its revolutionary character. Its view of human beings – to be destroyed at will, or to be forcibly redeemed – thrived in a revolutionary world of permanent, rapid change, where millions were on the move, the economy was undergoing complete transformation, and the messages of public culture made up a dramatic and total performance. The mentality of 'communism' amid mass mobilization facilitated the highest levels of creation and destruction. However cruel our own times can be, something akin to Stalinism seems unlikely to emerge unless such a revolution takes place again. Even so, people would be safer if the past could be remembered better, not least so they might think twice if the chance of revolution ever comes along again.

\*

What concerns many observers is not so much the return of a recognizably Stalinist system as the loss of a critical citizenry and the emergence of a cynical public culture. Oleg Khlevniuk, the biographer of Stalin, ends his 2015 book: 'Could it really be that Russia in the twenty-first century is in danger of repeating the mistakes of the twentieth?'[62] The blunting of a critical edge among political elites, the intelligentsia and the population generally seems to be the most likely mistake that could occur.

It seems unlikely, then, that Russia has become a country of Stalinists. For a start, worries about getting Stalinist history wrong are nothing new: they have always been part of the post-Soviet experience. Think of the presidential election campaign of 1996, when Gennady Zyuganov, the Communist Party candidate and no Stalinist, sent sub-Stalin signals in his election materials, which Yeltsin could call out. Some fringe groups openly admired Stalin in the 1990s, admittedly in confusing historical ways; Eduard Limonov's National Bolsheviks were a famous example. Alexander Yakovlev's Presidential Commission on the Rehabilitation of Victims of Political Repression was expressing concerns in 2000 that school textbooks were doing a poor job of describing and explaining Stalin's Terror.[63]

Two years before that, Yakovlev was campaigning to extend compensation for Stalin-era crimes to the children of the repressed, whom he saw also as victims, on the basis that the historical chains of consequence were long. 'Perhaps, from a strictly formal point of view, one could say that it was the parents, not the children, who were put on trial,' he wrote. 'What does one say about the hundreds of thousands of children who were in the concentration camps with their parents? And the children of parents who were shot – does one say they were not repressed, either?' But he had opponents who disputed that there could really be such a thing as a victim of Stalinism. 'What is this fund for political repression? asked Vladimir Zhirinovsky, a demagogue and self-styled nationalist, in the Duma, in February 1998. 'I'm categorically against all these victims of repression – there aren't any such victims of repression. All of Russia was repressed for the whole twentieth century.'[64]

Meanwhile, Russians today are not short of accurate historical information. There is some tendentious and even misleading history on TV, and sometimes it is the basis of shrill commentary, but there are also plenty of high-quality historical documentaries and dramas, including of the Stalin period. Many bookshops, at least in larger cities, contain a broad selection of useful books. The military historian Antony Beevor, author of several works on the Second World War, which emphasize excess and cruelty as well as courage among Red Army soldiers, wrote in 2015 that his books were banned in Russia,[65] but by 2018 they were ubiquitous in Moscow's bookshops, prominently displayed in glossy translations. One popular *History of Russia*, by Evgeny Anisimov, a leading historian and senior professor in St Petersburg, was published in 2006 and has run through four editions, the latest in 2018. Widely available, it contains sections on the Ukrainian famine (using the term *Holodomor*), Stalin's Terror, the mass repressions, the creation of the Gulag, the Molotov–Ribbentrop Pact and much more.[66] More detailed scholarship continues the work of excavating and explaining Stalinist violence and its wider social context. Sometimes drawing on collaborations with historians from outside Russia, many publications are widely available in bookshops, at least in Moscow.[67] Children's books often discuss the 'repressions' in one way or another, including the wildly popular picture-book history of the USSR told as the story of a single apartment and published in 2017.[68] The internet offers plenteous historical conspiracies and tall tales, but it also contains accurate historical information, attractively presented, and with a helpful presentist urgency, such as the ingenious Project 17, which tells the story of the Russian Revolution in real time. One should not underestimate Russia's history teachers, either, or the common sense and curiosity of their pupils. Russian education is highly systematic, and the role of the textbook is a very serious one, but the quality of history teaching does not depend on it alone. Much of this depends on individuals. If they want truth, they will find it easily enough.

And there is a context to this. History is debated with lower stakes in the contemporary West. But the bitter quarrels over Australia Day, which seems to deny the significance of Aboriginal peoples, or Confederate statues in the United States, which seem to normalize racial division, point to deep and unresolved issues where many people around the world refuse to think about the origins of their societies in the light of historical knowledge. Despite decades of teaching on the subject, knowledge of the atrocities and costs of European empires is not part of most Europeans' mental furniture. Just the opposite. Scrutiny of the recent past of post-Communist countries is susceptible to conspiracy theories and political conflict.

The problem is, perhaps, that national memory is not a subtle thing. It creates emotions rather than analysis. This is especially true of the Second World War. Like their contemporaries in Britain and the United States, Russians want to recall the war with confidence. In response to an opinion poll question in 2003 of what gave them most pride from their history, 87 per cent of Russians mentioned the war.[69] It's one of the things that gives legitimacy to them as a people. Like everywhere, however, collective memory in Russia is blunt and unsubtle. It is difficult enough for it to distinguish sharply between the 1940s and the 1930s, or even between the 1930s and the 1970s, or to look at the achievements of the victory without, for some, using 'Stalin' as a convenient label for them. 'Even if Europe *could* somehow cling indefinitely to a living memory of past crimes,' wrote Tony Judt, the great historian of post-war Europe, 'there would be little point. Memory is inherently contentious and partisan: one man's acknowledgement is another man's omission ... Some measure of neglect and even forgetting is the necessary condition for civil health.' For Judt, though, forgetting had to come after the work of memory had been achieved, and society was at ease about the past. The question for contemporary Russians is whether those who came before them – parents, grandparents, great-grandparents, depending on the generation to which one belongs – did enough during the Soviet period to pass on some kind of historical consolation to their children, and prepare them to keep useful memories alive. It might be that a whole society can never really answer such a question, and that families and individuals come to their own personal reckoning with the past, almost entirely invisible to observers.

However difficult this might be for the history industry to accept, forgetting and remembering are perhaps equally important. It's likely that Khrushchev understood it in 1956. Yet the memory work goes on, and at its most subtle, such as in the work of the Belarusian Nobel Prizewinner Svetlana Alexievich, it offers no easy answers. The process of accumulating novels and films that deal with the past might not have generated a popular consensus about the past – some works glorify, while others seek to condemn – but a contested process is still underway.[70]

Judt was an intellectual who believed in the power of honest books, public-service broadcasting and the classroom. Education could fill the gap of memory. 'If Europe's past is to continue to furnish Europe's present with admonitory meaning and moral purpose,' he concluded, 'then it will have to be *taught* afresh with each passing generation.'[71] Too often, though, the lesson plans are written by politicians, or are defined by an official consensus that it is difficult for teachers to transcend. Official materials from the EU or the UK government emphasize such myths as the apparent cooperation and friendliness, rather than the violence and civilizational failure, that marked Europe's 'dark ages' after the fall of Rome, or the peculiar assumption that England has been a democracy since 1215.[72] The failure to be critical about the past is therefore common in many places. Now that pupils in England can stop studying history at the age of fourteen, the failure is only exacerbated. It's unlikely that the 'memory boom' that has contributed to European politics since the 1990s has done much to sharpen people's critical engagement with the past; its effect is just as likely to be either soporific or entertaining depending on one's tastes.

'Our moral debt before history,' said Alexander Yakovlev on 30 October 2000, 'is to transmit to the coming generation, to our children, grandchildren, and great-grandchildren, our tormented memory of our calamity and guilt.' He was speaking at a mass meeting outside Moscow's Lubyanka, the headquarters of the secret police. Russians have achieved this difficult task before. Twice, after 1956 and again after 1987, Russians and other Soviet citizens felt an insistent need to confront, explain and record the tragedies of Stalinism. On both occasions, a gaping social urge coincided with political necessity. As winter approached Moscow on that day outside the Lubyanka, no one who heard him could doubt the moral value of Yakovlev's point. One response came seventeen years later, on 30 September 2017, when President Putin and Patriarch Kirill joined with the mayor of Moscow, Sergei Sobyanin, to open the new Wall of Grief in central Moscow. Right next to a busy interchange on the avenue named after

Andrei Sakharov, the space in which the Wall is set is wide open, visible to tens of thousands of people every day. Adjacent to the rush hour, visibility trumps peace. The sculptor, Georgy Frangulyan, carved images of prisoners into a long bronze expanse, into which awkward arches are cut, and the word 'remember' inscribed in twenty-two languages.[73]

But how can you make future generations feel the torment of memory when the past no longer directly threatens the present? No society really does this. And with good reason. Most of the time, it's better to think about the present and the future.[74] But the tools of memory need to be kept in stock, just in case.

As time goes on, the most important task of memory is not dutifully to attend a moral lesson, or listen repeatedly to a list of clichés. It is, instead, to educate oneself in thinking critically about the past. If a society lacks this resource, it loses self-awareness and analytical power, and compromises its own security. The Russia Anxiety will fade when the societies that feel it most sharply confront their own histories and the history of the Anxiety itself in this more honest and self-conscious way. Societies will always forget as well as remember, and tell stories about themselves that are part truth and part fiction. That's normal. For all of us, there's no simple choice between remembering and forgetting. But there is a lifelong necessity to keep our wits about us.

# 10

# The Putin Prospect

*Is Russia's Future Contained in Her Past?*

Once upon a time, a ferocious tsar with a fearsome countenance – he had one eye, one arm and one leg – decided the time had come for his portrait to be painted. He called on the services of one of the most famous painters in the land. When the tsar saw his portrait, he was furious. 'I look nothing like this!' he thundered. 'Why have you portrayed me as so handsome and complete, climbing a mountain and surveying the majesty of nature?' The painter was sent to be executed. Thus romanticism died a death in Russia.

The next-most famous artist arrived to see the tsar a few days later. He carefully appraised the monarch and worked efficiently and accurately. 'What have you done?' screamed the tsar, when the paining was unveiled. 'Why have you made me look like a weak and wizened man with one eye, one arm and one leg, standing feebly in front of a curtain?' The painter went to the scaffold. Thus realism was banished from the Russian lands.

After casting a little further into the provinces, the tsar's advisers found a young painter who combined all the artistic and personal virtues. He came to Moscow and paid homage to the tsar. Then he set to work, adjusting his view and casting a beady eye over his subject. He worked all day. Anticipating the results, the tsar began to fume. But when he saw the painting, his anger dissolved. Looking at an image of himself in profile, with eye, arm and leg in alignment, and with wisdom suffusing one-half of his face, he beamed at the artist. 'You have done a magnificent job,' he said, brushing down his robes and adjusting his crown. 'Let me ennoble you with all the riches of your province.' Thus was socialist realism born in Russia.

*

The joke – perhaps best told round a Russian kitchen table – is all about the Russia Anxiety. For a start, there's the tyrant. And not just any tyrant, but one who is grotesque, capricious and violent. Then there's the atmosphere around him: an air of fear and obsequiousness, in which the tsar might make any decision and his courtiers seek to please him in any way that seems right. Last of all is the absurdity of the situation: such a way of doing things is no way to live. But there is also a winning quality about the story. Around the kitchen table, as your host tells the joke, you sense the national self-deprecation and the ubiquity of culture in many Russians' lives. After all, which other nation tells jokes about romanticism and realism? And socialist realism? This was a Soviet aesthetic of mixed virtues. As the joke showed, it was sometimes a lacquering of reality, a production of fakery, but it was also a way of making accessible a vision of the future to all consumers of culture, including the barely literate. It blended past, present and future in a single work of art.

Socialist realism reminds us that the Russia Anxiety is not only illustrated by historical examples, but it's made out of history. In the last chapter, we saw that the relationship between history and memory is built into the Anxiety, but can also offer a remedy for it. What about the relationship between history and the future, out of which the Russia Anxiety is also constructed? This concluding chapter is about this relationship and how moving into the future defines the *cycles* of the Russia Anxiety: the movement from feelings of fear, to disregard, to contempt, and back to fear, as Russian power is perceived as overbearing, and then overstretched, and then inadequate. It shows how the problem of the Russian future has run through socialist realism, the post-Soviet transition and the attempts by Russia to 'catch up' with the West, helping to form the particular contours and problems of the Russia Anxiety. The chapter ends by describing six general principles that might help us to overcome the Russia Anxiety in the future.

## VISIONS OF THE FUTURE

In 1934, the Union of Soviet Writers held its first all-USSR congress. Maxim Gorky took the chair in front of 600 delegates from across the Soviet Union. Despite the talent in the room, the star of the show was Andrei Zhdanov, close ally of Stalin, and senior Party functionary. 'Your congress is meeting at a time when the socialist way of life has gained final and complete victory in our country – under the leadership of the Communist Party and under our leader of genius, Comrade Stalin,' he declared, breaking off to loud applause. 'Consequently,' he went on, 'advancing from milestone to milestone, from victory to victory, from the time of the Civil War to the reconstruction of the entire national economy, our Party has led the country to victory over capitalist elements, ousting them from all spheres of the national economy.'

Even more than in gentler times, in 1934 the economy was at the centre of every type of human activity. Zhdanov was at the congress to announce the new aesthetic that was to guide all cultural production in the USSR, but he was keen too to talk about the economy. For him, it was axiomatic that cultural and economic life could not be separated. He quoted Stalin's metaphor of writers as 'engineers of human souls', asking what it might mean. 'It means,' he declared, 'that we must know life so as to depict it truthfully in our works of art – and not to depict it scholastically, lifelessly or merely as "objective reality"; we must depict reality in its revolutionary development.'[1]

Zhdanov was describing the new Soviet style of socialist realism. Novels, films and paintings of the Stalin era were realist, in that the characters who populated them looked and sounded real enough and the action they performed was immediately comprehensible. This was not the impenetrable geometric imagery of the outer reaches of the avant-garde. But the world that the socialist realists depicted was at the same time not quite realistic. Instead, it was aspirational. It was full of the good things in life, and was bankrolled by communist promises. In line with the forward march of communism, it was the world of tomorrow.

Socialist realism depicted history, too. It drew on the example of nineteenth-century realism, whose history paintings brought prestige and wealth to the top artists, like Vasily Surikov, whom we met in chapter 7. The historical scenes favoured by the socialist realists were often from the very recent past, and especially the Revolution of 1917. A familiar subject was Lenin addressing a public meeting.

Revolutions are about the future, so such a painting depicts an historical promise about the world to come.

Socialist realism made the Soviet-era Russia Anxiety more concentrated. When fear of the Soviet Union was at its peak, socialist realism seemed to depict a threatening view of the Soviet future. But as fear gave way to contempt or disregard, socialist realism seemed little more than a risible vision of what a flailing regime still thought might be its destiny.

For all the flexibility of developed socialism, and the existence of 'permitted dissent' and cultural undergrounds, the USSR was always a revolutionary state, and socialist realism remained its official aesthetic. In 1985, a new statue was erected on October Square in central Moscow. Over the preceding two decades, the old square had been transformed into something on a different scale, surrounded by giant buildings. The enormous statue, the largest tribute to Lenin in the city (bigger than the Mausoleum), still stands.

It is instructive that this monument dates to the year that Gorbachev became general secretary. But it's not only a period piece. Embedded in its time and place, this massive, dynamic statue of Lenin, surveying the future with a fixed stare, grasping his cap, ready to address the crowd, surrounded by revolutionary supporters, reaching for the future, even today connects the Soviet past with the Russian present and an imagined future. In the 2010s, the future that Lenin looks towards is quite different than it was thirty years earlier. He looks out onto a skyscraper- and BMW-filled view of turbo-charged twenty-first-century capitalism.

The changing view from Lenin's plinth reminds us that the Russian future is a shifting target, likely to transform itself out of all recognition. In a history marked by unexpected turns, it seems unlikely that the scope of future change is circumscribed by past experience. At no time has the construction of new and unexpected futures been quicker than during the lifetime of this statue. In 1985, when it was erected, time seemed to be moving slowly in the Soviet Union. Viktor Grishin, who commissioned the monument, was the Party boss of the city of Moscow, and had been in post for eighteen years. Gorbachev would soon call this the era of 'stagnation', which captured something of the slowness of economic growth, but failed to explain the variety, complexity and even the legitimacy of Soviet life, in which many people led lives that they considered to be normal and appropriate. Gorbachev's reforms sped time up. On the one hand, *perestroika* ended the nuclear arms race and the Cold War, dismantled the Eastern bloc, opened up Soviet life properly to the outside world, and made the world much safer. Yet, on the other, it ripped the fabric of Soviet life apart. It caused the country to collapse, with devastating social and economic consequences for the next decade. As time accelerated, and countless new imminent futures suddenly became possible, Lenin's statue looked out at foreign cars, ugly neon, begging grandmothers and a tough-minded younger generation looking for a chance. To his left, if he could have turned his head, Lenin would have seen the city's central children's library, where calmness prevailed and culture was protected. In the Yeltsin years, anything seemed possible, though the range of probable futures narrowed with time. Across the road, Lenin could still see a famous old Soviet café, where lounge singers played on a Friday evening, but in a year or two it became the flagship branch of a successful chain. One future gave way to a different one. Near the end of the last century, on a cold late-winter night, I stepped out of that old Soviet café with a woman I'd met a month before. She became my wife. Our own future was just beginning.

We were all in transit to one future or another. Transition – the shift from the communist past to the capitalist future, from the Soviet yesterday to the American tomorrow – was all about movement through time. But it presupposed a particular future, one designed by the IMF and NATO, by Brussels and Bonn (Berlin only became the German capital again in 1999), and above all in the White House, where Bill Clinton seemed to have a handle on the future. The book that was on Washington reading lists in the year that Clinton was elected to the presidency was Francis Fukuyama's *The End of History and the Last Man*. It argued that liberal democracy was the logical endpoint of historical development, the only possible future for a society that wanted to be normal.

The sense of an impending future re-created the Russia Anxiety for the new age. What part would Russia play? Given the enormity of what had happened – the end of the Cold War, the collapse of the

Eastern bloc, the end of the Soviet Union, the demise of communism and the transformation of Russia, still one of the two great nuclear powers – Western governments responded in an unexciting way. They did not promise to make a completely new future, incorporating Russia in it, but to strive for a future that looked like the past, minus the USSR. The cycle of the Russia Anxiety clicked into disregard: we won't be hearing from the Russians again. European and global security architecture were left in place. The chance to rebuild institutions or create new ones so that they could incorporate both Russia and America, and that Russia could work alongside all the other countries of Europe, was missed. There are good reasons why the West was cautious. Times were unpredictable and dangerous. But there could only really be one reason for NATO to continue to exist, and that was as a vehicle for the Russia Anxiety – and for a conservatively imagined American power. Other security challenges would be better suited to a different set of institutions, yet to be built, but abandoning NATO might have led to the unravelling of cooperation between its member states. The risk was not taken, and the historic opportunity was missed. While the Russians might never have joined NATO, they might have joined something else. But the general sense was that the Russians were down, they wouldn't be coming back any time soon, and they could be disregarded. Better to prepare for a different strategy: of pushing American power, through NATO, ever closer to the Russian border. The bombing of Belgrade in 1999 was a low point: attacking a fraternal Slav people in a zone in which Russia had particular interests, but without consulting Moscow properly, seemed to signal total disrespect.

The future was, then, of America rising and Russia falling, but it was framed in ideological terms, and became what one historian called a 'failed crusade'.[2] 'Transitology' was indeed a doomed science, practised by men and women with a taste for fairy tales. The idea was one of suffering, redemption and recovery: post-Soviet Russia would go through a brief purgatory and emerge as America. It was the failed romantic epic of Russian economic history.

After the Soviet collapse, inflation ravaged people's savings, while employers were often unable to meet their monthly wage bill. By 1998, GDP was 55 per cent of what it had been in 1989.[3] Russian reformers and Western advisers were keen to turn Russia into a laboratory of market reform by imposing 'shock therapy' on an already desperate population. Despite the terrible pain the process caused, they argued that it was a price worth paying, and that a gradual approach would have been worse.[4] Even in 1992, shortages fell dramatically, but few could afford the range of goods on the newly filled shop shelves. The few who could were those who had acquired wealth by means that seemed opaque to ordinary Russians.

On the surface, the privatization programmes of the early 1990s had popular potential. People acquired formal ownership of their homes, though often they scarcely noticed this, as tenure had anyway been so secure. Voucher schemes for privatizing state enterprises, had they worked, would have given employees a share in the ownership of their workplace. They suggested a collaborative, inclusive and 'corporative' approach. But enterprises often ended up in the hands of their management. Many ordinary people lost out further thanks to pyramid schemes and faulty banks. In 1996, the so-called 'loans for shares' scheme transferred billions of rubles' worth of state assets and natural resources into the hands of a small number of 'oligarchs' who had helped Boris Yeltsin during his re-election campaign.

By 2007, society's top 10 per cent had incomes that were seventeen times those of the bottom 10 per cent; in 1992, when inequality was already accelerating, the gap had been eight times. The concentration of resources in very few hands was an even more pronounced development. In 2008, Russia had eighty-six billionaires, who owned (officially) one-third of GDP. Inequality set hackles rising and blood pressure racing. Crime was even more dangerous. By the mid-1990s, the Russian murder rate had soared to 30 per 100,000 people, fewer than in South Africa, but more than four times the rate in the USA. Even more worrying was natural mortality, which jumped by 60 per cent between 1990 and 1994. Once again, the best comparison was with the 1940s. In terms of public health, the state of affairs that marked Russia's departure from communist rule recalled the worst of the post-war crisis, including the famine of 1947.[5]

This was the problem. In the folk memory of Russians, they had not raced to the future but regressed half a century, and were living through the sort of experiences that had skipped two generations.

But a few were managing exceptionally well. This was an offence against natural justice as Russian culture long perceived it. Many Russians understandably interpreted the harshness of their lives as the consequence of capitalism and democracy. The brief chance to build a new Russia on the basis of a moral and political consensus slipped away. There was some renewed optimism from the middle of the 1990s, when the worst of the 'transition' was over. Incomes rose, people bought more washing machines and cars, and had more chances for foreign holidays. But the financial crisis of August 1998, when the Russian government defaulted on foreign debts, caused the loss of savings that were denominated in rubles. Unemployment increased; salaries were downgraded. 'Last time we still had some hope,' said an unemployed friend of mine to me.

The original sin had been committed. There was no going back on it. Russians could not rewind the clock to year zero. There was only the future. Yet Putin understood the appeal of hitting reset – and he also saw that this was usually an emotional desire, a matter of heart over head. During his presidency, the rhetoric of justice, so crucial in Russian culture, was borne out by increases in pensions and occasional high-profile corruption cases. Meanwhile, the bottom line of rising wages, foreign holidays and consumer choice broadened. The advantages of the post-Soviet economy over its predecessor were far from universally shared but were still obvious, and they were some consolation for the top-level corruption about which people could in any case do nothing.

Recovery in the early 2000s seemed to take Russia out of the 1990s and into the future once and for all. On the one hand, the ruble depreciated, and the price of oil and gas rose; on the other, more small businesses opened, productivity rose, and labour and investment shifted to where they were more needed. After the low point of 1998, GDP almost doubled by 2008, before falling slightly with a cyclical downturn in the economy.[6] As president, Dmitry Medvedev modishly emphasized the future, symbolized by the 'technology city' at Skolkovo. The price of oil was now falling. Foreign-policy risks and confrontation with the West led to sanctions. Society remained divided, but a thread of national unity ran through an economic policy of import substitution, especially in the food sector, where growing numbers of small businesses fed farmers' markets in the big cities, or a new range of Russian cheeses mimicked French flavours, to popular appeal.

Just like a hundred years before, the Russian future held out the promise of normality, of Russia again becoming a 'normal' great power with a 'normal' economy. Notwithstanding sanctions, Russian economic performance was becoming more normal. At the height of the 2000s boom, it was compared with another new normality, the BRICs: Brazil, Russia, India, China. The possibility of 'normal' development was sometimes set against, and sometimes inspired by, the confrontation with the West, but the big obstacles were domestic: the excessive focus on the energy sector, the scale of corruption, and uneven provincial investment. Russia's economy conformed to European norms over centuries, though there was one long exception – the Soviet period – when it had looked like something quite different, and the normal laws of economics had been suspended. But despite its flaws, the post-Soviet economy was part of the contemporary world, and its people were entirely plugged into its processes.

If the future was central to the two experiments conducted on Russians in the twentieth century – Soviet socialism and post-Soviet transition – then it played a deep part in Russian culture, too. Once again, the point was that past and future were deliberately connected. In medieval Muscovy, the past was a crucial resource for building the future. Literary works and theology were validated by the past. They also looked through the present to the future, emphasizing the great victory of Dmitry Donskoi at Kulikovo in 1380, which the chronicles repeatedly described as a crucial step in bringing the people of Muscovy closer to their heavenly future.[7] This was one expression of Muscovy's messianic destiny. The fourteenth century is too soon to start talking about the Russia Anxiety. But the concept of messianism – the future triumph of a chosen people – was important at one time or another in every century thereafter, and the outsiders' response to it was often to invoke the Russia Anxiety.

The future is at the heart of Russian culture, just as it is in other modern societies. Meanwhile, in a country where unexpected events and outsize personalities have played such an important role, a particularly wide range of futures has often been on display. Never more has the future determined the present than when Russia has sought to catch up and overtake its partners or adversaries.

## CATCH-UP

On 4 February 1931, Stalin made a famous speech at an industrial conference, promising that 'there are no fortresses that the Bolsheviks cannot seize'. With aggressive, bullet-like rhetoric, he placed his economic policy in historical context. 'The history of old Russia consisted, among other things, in her being ceaselessly beaten for her backwardness,' he insisted. 'She was beaten by the Mongol khans. She was beaten by the Turkish beys. She was beaten by the Swedish feudal rulers. She was beaten by the Polish-Lithuanian lords. She was beaten by the Anglo-French capitalists. She was beaten by the Japanese barons.' In case anyone had not yet got the point: 'Everyone gave her a beating for her backwardness.'

This was a tendentious and confusing description of the Russian past. But it provided perfect historical cover for breakneck industrialization. It was also an ideal subject for socialist realism, with its suggestion of the movement from darkness to light, from misery to paradise. In the middle, of course – the short Stalinist present that lay between past backwardness and future radiance – a generation would have to be sacrificed. Stalin showed how history could justify this sacrifice. But his narrative also explained industrialization in a patriotic tone; it was a response to international hostility. After all, international capitalism was in crisis, flailing and dangerous, and a communist-hating Nazi Party was on the cusp of power in Germany. The Soviet Union had to respond. 'We have fallen behind the advanced countries by fifty to a hundred years,' Stalin went on. 'We must close that gap in ten years. Either we do this or we'll be crushed. That is what our obligations before the workers and peasants of the USSR dictate to us.'[8]

Thirty years later, on 19 June 1961, Khrushchev presented the new Programme of the Communist Party to the Central Committee. This was the great statement of Khrushchev-era idealism. Its ethics had little to do with Stalinism. Instead, it drew its inspiration directly from the Revolution. Rather than demanding the sacrifice of Soviet citizens, it aimed to improve their personal conditions. But it did not circumvent Stalinism completely, because it also replicated the dynamism of the 1930s. It promised that communism would be delivered within twenty years, by 1980. Khrushchev claimed that the intervening period would see 'victory after victory' in economic terms against the United States, after which the USSR would 'rise to such a great height that, by comparison, the main capitalist countries will remain far below and way behind'.[9]

In October 1961, six months after Yuri Gagarin had flown in space, it was probably possible to believe in anything, certainly that the communist future really was in reach, and that the Soviet Union might indeed match the brute economic power of the United States within two decades. Stalin and Khrushchev were both true-believing communists, though their understandings of how to reach the communist future were dramatically different. Their catch-up attempts had contrasting effects on the Russia Anxiety. In the 1930s, the Soviet Union was not a threat, but was instead an object of distaste and disregard, and sometimes contempt, such as during the show trials. The few high-profile sympathizers who visited and proclaimed that the future belonged to Moscow were exceptions. This response was an historic error, making it more and more difficult to form the alliance against Hitler that was still feasible right up until 1939. Meanwhile, the response to Khrushchev was different. The launching of Sputnik in 1957, and then the Gagarin flight of 1961, seemed to indicate that the Soviet Union was a serious threat to American power, and the Russia Anxiety escalated. It took the form of a slightly bewildered but major fear. The natural result of this was the Cuban Missile Crisis the following year, when it was only good fortune, the immunity to the Anxiety of a small number of key aides, including Bobby Kennedy, and the unwillingness of the Soviet side to push things to their deadly conclusion, that prevented Armageddon.

Still, the West's military-industrial complex did not do badly out of the Russia Anxiety, and had vested interests, in the form of defence contracts and military power, in promoting the spectre of Soviet danger. But Khrushchev's vision of catching up with the American economy was, of course, not fulfilled. In 1987, by which time communism should long have been achieved, the United States and the USSR had broadly similar populations, though the USSR's was bigger: 244 million Americans, 283 million Soviet citizens. But Soviet

GDP was only 39 per cent of the American total, or 33 per cent per capita.[10] Soviet citizens had some advantages: stability, full employment, a fairly equal society, a 'social wage' that incorporated wide-ranging welfare and broadly 'democratic' access to education. It offered something, for some, to believe in. But these advantages had begun to dissipate since the late 1970s, and Gorbachev's *perestroika* was about to eviscerate them.

With so much of the Soviet budget focused on defence and the reinforcement of inefficiency, the cost of trying to catch up was heavy. The cost was borne by the people. 'When the state grew fat, the people grew lean,' wrote Vasily Klyuchevsky about the seventeenth century, in one of the most famous aphorisms in all of Russian historiography. By the late 1980s, the state wasn't even very fat, though the top elites were about to become so. And so the form of the Anxiety switched again. Disregard and contempt replaced the last vestiges of fear. The Russia Anxiety is a cycle. Disregard proved, once again, to be just as deleterious as fear.

Three hundred years before Stalin and Khrushchev, their predecessors faced some of the same concerns about economic development. Muscovy was connected to European trade networks, but from a position of relative weakness. Eastern Slavic civilization had never been isolated, as we have seen in earlier chapters; in fact, it was part of Europe.[11] But it was during the sixteenth century that Muscovy developed new trading ties with the West, following the pioneering voyage of Richard Chancellor into Muscovy in 1553.[12] Swashbuckling Tudor traders were familiar figures at the court of Ivan the Terrible.[13] They knew how to pay obeisance, but their contempt for the locals became a historical cliché. They were joined by adventurers from other parts of Western Europe. During the seventeenth century, they were embedded into the Muscovite economy, from Dutch shipbuilding on the Caspian in the 1630s to Italian silk manufacture in the 1670s.[14]

Western merchants had quasi-colonial expectations. Their job was to extract economic advantages from people they claimed to see as barbaric.[15] The Muscovite government needed their expertise and capital, but it was not at their mercy. The tsar's realm needed to catch up, and to be proactive in doing so. 'As a decisive means of terminating the commercial exploitation of Russia by foreigners,' wrote Juraj Križanic, a seventeenth-century Croatian priest turned Muscovite economic pundit, 'the tsar should take all foreign trade into his own hands.'[16] This was the core of a mercantilist approach: that the state should have a deliberate policy to favour its own economic concerns in competition with outsiders, by building up currency reserves, placing tariffs on imports, and taxing economic activity by foreigners in the homeland. These ideas were widely adopted across Europe in the seventeenth and eighteenth centuries.

'Catching up', then, also involved the normalization of Muscovy's place in the European economy. This only had much bearing on the Russia Anxiety later. It was under Peter the Great that the strategic aim of catching up became a frantic one. With his talk of earthly paradise, his aim was to telescope the future and bring its benefits to the Russian Empire as quickly as he could. As a young tsar, Peter had travelled across Europe in a 'grand embassy' that was one of the most important fact-finding missions in world history. He was interested in transferring technologies back to the Russian lands and using them to build a civilization that looked more like Western Europe. Shipbuilding fascinated him the most; he rolled up his sleeves in Amsterdam and south London to learn the techniques of the masters of the day. The Petrine economy was tough and extractive, funding wars against Sweden and the Ottomans and the construction of St Petersburg. This was only partly as a result of mercantilism – tariffs were only introduced on some imports in 1724[17] – but the catch-up dynamic was at its heart. As the eighteenth century went on, it became clearer that the relationship between Russia and 'the West' was becoming more equal. Between 1742 and 1797, Russian exports increased by twelve times, from a value of 4.5 million rubles to 69 million.[18]

This was the basis of the changed perceptions of the Russian Empire that we encountered in chapter 1. At any given moment, their form was shaped by the exigencies of war and diplomacy. But catching up was given a new boost in the three decades before the First World War, when Alexander III and Nicholas II opted to take their gamble on industrialization and modernization. Tempted to look back to the consolations of old Muscovy, they still made their bet on the future. They had foreign help. As a skilled dealmaker at the heights of international finance, Sergei Witte, who was first minister for railways and then minister of finance, arranged for enormous loans to come from France. In two big spurts of very rapid industrialization, in the 1880s–1890s and between 1907 and 1914, the Russian industrial economy seemed to become the engine room of Europe. Moscow and St Petersburg had more than doubled in size, becoming vast metropolises. In 1880, the population of St Petersburg was 877,000, and Moscow had 748,000 people. By 1910, the numbers were 1.9 million and 1.5 million. Industrial production grew by 5.6 times between 1880 and 1913, and the extent of railway track expanded from 22,865 kilometres to 70,156.[19] To Anxious onlookers, the future looked Russian. In the first spurt, the country's railway system was dramatically expanded, opening up the Empire as a single space of economic and political development. In the second spurt, the driver of industrial change was munitions and defence. Russia seemed to have catapulted itself into the future, though just how far it had come was often exaggerated. By 1914, in the minds of foreign observers, it was difficult to distinguish between the country's massive military and economic potential.[20] One of the causes of the First World War was Russia's attempt to catch up with its Western neighbours, and their mistaken perception of Russia's future.

## THE FUTURE

The future is, then, risky terrain. When Western policymakers – from Germans in 1914 to Americans in the 1960s – imagine the Russian future, their Anxiety increases. But the future might offer consolations, too. Let's move towards a conclusion of the book by making six suggestions about how we can think about history and the future in ways that diminish, not escalate, the Russia Anxiety.

### 1 Be modest about the claims of history

'The past is another country,' wrote L. P. Hartley, in what became one of the most famous clichés in the history of English letters. 'They do things differently there.' How they lived was different. How they thought was different. Their experience intersects with our own, but in subtle and complicated ways that historians and other commentators will perpetually debate.

In other words: it is probably a mistake to draw a thick red line from the deep past to the present and off into the future, which is the fundamental historical conceit of the Russia Anxiety. The American historian Leopold Haimson, a contemporary of Richard Pipes, surveyed the commanding heights of American-Russian historiography in the last third of the twentieth century from his Chair at Columbia. He was a man of the Left. Influenced by Marx, Haimson had a formidable capacity to explain modern Russian history as a consequence of structures that generated a working-class revolution in October 1917. But his first book, published in 1955, was about the psychology of Lenin and three other radical socialists before 1905. In this early work, Haimson drew on the Marxist categories of 'consciousness' and 'spontaneity', but the focus on personality and tactics in his argument really had little to do with the deep structures of Marxist history.[21] Even Haimson, then, felt the pull of historical contingency.

No doubt the structures of class might contribute to an explanation of the Revolution of 1917. But no explanation that ignores the circumstances of the First World War can account for the collapse of the monarchy or the rise of the Bolsheviks. And those circumstances were unique – a perfect storm. Can studying the Russian Revolution help us understand the stability of today's Russian government and the political prospects of the 'system' which it oversees? It can only do so obliquely. 1917's interplay of class tension, world war and individual psychology can't be a laboratory in which future political changes might be observed.

Although Russians themselves live constantly with history, including with a sense of its apparently deep and repetitive rhythms, their own recent past teaches them about the immediacy of historical chaos. Anyone in Russia born before 1980 had a visceral experience of the 1990s, a time when Russia's many immediate futures were dramatically different from each other.

Precedents, examples and long-term trends all tell us something about Russia's future, but they will always be controversial and vulnerable, open to counter-claims. History cannot offer the consolations of the natural sciences, though they are uncertain enough. At least as important as the detailed content of what we learn about Russian history is the process of how we learn it. Learning about the Russian past helps us to separate agreed-upon facts from grand theories and fake history; it draws attention to those who use history to take risks with peace; it allows us to imagine how Russians might respond to our governments' actions; it broadens our scope so that we can sense how other peoples might understand Russia. Above all, it helps us see that history is constantly being made anew, for good or bad – that vices and achievements alike can rapidly dissolve, that new roads are forever being taken, and that the apparent familiarity of the scenery can actually be a treacherous guide.

In this way, history can make a better future, but not through the scientific application of observed data. Instead, the connection between history and the future is drawn in the expansion of our imaginations that occurs when we study the past. It's a process that helps us understand the other point of view, and puts our own viewpoint and significance in perspective. If we could take the time to do this, perhaps we need not be so modest about the claims of history after all.

## 2 Keep in mind Russia's historic resources

Of all Russia's lost futures, it is the 1860s that look most full of promise. Alexander II's Great Reforms, which were focused on the emancipation of the serfs but extended across many areas of life, offered a means of resolving the Speransky Conundrum, by creating something like a functioning rule of law inside the Russian autocracy. Yet their promise was severely compromised by the assassination of Alexander in 1881 and the blinkered conservative turn of his successors. The Great Reforms are the kind of historic resource which, if they were used more rigorously, might diminish the Russia Anxiety in the future. Russians themselves are of course aware of the value of the precedent. Outside the front entrance of the Russian State University of Law, a post-Soviet institution in Moscow, is a new bust of Alexander, complete with generous words about the 'tsar liberator'.

The judicial reform of 1864, called by one of its historians 'Russia's first constitution',[22] made the judiciary formally independent of executive power. As judges now held lifetime appointments, they were protected from the interventions and whims of the monarch. Criminal trials were to be open and decided by jury. Justices of the Peace, who were elected by the new local assemblies (*zemstvos*), tried minor cases. Thanks also to those aspects of the Muscovite legal tradition which had facilitated due process, the great judicial reform of 1864 had foundations in the deeper past, and seemed directed towards a bright future.

This really was a great reform. More so than 1905, it was perhaps the most significant of all the moments when the tsarist autocracy showed it had the potential to reform itself and evolve towards a basis in rights-based citizenship. Yet it was not perfect. Even had circumstances been ideal, it might have failed. The biggest worry was the peasantry. In a nutshell, the dilemma of some contemporaries and historians alike has been: how on earth could one trust the peasants with the institutions of justice?

Emancipation in 1861 had created a new type of court: the *volost* (district) court, which only served peasants, and which existed in rural localities. It dealt with civil and criminal matters that had arisen in villages. The 1864 reform kept the *volost* court in place. Its proceedings were overseen by peasant judges, who lacked a legal education and were elected by peasants themselves. Although these courts were constituted as formal institutions, with extensive written records, they were based on the exercise of customary peasant law. Lawyers and intellectuals assumed that the courts and their peasant judges lacked a sense of abstract justice, were more concerned with morality than facts and tended to try the character of the accused rather than his or her actions. But the *volost* courts became extremely popular; peasants actively chose to make use of them in matters that could have been resolved in the commune, such as seeking redress for slanderous offences against one's dignity, or resolving disputes over property demarcations. In 1905, 47,761 cases, almost evenly divided between civil and criminal, were brought in the *volost* courts of Moscow Province alone. The premier historian of these courts argues that their existence between 1861 and 1917 created in the peasants nothing less than 'the formation of a legal consciousness – an accepted resort to law'.[23]

Separate peasant courts were, however, a problem for those who aspired to the rule of law. All subjects of the Empire should make use of the same courts; such universality would be the real incubator of citizenship. Instead, the *volost* courts preserved the separateness of the peasantry. They kept up the practical persistence of social estates, which divided people from each other. But the courts were a convenient institution to make emancipation work better – a comprehensible, accessible arena that peasants could visit to resolve disputes that emerged in their new post-emancipation world – and they were designed to be temporary. There was no intention that they should lock down a separate peasant juridical status.[24] And, in the end, their survival was no bad thing. By the time that Revolution came in 1917, the peasants had a sense of how to locate their own sense of justice in the bigger institutions of state power.

Outside of participating in their own courts, peasants were also called on for jury service. Nobles frequently dodged the duty, and so peasants made up more than 50 per cent of jurymen in late imperial Russia. But could they understand what was going on or what they were supposed to do? Some commentators have doubted this, claiming that the peasant jurors brought a village sensibility and a commitment to customary law to their duties.[25] One wonders what sensibility and view of law white jurors in the former Confederacy were bringing to court when trying a black man in the same period – and over many decades thereafter. The Russian-style jury system seemed to work as an evolving compromise between the adversarial contests of Anglo-American tradition and the inquisitorial tradition of Russian – and, say, French – jurisprudence.[26]

Meanwhile, the judicial reform spread into the Empire as a whole, which was imagined as a single judicial space. Over three decades, new-style courts spread into the Russian interior, the Ukrainian borderlands, the Caucasus, Poland, the Baltic provinces and as far as Turkestan. There were problems of disputed authority, worries that juries might rehearse arguments about national autonomy (and so they were not introduced in places such as Warsaw), and the obvious brute fact of imperial dominance.[27] And yet this might have been more similar to the rule of law than the governance by nineteenth-century Western European empires over their own imperial possessions, especially in Africa.

Today, there are good reasons to be concerned about the rule of law in Russia, not least because of the fears raised about 'telephone justice', where judicial independence is compromised. High-profile cases concerning businessmen and leaders in the arts – few in number but very public in effect – seem to reflect the witting or unwitting transgressions of unwritten rules rather than formal law. But there is evidence to show the regularized, reasonable workings of the civil legal system in disputes between ordinary Russians.[28] Alexander's reforms offer a powerful precedent for further improvement, based as they are on values that cut across Russian time from past to future. Of Russia's many historic resources – its great-power heritage, cultural and scientific achievements, the education and endurance of its people – it might be that the capacity to embrace a paradox turns out to be the most valuable. After all, Russia has been the nation that was also an empire, the dictatorship obsessed with democracy, and the autocracy governed briefly by law. Making a contradiction work might be better than shattering it to pieces in a lethal revolution.

## 3 Think of Russia as a 'normal' country

When the *perestroika*-era Moscow correspondent of the *Washington Post*, David Remnick, returned to Russia in the 1990s, he concluded that Russians wanted above all for their country to become 'normal'.[29] In the turbulence of that time, Russia did not seem 'normal' at all. People lived lives of exceptional difficulty, the scale of which the outside world has never really acknowledged. Their society seemed about to collapse. Its political leaders' claim to be the face of democracy was a disastrous advertisement for the utility of elections. Russians themselves sometimes compare those years to the chaotic periods that immediately followed the Second World War or the Civil War; it was the toughest time for half a century. No wonder that Remnick found people who wanted 'normality', just as people across Europe wanted normality in the decade after 1945.

Remnick's comment was related to the dynamic of transition. The 1990s was another period of Russian history when the past was being destroyed in the name of the future. But within a decade, Russian life looked more normal. And although living conditions and even local politics varied widely across Russia at the onset of Putin's fourth presidential term, with examples of misery in parts of the country, life had normalized for many people. At least in the major cities, people plan careers, borrow money to buy apartments, fit them out at IKEA, accumulate possessions, enjoy holidays, look for the best doctors and schools, seek out hints of hope in the future. Poverty levels are high but people on average live better than ever before. The worldview of most Russians is probably similar to that of most other citizens of Europe – a familiar mix of aspiration, caution, national feeling but openness to the outside world, and desire for individual respect. Despite the particular scale of some of their everyday economic struggles, notably the excessive concentration of wealth in a few cities, the persistence of corruption, and the existence of a super-rich elite, there was also something normal about their problems.

In the West, 'oligarchs' had become cartoon villains for a specifically Russian abnormality, and often with good reason. Yet the universalization of this term, sometimes applied by Western journalists to any Russian businessperson, however ingenious, popular or legitimate their operations, was an echo of the Russia Anxiety. The wider Western fears of Russian big money and contempt for Russian corruption, which spiralled in the 2010s, were sometimes justified, sometimes Anxious, but sometimes a general anger about international finance that transcended Russia. You did not have to like what had happened in the Russian 1990s to accept that life had moved on, and sometimes big money had become respectable and responsible, both in Russia itself and abroad. The possibility of a new just order that had briefly existed in 1991 was ancient history, and perhaps it was simply capitalism, rather than oligarchs or mafias, that had embedded inequality, innovation, consumerism, welfare cutbacks and a sometimes-ferocious work ethic in Russian society. After all, the sanctions that were imposed on Russia from 2014 were testament to the interlocking of the country in global business. In the world that came after the global financial crash of 2008, Russia's oligarchs were caught not just in the shadow of the Russia Anxiety but in the glare of a wider millennial crisis: the fury at the 1 per cent, the distrust of big business, the contempt for the global money elite. Many of the young Western protestors born after 1991 saw little difference between Russian wealth and that of some of their own business elites. Rage about money-laundering, exploitative corporations, tax-havens, impoverished workforces, impenetrable high finance and amoral globalization was so acute precisely because they were so unrestrained by nation states; they were generalized, and not specifically about Russia. In weird ways, big money might have normalized Russia as well as pathologized it.

Yet in the 2010s, many Russians refused to think that their country's economic and social system was normal at all. Some of them, understandably enough, could never come to terms with what had happened during the 1990s, which to them seemed like the theft of their economy. A younger generation, some of them very young, usually indistinguishable in dress and manners from other Europeans of their age, expressed their frustration in public demonstrations or private tirades about corruption. For them, it was an undignified affront to normality that encroached on their own life chances. The purpose of this book is not to tell them what to think or to offer them solutions. Yet seeing Russia as a normal country allows us, from outside, to take seriously the incremental improvements that would not topple the government or foment a revolution: those plausible, specific policies aimed at reducing corruption (targeting an individual government agency), increasing local accountability (more competitive elections in selected districts), and improving regional development (including innovation zones), none of which is beyond the realm of possibility.

## 4 Remember that Russia is the biggest country in Europe

Russia is the biggest country in the world: this makes it exceptional. But it is also the biggest country in Europe, which makes it seem more normal.

If we were more modest about the master-narratives of European history, we might find a common European home in the future. This might be one in which Britain as well as Russia feels comfortable. The leading figures in the Brexit referendum of June 2016 did not exactly debate Britain's European identity with the elegance of

Russia's Slavophiles and Westerners two centuries earlier. But the separately minded in both cases had something in common: the sense of a country that was in Europe but not really of it. Even today, many British people talk about 'the continent' as if it is not their continent. British university courses in European history traditionally include Russia but exclude Britain. Yet European institutions are less European for their failure to incorporate the United Kingdom and the Russian Federation. In one sense, British and Russian people have chosen this outcome; in another, there are very many elements of chance in both the circumstances of post-Soviet politics and the outcome of Brexit. It's too easy to put this down to ignorance, chauvinism or an imagined dead weight of the past.

For Russians in the 1990s, it seemed that their country had fallen off the edge of Europe: that it was irrelevant, not respected, a troubled, poor relation who was better off kept at arm's length, behind, for example, punishingly tough visa regimes. Vladimir Putin offered a convincing counter-narrative that responded to the crisis of the 1990s. But there was no obvious path from NATO's bombing of Belgrade to Russia's annexation of Crimea. Multiple futures remained open: collaboration with NATO in the early 2000s, a combined anti-terrorism policy, close personal relations with Western leaders, not least Tony Blair and George W. Bush, but more controversially with Silviano Berlusconi and Gerhard Schroeder. The logic of these alternative futures was closed off in the first instance by the invasion of Iraq in 2003, during which the American and British governments disregarded Russia's interests. With Western troops in Central Asia and Kurdistan – not to mention the Middle East and the Gulf region – it was impossible for Russians not to feel that the West had its own standards of hypocrisy when it came to threatening or invading foreign countries. For many Russians, NATO's encouragement of Georgia to seek membership, or the support of the State Department for Ukraine to look towards the European Union, were part of the same wilfully robust disregard of what they thought of as Russian interests. From 2014, the conflict in Ukraine and the dangerous deterioration in relations with the United States was at least partly explicable in the context of the history of the 1990s. Although the crisis was also caused by internal Russian and Ukrainian politics, another explanation – that Russia was reverting to its natural instinct for regional violence and world domination – had little credibility.

For all their talk of 'the West' as another place, most Russians, therefore, probably see themselves as Europeans – bruised and unwelcome, second-class, but Europeans nonetheless. Even though other identities are possible, none has ever been wholeheartedly pursued. But the less welcome Russians feel – the more Europe designs itself in distinction to Russia, and also to Britain and Turkey – the greater the chance that they will seek out the other identities that might allow them to feel like first-class human beings: great Russian nationalism, Eurasianism. The effect of this on international politics is unclear, though one possibility is closer ties with China. But the European future remains the most likely one; relations can, after all, change as quickly as leaders wish them so to do. Russia's relationship to the West is defined by variety and inconsistency, by fits and starts. History suggests not only that Europe works best and is safest when Russia is one of its main players, but that this option remains open in the future.

## 5 Don't fall for the claim that Russia is an historic foe

Every century between the twelfth and nineteenth saw a war between England (later, Britain) and France. The Hundred Years' War stretched from 1337 to 1453. Given this long history of conflict and the popular attitudes that endured after it ended, it seems improbable that Britain and France should later become allies, let alone close ones, but events and circumstances made this happen.

A millennium of Anglo-French encounters clarifies the Russia Anxiety in two ways: it reminds us to ask what we are afraid of, and how quickly international relationships change. Russia has no more a violent history of relations with its neighbours than either Britain or France, especially if we make a distinction between international warfare and imperial expansion. And anything can happen in international affairs, even 200 years of peace between Britain and France.[30] Compared with Franco-British enmity, Russia is not an historic foe.

Despite its violent incursions into Budapest (1956), Prague (1968), Georgia (2008) and Ukraine (2014–), Russia has only once been at war with another European country since 1856 – with the Ottoman Empire in 1877–8 – apart from during the world wars and the Civil War. Russia has often been the crucial ally, not only on the famous occasions: take the foolhardy Anglo-Russian invasion of Holland in 1799. Most important and easily forgotten of all, Russia has never been to war with the United States, despite American intervention in the Russian Civil War and some Cold War skirmishing. Many of its medieval and early-modern wars were conflicts over borders and resources, just as was the case for other European states, while it behaved like a 'normal' great power in the European system from the time of Peter the Great. In many ways the most important wars to afflict the Russian lands were invasions from outside, by the Mongols in 1240, the Swedes in 1708, the French in 1812 and the Germans in 1941. In other words, Russia does not seem unusually prone to war. It is not an historic enemy.

Why, then, can people think of Russia as an enduring adversary, reverting to type? Perhaps there are two main reasons. One of these is the Russian Empire, with its capacity for inexorable expansion over centuries, and the other is the Cold War, when the Soviet Union effectively took ultimate control of East Germany, Poland, Hungary, Czechoslovakia, Bulgaria and Romania, and ensured that they were governed by socialist dictatorships. The fact that Russia is the biggest country in the world and retains some of its old imperial borders is a standing reminder of its expansionist past. Britain is different: the contrast between its lost global empire and today's United Kingdom is so out-of-scale that its unrestrained imperialism, though recent, seems merely a quaint fragment of history. For all its size, the Russian Empire was part of the international standard, and the translation of a significant part of it into a nation state, today's Russian Federation, is evidence for the long-term accommodations and 'management of difference' that underwrote parts of the Russian imperial project. Meanwhile, the creation of the socialist dictatorships and the forceful insistence that they remain tied to Moscow, exemplified in the crushing of the Hungarian uprising of 1956, was never in the long-term interests of the Soviet Union, or even part of its characteristic behaviour.

The emergence of the Eastern bloc in the form of socialist dictator-ships whose institutions were analogous to those of the Soviet Union was contingent on events; the Cold War could easily have taken a different form. In the 1940s and 1950s, this way of solving the 'Ger-man question' was controversial even in the Kremlin. *Perestroika* was partly driven by an acknowledgement of the counterproductiveness of this strategy, as well as its moral failings. Yet the Russia Anxiety sees the Iron Curtain and the Eastern bloc as the fundamental reality of Soviet power, rather than as a malfunction of international polit-ics; in 1945, it was probably still possible for the superpowers to have created a less militarized Europe, even one with neutral zones, that would more economically and less dangerously have protected the interests of both the USA and the USSR. Meanwhile, the member-ship of the former 'People's Democracies' in NATO, and the influence of their governments on NATO policy, ensures that this perception of Russian interests remains live. At its riskiest, this gives new life to the security architecture of the Cold War, tipped by nuclear weapons. However understandable this is, the danger is that it perpetuates the past, and becomes a self-fulfilling prophecy of mass destruction.

## 6 Remember your own history

At its most fundamental, the Russia Anxiety interprets Russia in iso-lation. The country's past and present are absolute quantities, not open to comparison. (The more extreme point is that Russia is bad on its own terms, and failing to accept this merely relativizes evil.) Pro-ponents of the Anxiety are quick to call out 'whataboutism', the rhetorical device whereby one responds to a charge by asking's one's interlocutor: but what about what you did? Yet the willingness to look at one's own history as a point of comparison not only enriches understanding of the Russian past, but also makes it much more dif-ficult to succumb to the Anxiety.

In the 1990s, messianism seemed absurd unless it was that of the Washington Consensus, whose central text was Fukuyama's *End of History*. But there was a counter-narrative to Fukuyama's. In 1998, the historian Mark Mazower published *Dark Continent*, a history of twentieth-century Europe. The clue to Mazower's argument lay in his title. When people talk of the 'dark continent', the world assumes that they mean Africa. But this was a book about Europe. Mazower wanted to show that the destruction that the British, French, Belgian, German and Italian Empires wrought on Africa in the nineteenth and twentieth centuries was transferred to Europe itself in the 1930s and 1940s. The technologies of the concentration camp, the targeting of civilians during war, the elimination of opposing groups, the purification of populations on the basis of ethnic identity, the exploitation of labour and the insistence that local investment came at the cost of the local population, the attempt to extract resources and profits, the opening-up of zones for settlement by colonists – these were the practices that were imported to 'Hitler's Empire'. This was a crucial part of what it meant to be European, not less than Magna Carta, Kant or the Rights of Man. If Europe's twentieth century was a contest between the three ideologies of the time, liberal democracy, fascism and communism, the ultimate triumph of liberal democracy was contingent on events and quite possibly temporary. After all, existing democracies had been eliminated in places such as Germany and Spain in the 1930s, while the democratization programme that followed 1945 depended for its success on American intervention, not indigenous instincts and traditions.

Mazower's book remains a must-read for students of twentieth-century European history. But it is also of its time, a primary source as well as a secondary source. Standing alongside *The End of History*, it helps us to recover the dynamics and assumptions of the transition period, and the various futures that were then self-consciously open.

Reading European history in a way that acknowledges contingency and comparison – taking up the burden of Mazower rather than Fukuyama – makes it much easier to find a comprehensible place for Russia and the Soviet Union in the story; the assumption of inevitable democratic triumph paints Russia as an outlier. By abandoning the narratives of darkness to light, which are based on the idea that the future should take a particular form, and if Russia does not take that form, it must be a bad learner, we can write a history of Europe in which Russia is a normal part. And the willingness to make comparisons places Russian experiences in a common framework with the rest of Europe, clarifying them, showing that they are usually in line with wider expectations. This takes the heat out of the Russia Anxiety. Reading history in more complex and sophisticated ways, abandoning the fairy tales of self-congratulation, makes Europe safer.

The world of Sophia Kovalevskaya (*née* Korvin-Krukovskaya), one of Russia's great mathematicians, was not dissimilar from that of Ivan Turgenev, whom we met in some of the earlier chapters of this book. Like him, Kovalevskaya offers readers a certain view of the Russia Anxiety, and she allows me to make a final point about it.

She was born in Moscow in 1850. Her father was a lieutenant general in the Russian Army. She spent her childhood in St Petersburg and especially at the family estate at Polibino, which belonged to her father's family. As a child in the 1860s, her world, like that of Turgenev, offered multiple trajectories into the future. The nostalgic scenes she describes in her autobiography don't suggest an impending revolution. 'The coachman lit a campfire in the clearing where the unharnessed horses were grazing. A lackey ran to the nearby stream to fill the carafes with water. The maids spread a tablecloth on the grass, started the samovar going,' she writes, describing how the 'masters' and the servants then sat apart from each other as the picnic got under way. 'But this division lasted no more than the first fifteen minutes,' she went on. 'Today was such a special day that class divisions seemed not to exist. Everyone was possessed by the same all-consuming interest: mushrooms.'[31] Hunting for mushrooms in the forest, however enjoyable it can be, is a cliché of Russian life and culture. As we look back, Kovalevskaya's childhood seems to be a sequence of familiar pictures, though ones that never prefigure what would happen next.

As she grew up, she developed a passion for mathematics, first of all geometry and analytical arithmetic. Her family estate, for all its Russian qualities, was an outward-looking place. Her father was marshal of the nobility for the province where they lived, Vitebsk, and her mother, whose maiden name was Schubert, derived from a family of Russian-Germans. Later, when Sophia was still a teenager, her sister got involved with Dostoevsky. One way and another, on the country estate, Sophia was confronted with radical ideas, just as her encounter intensified with higher mathematics.

Russia is famous for its achievements in mathematics, in a tradition that dates back long into the tsarist period. Leonty Magnitsky, for instance, was a favourite of Peter the Great. Together with colleagues from Germany and France, Russian mathematicians criss-crossed Europe in the nineteenth century in the name of scholarly advances. During Soviet times, mathematics was privileged in schools and universities, with its leading practitioners also making major strides in economics and physics. After the end of the Cold War, mathematics departments in Western universities came to depend on Russian mathematical talent, and global banks filled up with Russian computer programmers.

In the nineteenth century, women could study but not be awarded a degree at a Russian university. Committed to the world of mathematics more than to the world of the Russian provinces – or perhaps finding a way of integrating them – she married and went to Heidelberg before she was twenty, enrolling in the university. But it was not that Russia was 'backward'; Oxford and Cambridge, for example, were not awarding degrees to women, and in many ways Russian women blazed the trail in Western Europe. Kovalevskaya and Yulya Lermontova were the first female students of any nationality at Heidelberg. It was a similar story at Zurich, where Nadezhda Suslova was the first woman to enrol on a degree course, and Russian women dominated the first female cohorts at several other leading universities.

Sophia completed her studies in mathematics in Germany and found herself in a Russian-style intelligentsia milieu. Despite her noble upbringing, this seemed a natural progression from the ideas, people and opportunities that had populated her childhood. As a Russian *intelligent* abroad, she became one of the great mathematicians of the century from a base as a professor at Stockholm University. She was the first woman professor of mathematics since the Italian Renaissance, and modern Europe's first female holder of a doctorate in the subject. Her work was recognized by prestigious awards from the Academies of Science in both France and Sweden.[32] She was the first female academician of the Russian Academy of Sciences. Mathematics was not a world in which the Russia Anxiety could thrive. It depended upon international exchanges of knowledge in which Russia was an indispensable part. Kovalevskaya served as editor of the major scholarly journal *Acta Mathematica*, and shuttled between meetings of scholars in Russia and Sweden, France and Germany. She had scholarly, cultural and personal connections across Europe.

Her interests extended across literature, too, in ways that also reflected Russia's crucial place in international developments. She had known Dostoevsky back in Russia. As a student abroad, she travelled to England and wrote to George Eliot, who invited her to tea at her house at St John's Wood in London, and a friendship began. Turgenev was a mutual friend.[33] Her encounters with Eliot opened her mind further about what women could achieve. Kovalevskaya kept an eye on radical politics, too, and visited the Paris Commune. Her mathematical brilliance was only part of a capacious worldview, defined by a sense of possibility and also a certain caution. 'I would be ecstatic to open up a career for women,' she wrote in a letter of June 1881. 'But, I repeat, I do not want to give of myself too much to these wonderful projects, which, probably, will meet the same fate as the majority of wonderful projects on this earth.'[34] She was prepared to look towards a better future and actively to bring it about, but the optimistic path she walked was hedged with pragmatism. Kovalevskaya had been a committed feminist since her youth in the Russian provinces, and her first encounters with the Russian radical movement. But she was no Bolshevik: her dreams about the future did not require the destruction of the past, or the refusal to acknowledge human nature. No wonder Russians remember her so fondly.

Sophia Kovalevskaya is a reproach to the Russia Anxiety. Her life reminds us of the themes that have run through this book. She was buffeted by events that were beyond her control, though she learned to make the best of them: contingent circumstances rather than deep unchanging historical structures were her first reality. The world of the Russian provinces in which she was raised was more 'democratic' than appearances suggested. Her encounter with the Russian state suggested to her its capacity for violence, but also that this capacity was limited and under control. All of her achievements were an example of Russians' periodic ability to bet on the future and occupy the vanguard of progress in Europe. In her own career and personal relationships she actively reminded 'the West' that it was stronger when Russia was a part of it – although it could not make sense to say that

Russia would ever be only of the West. In fact, she simultaneously occupied the worlds of both Russia and Europe before the First World War precisely because they were the same place. Her ambitions and mentality grew out of the past of the whole continent, and were focused on its future, especially her hopes about the role and status of women. She reminds us that the Russian past opens up many possible futures. Some of these are bright. But others are catastrophically lethal on a global scale.

A bright future is perhaps more likely for us all if we are pragmatic and reflective in the way we work with Russia, recognizing that its vices have usually been the same as ours, and its virtues, like ours, are its own. History offers one of the keys to this future, because the Russia Anxiety cannot dominate international politics when people study the Russian past in a critical and open-minded way. For sure, it is a cyclical syndrome, and it might always rise and fall. But it is only when the cycle is broken and the Anxiety is gone that Europe will have a chance of being at peace with itself.

# Acknowledgements

This is a personal book, but I have relied on the support of colleagues while I have been writing it. Lawrence Klein and Tim Harper, successive Chairs of the Faculty of History at the University of Cambridge, were quick to help me in practical ways when I needed it, and John Arnold and Gareth Austin did the same at King's College. Christopher Clark, Marcus Colla and Geoffrey Hosking between them read all of the manuscript in one stage or another of its development, and provided extensive, acute and inspiring feedback.

This book could not have seen the light of day without Andrew Gordon of David Higham Associates, who arranged publication and provided essential comments on the manuscript, as well as Simon Winder of Penguin Books, whose editorial work on the big picture and the small detail was always brilliant. I am grateful too to David Watson for his meticulous copyediting. In New York, Wendy Strothman arranged for the publication of a US edition, and Tim Bent of Oxford University Press provided an American perspective on the manuscript. I would like to thank all the agency and publishing teams in London and New York whose ingenuity and hard work created the book. All of these people made the book much better, and its faults are the result of my stubborn refusal to follow wise advice.

More personally, I still owe the deepest of debts to my parents, which only increased during my work on this book. I am grateful too for the insights and help of my mother-in-law.

I dedicate *The Russia Anxiety* to two people who inhabit Russia and 'the West' as a single, uninterrupted space, in good times and bad: my daughter Sonia, who inspires me to start writing, and my wife Laura, who inspires me to keep going.

# Notes

*Note on Russian words, names and transliteration*: In the main text of the book, I have transliterated Russian from the Cyrillic alphabet in the way that I think is most accessible to English-language readers for any given word, name or phrase, facilitating readability and pronunciation. I have avoided a fixed system, taking every case on its own terms. Russianists (and perhaps Russians) will spot occasional inconsistent or unconventional forms, which are the result of my own judgement and not editorial error. The Library of Congress transliteration system commonly used by Anglophone Russia experts is followed in the Notes, though I present the titles of cited works and quotations from them in the forms adopted by their authors.

## INTRODUCTION TO PART I:
### FEAR, CONTEMPT AND DISREGARD

1 Colin Thubron, *Among the Russians*, London: Penguin, 1985, 1; Lady Verney, *How the Peasant Owner Lives in Parts of France, Germany, Italy, Russia*, London and New York: Macmillan, 1888, 110; Joe Biden, 23 January 2018 at Council for Foreign Relations, Washington, DC: https://www.apnews.com/4414f999aca94d228228c6e9f20d3762, accessed 27 November 2018; Evgenia Ginzburg, *Into the Whirlwind*, London: Harvill, 1999, 90; Alexander Werth, *Moscow '41*, London: Hamish Hamilton, 1942, 268.

## 1. THE BEAR PHANTASMAGORIA

1 Marquis de Custine, *Letters from Russia*, trans. and ed. Robin Buss, London: Penguin, 1991, 144.

2 *The Economist*, 30 December 1848, 1468; 10 September 2011, 29; 15 February 2014, 28.

3 Christopher Clark, *The Sleepwalkers: How Europe Went to War in 1914*, London: Penguin, 2013, 421.

4 Olga Oliker, interviewed in Keith Gessen, 'The Quiet Americans Behind the US-Russia Imbroglio', *The New York Times Magazine*, 8 May 2018.

5 See video of 21 September 2017: https://www.realclearpolitics.com/video/2017/09/21/morgan_freeman_we_are_at_war_with_russia.html? D, accessed 27 November 2018.

6 Franklin Foer, 'Putin's Puppet', *Slate*: http://www.slate.com/articles/news_and_politics/cover_story/2016/07/vladimir_putin_has_a_plan_for_destroying_the_west_and_it_looks_a_lot_like.html, accessed 27 November 2018.

7 Steele ('Trump-Russia') dossier, Company Intelligence Report of 20 June 2016.

8 Office of the Director of National Intelligence, 'Background to "Assessing Russian Activities and Intentions in Recent US Elections": The Analytical Process and Cyber Incident Attribution', 6 January 2017, ii: https://www.dni.gov/files/documents/ICA_2017_01.pdf, accessed 27 November 2018.

9 Hillary Rodham Clinton, *What Happened*, New York and London: Simon and Schuster, 2017, 325–6.

10 Sean Guillory, 'A Genealogy of American Russophobia', *InRussia*, 2017: http://inrussia.com/a-genealogy-of-american-russophobia, accessed 27 November 2018.

11 Company Intelligence Report 2016/100, 5 August 2016: 'Russia / USA: Growing Backlash in Kremlin'.

12 http://www.bbc.co.uk/news/uk-42828218?intlink_from_url=http://www.bbc.co.uk/news/topics/cwlw3xzo1e5t/gavin-williamson&link_location=live-reporting-story, accessed 27 November 2018.

13 Dzhul'etto K'eza [Giulietto Chiesa], *Rusofobiia 2.0: bolezn' ili oruzhie zapada?*, Moscow: 'E', 2016, e.g. 39.

14 This is the basic argument of Guy Mettan, *Russie-Occident, une guerre de mille ans: La Russophobie de Charlemagne à la crise ukrainienne*, Paris: Editions des Syrtes, 2015.

15 Sigismund von Herberstein, *Notes upon Russia: Being a Translation of the Earliest Account of that Country, Entitled Rerum Moscoviticarum Commentarii*, London: Hakluyt Society, 1851 [first published 1549], 94–5.

16 Marshall T. Poe, *'A People Born to Slavery': Russia in Early Modern European Ethnography, 1476–1748*, Ithaca, NY, and London: Cornell University Press, 2000, 32.

17  Giles Fletcher, *Of the Russe Commonwealth*, London: Thomas Charde, 1591, dedicatory epistle.

18  See, e.g., Nancy Shields Kollmann, *Crime and Punishment in Early Modern Russia*, Cambridge: Cambridge University Press, 2012; Daniel H. Kaiser, *The Growth of the Law in Medieval Russia*, Princeton, NJ: Princeton University Press, 1980, Jarno T. Kotilaine, 'Mercantilism in Pre-Petrine Russia', in Kotilaine and Marshall Poe (eds.), *Modernizing Muscovy: Reform and Social Change in Seventeenth-Century Russia*, London: RoutledgeCurzon, 2004, 143–74.

19  As quoted in M. S. Anderson, *Britain's Discovery of Russia, 1553–1815*, London: Macmillan, 1958, 112.

20  Anthony Cross, *By the Banks of the Neva: Chapters from the Lives and Careers of the British in Eighteenth-Century Russia*, Cambridge: Cambridge University Press, 1997, chs. 3, 8 (quotation on 390).

21  P. P. Cherkasov, *Dvuglavyi orel i korolevskie lilii: Stanovlenie russko-frantsuzskikh otnoshenii v XVIII veke 1700–1775*, Moscow: Nauka, 1995.

22  Albert Resis, 'Russophobia and the "Testament" of Peter the Great, 1812–1980', *Slavic Review* 44:4 (1985): 681–93.

23  David Kunzle, 'Gustave Doré's History of Holy Russia: Anti-Russian Propaganda from the Crimean War to the Cold War', *Russian Review* 42:3 (1983): 271–99 (see esp. 295).

24  Raymond T. McNally, 'The Origins of Russophobia in France: 1812–1830', *American Slavic and East European Review* 17:2 (April 1958): 173–89.

25  Orlando Figes, *Crimea: The Last Crusade*, London: Penguin, 2011, 73–4, 78.

26  Barbara Jelavich, 'British Means of Offence against Russia in the Nineteenth Century', *Russian History* 1:2 (1974): 119–35 (124).

27  Simon Dixon, 'Allegiance and Betrayal: British Residents in Russia during the Crimean War', *Slavonic and East European Review* 94:3 (2016): 431–67.

28  Malcolm Yapp, 'The Legend of the Great Game', *Proceedings of the British Academy* 111 (2001): 179–98.

29  Alexander Morrison, 'Beyond the "Great Game": The Russian Origins of the Second Anglo-Afghan War', *Modern Asian Studies* 51:3 (2017): 686–735.

30  Evgeny Sergeev, *The Great Game 1856–1907: Russo-British Relations in Central and East Asia*, Baltimore, MD: Johns Hopkins University Press, 2013.

31  Troy R. E. Paddock, 'Still Stuck at Sevastopol: The Depiction of Russia during the Russo-Japanese War and the Beginning of the First World War in the German Press', *German History* 16:3 (1998): 358–76 (366); see also Paddock, *Creating the Russian Peril: Education, the Public Sphere, and National Identity in Imperial Germany, 1890–1914*, Rochester, NY: Camden House, 2010.

32  Alexander Watson, *Ring of Steel: Germany and Austria-Hungary at War, 1914–1918*, London: Penguin, 2015.

33  Sean Guillory, 'A Genealogy of Russophobia in America', talk at Kennan Institute, Washington, DC, 11 April 2017 (audio recording at Sean's Russia Blog).

34  In this paragraph I draw on Natal'ia Ten, *Ot Pushkina do Putina: Obraz Rossii v sovremennom Kitae, 1991–2010gg*, Moscow: Novoe literaturnoe obozrenie, 2016, passim and esp. 266–70.

35  Elizabeth McGuire, *Red at Heart: How Chinese Communists Fell in Love with the Russian Revolution*, New York: Oxford University Press, 2017.

36  Tom Røseth, 'Moscow's Response to a Rising China: Russia's Partnership Policies in Its Military Relations with Beijing', *Problems of Post-Communism*, 2018.

37  Constantin Katsakioris, 'Burden or Allies? Third World Students and Internationalist Duty through Soviet Eyes', *Kritika: Explorations in European History* 18:3 (2017): 539–67 (541).

38  E. N. Korendriasov, 'Obshchee i osobennoe v formirovanii obraza Rossii v Afrike', in T. L. Deich and Korendriasov (eds.), *Rossiisko-Afrikanskoe otnosheniia i obraz Rossii v Afrike: Sbornik statei*, Moscow: RAN Institut Afriki, 2007, 10–20.

39  I. A. Mal'kovskaia (ed.), *Rossiia – Braziliia: Transkul'turnye dialogi*, Moscow: URSS, 2012.

40  Katsakioris, 'Burden or Allies?', 541.

41  Ekaterina Kosevich, 'Neset li Rossiia ugrozu budushchemu Meksiku', *Nezavisimaia gazeta*, 15 March 2018, 3.

42  Kelly was speaking to a US Senate committee: Reuters.com, 6 April 2017.

43  Tony Wilson, 'Russophobia and New Zealand–Russian Relations, 1900s to 1939', *New Zealand Slavonic Journal*, 1999: 273–96 (esp. 277, 287–9, 292).

44  Anatole Lieven, 'Against Russophobia', *World Policy Journal* 17:4 (Winter 2000–2001): 25–32 (26).

45  Andrei P. Tsygankov, *Russophobia: Anti-Russian Lobby and American Foreign Policy*, New York: Palgrave Macmillan, 2009, 166.

46 Mircea Platon, 'Astolphe de Custine's Letters from Russia and the Defence of the West: Patterns of Prejudice from Henri Massis to Walter Bedell Smith', *Russian History* 43 (2016): 142–80.

47 For biographical details, I have relied on Anka Muhlstein, *A Taste for Freedom: The Life of Astolphe de Custine*, trans. Teresa Waugh, New York: Helen Marx, 1999.

48 Muhlstein, *A Taste for Freedom*, 344–5.

49 Custine, *Letters from Russia*, 133, 72, 102.

50 Custine, *Letters from Russia*, 233.

51 Geoffrey Hosking, *Russia: People and Empire 1552–1917*, London: Fontana, 1998.

52 Lawrence Freedman, *The Future of War: A History*, New York: Public Affairs, 2017, ch. 20; also Freedman, 'Stop Overestimating the Threat Posed by Russia's "New" Form of Warfare', *World Economic Forum*, 4 January 2017: https://www.weforum.org/agenda/2017/01/stop-over estimating-the-threat-posed-by-russia-s-new-form-of-warfare/, accessed 27 November 2018.

53 For more on this, see Masha Gessen, *The Man Without a Face: The Unlikely Rise of Vladimir Putin*, London: Granta, 2012, 179–80, though I cite line 11 of the 1944 and 1977 anthems and line 7 of the 1977 and 2001 anthems for stricter comparability.

54 N. M. Karamzin, *A Memoir on Ancient and Modern Russia*, trans. Richard Pipes, New York: Atheneum, 1966, 103.

55 Muhlstein, *A Taste for Freedom*, 347.

56 Vladimir Medinsky, *Mify o Rossii*, 3 vols., Moscow: Olma, 2016 (first published 2011), vol. I, 36, 54–5, 59–60. The books were associated with a TV series.

57 Igor Prokopenko, *Zlye mify o Rossii; chto o nas govoriat na zapade?*, Moscow: 'E', 2016, 7–8. The book is based on the TV series *Military Secrets*.

58 Raymond T. McNally (ed.), *The Major Works of Peter Chaadaev*, South Bend, IN: University of Notre Dame Press, 1969, 37.

59 Custine, *Letters from Russia*, 236.

60 George F. Kennan, *The Marquis de Custine and His Russia in 1839*, London: Hutchinson, 1972, 39–41.

61 Although she does not mention Radishchev directly, this general argument is made by Irena Grudzinska Gross, 'The Tangled Tradition: Custine, Herberstein, Karamzin, and the Critique of Russia', *Slavic Review* 50:4 (1991): 989–98.

62  Aleksandr Nikolaevich Radishchev, *A Journey from St Petersburg to Moscow*, trans. Leo Weiner, ed. Roderick Page Thaler, Cambridge, MA: Harvard University Press, 1958, 43.

63  Yuri Olesha, *Envy*, trans. Marian Schwartz, New York: New York Review of Books, 2004, 27.

64  Vladimir Sorokin, *The Queue*, trans. Sally Laird, New York: New York Review of Books, 2008, 73.

65  Oleg Gordievsky, *Next Stop Execution*, London: Macmillan, 1985, 197.

66  George F. Kennan, *Memoirs, 1925–1950*, Boston: Little, Brown, 1967, 189.

67  George F. Kennan, *Memoirs, 1950–1963*, London: Hutchinson, 1973, 155.

68  John Lewis Gaddis, *George F. Kennan: An American Life*, New York: Penguin Press, 695.

69  Kennan, *Memoirs 1925–1950*, 68.

70  Kennan, *Memoirs 1925–1950*, 57.

71  Kennan, *Memoirs 1925–1950*, 54.

72  The Long Telegram: Woodrow Wilson Center Digital Archive, digital archive.wilsoncenter.org.

73  Kennan, *Memoirs 1950–1963*, 135–7.

74  Kennan, *Memoirs 1950–1963*, 90–92 (quotation on 92).

75  Kennan, *Memoirs 1950–1963*, 40–43, 49–51.

76  Kennan, *Memoirs 1925–1950*, 53.

77  George F. Kennan, 'Containment: 40 Years Later', *Foreign Affairs*, spring 1987.

78  George F. Kennan, *Around the Cragged Hill: A Personal and Political Philosophy*, New York and London: W. W. Norton, 1993, 182–3.

79  Kennan, *Around the Cragged Hill*, 198.

80  Kenann, *Around the Cragged Hill*, 210.

81  Stephen F. Cohen, *Failed Crusade: America and the Tragedy of Post-Communist Russia*, New York and London: W. W. Norton, 2000.

82  A position identified and critiqued by Iver B. Neumann, 'Russia as Europe's Other', *Journal of Area Studies* 6:12 (1989): 26–73 (29–30).

83  George F. Kennan, 'The New Russia as a Neighbor', in Kennan, *At a Century's Ending: Reflections, 1982–1995*, New York and London: W. W. Norton, 1996, 320–21, 330, 333.

84  Kennan, *The Marquis de Custine*, 122–3.

85  Kennan, *The Marquis de Custine*, 124–33.

86  David S. Foglesong, 'The Perils of Prophecy: American Predictions about Russia's Future since 1881', in *Rossiia i SShA: poznavaia drug druga: Sbornik pamiati akademika Aleksandra Aleksanrovicha Fursenko*, St Petersburg: Rossiiskaia Akademiia nauk Sankt-Peterburgskii Institut

istorii RAN, 2015. For a sparkling overview of US expertise on Russia, see David C. Engerman, *Know Your Enemy: The Rise and Fall of America's Soviet Experts*, New York: Oxford University Press, 2009.

## 2. THE DESTINY PROBLEM

1 This account draws on Jonathan Shepard, 'The Origins of Rus' (*c.*900–1015)', in Maureen Perrie (ed.), *The Cambridge History of Russia*, vol. 1 of 3: *From Early Rus' to 1689*, 47–72, and Janet Martin, *Medieval Russia 980–1584*, Cambridge: Cambridge University Press, 1995, ch. 1.

2 As recounted in *Novaia Gazeta*, 4 November 2016.

3 Serhii Plokhy disentangles the symbolism a little differently in *Lost Kingdom: A History of Russian Nationalism from Ivan the Great to Vladimir Putin*, London: Allen Lane, 2017, vii–viii.

4 Exchange on Twitter, 11–12 August 2016: Josh Marshall (127,000 followers) and Gerard di Trolio (1,148). Numbers correct on 14 August 2016.

5 The term 'black legend' has been influential in Spanish historiography to denote a similar issue. See, e.g., J. N. Hillgarth, 'Spanish Historiography and Iberian Reality', *History and Theory* 24:1 (1985): 23–43.

6 Richard Stengel, 'Choosing Order Before Freedom', *Time Magazine* 19 December 2007.

7 Tibor Szamuely, *The Russian Tradition*, London: Secker and Warburg, 1974, 9. The well-known quotation is also used by Stefan Hedlund as the epigraph of his book *Russian Path Dependence*, Abingdon: Routledge, 2005, as he seeks to make a similar point.

8 The Russian *longue durée* historiographical canon was formed by the nineteenth-century historians Nikolai Karamzin, Sergei Solov'ev and Vasily Klyuchevsky. Anglophone scholars with an eye for structure who have written long-range Russian histories are led by Richard Pipes, *Russia under the Old Regime*, London: Penguin, 1974; Geoffrey Hosking, *Russia and the Russians: From Earliest Times to 2001*, London: Penguin, 2001; Nicholas V. Riasanovsky, *A History of Russia*, New York: Oxford University Press, 1963; George Vernadsky, *A History of Russia*, New Haven, CT: Yale University Press, 1943–69. Less conventional long-range structural accounts include Boris Akunin, *Istoriia Rossiiskogo gosudarstva*, Moscow: AST, 2013–, 6 vols. and ongoing, and L. N. Gumilev, *Ot Rusi k Rossii*, Moscow: Progress-Pangeiia, 1992. Historians who have shown at less length how one variable has over time shaped the Russian past include Arch Getty, *Practicing Stalinism: Bolsheviks, Boyars, and the Persistence of Tradition*,

New Haven, CT: Yale University Press, 2013; Alexander Etkind, *Internal Colonization: Russia's Imperial Experience*, Cambridge: Polity, 2011; L. V. Milov, *Velikorusskii pakhar i osobennosti rossiiskogo istoricheskogo protsessa*, Moscow, 1998; B. N. Mironov, *Sotsial'naia istoriia Rossii perioda imperii (XVIII–nachalo XX vv.)*, 2 vols, St Petersburg: Dmitrii Bulanin, 1999. The scholarly polemics most influential among students and an earlier generation of policymakers are Edward L. Keenan, 'Muscovite Political Folkways', *Russian Review* 45:2 (1986): 115–81; and Richard Hellie, 'The Structure of Russian History: Toward a Dynamic Model', *Russian History* 4:1 (1977): 1–22. Historians who have balanced the long range with a focus on individuals as agents of change include Orlando Figes, *Natasha's Dance: A Cultural History of Russia*, London: Allen Lane, 2002; Catherine Merridale, *Red Fortress: The Secret Heart of Russia's History*, London: Allen Lane, 2013; Simon Sebag Montefiore, *The Romanovs: 1618–1918*, London: Weidenfeld and Nicolson, 2016. An overall interpretation of Russian history that takes a different view from mine but which also emphasizes contingency is Marshall T. Poe, *The Russian Moment in World History*, Princeton, NJ: Princeton University Press, 2003.

9  Ivan Turgenev, 'Khor and Kalinych', in *Sketches from a Hunter's Album*, trans. Richard Freeborn, London: Penguin, 1990, 25.

10  Richard Hellie, *Slavery in Russia 1450–1725*, Chicago: University of Chicago Press, 1982.

11  Richard Hellie, 'The Peasantry', in Perrie (ed.), *The Cambridge History of Russia*, vol. 1, 286–97 (esp. 294–7).

12  Richard Hellie, 'The Economy, Trade and Serfdom', in Perrie (ed.), *The Cambridge History of Russia*, vol. 1, 539–58 (551–7).

13  George L. Yaney, *The Systematization of Russian Government: Social Evolution in the Domestic Administration of Imperial Russia, 1711–1905*, Urbana, IL: University of Illinois Press, 1973, 129–35.

14  Richard Stites, *Serfdom, Society and the Arts in Imperial Russia: The Pleasure and the Power*, New Haven, CT: Yale University Press, 2005.

15  Tracy Dennison, *The Institutional Framework of Russian Serfdom*, Cambridge: Cambridge University Press, 2011.

16  See the account in James H. Billington, *The Icon and the Axe: An Interpretive History of Russian Culture*, New York: Knopf, 1966, III.

17  Gregory Freeze, 'Church and Politics in Late Imperial Russia', in Anna Geifman (ed.), *Russia under the Last Tsar*, Oxford: Blackwell, 1999, 269–97.

18  Simon Dixon, 'Orthodoxy and Revolution: The Restoration of the Russian Patriarchate in 1917', Prothero Lecture, Royal Historical Society

(read at University College London, 7 July 2017): https://royalhistsoc .org/prothero-lecture-2017/, accessed 27 November 2018.

19  Leonid Hertz, *Russia on the Eve of Modernity: Popular Religion and Traditional Culture under the Last Tsars*, Cambridge: Cambridge University Press, 2008, 22–6.

20  Tat'iana Nikolskaia, *Russkii protestantizm i gosudarstvennaia vlast' v 1905–1991 godakh*, St Petersburg: Evropeiskii universitet v Sankt Peterburge, 2009.

21  A. Shitov, *Iurii Trifonov: Khronika zhizni i tvorchestva 1925–1981gg*, Ekaterinburg: Izdatel'stvo Ural'skogo universiteta, 1997, 261–2 (March 1955).

22  Marc Raeff, *Origins of the Russian Intelligentsia: The Eighteenth-Century Nobility*, New York: Harcourt, 1966.

23  G. M. Hamburg, 'Russian Intelligentsias', in William Leatherbarrow and Derek Offord (eds.), *A History of Russian Thought*, Cambridge: Cambridge University Press, 2010, 44–69.

24  Dina R. Spechler, *Permitted Dissent in the USSR: Novy Mir and the Soviet Regime*, New York: Praeger, 1982.

25  Janet Martin, *Medieval Russia 980–1584*, Cambridge: Cambridge University Press, 1995, 139.

26  Stefan Hedlund, *Russian Path Dependence*, Abingdon: Routledge, 2005. On the Muscovy and Novgorod counterfactuals: 45–6, 66–7.

27  Valerie Kivelson, 'Muscovite "Citizenship": Rights without Freedom', *Journal of Modern History*, 74:3 (2002): 465–89.

28  Marie-Pierre Rey, *Alexander I: The Tsar Who Defeated Napoleon*, DeKalb, IL: Northern Illinois University Press, 2012, chs. 1 and 2.

29  Elise Kimerling Wirtschafter, *Russia's Age of Serfdom, 1649–1861*, Oxford: Blackwell, 2008, 104.

30  John Gooding, 'The Liberalism of Michael Speransky', *Slavonic and East European Review*, 64:3 (1986): 401–24.

31  Marc Raeff, *Understanding Imperial Russia: State and Society in the Old Regime*, trans. Arthur Goldhammer, New York: Columbia University Press, 1984, 115–19.

32  Marc Raeff, *The Well-Ordered Police State: Social and Institutional Change through Law in the Germanies and Russia, 1600–1800*, New Haven, CT: Yale University Press, 1983.

33  Marc Raeff, *Michael Speransky: Statesman of Imperial Russia, 1772–1839*, The Hague: Martinus Nijhoff, 1969 (2nd edn), 37–46.

34  Raeff, *Michael Speranksy*, 361–2.

35  Richard Pipes, *Karamzin's Memoir on Ancient and Modern Russia: A Translation and Analysis*, New York: Atheneum, 1966, 197.

36  Richard S. Wortman, *The Development of a Russian Legal Consciousness*, Chicago, IL: University of Chicago Press, 1976, ch. 2.

37  W. Bruce Lincoln, *In the Vanguard of Reform: Russia's Enlightened Bureaucrats, 1825–1861*, DeKalb, IL: Northern Illinois University Press, 1982.

38  Georgy Bovt, 'Putin Is Inspired by Russian Empire', *Moscow Times*, 25 November 2014: https://themoscowtimes.com/articles/putin-is-ins pired-by-russian-empire-41711, accessed 26 July 2016.

## 3. THE NARRATIVE CORRECTION

1  As this chapter selects from agreed-upon facts, I do not cite individual sources, but I rely most of all on the general works on Russian history that are cited elsewhere in this book, including the standard massive work A. N. Sakharov, et al., *Istoriia Rossii s drevneishiikh vremen do nashikh dnei*, Moscow: AST, 2018.

## INTRODUCTION TO PART II: NORMALITY, FRIENDSHIP AND LIBERTY?

1  Mikhail Gorbachev, *Perestroika*, 1987; from Catherine to Alexander Vyazemsky, leading adviser, on his appointment, as quoted in Simon Dixon, *Catherine the Great*, London: Profile, 2009, 134; Sally Belfrage, *A Room in Moscow*, London: Andre Deutsch, 1958, 189–90.

## 4. THE DICTATORSHIP DECEPTION

1  For a fuller account of the assassination, see W. Bruce Lincoln, *In War's Dark Shadow: The Russians before the Great War*, New York: Oxford University Press, 1983, 163–74.

2  Turgenev to P. V. Annenkov, 6–7 March 1881 (old style). I. S. Turgenev, *Polnoe sobranie sochenenii i pisem v dvadtsati vos'mi tomakh. Pis'ma*, vol. 13 of 13: *1880–1882*, Leningrad: Nauka, 1968, 72–3.

3  Turgenev, 'Alexander III', in *Polnoe sobranie sochinenii i pisem v 28-kh tomakh. Sochineniia*, vol. 14 of 15, 280.

4  Ivan Turgenev, *Virgin Soil*, trans. Ashton W. Dilke, London: Macmillan, 1878, 14, 84, 98–9.

5  Cited in Henri Troyat, *Turgenev*, London: W. H. Allen, 1989, 53.

6　Alison Smith, *For the Common Good and Their Own Wellbeing: Social Estates in Imperial Russia*, Oxford: Oxford University Press, 2014.

7　Peter Waldron, *Governing Tsarist Russia*, Basingstoke: Palgrave Macmillan, 2007, 108.

8　Catherine Evtuhov, *Portrait of a Russian Province: Economy, Society, and Civilization in Nineteenth-Century Nizhnii Novgorod*, Pittsburgh, PA: University of Pittsburgh Press, 2011, ch. 7.

9　Isabel de Madariaga, *Russia in the Age of Catherine the Great*, London: Phoenix, 2003, 299–304.

10　Simon Dixon, *Catherine the Great*, London: Profile, 2009, 173.

11　Simon Franklin, 'Kieven Rus' (1015–1125)', in Perrie (ed.), *The Cambridge History of Russia*, vol. 1, 73–97 (83).

12　V. L. Ianin, 'Medieval Novgorod', in Perrie (ed.), *The Cambridge History of Russia* , vol. 1, 188–210 (203).

13　Marshall Poe, 'The Central Government and Institutions', in Perrie (ed.), *The Cambridge History of Russia*, vol. 1, 435–63 (458–60).

14　Isabel de Madariaga, *Ivan the Terrible: First Tsar of Russia*, New Haven, CT: Yale University Press, 2005, ch. 12.

15　Almut Bues, 'The Formation of the Polish-Lithuanian Monarchy in the Sixteenth Century', in Richard Butterwick (ed.), *The Polish-Lithuanian Monarchy in European Context, c. 1500–1795*, Basingstoke: Palgrave, 2001, 58–81 (60, 69, 77).

16　Mariusz Markiewicz, 'The Functioning of the Monarchy during the Reigns of the Electors of Saxony, 1697–1763', in Butterwick (ed.), *The Polish-Lithuanian Monarchy*, 172–92 (173).

17　Donald Ostrowski, 'The Assembly of the Land (Zemskii Sobor) as a Representative Institution', in Jarno Kotilaine and Marshall Poe (eds.), *Modernizing Muscovy: Reform and Social Change in Seventeenth-Century Russia*, London: Routledge, 2004, 117–42 (135–42).

18　V. O. Klyuchevsky, *A Course in Russian History: The Seventeenth Century*, trans. Natalie Duddington, ed. Alfred J. Rieber, Chicago: Quadrangle, 1968, 71, 44, 91.

19　George Carson, *Electoral Practices in the USSR*, London: Atlantic, 1956, 2–3.

20　Victor Leontovitsch, *The History of Liberalism in Russia*, Pittsburgh, PA: University of Pennsylvania Press, 2012, 273–4 and 280.

21　Peter Vanneman, *The Supreme Soviet: Politics and the Legislative Process in the Soviet Political System*, Durham, NC: Duke University Press, 1977, 20.

22 Leontovitsch, *History of Liberalism*, 285.

23 Geoffrey Hosking, *The Russian Constitutional Experiment: Government and Duma 1907-1914*, Cambridge: Cambridge University Press, 1973.

24 Aleksandr Solzhenitsyn, *The Gulag Archipelago 1918-1956: An Experiment in Literary Investigation*, Parts I and II, New York: Harper and Row, 1973, 70.

25 Ivan Turgenev, *Fathers and Sons*, trans. Peter Carson, London: Penguin, 2009 (first published 1862), 81.

26 Cited in Isaiah Berlin, *Russian Thinkers*, London: Penguin, 1984, 287.

27 Robert Tombs, *France 1814-1914*, London and New York: Longman, 1996, 396-7.

28 Fedor H. Friedgut, *Political Participation in the USSR*, Princeton, NJ: Princeton University Press, 1979, 34-6.

29 Tombs, *France 1814-1914*, 429-31.

30 Robert Tombs, *The Paris Commune of 1871*, London and New York: Longman, 1999, 76-7.

31 Andy Willimott, *Living the Revolution: Urban Communes and Soviet Socialism, 1917-1932*, Oxford: Oxford University Press, 2017, 28, 42.

32 Tombs, *The Paris Commune*, 176, 199, 200-201.

33 Wendy Z. Goldman, *Terror and Democracy in the Age of Stalin: The Social Dynamics of Repression*, Cambridge: Cambridge University Press, 2007.

34 Goldman, *Terror and Democracy*, 146.

35 A. S. Kiselev et al. (eds.), *Moskva poslevoennaia 1945-1947gg: Arkhivnye dokumenty i materialy*, Moscow: Mosgorarkhiv, 2000, 103 (doc. 54).

36 E. S. Zubkova et al. (eds.), *Sovetskaia zhizn' 1945-1953gg*, Moscow: ROSSPEN, 2003, 406 (doc. 134).

37 Zubkova et al. (eds.), *Sovetskaia zhizn'*, 399 (doc. 131).

38 Kiselev (ed.), *Moskva poslevoennaia*, 104 (doc. 55).

39 Friedgut, *Political Participation in the USSR*, 72.

40 Carson, *Electoral Practices*, 93-5.

41 Anatoly Sobchak, *For a New Russia: The Mayor of St Petersburg's Own Story of the Struggle for Justice and Democracy*, London: HarperCollins, 1992, 5-19.

42 'Appeal to Leningraders' by the Public Committee of Voters 'Elections-89', end of March 1989: A. D. Margolis et al. (eds.), *Obshchestvennaia zhizn' Leningrada v gody perestroiki 1985-1991: Sbornik materialov*, St Petersburg: Serebrianyi vek, 2009, 148-50.

43 Geoffrey Hosking, *The Awakening of the Soviet Union*, Cambridge: MA: Harvard University Press, 1991.

44 Letter to editor, *Izvestiya*, 6 January 1989, reproduced in *Current Digest of the Soviet Press* (hereafter CDSP) 41 (1989): 3, 28.

45 Abel Aganbegyan, *Moving the Mountain: Inside the Perestroika Revolution*, London: Bantam, 1989, 174–5.

46 Robin Blackburn, 'Economic Democracy: Meaningful, Desirable, Feasible?', *Daedalus* (summer 2007): 36–45 (esp. 40–41).

47 For a thorough account, see David White, *The Russian Democratic Party Yabloko: Opposition in a Managed Democracy*, Aldershot: Ashgate, 2006.

48 Grigory Yavlinsky, 'An Uncertain Prognosis', *Journal of Democracy* 8:1 (1997): 3–11 (8–9).

49 As reported on the evening TV news, *Vremia*, Channel 1, 25 February 2018, 9 p.m.

50 Klyuchevsky, *Course of Russian History: The Seventeenth Century*, 41.

51 Leontovitsch, *History of Liberalism*, 38–9.

52 Marc Raeff, *Origins of the Russian Intelligentsia: The Eighteenth-Century Nobility*, New York: Harcourt, 1966.

53 Richard Stites, 'Decembrists with a Spanish Accent', *Kritika: Explorations in Russian and Eurasian History* 12:1 (2011): 5–23.

54 Michael Hamm, 'Liberal Policies in Wartime Russia: An Analysis of the Progressive Bloc', *Slavic Review* 33:3 (1974): 453–68 (456).

55 Paul Miliukov, *Russia and Its Crisis*, London: Collier, 1962, 403.

56 V. P. Litvinov-Falinskii, *Organizatsiia i praktika strakhovaniia rabochykh v Germanii i usloviia vozmozhnogo obespecheniia rabochikh v Rossii*, St Petersburg, 1903.

57 Baron Tizengauzen of labour commission in opening speech to Duma, 19 April 1911: *Gosudarstvennaia Duma stenograficheskii otchet 1911g, sessiia 4-aia*, ch. 3, zas. 74–113.

58 Francis W. Wcislo, *Tales of Imperial Russia: The Life and Times of Sergei Witte, 1849–1915*, Oxford: Oxford University Press, 2011, 104.

59 Konstantin P. Pobedonostsev, *Reflections of a Russian Statesman*, Ann Arbor, MI: University of Michigan Press, 1965, 26–35.

60 Richard Pipes, *Russian Conservatism and Its Critics: A Study in Political Culture*, New Haven, CT: Yale University Press, 2005.

61 William Leatherbarrow, 'Conservatism in the Age of Alexander I and Nicholas I', in William Leatherbarrow and Derek Offord (eds.), *A History of Russian Thought*, Cambridge: Cambridge University Press, 2010, 95–115 (esp. 98–102).

62 V. A. Gusev, *Russkii konservatizm: osnovnye napravleniia i etapy razvitiia*, Tver': Tverskoi gosudarstvennyi universitet, 2001, 153–4, 171, 175.

63  As revealed in the Wikileaks scandal: *Guardian*, 2 December 2010.

64  Evan Osnos, David Remnick and Joshua Yaffa, 'Active Measures', *New Yorker*, 6 March 2017; Michael Crowley, 'What Worries Ben Rhodes about Trump', *Politico Magazine*, January 2017.

65  See, e.g., *The Economist*, 31 January 2008.

66  John le Carré, *A Small Town in Germany*, London: Sceptre, 2006 (first published 1968), 328.

67  Stephen White, *Russia's New Politics: The Management of a Postcommunist Society*, Cambridge: Cambridge University Press, 2000, 273.

68  For an elaboration of these two defences of democracy, especially the first, see Amartya Sen, 'Democracy as a Universal Value', *Journal of Democracy* 10:3 (1999): 3–16.

69  David Daley, *Ratf**ked: The True Story Behind the Secret Plan to Steal America's Democracy*, New York: Liveright, 2016, xxi–xxii.

70  Ethan Scheiner, *Democracy Without Competition in Japan: Opposition Failure in a One-Party Dominant State*, Cambridge: Cambridge University Press, 2006, 211.

71  Justin Buckler, *Hiring and Firing Public Officials: Rethinking the Purpose of Elections*, Oxford: Oxford University Press, 2011, 226–7.

72  John Dunn, *Setting the People Free: The Story of Democracy*, London: Atlantic, 2005, 160–61.

73  The case for sortition is laid out in David Van Reybrouck, *Against Elections: The Case for Democracy*, London: Bodley Head, 2016.

74  David Runciman, *The Confidence Trap: A History of Democracy in Crisis from World War I to the Present*, Princeton, NJ: Princeton University Press, 2013, 324.

75  Arch Puddington and Tyler Roylance, 'The Dual Threat of Populists and Anarchists', *Journal of Democracy* 28:2 (2017): 105–19 (108–9).

## 5. THE TERROR MOMENT

1  Charles J. Halperin, 'Ivan IV's Insanity', *Russian History* 34:1–4 (2007): 207–18.

2  Charles J. Halperin, 'Did Ivan IV's Oprichniki Carry Dogs' Heads on Their Horses?', *Canadian–American Slavic Studies* 46 (2012): 40–67.

3  Descriptions of these events can be found in Isabel de Madariaga, *Ivan the Terrible: First Tsar of Russia*, New Haven and London: Yale University Press, 2005, 210–11, 245–7, 255–9.

4 Ronald Hingley, *The Russian Secret Police: Muscovite, Imperial Russian and Soviet Political Security Operations 1565–1970*, London: Hutchinson, 1970, 1–4.

5 Robert O. Crummey, 'Reform under Ivan IV: Gradualism and Terror', in Crummey (ed.), *Reform in Russia and the USSR: Past and Prospects*, Urbana and Chicago: University of Illinois Press, 1989, 12–27.

6 Martin Luther, 'Against the Robbing and Murdering Hordes of Peasants' (1525) in Carter Lindberg (ed.), *The European Reformations Sourcebook*, Oxford: Blackwell, 2000, 97–8.

7 John Guy, *Henry VIII: The Quest for Fame*, London: Allen Lane, 2014, vii.

8 Natalie Zemon Davis, 'The Rites of Violence: Religious Riot in Sixteenth-Century France', *Past and Present* 59 (1973): 51–91 (62).

9 Sara Beam, 'Rites of Torture in Reformation Geneva', *Past and Present* special supplement 7 (2012): 197–219 (204–5).

10 Act of Supremacy, 1534, in Lindberg (ed.), *The European Reformations Sourcebook*, 223, doc. 12.7.

11 Andy Wood, 'The Deep Roots of Albion's Fatal Tree: The Tudor State and the Monopoly of Violence', *History* 99:336 (2014): 403–17 (407, 410, 414); for the statistics, Wood cites Sarah Covington, *The Trail of Martyrdom: Persecution and Resistance in Sixteenth-Century England*, Notre Dame, IN, 2003, 158.

12 Brendan Kane, 'Ordinary Violence? Ireland as Emergency in the Tudor State', *History* 99:336 (2014): 444–67 (460).

13 Peter H. Wilson, *Europe's Tragedy: A New History of the Thirty Years War*, London: Penguin, 2010, 787.

14 Peter H. Wilson, *The Thirty Years War: A Sourcebook*, Basingstoke: Palgrave, 2010, 144, 149.

15 Blair Worden, *The English Civil Wars 1640–1660*, London: Weidenfeld and Nicolson, 2009, 73.

16 Susan K. Morrissey, 'The "Apparel of Innocence"': Toward a Moral Economy of Terrorism in Late Imperial Russia', *Journal of Modern History* 84 (2012), 607–42 (626).

17 Vladimir Sorokin, 'Let the Past Collapse on Time!', *New York Review of Books*, 8 May 2014.

18 For more of this, see James Harris, *The Great Fear: Stalin's Terror of the 1930s*, Oxford: Oxford University Press, 2016.

19 According to Filip Filippovich Vigel', quoted in Alexander Martin, *Romantics, Reformers, Reactionaries: Russian Conservative Thought*

*and Politics in the Reign of Alexander I*, DeKalb, IL: Northern Illinois University Press, 1997, 53.

20 In the words of a priest from Arakcheev's estate: Michael Jenkins, *Arakcheev: Grand Vizier of the Russian Empire*, London: Faber and Faber, 1969, 11.

21 Quoted in Dominic Lieven, *Russia against Napoleon: The Battle for Europe, 1807 to 1814*, London: Allen Lane, 2009, ch. 4.

22 K. M. Iachmenikhin, 'Aleksei Andreevich Arakcheev', in A. I. Bokhanov (ed.), *Rossiiskie konservatory*, Moscow: Russkii mir, 1997, 17–62.

23 On the significance of the Gruzino visit, see Richard Pipes, 'The Russian Military Colonies', *Journal of Modern History* 22:3 (September 1950): 205–19 (206). Marc Raeff argues that the colonies appealed to Alexander's military obsessions, or his 'paradomania', in *Michael Speransky*. On the decision of 1809 and for a more detailed but less provocatively phrased account, see Kenneth R. Whiting, 'Aleksei Andreevich Arakcheev', PhD dissertation, Harvard University, 1951, 147.

24 Janet M. Hartley, *Alexander I*, London and New York: Longman, 1994, 180.

25 John L. H. Keep, *Soldiers of the Tsar: Army and Society in Russia, 1462–1874*, Oxford: Clarendon Press, 1985, 290–91.

26 On midwives: Janet Hartley, *Russia, 1762–1825: Military Power, the State, and the People*, Westport, CN: Praeger, 2008, 198; on school-teachers: Pipes, 'Russian Military Colonies', 216.

27 Cited in V. A. Fedorov, *M. M. Speranskii i A. A. Arakcheev*, Moscow: Izdatel'stvo Moskovskogo Universiteta. 1997, 172.

28 Quoted in Rey, *Alexander I*, 326.

29 Keep, *Soldiers of the Tsar*, 297–301.

30 Robert Lyall, *An Account of the Organization, Administration, and Present State of the Military Colonies of Russia*, London: T. Cadell and W. Blackwood, 1824, 44.

31 James Cracraft, *The Petrine Revolution in Russian Architecture*, Chicago and London: University of Chicago Press, 1988, 176–8.

32 Lindsey Hughes, *Russia in the Age of Peter the Great*, New Haven and London: Yale University Press, 1998, 213.

33 As cited in W. Bruce Lincoln, *Sunlight at Midnight: St Petersburg and the Rise of Modern Russia*, Oxford: Perseus, 2000, 20–21.

34 Simon Dixon, *The Modernisation of Russia 1676–1825*, Cambridge: Cambridge University Press, 1999, 5.

35 Abraham Ascher, *The Revolution of 1905*, vol. 1: *Russia in Disarray*, Stanford, CA: Stanford University Press, 1988, ch. 3.

36  Ascher, *The Revolution of 1905*, vol. 1, 322.

37  John Merriman, *Massacre: The Life and Death of the Paris Commune of 1871*, New Haven and London: Yale University Press, 2014.

38  Norman N. Naimark, 'Terrorism and the Fall of Imperial Russia', *Terrorism and Political Violence* 2:2 (1990): 171–92 (174).

39  Morrissey, Apparel of Innocence'.

40  Orlando Figes, *A People's Tragedy: The Russian Revolution 1891–1924*, London: Pimlico, 1997, 201–2.

41  Askoldov's interview is recorded in the DVD of *The Commissar* produced by Artificial Eye.

42  Peter Holquist, 'Violent Russia, Deadly Marxism? Russia in the Epoch of Violence, 1905–21', *Kritika: Explorations in Russian and Eurasian History* 4:3 (2003): 627–52.

43  Peter Holquist, *Making War, Forging Revolution: Russia's Continuum of Crisis, 1914–1921*, Cambridge, MA: Harvard University Press, 2002; Peter Gatrell, *A Whole Empire Walking: Refugees in Russia during World War I*, Bloomington, IN: Indiana University Press, 1999; Alexander Watson, *Ring of Steel: Germany and Austria at War, 1914–1918*, London: Allen Lane, 2014.

44  Alexander Yakovlev, *A Century of Violence in Soviet Russia*, New Haven and London: Yale University Press, 2002, 65, 67, 79.

45  J. Arch Getty and Oleg V. Naumov, *The Road to Terror: Stalin and the Self-Destruction of the Bolsheviks, 1932–1939*, New Haven and London: Yale University Press, 1999, 588 [table 5].

46  I refer readers to the detailed scholarship of Terry Martin, *The Affirmative Action Empire: Nations and Nationalities in the Soviet Union, 1932–1939*, Ithaca, NY, and London: Cornell University Press, 2001, and in contrast, Robert Conquest, *Harvest of Sorrow: Soviet Collectivization and the Terror-Famine*, New York: Oxford University Press, 1986, and Anne Applebaum, *Red Famine: Stalin's War on Ukraine*, London: Allen Lane, 2017.

47  For a historiographical review, see Mark Edele, *Stalinist Society 1928–1953*, Oxford: Oxford University Press, 2011, ch. 9.

48  Oleg Khlevniuk, *Stalin: New Biography of a Dictator*, New Haven, CT: Yale University Press, 2014; Stephen Kotkin, *Stalin*, vol. 2: *Waiting for Hitler 1928–1941*, London: Allen Lane, 2017, part II.

49  Harris, *The Great Fear*.

50  J. Arch Getty, Gábor T. Rittersporn and Viktor N. Zemskov, 'Victims of the Soviet Penal System in the Pre-War Years: A First Appraisal on

the Basis of Archival Evidence', *American Historical Review* 98:4 (October 1993): 1017–49 (1039).

51 Lynne Viola, *The Unknown Gulag: The Lost World of Stalin's Special Settlements*, Oxford: Oxford University Press, 2007.

52 Steven A. Barnes, *Death and Redemption: The Gulag and the Shaping of Soviet Society*, Princeton, NJ, and Oxford: Princeton University Press, 2011.

53 As told by 'Pasha' himself to the author in March 2000.

54 Simon Sebag Montefiore, *Stalin: The Court of the Red Tsar*, London: Weidenfeld and Nicolson, 2003, 448–9.

55 Jeffrey S. Hardy, *The Gulag After Stalin: Redefining Punishment in Khrushchev's Soviet Union, 1953–1964*, Ithaca, NY, and London: Cornell University Press, 2016, 23.

56 Elena Monastireva-Ansdell, 'Redressing the Commissar: Thaw Cinema Revises Soviet Structuring Myths', *Russian Review* 65 (April 2006): 230–49 (quotation on 230).

57 William Wolf, 'Askoldov! The Man Who Made Commissar', *Film Comment* 24:3 (June 1988): 68–72.

## 6. THE EUROPE QUESTION

1 Vladimir Polushin, *Natalia Goncharova: Tsaritsa russkogo avangarda*, Moscow: Molodaia gvardiia, 2016, 185. The train journey took place on 29 April according to the Julian calendar that was in operation in Russia until 1918.

2 John E. Bowlt and Matthew Drutt, *Amazons of the Avant-Garde*, London: Royal Academy of Arts, 1999.

3 Polushin, *Natalia Goncharova*, 185.

4 Kazimir Malevich, 'From Cubism and Futurism to Suprematism: The New Painterly (*Zhivopisnyi*) Realism', 1915, in John E. Bowlt (ed.), *Russian Art of the Avant Garde: Theory and Criticism*, London: Thames and Hudson, 1988, 121–3.

5 Jane Ashton Sharp, *Russian Modernism Between East and West: Natal'ia Goncharova and the Moscow Avant-Garde*, Cambridge: Cambridge University Press, 2006, 11.

6 Natalia Goncharova, 'Preface to Catalogue of One-Man Exhibition', 1913, in Bowlt (ed.), *Russian Art of the Avant Garde*, 55–6.

7 As did the Russian avant-garde in general: Evgeniia Petrova, 'Narodnye istochniki i russkii avangard nachalo XX-ogo veka', in *Avangard i*

*ego russkie istochniki*, St Petersburg: Gosudarstvennyi Russkii Muzei, 1993; Robin Milner-Gullard, *The Russians*, Oxford: Oxford University Press, 1997, 197–208; Lindsey Hughes, 'Restoring Religion to Russian Art', in Geoffrey Hosking and Robert Service (eds.), *Reinterpreting Russia*, London: Arnold, 1999, 40–53.

8  John E. Bowlt, 'Orthodoxy and the Avant-Garde: Sacred Images in the Work of Goncharova, Malevich, and Their Contemporaries', in William C. Brumfield and Milos M. Velimirovic (eds.), *Christianity and the Arts in Russia*, Cambridge: Cambridge University Press, 1991, 145–50.

9  I owe the description of the tent and the dome, and the overall sense of Muscovy in this section, to James H. Billington, *The Icon and the Axe: An Interpretive History of Russian Culture*, New York: Vintage, 1970, 47–8.

10  Scott M. Kenworthy, *The Heart of Russia: Trinity-Sergius, Monasticism, and Society after 1825*, New York: Oxford University Press, 2010.

11  Nicholas V. Riasanovsky, *Russian Identities: An Historical Survey*, Oxford: Oxford University Press, 2005, ch. 1.

12  Yuval Noah Harari, *Sapiens: A Brief History of Humankind*, London: Vintage, 2011.

13  Norman Davies, *Europe: A History*, Oxford: Oxford University Press, 1996, Introduction.

14  Milan Kundera, 'The Tragedy of Central Europe', *New York Review of Books*, April 1986.

15  These paragraphs draw on Norman Davies, 'Fair Comparisons, False Contrasts: East and West in Modern European History', in Davies, *Europe East and West*, London: Jonathan Cape, 2006, 22–45 (esp. 34–9), and Larry Wolff, *Inventing Eastern Europe: The Map of Civilization on the Mind of the Enlightenment*, Stanford, CA: Stanford University Press, 1994.

16  Edward W. Said, *Orientalism*, London: Penguin, 2003 (first published 1978), e.g. 26, 100, 191.

17  These details and interpretations rely on Dimitri Obolensky, *Six Byzantine Portraits*, Oxford: Clarendon Press, 1988, ch. 3, Vladimir Monomakh, 83–114.

18  V. L. Ianin, 'Medieval Novgorod', in Perrie (ed.), *The Cambridge History of Russia*, vol. 1, 188–210 (196).

19  Sergei Bogatyrev, 'Ivan the Terrible Discovers the West: The Cultural Transformation of Autocracy during the Early Northern Wars', *Russian History* 34:1–4 (2007): 161–88 (166–7).

20 Chester Dunning, 'A "Singular Affection" for Russia: Why King James Offered to Intervene in the Time of Troubles', *Russian History* 34:1–4 (2007): 277–302 (286–7).

21 Erika Monahan, *Merchants of Siberia: Trade in Early Modern Eurasia*, Ithaca, NY, and London: Cornell University Press, 2016.

22 Dimitri Obolensky, *The Byzantine Commonwealth: Eastern Europe, 500–1453*, London: Weidenfeld and Nicolson, 1971, 367.

23 Lindsey Hughes, *Russia in the Age of Peter the Great*, New Haven and London: Yale University Press, 2000, 299.

24 John T. Faris, *The Romance of Forgotten Towns*, New York and London: Harper and Brothers, 1924, 13–37.

25 Peter J. S. Duncan, *Russian Messianism: Third Rome, Revolution, Communism and After*, London and New York: Routledge, 2000, 11.

26 Obolensky, *The Byzantine Commonwealth*, 364–7.

27 Katerina Clark, *Moscow, The Fourth Rome: Stalinism, Cosmopolitanism, and the Evolution of Soviet Culture, 1931–1941*, Cambridge, MA: Harvard University Press, 2011, 1.

28 Dominic Lieven, *Russia against Napoleon: The Battle for Europe, 1807 to 1914*, London: Allen Lane, 2011.

29 Rey, *Alexander I*, 282.

30 Geoffrey Hosking, *Russia: People and Empire, 1552–1917*, London: Fontana, 1998, 271–4.

31 Vera Tolz, *Russia: Inventing the Nation*, London: Hodder, 2001, 93–4. See also Martin Malia, *Russia under Western Eyes: From the Bronze Horseman to the Lenin Mausoleum*, Cambridge, MA: Belknap Press of Harvard University Press, 1999, ch. 2.

32 V. V. Alekseev, *Opyt rossiiskikh modernizatsii XVIII–XX veka*, Moscow: Nauka, 2000.

33 Larry Siedentop, *Inventing the Individual: The Origins of Western Liberalism*, London: Allen Lane, 2014, 2–3.

34 Peter Mandler, *Return from the Natives: How Margaret Mead Won the Second World War and Lost the Cold War*, New Haven and London: Yale University Press, 2013, ch. 6 (esp. 229–30).

35 As quoted in Neil O'Sullivan, 'The Weekend Started Here', *FT Weekend*, 24 May 2015.

36 Sarah B. Snyder, *Human Rights Activism and the End of the Cold War: A Transnational History of the Helsinki Network*, Cambridge: Cambridge University Press, 2011; Daniel C. Thomas, *The Helsinki Effect: International Norms, Human Rights, and the Demise of Communism*, Princeton, NJ: Princeton University Press, 2001.

37 Samuel Moyn, *The Last Utopia*, Cambridge, MA: Harvard University Press, 2012.

38 Benjamin Nathans, 'The Dictatorship of Reason: Aleksandr Vol'pin and the Idea of Rights under Developed Socialism', *Slavic Review* 66:4 (2007): 630–63.

39 David Priestland, *Stalinism and the Politics of Mobilization: Ideas, Power, and Terror in Inter-war Russia*, Oxford: Oxford University Press, 2007.

40 Hosking, *Russia: People and Empire*, 345–66; Tolz, *Russia: Inventing the Nation*, 94–9.

41 Mark B. Smith, 'Social Rights in the Soviet Dictatorship: The Constitutional Right to Welfare from Stalin to Brezhnev', *Humanity* 3:3 (2012): 385–406.

42 *Daily Sketch*, 9 December 1955; *The Times*, 27 April 1956. See also Mark B. Smith, 'Peaceful Coexistence at All Costs: Cold War Exchanges between Britain and the Soviet Union in 1956', *Cold War History* 12:3 (2012), 537–58.

43 http://www.wfdy.org/festivals/, accessed 4 July 2016.

44 https://www.olympic.org/melbourne-stockholm-1956, accessed 4 July 2016.

45 *Pravda*, 30 July 1957, 1; 2 August 1957, 3; 11 August 1957, 3; 12 August 1957, 1; F. Novikov and I. Pokrovskii, 'V Moskve, gorode festivalia', *Arkhitektura SSSR* 1957, 7, 6–8.

46 *Opinions about the VI World Festival of Youth and Students for Peace and Friendship*, Budapest, 1957, 19.

47 Kristin Roth-Ey, ' "Loose Girls" on the Loose? Sex, Propaganda, and the 1957 Youth Festival', in Melanie Ilic, Susan E. Reid and Lynne Attwood (eds.), *Women in the Khrushchev Era*, Basingstoke: Palgrave, 2004, 75–95.

48 *Literaturnaia gazeta*, 27 July 1957, 1 and 3.

49 *New Statesman*, 17 August 1957, 187.

50 Vladislav Zubok, *Zhivago's Children: The Last Russian Intelligentsia*, Cambridge, MA: Belknap Press of Harvard University Press, 2009, ch. 3.

51 Anne E. Gorsuch, *All This Is Your World: Soviet Tourism at Home and Abroad after Stalin*, Oxford: Oxford University Press, 2011, ch. 4 (esp. 109).

52 Georgii Arbatov, *Chelovek sistemy: nabliudeniia i razmyshleniia ochevidtsa ee raspada*, Moscow: Vagrius, 2002, 136.

53 O. V. Volobuev, 'Prioritety sovetskogo gosudarstva', in Volobuev et al. (eds.), *Rossiia: gosudarstvennye prioritety i natsional'nye interesy*, Moscow: Rosspen, 2000, 247–96 (285).

54  E. A. Ivanian, *Kogda govoriat muzy: Istoriia rossiisko-amerikanskikh kul'turnykh sviazei*, Moscow: Mezhdunarodnye otnosheniia, 2007, 383.

55  Steven Lee Myers, *The New Tsar: The Rise and Reign of Vladimir Putin*, New York: Knopf, 2015, 19.

56  Geoffrey Hosking, *Rulers and Victims: The Russians in the Soviet Union*, Cambridge, MA: Belknap Press of Harvard University Press, 2006.

57  Nikolai Mitrokhin, *Russkaia partiia: dvizhenie russkikh natsionalistov v SSSR 1953–1985gg*, Moscow: Novoe literaturnoe obozrenie, 2003.

58  Andés Artal-Tur, Galina Romanova and Maria del Mar Vacquez-Mendez, 'Tourism in Russia', in Frédéric Dimanche and Lidia Andrades Caldito (eds.), *Tourism in Russia: A Management Handbook*, Bingley: Emerald, 2015, 9–56 (35, 39, 45).

59  Donald Ostrowski, *Muscovy and the Mongols: Cross-Cultural Influences on the Steppe Frontier, 1304–1589*, Cambridge: Cambridge University Press, 1998, 3 n. 9.

60  Lawrence N. Langer, 'Muscovite Taxation and the Problem of Mongol Rule in Rus'', *Russian History* 34:1–4 (2007): 101–29.

61  This paragraph as a whole broadly follows the arguments of Ostrowski, *Muscovy and the Mongols*. A contrasting and equally important account emphasizes devastation and the influences that flow from that, as well as growing wealth and a subordinate cooperation between Muscovites and Mongols: Charles J. Halperin, *Russia and the Golden Horde: The Mongol Impact on Medieval Russian History*, Bloomington, IN: Indiana University Press, 1985.

62  For Russia's two would-be Asian moments, see the works of Dimitri Obolensky.

63  Alexandra Harrington, 'Anna Akhmatova (1889–1966)', in Stephen M. Norris and Willard Sunderland (eds.), *Russia's People of Empire: Life Stories from Eurasia, 1500 to the Present*, Bloomington and Indianapolis, IN: Indiana University Press, 2012, 254–63.

64  In discussing Gumilev, I have drawn on Mark Bassin, *The Gumilev Mystique: Biopolitics, Eurasianism, and the Construction of Community in Modern Russia*, Ithaca, NY: Cornell University Press, 2016.

65  Adapting John P. LeDonne, 'Definitions, Methodology, and Argument', *Kritika: Explorations in Russian and Eurasian History* 16:4 (2015): 943–50 (943–4).

66  Stephen Kotkin, 'Mongol Commonwealth? Exchange and Governance across the Post-Mongol Space', *Kritika: Explorations in Russian and Eurasian History* 8:3 (2007): 487–531.

67  Tat'iana Gurova, 'Zapandnyi put' Rossii zakonchen', *Ekspert*, 16 April 2018.

68  *Nezavisimaia gazeta*, 18 April 2018, 2.

69  Uniqueness, in the end, is how Marshall T. Poe characterizes Russia in his important discussion of this matter: *The Russian Moment in World History*, Princeton and Oxford: Princeton University Press, 2003.

## 7. THE EMPIRE RELATIONSHIP

1  This account draws heavily from Richard Pipes, *Vixi: Memoirs of a Non-Belonger*, New Haven and London: Yale University Press, 2003, esp. 13–14.

2  Richard Pipes, *Survival Is Not Enough: Soviet Realities and America's Future*, New York: Simon and Schuster, 1984, 37–9. The historical substance of the argument was laid out in Richard Pipes, *Russia Under the Old Regime*, London: Penguin, 1995 (1st edn, 1974), 79–84 and passim.

3  Pipes, *Survival Is Not Enough*, 67 (quotation), 71–7, 279–80.

4  Gordon Barrass, 'Able Archer 83: What Were the Soviets Thinking?' *Survival: Global Politics and Strategy* 58:6 (2016): 7–30.

5  David Rothkopf, *Running the World: The Inside Story of the National Security Council and the Architects of American Power*, New York: Public Affairs, 2004, 224–5.

6  Pipes, *Vixi*, 250.

7  Hosking, *Russia and the Russians*, 42.

8  Janet Martin, *Treasure of the Land of Darkness: The Fur Trade and Its Significance for Medieval Russia*, Cambridge: Cambridge University Press, 1986.

9  Martin Dimnik, 'The Rus' principalities (1125–1246)', in Perrie (ed.), *The Cambridge History of Russia*, vol. 1, 98–126.

10  Plokhy, *Lost Kingdom*, parts II and III.

11  Faith Hollis, *Children of Rus': Right-Bank Ukraine and the Invention of a Russian Nation*, Ithaca, NY, and London: Cornell University Press, 2013.

12  Plokhy, *Lost Kingdom*, 347–51.

13  Jane Burbank and Frederick Cooper, *Empires in World History: Power and the Politics of Difference*, Princeton, NJ: Princeton University Press, 2010.

14  The statistic is cited in Stephen Kotkin, *Stalin*, vol. 1: *Paradoxes of Power 1878–1928*, London: Penguin, 2014, 11.

15 Serhii Plokhy, *The Gates of Europe: A History of Ukraine*, London: Penguin, 2015, 179.

16 Hans Rogger, *Russia in the Age of Modernisation and Revolution 1881–1917*, London and New York: Longman, 1983, 187.

17 Valerie A. Kivelson and Ronald Grigor Suny, *Russia's Empires*, Oxford: Oxford University Press, 2017, 144.

18 Rogger, *Russia in the Age of Modernisation and Revolution*, 190.

19 Krista Sigler, 'Mathilde Kshesinskaia (1872–1971)', in Stephen M. Norris and Willard Sunderland (eds.), *Russia's People of Empire: Life Stories from Eurasia, 1500 to the Present*, Bloomington and Indianapolis, IN: Indiana University Press, 2012, 232–41 (240).

20 Elizabeth Valkenier, *Russian Realist Art. The State and Society: The Peredvizhniki and Their Tradition*, Ann Arbor, MI: Ardis, 1977, 59–61.

21 Elizabeth Kridl Valkenier, *Ilya Repin and the World of Russian Art*, New York: Columbia University Press, 1990, 131–3.

22 Paul W. Werth, 'The Emergence of "Freedom of Conscience" in Imperial Russia', *Kritika: Explorations in Russian and Eurasian History* 13:3 (2012): 585–610 (quotation on 596).

23 Michael Khodarkovsky, ' "Ignoble Savages and Unfaithful Subjects": Constructing Non-Christian Identities in Early Modern Russia', in Daniel K. Brower and Edward J. Lazzerini (eds.), *Russia's Orient: Imperial Borderlands and Peoples, 1700–1917*, Bloomington and Indianapolis, IN: Indiana University Press, 1997, 9–26 (10, 20).

24 Eugene M. Avrutin, *Jews and the Imperial State: Identification Politics in Tsarist Russia*, Ithaca, NY: Cornell University Press, 2010.

25 Ekaterina Pravilova, 'From the Zloty to the Ruble: The Kingdom of Poland in the Monetary Politics of the Russian Empire', in Jane Burbank, Mark von Hagen and Anatoly Remnev (eds.), *Russian Empire: Space, People, Power, 1700–1930*, Bloomington and Indianapolis, IN: Indiana University Press, 2007, 295–319.

26 A. G. Hopkins, *American Empire: A Global History*, Princeton, NJ, and Oxford: Princeton University Press, 2018, 39.

27 Burbank and Cooper, *Empires*, 286.

28 Nancy Shields Kollmann, *The Russian Empire 1450–1801*, Oxford: Oxford University Press, 2017, 450–52, 457.

29 Alexander Etkind, *Internal Colonization: Russia's Imperial Experience*, Cambridge: Polity, 2011, 72–8.

30 John Elliott, *Empires of the Atlantic World: Britain and Spain in America, 1492–1830*, New Haven and London: Yale University Press, 2006.

31  James Belich, *Replenishing the Earth: The Settler Revolution and the Rise of the Angloworld*, Oxford: Oxford University Press, 2009.

32  Howard Zinn, *A People's History of the United States*, New York: Harper Perennial Modern Classics, 2005 (first published 1980), 140.

33  This account of Surikov's early life relies on G. Gor and V. Petrov, *Vasilii Ivanovich Surikov 1848-1916*, Moscow: Molodaia gvardiia, 1955, chs. 1-2. See also E. Iu. Bezyzvestnykh, *Surikiov i Sibir'*, Krasnoiarsk: Russkaia entsiklopediia, 1995, 10-14.

34  William Sunderland, 'Ermak Timofeevich', in Norris and Sunderland (eds.), *Russia's People of Empire*, 17-26. See also W. Bruce Lincoln, *The Conquest of a Continent: Siberia and the Russians*, New York: Random House, 1994, 40-43.

35  G. L. Vasil'eva-Shliapina, *Sibirskie krasavitsy V. Surikova: portret v tvorchestve khudozhnika*, St Petersburg, 2002, 130; N. G. Mashkovtsev, *V. I. Surikov*, Moscow, 1994, 29.

36  Richard Wortman, *Scenarios of Power: Myth and Ceremony in Russian Monarchy*, vol. 2, Princeton, NJ: Princeton University Press, 2000, 328.

37  Nicholas V. Riasanovsky, 'Asia through Russian Eyes', in Wayne S. Vucinich (ed.), *Russia and Asia: Essays on the Influence of Russia on the Asian Peoples*, Stanford, CA: Stanford University Press, 1972, 3-29 (here, 18).

38  David Schimmelpennick van der Oye, *Toward the Rising Sun: Russian Ideologies of Empire and the Path to the War with Japan*, DeKalb, IL: Northern Illinois University Press, 2001, 24ff and 42ff.

39  Wortman, *Scenarios of Power*, vol. 2, 175, 319-20.

40  For John LeDonne, expansionism was an 'inclusive policy', in the way that it involved local elites, Cossacks among many others. John P. LeDonne, *The Russian Empire and the World, 1700-1917: The Geopolitics of Expansion and Containment*, New York: Oxford University Press, 1999.

41  Letter from Surikov to his mother and brother Alexander, St Petersburg, 24 February 1895. V. I. Surikov, *Pis'ma, vospominaniia o khudozhnike*, Leningrad: Iskusstvo, 1977, 97, letter 119.

42  Hosking, *Rulers and Victims*.

43  Hélène Carrère, *The Great Challenge: Nationalities and the Bolshevik State, 1917-1930*, trans. Nancy Festinger, New York, 1992, chs. 1 and 2.

44  Terry Martin, *The Affirmative Action Empire: Nations and Nationalism in the Soviet Union, 1923-1939*, Ithaca, NY: Cornell University Press, 2001.

45  Yuri Slezkine, *The Jewish Century*, Princeton, NJ: Princeton University Press, 2004.

46 Martin, *Affirmative Action Empire*, 146, 377 (59 per cent figure is for 1935).

47 Douglas Northrop, *Veiled Empire: Gender and Power in Stalinist Central Asia*, Ithaca, NY: Cornell University Press, 2004.

48 Marianne Kamp, 'Jahon Obidova (1900–1967)', in Norris and Sunderland (eds.), *Russia's People of Empire*, 308–16 (313).

49 James Harris, *The Great Fear: Stalin's Terror of the 1930s*, Oxford: Oxford University Press, 2016, 178–80.

50 Martin, *Affirmative Action Empire*, 102, 108.

51 Applebaum, *Red Famine*, xiii–xiv, xxiv.

52 Martin, *Affirmative Action Empire*, 345.

53 Applebaum, *Red Famine*, 353–62.

54 Martin, *Affirmative Action Empire*, 305.

55 Quoted in Kathleen E. Smith, *Moscow 1956: The Silenced Spring*, Cambridge. MA: Harvard University Press, 2017, 52.

56 Tarik Cyril Amar, *The Paradox of Lviv: A Borderland City between Stalinists, Nazis, and Nationalists*, Ithaca, NY: Cornell University Press, 2015.

57 Dmitrii Shepilov, *The Kremlin's Scholar: A Memoir of Soviet Politics under Stalin and Khrushchev*, New Haven and London: Yale University Press, 2007, ed. Stephen V. Bittner, trans. Anthony Austin, 309–11.

58 Plokhy, *Gates of Europe*, 298–9.

59 Plokhy, *Gates of Europe*, 304.

60 Benjamin Tromly, *Making the Soviet Intelligentsia: Universities and Intellectual Life under Stalin and Khrushchev*, Cambridge: Cambridge University Press, 2014, ch. 8.

61 William Jay Risch, *The Ukrainian West: Culture and the Fate of Empire in Soviet Lviv*, Cambridge, MA: Harvard University Press, 2011, 234–41; also 1–2.

62 Valerii Tishkov, *The Mind Aflame: Ethnicity, Nationalism, and Conflict in and after the Soviet Union*, London: Sage, 1997, 40–42.

63 Yuri Slezkine, *Arctic Mirrors: Russia and the Small Peoples of the North*, Ithaca, NY, and London: Cornell University Press, 1994, 373–5.

64 See Hosking, *Russia: People and Empire*, and idem, *Rulers and Victims*.

## 8. THE INVADER OBSESSION

1 Margaret Thatcher speech at Kensington Town Hall, 19 January 1976: https://www.margaretthatcher.org/document/102939. See also Charles Moore, *Margaret Thatcher: The Authorized Biography*, vol. 1, London:

Penguin, 2014, 332. On Pearl Harbor: Mark Hertling and Molly K. McKew in Politico Magazine (https://www.politico.com/magazine/story/2018/07/16/putin-russia-trump-2016-pearl-harbor-219015).

2 Cathy Porter, *The Lonely Struggle of the Woman Who Defied Lenin*, New York: Dial Press, 1980, 11–21.

3 Porter, *The Lonely Struggle*, 180.

4 Aleksandra Kollontai, *Letopis' moei zhizni*, Moscow: Academia, 2004, 268.

5 Leonid Mlechin, *Kollontai*, Moscow: Molodaia gvardiia, 2013, 263.

6 Porter, *The Lonely Struggle*, 423.

7 A. M. Aleksandrov-Alentov, *Ot Kollontai do Gorbacheva*, Moscow: Mezhdunarodnye otnosheniia, 1994, 24 (italics added).

8 A. M. Kollontai, *Diplomaticheskie dnevniki 1922–1940*, vol. 2 of 2, Moscow: Academia, 2001, 257.

9 Kollontai, *Diplomaticheskie dnevniki*, vol. 2, 295.

10 Tobias Buck, 'How Russian Gas Became Europe's Most Divisive Commodity', *Financial Times*, 17 July 2018.

11 Roger Moorhouse, *The Devils' Alliance: Hitler's Pact with Stalin 1939–41*, London: Bodley Head, 2014, 4; Timothy Snyder, *Bloodlands: Europe between Hitler and Stalin*, London: Bodley Head, 2011, xi; the diametrically opposite case is made by Geoffrey Roberts, *Stalin's Wars: From World War to Cold War, 1939–1953*, New Haven, CT: Yale University Press, 2006.

12 A. J. P. Taylor, *The Origins of the Second World War*, London: Penguin, 1961.

13 Taylor's favourite among his books was *The Trouble Makers: Dissent over Foreign Policy 1792–1939*, London: Hamish Hamilton, 1957, and one of his biographies has a related title: Kathleen Burk, *Troublemaker: The Life and History of A. J. P. Taylor*, New Haven, CT: Yale University Press, 2000.

14 Kotkin, *Stalin*, vol. 2, 582–83.

15 Zara Steiner, *The Triumph of the Dark: European International History 1933–1939*, Oxford: Oxford University Press, 2013, 427–30.

16 Jonathan Haslam, *The Soviet Union and the Struggle for Collective Security in Europe, 1933–39*, London: Macmillan 1984, 169.

17 David Reynolds, *Summits: Six Meetings that Shaped the Twentieth Century*, London: Penguin, 2008, ch. 2 (95 for Churchill on Chamberlain).

18 R. Gerald Hughes, 'The Ghosts of Appeasement: Britain and the Legacy of the Munich Agreement', *Journal of Contemporary History* 48:4 (2013): 715 for Blair on Chamberlain.

19 *Guardian*, 2 September 2014; *Time*, 1 April 2014; *The Economist*, 20 September 2014.

20 *Daily Telegraph*, 10 September 2014.

21 Brendan Simms, *Europe: The Struggle for Supremacy 1453 to the Present*, London: Penguin, 2014, 178–9.

22 Philip Bobbitt, *The Shield of Achilles: War, Peace and the Course of History*, London: Penguin, 2003, 551.

23 For more speculation along these lines, see Alexander Titov, '19th-Century Diplomacy Can Help with 21st-Century Russia', *The Conversation*, 11 September 2014.

24 See Richard Sakwa, *Frontline Ukraine: Crisis in the Borderlands*, London: IB Tauris, 2016.

25 Fiona Hill and Clifford G. Gaddy, *Mr Putin: Operative in the Kremlin*, Washington, DC: Brookings Institution Press, 2015, 308: archive. kremlin.ru/eng speech of 2008/04/04.

26 As archived on 1tv.ru: *Putin: dokumental'nyi fil'm Oliver Stouna* (examples from episodes 3 and 4). Produced in English version by Showtime.

27 Michael McFaul, *From Cold War to Hot Peace: The Inside Story of Russia and America*, London: Allen Lane, 2018.

28 Richard Sakwa, *Russia Against the Rest: The Post-Cold War Crisis of World Order*, Cambridge: Cambridge University Press, 2017, 325, 328.

29 David Bromwich, 'American Breakdown', *London Review of Books*, 9 August 2018.

30 On the connections between NATO expansion and Russian policy, see Constantine Pleshakov, *The Crimean Nexus: Putin's War and the Clash of Civilizations*, New Haven and London: Yale University Press, 2017 (Kennan quotation cited on 26).

31 Michael Jabara Carley, 'Fiasco: The Anglo-Franco-Soviet Alliance That Never Was and the Unpublished British White Paper, 1939–1940', *International History Review*, 2018 (advance publication online).

32 Steiner, *The Triumph of the Dark*, 885–90.

33 Kotkin, *Stalin*, vol. 2, 648.

34 Richard Pipes, *Survival Is Not Enough: Soviet Realities and America's Future*, New York: Simon and Schuster, 1984.

35 Heather A. Conley et al., *Understanding Russian Influence in Central and Eastern Europe*, Center for Strategic and International Studies, Washington, DC, October 2016, x.

36 Christopher Clark, *The Sleepwalkers: How Europe Went to War in 1914*, London: Penguin, 2013, 475.

37 Patricia A. Weitsman, *Dangerous Alliances: Proponents of Peace, Weapons of War*, Stanford, CA: Stanford University Press, 2004, 23, 173.

38 Norman Stone, *The Eastern Front, 1914–1917*, London: Penguin, 1998, 28.

39 Weitsman, *Dangerous Alliances*, 184–5.

40 Dominic Lieven, *The End of Tsarist Russia: The March to World War I and Revolution*, New York: Viking, 2015, 148.

41 For more on these calculations, which lie at the centre of my argument, see Clark, *The Sleepwalkers*.

42 Lieven, *The End of Tsarist Russia*, 284–7.

43 Sean McMeekin, *The Russian Origins of the First World War*, Cambridge, MA: Belknap Press of Harvard University Press, 2011.

44 Niall Ferguson, *The Pity of War*, London: Allen Lane, 1998, 158–73.

45 Alexander Watson, *Ring of Steel: Germany and Austria-Hungary at War, 1914–1918*, London: Penguin, 2015, 35.

46 Lieven, *The End of Tsarist Russia*, 341.

47 Henry Kissinger, *World Order*, London: Penguin, 2015, 373 and passim.

48 House of Lords European Union Committee, 6th Report of Session 2014–15, 'The EU and Russia: Before and Beyond the Crisis in Ukraine', 6, 29.

49 Andrei P. Tsygankov, *Russia and the West from Alexander II to Putin: Honor in International Relations*, Cambridge: Cambridge University Press, 2012.

50 I. N. Nikitin, 'Rasshirenie territorii kak geopoliticheskii faktor rossiiskoi gosudarstvennosti: kontseptual'nye voprosy', in A. I. Aksenov et al. (eds.), *Rossiiskaia imperiia ot istokov do nachala XIX veka: ocherki sotsial'no-politicheskoi i ekonomicheskoi istorii*, Moscow: Russkaia panorama, 2011, 28–49 (44).

51 For overviews of Russian war and diplomacy, see William C. Fuller, Jr, *Strategy and Power in Russia 1600–1914*, New York: Free Press, 1992; Brian Davies, 'Muscovy at War and Peace', in Perrie (ed.), *The Cambridge History of Russia*, vol. 1, 486–520; the essays in Part VI of Dominic Lieven (ed.), *The Cambridge History of Russia*, vol. 2: *Imperial Russia, 1689–1917*; Barbara Jelavich, *A Century of Russian Foreign Policy 1814–1914*, Philadelphia: J. B. Lippincott, 1964.

52 Dominic Lieven, *Russia Against Napoleon: The Battle for Europe 1807–1914*, London: Allen Lane, 2010.

53 See Jonathan Haslam, *Russia's Cold War: From the October Revolution to the Fall of the Wall*, New Haven, CT: Yale University Press, 2012, ch. 1; Odd Arne Westad, *The Cold War: A World History*, London: Allen Lane, 2017, 4–5, 19, 68–9.

54 The same authors demonstrate connections between structural and contingent causes of the Cold War: Westad, *The Cold War*, 52–3, and Haslam, *Russia's Cold War*, 32–3, 76.

55 Taylor, *Origins of the Second World War*.

56 Peter Beinart, 'The US Needs to Face Up to Its Long History of Electoral Meddling', *The Atlantic*, 22 July 2018; Don H. Levin, 'Partisan Electoral Interventions by the Great Powers: Introducing the PEIG Dataset', *Conflict Management and Peace Science*, 2016.

57 Joan Kruckewitt, 'US Militarization of Honduras in the 1980s and the Creation of CIA-Backed Death Squads', in Cecilia Menjívar and Néstor Rodriguez (eds.), *When States Kill: Latin America, the U.S., and Technologies of Terror*, Austin, TX: University of Texas Press, 2005, 170–97 (175, 182–3).

58 Patrick Iber, *Neither Peace Nor Freedom: The Cultural Cold War in Latin America*, Cambridge, MA: Harvard University Press, 2015.

59 Bob Woodward, *Veil: The Secret Wars of the CIA, 1981–1987*, New York: Simon and Schuster, 1987; idem, *Fear: Trump in the White House*, New York: Simon and Schuster, 2018.

60 Gabriel Gorodetsky (ed.), *The Maisky Diaries: Red Ambassador to the Court of St James's, 1932–43*, New Haven, CT: Yale University Press, 2015, 230–33 (6 October 1939).

61 Robert Caro, *The Passage of Power: The Years of Lyndon Johnson*, vol. 4, London: Bodley Head, 2012, 235–6.

62 Arthur Schlesinger, Jr, *Robert Kennedy and His Times*, New York: Ballantine, 1978, 127.

63 Denis Healey, *The Time of My Life*, London: Penguin, 1989, 309, 362.

64 *New York Times*, 27 May 2016.

65 Jonathan Haslam, *Russia's Cold War: From the October Revolution to the Fall of the Wall*, New Haven, CT: Yale University Press, 2011, 62–3.

66 Kai Bird, *The Color of Truth: McGeorge Bundy and William Bundy: Brothers in Arms*, New York, 1998, 94.

67 George F. Kennan, *The Kennan Diaries*, ed. Frank Costigliola, New York, 2014, 642

68 Haslam, *Russia's Cold War*, 62–3; Bird, *The Color of Truth*, 94; Kennan, *The Kennan Diaries*, 642.

69 Tass.com, 5 July 2018.

70 Giles Whittell, 'This Is Russia's Real Revolution', *The Times*, 14 July 2018, 32–3.

71 Dmitri Trenin, *Should We Fear Russia?*, Cambridge: Polity, 2016, 54–5.

## PART III: THE FIREGLOW OF HISTORY

1   Cathy Porter, *Alexandra Kollontai: The Lonely Struggle of the Woman Who Defied Lenin*, New York: Dial Press, 1980, 489; Ivan Gorcharov, *Oblomov*, trans. David Magarshack, London: Penguin 1954 [1859], 68; Vladimir Sokolov, *Eto vechnoe stikhotvoren'e Kniga liriki*, Moscow: Literaturnaia gazeta, 2007, 514

## 9. THE STALIN INHERITANCE

1   Evgenia Ginzburg, *Journey into the Whirlwind*, New York: Harcourt, 1967; *Within the Whirlwind*, New York: Harcourt, 1981; see also www.sakharov-center.ru.

2   Iurii Trifonov, *Otblesk kostra*, in *Izbrannye proizvedeniia*, vol. 1, Moscow: Mir knigi, 2005, 212.

3   Iurii Trifonov, 'Bul'varnoe kol'tso', in Trifonov, *Kak slovo nashe otzovetsia*, Moscow: Sovetskaia Rossiia, 1985, 118.

4   Trifonov, 'Bul'varnoe kol'tso', 116.

5   Yuri Trifonov, *Disappearance*, trans. David Lowe, Evanston, IL: Northwestern Illinois University Press, 1996, 63.

6   Yuri Slezkine, *The House of Government: A Saga of the Russian Revolution*, Princeton, NJ: Princeton University Press, 2017, 379.

7   Slezkine, *The House of Government*, 777.

8   Trifonov, *Disappearance*, 7.

9   A. Shitov, *Iurii Trifonov: Khronika zhizni i tvorchestva 1925–1981*, Ekaterinburg: Izdatel'stvo Ural'skogo Universiteta, 1997, 506.

10  Trifonov to I. Ia. Chernukhina, 10 April 1977: Shitov, *Khronika*, 548.

11  Trifonov, 'Zapiska soseda', *Kak slovo*, 138–74 (1972).

12  Geoffrey Hosking, *Beyond Socialist Realism: Soviet Fiction Since 'Ivan Denisovich'*, London: Elek, 1980.

13  Yuri Trifonov, *Another Life and The House on the Embankment*, trans. Michael Glenny, Evanston, IL: Northwestern University Press, 2004, 350.

14  Dina R. Spechler, *Permitted Dissent in the USSR: Novy Mir and the Soviet Regime*, New York: Praeger, 1982.

15  Shitov, *Khronika*, 504.

16  *Literaturnaia gazeta*, 23 June 1976, 2; 30 June 1976, 4.

17  Quoted in David Gillespie, *Iurii Trifonov: Unity Through Time*, Cambridge: Cambridge University Press, 1993, 8. Markov's professional

position is recorded in Iu. V. Goriachev, *Tsentral'nyi komitet KPSS, VKP(b), PRK(b), RSDRP (b) 1917–1991: Istoriko-biograficheskii spravochnik*, Moscow: Parad, 2005, 289.

18 Shitov, *Khronika*, 519.

19 Böll in conversation with G. Formvege; Shitov, *Khronika*, 628.

20 Shitov, *Khronika*, 636–7.

21 Zhores Medvedev and Roi Medvedev, *Neizvestnyi Stalin*, Moscow: Prava cheloveka, 2001, 123.

22 Sheila Fitzpatrick, *On Stalin's Team: The Years of Living Dangerously in Soviet Politics*, Princeton, NJ: Princeton University Press, 2015, 224ff.

23 Steven A. Barnes, *Death and Redemption: The Gulag and the Shaping of Soviet Society*, Princeton, NJ, and Oxford: Princeton University Press, 2011, 205.

24 Miriam Dobson, *Khrushchev's Cold Summer: Gulag Returnees, Crime, and the Fate of Reform under Stalin*, Ithaca, NY, and London: Cornell University Press, 2009, esp. Part II.

25 Stephen V. Bittner, *The Many Lives of Khrushchev's Thaw: Experience and Memory in Moscow's Arbat*, Ithaca and London: Cornell University Press, 2008, ch. 2 (e.g. 54).

26 Denis Kozlov, *The Readers of Novyi Mir: Coming to Terms with the Stalinist Past*, Cambridge, MA: Harvard University Press, 2013.

27 Miriam Dobson, 'Contesting the Paradigms of De-Stalinization: Readers' Responses to *One Day in the Life of Ivan Denisovich*', *Slavic Review* 64:3 (2005): 580–600.

28 Kathleen E. Smith, *Moscow 1956: The Silenced Spring*, Cambridge, MA: Harvard University Press, 2017, 36–42.

29 V. F. Morozov to Central Committee of CPSU, 10 January 1956: K. Aimermakher et al. (eds.), *Doklad N. S. Khrushcheva o kul'te lichnosti Stalina na XX s'ezde KPSS: Dokumenty*, Moscow, Rosspen, 2002, 173 (doc. 6).

30 *Memoirs of Nikita Khrushchev*, vol. 2: *Reformer, 1945–1964*, ed. Sergei Khrushchev, trans. George Shriver, University Park, PA: Pennsylvania University Press, 2006, 204, 212.

31 See the conclusion of Polly Jones, *Myth, Memory, Trauma: Rethinking the Stalinist Past in the Soviet Union, 1953–70*, New Haven and London: Yale University Press, 2013.

32 Marcus Colla, 'Prussian Palimpsests: Historic Architecture and Urban Spaces in East Germany, 1945–1961', *Central European History* 50 (2017): 184–217.

33  Dan Stone, *Goodbye to All That? The Story of Europe since 1945*, Oxford: Oxford University Press, 2014, 46, 50–55.

34  Tony Judt, *Postwar: A History of Europe since 1945*, London: Heinemann, 2005, 805.

35  Dan Stone, 'Memory Wars in the "New Europe"', in Dan Stone (ed.), *The Oxford Handbook of Postwar European History*, Oxford: Oxford University Press, 2012, 713–31 (esp. 717–26). Tina Rosenberg, *The Haunted Land: Facing Europe's Ghosts after Communism*, New York: Vintage, 1996, 320–21.

36  Smith, *Moscow 1956*, 37.

37  Anne Applebaum, *Red Famine: Stalin's War on Ukraine*, London: Allen Lane, 2017, ch. 15.

38  Geoffrey Hosking, *Rulers and Victims: The Russians in the Soviet Union*, Cambridge, MA: Belknap Press of Harvard University Press, 2006, ch. 9.

39  Arkady Ostrovsky, *The Invention of Russia: The Journey from Gorbachev's Freedom to Putin's War*, London: Atlantic, 2015, 75.

40  Leon Aron, *Roads to the Temple: Truth, Memory, and Ideals in the Making of the Russian Revolution, 1987–1991*, New Haven and London: Yale University Press, 2012, 72.

41  David Remnick, *Lenin's Tomb*, London: Penguin, 1994, 70–86.

42  Cited in R. W. Davies, *Soviet History in the Gorbachev Revolution*, Basingstoke: Macmillan, 1989, 137.

43  *Pravda*, 6 January 1989. Translation: *Current Digest of the Soviet Press* 41:1 (1989): 13.

44  *Moskovskie Novosti*, 27 November 1988, 11. Translation: *Current Digest of the Soviet Press* 41:1 (1989): 15.

45  Adam Hochschild, *The Unquiet Ghost: Russians Remember Stalin*, New York: Viking, 1994.

46  *Pravda*, 25 May 1989, 4.

47  Interview undated, but it took place after Chubais became chair of Rosnano in 2011: http://strana.lenta.ru/russia/chubais.htm, accessed 27 November 2018.

48  Arup Banerji, *Writing History in the Soviet Union: Making the Past Work*, New Delhi: Esha Béteille Social Science Press, 2008, 261.

49  Catriona Kelly, *St Petersburg: Shadows of the Past*, New Haven and London: Yale University Press, 2014, 251.

50  Alex Luhn, 'New Wave of Musicians Tune in to the Soviet Past', *Guardian*, 29 July 2015, 17.

51  Guy Chazan, 'Grandmother Russia' ('Dinner with the FT: Svetlana Alexievich'), *FT Weekend*, 17–18 June 2017.

52  Pyotr Chaadaev, *Philosophical Letters* I, in McNally (ed.), *Major Works*.

53  Andreas Schönle, *Architectures of Oblivion: Ruins and Historical Consciousness in Modern Russia*, DeKalb, IL: Northern Illinois University Press, 2011.

54  Oleg V. Khlevniuk, *Stalin: New Biography of a Dictator*, New Haven and London: Yale University Press, 2015, 330.

55  Tatyana Tsyrlina-Spady and Alan Stotskopf, 'Russian History Textbooks in the Putin Era: Heroic Leaders Demand Loyal Citizens', in Joseph Zajda et al. (eds.), *Globalisation and Historiography of National Leaders*, Dordrecht, Netherlands: Springer, 2017, 15–33.

56  Steven Lee Myers, *The New Tsar: The Rise and Reign of Vladimir Putin*, New York: Knopf, 2015, 415, 424.

57  Mikhail Zygar, *All the Kremlin's Men: Inside the Court of Vladimir Putin*, New York: Public Affairs, 2016, 152, 186–7.

58  Fiona Hill and Clifford G. Gaddy, *Mr Putin: Operative in the Kremlin*, Washington, DC: Brookings Institution, 2015 (new and expanded edition), 70–71.

59  Mark Edele, 'Fighting Russia's History Wars: Vladimir Putin and the Codification of World War II', *History and Memory* 29:2 (2017): 90–124. See also Shaun Walker, *The Long Hangover: Putin's New Russia and the Ghosts of the Past*, New York: Oxford University Press, 2018. More generally on the legacies of the Second World War: Stephen Lovell, *The Shadow of War: Russia and the Soviet Union, 1941 to the Present*, Oxford: Wiley-Blackwell, 2010.

60  Natalia Shkurenok, 'The Historian Who Dug Too Deep', *openDemocracy*, 4 September 2017: https://www.opendemocracy.net/od-russia/natalia-shkurenok/yuri-dmitriev-sandarmoh, accessed 27 November 2018.

61  Donald Filtzer, 'Russia's Archives Are Still Open for Business', Letter to Editor, *Guardian*, 16 February 2018.

62  Khlevniuk, *Stalin*, 330.

63  Arup Banerji, *Writing History in the Soviet Union: Making the Past Work*, New Delhi: Esha Béteille Social Science Press, 2008, 269.

64  Alexander N. Yakovlev, *A Century of Violence in Soviet Russia*, New Haven and London: Yale University Press, 2002, 46–7 (Russian version published in Moscow in 2000).

65  Antony Beevor, 'By Banning My Book, Russia Is Deluding Itself about Its Past', *Guardian*, 5 August 2015.

66 Evgenii Anisimov, *Istoriia Rossii ot Riurika do Putina: Liudi, sobyt-iia, daty*, Moscow, St Petersburg (etc.): Piter, 2018.

67 From many examples: S. Papkova and K. Teraiama, *Politicheskie i sotsial'nye aspekty istorii Stalinizma: Novye fakty i interpretatsii*, Moscow: Rosspen, 2015.

68 Aleksandra Litvina and Ania Desnitskaia, *Istoriia staroi kvartiry*, Moscow: Memorial, 2017.

69 Roger Markwick, 'The Great Patriotic War in Soviet and Post-Soviet Collective Memory', in Stone (ed.), *Oxford Handbook of Postwar European History*, 692–713 (712).

70 Alexander Etkind, *Warped Mourning: Stories of the Undead in the Land of the Unburied*, Stanford, CA: Stanford University Press, 2013, 246.

71 Judt, *Postwar*, 829, 831.

72 Bryan Ward Perkins, *The Fall of Rome and the End of Civilization*, Oxford: Oxford University Press, 2005.

73 Interview with Georgy Frangulyan, *Istorik* 10:34 (October 2017): 44–5.

74 David Rieff, *In Praise of Forgetting: Historical Memory and Its Ironies*, New Haven and London: Yale University Press, 2016.

## 10. THE PUTIN PROSPECT

1 John Bowlt (ed.), *Russian Art of the Avant Garde: Theory and Criticism, 1902–1934*, New York: Viking, 1976, 293 ('From Andrei Zhdanov's Speech').

2 Stephen F. Cohen, *Failed Crusade: America and the Tragedy of Post-Communist Russia*, New York: W. W. Norton, 2000.

3 Vladimir Popov, 'Transformational Recession', in Michael Alexeev and Shlomo Weber (eds.), *The Oxford Handbook of the Russian Economy*, Oxford: Oxford University Press, 2013, 102–31 (102).

4 E.g. Maxim Boyco, Andrei Shleifer and Robert Vishny, *Privatizing Russia*, Cambridge, MA: MIT Press, 1996, 153.

5 Popov, 'Transformational Recession', 104–5.

6 Revold M. Entov and Oleg V. Lugovoy, 'Growth Trends in Russia after 1998', in Alexeev and Weber (eds.), *The Oxford Handbook of the Russian Economy*, 132–160 (132–3).

7 James H. Billington, *The Icon and the Axe: An Interpretive History of Russian Culture*, New York: Vintage, 1970, 55.

8 *Pravda*, 5 February 1931: see Robert Service, *Stalin: A Biography*, London: Macmillan, 2005, 272–3.

9 William Taubman, *Khrushchev: The Man and His Era*, New York: Free Press, 2003, 511.

10 Vladimir Mau and Tatiana Drobyshevskaya, 'Modernization and the Russian Economy: Three Hundred Years of Catching Up', in Alexeev and Weber (eds.), *The Oxford Handbook of the Russian Economy*, 29–51 (41).

11 See, e.g. Christian Raffensperger, *Reimagining Europe: Kievan Rus in the Medieval World*, Cambridge, MA: Harvard University Press, 2012; and Boris Akunin, *Chast' Evropy: Istoriia Rossiiskogo gosudarstva. Ot istokov do mongol'skogo nashestviia*, Moscow: AST, 2014 (though his point is that from being a 'part of Europe' until 1240, things change thereafter).

12 Denis J. B. Shaw, 'Towns and Commerce', in Perrie (ed.), *The Cambridge History of Russia*, vol. 1, 298–316 (313–15).

13 Stephen Alford, *London's Triumph: Merchant Adventurers and the Tudor City*, London: Allen Lane, 2017.

14 Richard Hellie, 'The Economy, Trade and Serfdom', in Perrie (ed.), *The Cambridge History of Russia*, vol. 1, 539–58 (544–5).

15 Marshall Poe, *'A People Born to Slavery': Russia in Early-Modern Ethnography, 1476–1748*, Ithaca, NY, and London: Cornell University Press, 2000.

16 Jarno T. Kotilaine, 'Mercantilism in Pre-Petrine Russia', in Kotilaine and Marshall Poe (eds.), *Modernizing Muscovy: Reform and Social Change in Seventeenth-Century Russia*, London: RoutledgeCurzon, 2004, 143–74 (148–50).

17 Lindsey Hughes, *Russia in the Age of Peter the Great*, New Haven and London: Yale University Press, 2000, 158.

18 Arcadius Kahan, *The Plow, the Hammer, and the Knout: An Economic History of Eighteenth-Century Russia*, Chicago: University of Chicago Press, 1985, 163–5.

19 Brian R. Mitchell, *International Historical Statistics: Europe 1750–1993*, Basingstoke: Macmillan, 1998, 75, 422, 424, 818, 821.

20 Alexander Gerschenkron, 'Economic Backwardness in Historical Perspective' and 'Russia: Patterns and Problems of Economic Development, 1861–1958', in Gerschenkron, *Economic Backwardness in Historical Perspective: A Book of Essays*, Cambridge, MA: The Belknap Press of Harvard University Press, 1966, 5–30 and 119–51.

21 Leopold Haimson, *The Russian Marxists and the Origins of Bolshevism*, Cambridge, MA: Harvard University Press, 1955; see the discussion in Jonathan Daly, 'The Pleiade: Five Scholars Who Founded Russian Historical Studies in the United States', *Kritika: Explorations in Russian and Eurasian History* 18:4 (2017): 785–826 (813).

22 Jorg Baberowski, 'Law, the Judicial System and the Legal Profession', in Dominic Lieven (ed.), *The Cambridge History of Russia*, vol. 2: *Imperial Russia, 1689–1917*, Cambridge: Cambridge University Press, 2006, 344–68 (344).

23 Jane Burbank, 'Legal Culture, Citizenship, and Peasant Jurisprudence: Perspectives from the Early Twentieth Century', in Peter H. Solomon, Jr (ed.), *Reforming Justice in Russia 1864–1996: Power, Culture, and the Limits of Legal Order*, Armonk, NY: M. E. Sharpe, 1997, 82–106 (esp. 95–6).

24 Larisa Zakharova, 'The Reign of Alexander II: A Watershed?', in Lieven (ed.), *Cambridge History of Russia*, vol. 2, 593–616 (609).

25 Baberowski, 'Law, the Judicial System and the Legal Profession', 351–2.

26 Girish N. Bhat, 'The Consensual Dimension of Late Imperial Russian Criminal Procedure: The Example of Trial by Jury', in Peter H. Solomon, Jr (ed.), *Reforming Justice in Russia 1864–1996: Power, Culture, and the Limits of Legal Order*, Armonk, NY: M. E. Sharpe, 1997, 61–81.

27 Baberowski, 'Law, the Judicial System and the Legal Profession', 356–9.

28 Kathryn Hendley, *Everyday Law in Russia*, Ithaca, NY: Cornell University Press, 2017.

29 David Remnick, *Resurrection*, London: Picador, 1998, 382.

30 Robert Tombs and Isabelle Tombs, *That Sweet Enemy: The French and the British from the Sun King to the Present*, London: Pimlico, 2007.

31 Sofya Kovalevskaya, *A Russian Childhood*, trans. Beatrice Stillman, New York: Springer Verlag, 1978, 91.

32 Ann Hibner Koblitz, *A Convergence of Lives: Sofia Kovalevskaia: Scientist, Writer. Revolutionary*, Boston, Basel and Stuttgart: Birkhauser, 1983, xv, 6, 270.

33 S. V. Kovalevskaia, *Vospominaniia i pis'ma: izdanie ispravlennoe*, Moscow: Akademiia Nauk SSSR, 1961, 148–65.

34 To G. Mittag-Leffler, 7 June 1881, in Kovalevskaia, *Vospominaniia i pis'ma*, 255.

# *Index*

ALLEN LANE
*an imprint of*
PENGUIN BOOKS

## Also Published

David Brooks, *The Second Mountain*

Roberto Calasso, *The Unnamable Present*

Lee Smolin, *Einstein's Unfinished Revolution: The Search for What Lies Beyond the Quantum*

Clare Carlisle, *Philosopher of the Heart: The Restless Life of Søren Kierkegaard*

Nicci Gerrard, *What Dementia Teaches Us About Love*

Edward O. Wilson, *Genesis: On the Deep Origin of Societies*

John Barton, *A History of the Bible: The Book and its Faiths*

Carolyn Forché, *What You Have Heard is True: A Memoir of Witness and Resistance*

Elizabeth-Jane Burnett, *The Grassling*

Kate Brown, *Manual for Survival: A Chernobyl Guide to the Future*

Roderick Beaton, *Greece: Biography of a Modern Nation*

Matt Parker, *Humble Pi: A Comedy of Maths Errors*

Ruchir Sharma, *Democracy on the Road*

David Wallace-Wells, *The Uninhabitable Earth: A Story of the Future*

Randolph M. Nesse, *Good Reasons for Bad Feelings: Insights from the Frontier of Evolutionary Psychiatry*

Anand Giridharadas, *Winners Take All: The Elite Charade of Changing the World*

Richard Bassett, *Last Days in Old Europe: Triste '79, Vienna '85, Prague '89*

Paul Davies, *The Demon in the Machine: How Hidden Webs of Information Are Finally Solving the Mystery of Life*

Toby Green, *A Fistful of Shells: West Africa from the Rise of the Slave Trade to the Age of Revolution*

Paul Dolan, *Happy Ever After: Escaping the Myth of The Perfect Life*

Sunil Amrith, *Unruly Waters: How Mountain Rivers and Monsoons Have Shaped South Asia's History*

Christopher Harding, *Japan Story: In Search of a Nation, 1850 to the Present*

Timothy Day, *I Saw Eternity the Other Night: King's College, Cambridge, and an English Singing Style*

Richard Abels, *Aethelred the Unready: The Failed King*

Eric Kaufmann, *Whiteshift: Populism, Immigration and the Future of White Majorities*

Alan Greenspan and Adrian Wooldridge, *Capitalism in America: A History*

Philip Hensher, *The Penguin Book of the Contemporary British Short Story*

Paul Collier, *The Future of Capitalism: Facing the New Anxieties*

Andrew Roberts, *Churchill: Walking With Destiny*

Tim Flannery, *Europe: A Natural History*

T. M. Devine, *The Scottish Clearances: A History of the Dispossessed, 1600-1900*

Robert Plomin, *Blueprint: How DNA Makes Us Who We Are*

Michael Lewis, *The Fifth Risk: Undoing Democracy*

Diarmaid MacCulloch, *Thomas Cromwell: A Life*

Ramachandra Guha, *Gandhi: 1914-1948*

Slavoj Žižek, *Like a Thief in Broad Daylight: Power in the Era of Post-Humanity*

Neil MacGregor, *Living with the Gods: On Beliefs and Peoples*

Peter Biskind, *The Sky is Falling: How Vampires, Zombies, Androids and Superheroes Made America Great for Extremism*

Robert Skidelsky, *Money and Government: A Challenge to Mainstream Economics*

Helen Parr, *Our Boys: The Story of a Paratrooper*

David Gilmour, *The British in India: Three Centuries of Ambition and Experience*

Jonathan Haidt and Greg Lukianoff, *The Coddling of the American Mind: How Good Intentions and Bad Ideas are Setting up a Generation for Failure*

Ian Kershaw, *Roller-Coaster: Europe, 1950-2017*

Adam Tooze, *Crashed: How a Decade of Financial Crises Changed the World*

Edmund King, *Henry I: The Father of His People*

Lilia M. Schwarcz and Heloisa M. Starling, *Brazil: A Biography*

Jesse Norman, *Adam Smith: What He Thought, and Why it Matters*

Philip Augur, *The Bank that Lived a Little: Barclays in the Age of the Very Free Market*

Christopher Andrew, *The Secret World: A History of Intelligence*

David Edgerton, *The Rise and Fall of the British Nation: A Twentieth-Century History*

Julian Jackson, *A Certain Idea of France: The Life of Charles de Gaulle*

Owen Hatherley, *Trans-Europe Express*

Richard Wilkinson and Kate Pickett, *The Inner Level: How More Equal Societies Reduce Stress, Restore Sanity and Improve Everyone's Wellbeing*

Paul Kildea, *Chopin's Piano: A Journey Through Romanticism*

Seymour M. Hersh, *Reporter: A Memoir*

Michael Pollan, *How to Change Your Mind: The New Science of Psychedelics*

David Christian, *Origin Story: A Big History of Everything*

Judea Pearl and Dana Mackenzie, *The Book of Why: The New Science of Cause and Effect*

David Graeber, *Bullshit Jobs: A Theory*

Serhii Plokhy, *Chernobyl: History of a Tragedy*

Michael McFaul, *From Cold War to Hot Peace: The Inside Story of Russia and America*

Paul Broks, *The Darker the Night, the Brighter the Stars: A Neuropsychologist's Odyssey*

Lawrence Wright, *God Save Texas: A Journey into the Future of America*

John Gray, *Seven Types of Atheism*

Carlo Rovelli, *The Order of Time*

Mariana Mazzucato, *The Value of Everything: Making and Taking in the Global Economy*

Richard Vinen, *The Long '68: Radical Protest and Its Enemies*

Kishore Mahbubani, *Has the West Lost It?: A Provocation*

John Lewis Gaddis, *On Grand Strategy*

Richard Overy, *The Birth of the RAF, 1918: The World's First Air Force*

Francis Pryor, *Paths to the Past: Encounters with Britain's Hidden Landscapes*

Helen Castor, *Elizabeth I: A Study in Insecurity*

Ken Robinson and Lou Aronica, *You, Your Child and School*

Leonard Mlodinow, *Elastic: Flexible Thinking in a Constantly Changing World*

Nick Chater, *The Mind is Flat: The Illusion of Mental Depth and The Improvised Mind*

Michio Kaku, *The Future of Humanity: Terraforming Mars, Interstellar Travel, Immortality, and Our Destiny Beyond*

Thomas Asbridge, *Richard I: The Crusader King*

Richard Sennett, *Building and Dwelling: Ethics for the City*

Nassim Nicholas Taleb, *Skin in the Game: Hidden Asymmetries in Daily Life*

Steven Pinker, *Enlightenment Now: The Case for Reason, Science, Humanism and Progress*

Steve Coll, *Directorate S: The C.I.A. and America's Secret Wars in Afghanistan, 2001 - 2006*

Jordan B. Peterson, *12 Rules for Life: An Antidote to Chaos*

Bruno Maçães, *The Dawn of Eurasia: On the Trail of the New World Order*

Brock Bastian, *The Other Side of Happiness: Embracing a More Fearless Approach to Living*

Ryan Lavelle, *Cnut: The North Sea King*

Tim Blanning, *George I: The Lucky King*

Thomas Cogswell, *James I: The Phoenix King*

Pete Souza, *Obama, An Intimate Portrait: The Historic Presidency in Photographs*

Robert Dallek, *Franklin D. Roosevelt: A Political Life*

Norman Davies, *Beneath Another Sky: A Global Journey into History*

Ian Black, *Enemies and Neighbours: Arabs and Jews in Palestine and Israel, 1917-2017*

Martin Goodman, *A History of Judaism*

Shami Chakrabarti, *Of Women: In the 21st Century*

Stephen Kotkin, *Stalin, Vol. II: Waiting for Hitler, 1928-1941*

Lindsey Fitzharris, *The Butchering Art: Joseph Lister's Quest to Transform the Grisly World of Victorian Medicine*

Serhii Plokhy, *Lost Kingdom: A History of Russian Nationalism from Ivan the Great to Vladimir Putin*

Mark Mazower, *What You Did Not Tell: A Russian Past and the Journey Home*

Lawrence Freedman, *The Future of War: A History*

Niall Ferguson, *The Square and the Tower: Networks, Hierarchies and the Struggle for Global Power*